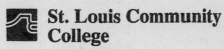

The Salem World of Nathaniel Hawthorne

The Salem World of Nathaniel Hawthorne

Margaret B. Moore

UNIVERSITY OF MISSOURI PRESS
Columbia and London

Copyright © 1998 by
The Curators of the University of Missouri
University of Missouri Press, Columbia, Missouri 65201
Printed and bound in the United States of America
All rights reserved
5   4   3   2   1   02   01   00   99   98

Library of Congress Cataloging-in-Publication Data

Moore, Margaret B., 1925–
    The Salem world of Nathaniel Hawthorne / Margaret B. Moore.
        p.   cm.
    Includes bibliographical references and index.
    ISBN 0-8262-1149-6 (alk. paper)
    1. Hawthorne, Nathaniel, 1804–1864—Homes and haunts—
Massachusetts—Salem.   2. Hawthorne, Nathaniel, 1804–1864—
Knowledge—Massachusetts—Salem.   3. Historical fiction, American—
History and criticism.   4. Novelists, American—19th century—
Biography.   5. Salem (Mass.)—In literature.   6. Salem (Mass.)—
Biography.   7. Salem (Mass.)—History.   I. Title.
PS1884.M66   1997
813'.3—dc21
[B]   97-38150
                                                                              CIP

∞™ This paper meets the requirements of the
American National Standard for Permanence of Paper
for Printed Library Materials, Z39.48, 1984.

Designer: Mindy Shouse
Typesetter: BOOKCOMP
Printer and binder: Thomson-Shore, Inc.
Typefaces: Garmond light Cochin

For Rayburn

Contents

Acknowledgments

A NY BOOK based upon primary research incurs many debts to numerous people and institutions. For whetting my interest in Salem,
I am grateful to my late mother, Margaret White Bear, and to two
aunts, Gertrude White Irvine and the late Nancy White Allen, whose
enthusiasm and informed interest in a large and old archive of family
letters was catching. For encouraging an independent scholar to work
on Hawthorne, I am grateful to David B. Kesterson, Vice Provost and
Associate Vice President of Academic Affairs at the University of North
Texas and a founder of the Nathaniel Hawthorne Society; to John L.
Idol Jr., Professor Emeritus of English at Clemson University; and to Joel
Myerson, Professor of English at the University of South Carolina.

I wish to thank the following institutions, which graciously gave
me permission to quote from their manuscript holdings: Hawthorne-
Longfellow Library, Bowdoin College, Brunswick, Maine; Bancroft Library of the University of California at Berkeley; Henry W. and Albert
A. Berg Collection, The New York Public Library, Astor, Lenox and
Tilden Foundations; Clifton Waller Barrett Library, Special Collections
Department, University of Virginia Library; the Beverly Historical Society, Beverly, Massachusetts; the Trustees of the National Library of
Scotland, Edinburgh; and the Hargrett Rare Book and Manuscript Library, University of Georgia. I owe a debt to the following editors
who have allowed me to use my articles that appeared in their journals: Joel Myerson of *Studies in the American Renaissance;* Will LaMoy
of *Essex Institute Historical Collections;* John L. Idol Jr. and Frederick
Newberry of the *Nathaniel Hawthorne Review;* and Debra C. Boyd and

Patricia Ward of *Postscript: Publication of the Philological Association of the Carolinas*. I especially thank both former and present staff at the James Duncan Phillips Library of the Peabody Essex Museum in Salem: among others, the late Anne Farnam, Katherine W. Richardson, Eugenia Fountain, Richard Fyffe, Prudence K. Backman, current editor William T. La Moy, and Curator of Manuscripts Jane E. Ward, who have patiently answered all questions with grace and given me permission to both use and cite their holdings.

I am grateful for many scholarly courtesies that space does not permit me to detail. I thank the following: Professor Helen R. Deese, Tennessee Tech University; Professor Joseph Flibbert, Salem State College; Professor Thomas Woodson, Ohio State University; Dr. Gwen Nagel, Athens, Georgia; Marie Ellis, Anne Hurst, and Danny Bridges, librarians at the University of Georgia; Joyce King and Mark Nystedt, researchers in Salem; Ed Stevenson, former Director of the Historic Site of the Seven Gables; Jennifer Gosse and Mary Bellhouse of Cold Ash, Berkshire, England; Janet Appleton of Beverly; and especially Jane Reed, formerly of Salem and now of Beverly, whose aid has been invaluable.

A special expression of thanks goes to Beverly Jarrett, Director and Editor-in-Chief of the University of Missouri Press, for her encouragement and for patiently enduring the long gestation of this manuscript. I am grateful too to Jane Lago and John Brenner, editors at the Press. Most of all, I thank my husband, Professor Emeritus Rayburn S. Moore of the University of Georgia, whose support and unfailing humor upholds me in this book and in life.

Margaret B. Moore
Athens, Georgia

Abbreviations

AL	American Literature
AMUEK	American Magazine of Useful and Entertaining Knowledge
CE	The Centenary Edition of the Works of Nathaniel Hawthorne
EA	Essex Antiquarian
EIHC	Essex Institute Historical Collections
ECH	Elizabeth Clarke Hawthorne
EMH	Elizabeth Manning Hawthorne
EPP	Elizabeth Palmer Peabody
ER	Essex Register
JH	Julian Hawthorne
MLH	Maria Louisa Hawthorne
MHSC	Massachusetts Historical Society Collections
MHSP	Massachusetts Historical Society Proceedings
NEHGR	New England Historical and Genealogical Register
NEQ	New England Quarterly
NH	Nathaniel Hawthorne
NHJ	Nathaniel Hawthorne Journal
NHR	Nathaniel Hawthorne Review
RHL	Rose Hawthorne Lathrop
SAR	Studies In the American Renaissance
SG	Salem Gazette
SPH	Sophia Peabody Hawthorne
WB	William Bentley

The Salem World of Nathaniel Hawthorne

Introduction

In "Grimshawe," Nathaniel Hawthorne has the old Doctor ask: "Whence did you come? Whence did any of us come? Out of the darkness and mystery, out of nothingness, out of a kingdom of shadows, out of dust, clay, impure mud, I think, and to return to it again" (*CE* 12:356). On a less philosophical level, however, Hawthorne knew very well from whence he came and he always had mixed feelings about it, what Henry James called "the mingled tenderness and rancour." With his usual obtuseness about his parent, Julian Hawthorne said that his father's "instinct for localities was not strongly developed."[1] I believe that his father had a very clear sense of place, and for nowhere so much as Salem.

On the one hand, he felt a strong attachment to the town. It was, he thought, the "mere sensuous sympathy of dust for dust," or the "kindred between the human being and the locality" (*CE* 1:9,11). He

1. NH, *The Centenary Edition of the Works of Nathaniel Hawthorne*, ed. William Charvat et al., 23 vols. to date (Columbus: Ohio State University Press, 1962–1997). These include 1. *The Scarlet Letter;* 2. *The House of the Seven Gables;* 3. *The Blithedale Romance and Fanshawe;* 4. *The Marble Faun, or The Romance of Monte Beni;* 5. *Our Old Home: A Series of English Sketches;* 6. *True Stories;* 7. *A Wonder Book and Tanglewood Tales;* 8. *The American Notebooks;* 9. *Twice-Told Tales;* 10. *Mosses From an Old Manse;* 11. *The Snow-Image and Uncollected Tales;* 12. *The American Claimant Manuscripts;* 13. *The Elixir of Life Manuscripts;* 14. *The French and Italian Notebooks;* 15. *The Letters, 1813–1843;* 16. *The Letters, 1843–1853;* 17. *The Letters, 1853–1856;* 18. *The Letters, 1857–1864;* 23. *Miscellaneous Prose and Verse,* 1994. *The Consular Letters* (vols. 19 and 20) I did not use. Volumes 21 and 22 *(The English Notebooks)* arrived too late for me to use. References to the volumes are inserted in the text with volume and page number; Henry James, *Hawthorne,* 11; JH, "The Salem of Hawthorne," 3.

felt, as did his character Peter Goldthwaite, "a fatality that connected him with his birth-place" (*CE* 9:385). In *Our Old Home* he wrote with the perspective of England upon him of "my own dear native place" (*CE* 5:165). No matter what he said about it, Salem was the locale for many of his stories, sketches, a novel, and a fragmentary novel. Salem history haunted him, and Salem people fascinated him.

Yet he also hated Salem. He confessed to Sophia in January 1841, "I ought to love Salem better than I do; for the people have always had a pretty generous faith in me, ever since they knew me at all" (*CE* 15:518). That same year in November he again wrote Sophia: "I am intolerably weary of this old town. . . . Dost Thou not think it really the most hateful place in all the world? My mind becomes heavy and nerveless, the moment I set my foot within its precincts. Nothing makes me wonder more than that I found it possible to write all my tales in this same region of sleepy-head and stupidity" (*CE* 15:596). He often saw Salem as a sleepy, run-down town full of unpainted wooden buildings, living on past glories in a present that was dull and unalluring. This feeling was especially evident, of course, after he was fired in 1849, and his sketch, "The Custom-House," was particularly biting. He spoke of his "strange, indolent, unjoyous attachment" to the city, caused, he thought, by his "deep and aged roots," which gave him "a sort of home-feeling with the past" (*CE* 1:12, 8, 9). He said "[T]he spell survives and just as powerfully as if the natal spot were an earthly paradise . . . as if Salem were for me the inevitable centre of the universe" (*CE* 1:11, 12). In letters he called it "this abominable city" and "that wretched old town" (*CE* 16:293, 346). He looked on it with "infinite contempt" (*CE* 16:329). Though he did not live there again after his "decapitation," as he referred to his firing, he was never able to shake Salem loose. In a last incomplete novel, Salem was again the place for the initial action. In "Grimshawe," Hawthorne described post-Revolutionary Salem as "a town that was as yet but a large village, where everybody knew everybody, and claimed the privilege to know and discuss their characters, and where there were few topics of public interest to take off the attention" (*CE* 12:380). In something of an anticipation of Quentin Compson in *Absalom, Absalom!* he seemed in "the cold air, the iron New England dark" to be saying "I don't hate it! I don't hate it," yet the compulsion remained to tell the story again.

What Salem thought of Hawthorne was somewhat more one-sided for a long time. Caroline King characterized him as "a strange and picturesque figure with gloomy brow and repellent manners" who was "mooning about the streets of Salem." George Holden spoke of the "muck-heaps of local prejudice" still apparent in 1881 in those who could not forgive his treatment of Salemites, especially in "The Custom-House." Henry M. Brooks noted in 1894 that he well remembered seeing Hawthorne before he went into the Custom House. "He was a very retiring man, and seldom was seen to speak to any one in the street, rarely raising his eyes from the ground. . . . In the Custom House he never made any advances to any one or took notice of any except political friends. If you said 'good morning' to him he would make no reply." A decade earlier Captain William Cheever wrote to Francis Lee that Hawthorne "was probably less known by sight than almost any other man in the City," and Mrs. L. J. Jarvis, in her reminiscences of 18 Chestnut Street, noted with thinly veiled sarcasm, "I did not know that Hawthorne ennobled our dwelling." Annie Fields, on the other hand, took delight from an incident during a visit from a Salem lady, who, in speaking of Hawthorne, drew herself up and sniffed, "Yes, he was born in Salem, but we never knew anything about him." Remarking that the lady "was the last person to appreciate him," Fields continued, "[f]ortunately Miss Howes was present, whose father was one of Hawthorne's best friends; so matters were made clear there." Yet, as William Dean Howells affirmed, "there was, in fact, no love lost between Hawthorne and his birthplace, but probably neither knew how much was their mutual debt."[2]

Many others also felt that Salem was absolutely indispensable to Hawthorne's work. Robert S. Rantoul at the celebration of the Hawthorne Centenary remarked, "I doubt if any other place could have produced just such a personality. . . . Salem may be regarded as his workshop." Joseph H. Choate held that "[h]e was inspired in a most remarkable degree, by the *genius loci*—the spirit of the place where he was born and bred." George B. Loring thought that "[t]he fact that he was born in Salem may not amount to much to other people, but it amounted to a great deal to him." Rose Hawthorne Lathrop, too, commented on her father's "inheritance":

> He undoubtedly had a large store of *inherited* experiences to draw upon; he was richly endowed with these, and could sit and walk alone, year after year (except for occasional warm reunions with friends of the cleanest joviality), and feel the intercourse with the world, of

2. Caroline Howard King, *When I Lived in Salem,* 32; George H. Holden, "Hawthorne among His Friends," 263; Henry M. Brooks, "Some Localities about Salem," 108; William Cheever to Francis Lee, February 3, 1884, and Mrs. L. J. Jarvis to Lee, January 28, 1884, Scrapbook, 1:55, 74, copies, Francis Henry Lee Papers; Mark Anthony DeWolfe Howe, *Memories of a Hostess,* 236; William Dean Howells, "The Personality of Hawthorne," 874.

his ancestors, stirring in his veins. He tells us that this was a ghostly pastime; but it is an inheritance that makes a man well equipped and self-sustained, for all that.[3]

Part of the problem, I believe, was the intuition by Hawthorne that he never quite belonged in Salem or anyplace else. In "The Intelligence Office," which, contrary to our notion of intelligence, was a combination employment office and lost and found, Hawthorne depicts a person who wore "the characteristic expression of a man out of his right place." He demands "my place!—my own place!—my true place in the world!—my proper sphere—my thing to do, which nature intended me to perform when she fashioned me thus awry, and which I have vainly sought, all my lifetime!" (*CE* 10:323). When Hawthorne was editing the *American Magazine of Useful and Entertaining Knowledge,* he abstracted from "Curiosities of Literature" the idea of a "round man stuck into the three-cornered hole."[4] Elizabeth Hawthorne compared her brother to a square peg in a round hole: "if the peg could relate its feelings, and its thoughts, they would be better worth hearing than any it would have in a more congenial position. Now, my brother was all of his life just so misplaced."[5] This feeling of being "strangely ajar with the human race," as was true of Septimius Felton, permeates many of his tales and was, I believe, a part of Hawthorne's view of the world, and of Salem as well (*CE* 13:23).

In this book I have endeavored to put Hawthorne in his Salem context—especially that Salem from 1804 to 1821, from 1825 to 1842, and from 1845 to 1850, when he lived there. I do not deal with his Maine experience except tangentially, but I consider him still a citizen of Salem during his times in Boston or at Brook Farm. The Salem of those times was pervaded by its past, and so was Hawthorne. I have not sought to trace every Salem incident through his works, although I have tried to give enough of the context to make plain the uses that Hawthorne made of the town and the ways in which it nourished the writer's imagination. I have also attempted to answer some of the questions that have always interested me—who were these fellow Salemites who impinged, however lightly or heavily, on Hawthorne's life, and what were they like? What did Salem offer Hawthorne in stimulation or

3. Robert S. Rantoul, "Opening Remarks," 3; Joseph H. Choate, "Letter on Birth at Salem, July 4, 1904," in Kenneth Walter Cameron, *Hawthorne among His Contemporaries,* 473; George Bailey Loring, "Nathaniel Hawthorne," in Cameron, *Hawthorne among Contemporaries,* 213; RHL, *Memories of Hawthorne,* 462.

4. "Bent of the Mind," 294.

5. Randall Stewart, "Recollections of Hawthorne by His Sister Elizabeth," 337.

culture? At any rate, he was Salem born and Salem bred (even though not Salem dead), and that matters.

So many biographers seem to dismiss Hawthorne's childhood with a few of his sister's memories or Elizabeth Peabody's recollections of that time. Some also see Hawthorne's solitary years after college as though they were empty years, not years in which ideas abounded in the town. Events big and small occurred; other people were born and lived and died. Hawthorne may have been the disinterested "spectator" to all this (though I wonder about the extent of his lack of involvement), but he did look on or out at Salem. His youth was spent, for the most part, in Salem, and although recent studies have filled in those years somewhat, there are still gaps in our knowledge. Some of those spaces cannot be replenished, but others can either be known or speculated about with some certainty. Certain errors have been repeated through the years. I have ventured to point out such errors, knowing full well that I may be making some of my own.

Salem is in many ways a unique town, if only for its history. Even though most of the witchcraft events took place in Salem Village (now Danvers), it is Salem, not Danvers, that carries the burden of the past. In many ways Salem carries the history of the whole North Shore, and much of what I have to say is more properly the history of Ipswich or Marblehead or Lynn or Beverly or Danvers. Some of these towns were once part of Salem, and their history is often inextricably intertwined with that particular port city. I treat them all as though they were at that time greater Salem, which in many ways they were.

The town was not unique for its time, however, in the naming of children. Until Hawthorne's children's generation, offspring were given family Christian names, except for those early Puritans who used such names as Thankful or Preserved. After three Caleb Footes in a row, Mary and Caleb Foote turned to other names for their sons. Sophia and Nathaniel Hawthorne had two paternal "Nathaniels" as well as the father's name, but their son went unnamed for a considerable time until they decided on Julian.[6] The earlier use of family names was such a regular practice that there is genuine danger that later scholars may mix generations or even families.

Hawthorne used Salem or North Shore surnames in all his works. Robert S. Rantoul said that Hawthorne had told Edwin P. Whipple that

6. A perusal of the six-volume set of *Vital Records of Salem to the End of the Year 1849* shows clearly the repeated use of names.

"for names he adopted, without scruple, those he found about him."[7] His use of the Pynchon name (which he spelled Pyncheon) was challenged by descendants, and Hawthorne expressed complete surprise at the accusation, but he protested too much. He knew the name had been local long after the Springfield William Pynchon was dead. Any writer uses names with which he is familiar, but Hawthorne's works are dotted with those that can be seen in any stroll through Salem's cemeteries.

The very spelling of names is another difficulty. The choosing of "Hawthorne" by the writer over Hathorne was deliberate, but the two spellings had been mixed up before his time. In this book I have used the spelling Hathorne except for the writer, his mother, sisters, wife, and children who *chose* to be Hawthornes. Betsy was often spelled Betsey in that time, and Hawthorne's mother usually retained that spelling. I have tried to be consistent, whenever possible, in such references— using Endicott instead of Endecot, Ann instead of Anne Hutchinson.

I am aware of various critical approaches in recent Hawthornean studies. I know, of course, that the narrator of the various tales and sketches is not necessarily Hawthorne himself, that he has chosen a persona or personae to tell or sometimes to obfuscate the narrative. I do not always make the distinction in discussing his work. My purpose is to show what there was in Salem to give Hawthorne material—not so much how he used it as what he used. There are relevant investigations that do discuss his methods of writing.[8] I may seem to tell more about some friends than many readers want to know, but, at the same time, to have slighted people in Hawthorne's life about whom we know a great deal already. I have tried not to elaborate known facts other than those needed for clarification.

In short, it has seemed to me that the Salem world of Nathaniel Hawthorne has needed more study than is now available, although much has been done, particularly by some of the early biographers such as George P. Lathrop or later by Robert Cantwell and Hubert Hoeltje. Arlin Turner has contributed much to our understanding. James R. Mellow has put Hawthorne in a wider geographical context than have I. Gloria Erlich has filled in much useful material on the Manning family. I disagree with the interpretation of T. Walter Herbert in *Dearest Beloved*. Edwin Haviland Miller's book, *Salem Is My Dwelling Place,* is more about Hawthorne's inner psyche than the dwelling place. But I could not be

---

7. Rantoul, "Opening Remarks," 4.
8. See, among others, Michael Dunne, *Hawthorne's Narrative Strategies* and Gary Richard Thompson, *The Art of Authorial Presence: Hawthorne's Provincial Tales.*

more grateful for all the work that has been done by these and other scholars. They all enlarge our understanding. What could any of us do without the work of the editors of *The Centenary Edition* from William Charvat on? Especially are we indebted to Thomas Woodson for his thorough annotation of the helpful volumes of letters.

I do not mean to say, by concentrating on the world of Salem, that this writer's environment shaped him or his writings altogether. Hawthorne is too complicated for that. He remains a mystery despite all the attempts to solve the riddle. But as Henry James said in a letter to the Essex Institute on the centennial celebration of the writer's birth:

> What was admirable and instinctive in Hawthorne was that he saw the quaintness or the weirdness, the interest *behind* the interest, of things, as continuous with the very life we are leading, or that we were leading—you, at Salem, certainly were leading—round about him and under his eyes; saw it as something deeply within us, not as something infinitely disconnected from us; saw it in short in the very application of the spectator's, the poet's mood, in the kind of reflection the things we know best and see oftenest may make in our minds.[9]

Salem and Hawthorne are not and were not interchangeable, but it is hard to know the one without the other. Accordingly, we would do well to remember the observation of Salem historian James Duncan Phillips that though "most of the contemporary knowledge of Salem history is derived from Nathaniel Hawthorne. . . . he wrote to make fiction exciting and picturesque without much attention to historical accuracy."[10]

Keeping in mind the difference between factual history, so far as we can know it, and the shaping power of Hawthorne's imagination, this study will examine the Salem world of Nathaniel Hawthorne in chapters that seek to provide context for and insight into that world. Accordingly, Salem and some of its history and legends are sketched; Hawthorne's ancestors and their connections with the large events of their own day are scanned; the writer's family is investigated; his education is discussed; his religious context characterized; his days in Salem after college amplified, and his Salem experiences with politics, friends, and women are elucidated in the hope that such knowledge and interpretation will contribute to a better understanding of Hawthorne as man and writer and of Salem's vital part in his life and work.

9. Henry James, "A Letter from Henry James," 58–59.
10. James Duncan Phillips, *Salem in the Eighteenth Century,* preface.

1

"A Legend, Prolonging Itself"

[It is an] attempt to connect a by-gone time with the very Present that is flitting away from us. It is a Legend, prolonging itself, from an epoch now gray in the distance, down into our own broad daylight. —(*CE* 2:2)

THE SALEM into which Hawthorne was born was in the last stages of its glory days. Between the Revolutionary War and the Embargo of 1807, Salem ships sailed the world, bringing back strange and exotic cargoes from distant lands. No journey seemed too difficult, no land too strange. America too felt that all things were possible. It had declared its independence and had won it. It was indeed a brave new world. New England was imbued still with the Puritan conviction that God had chosen this people and this time to work out what would later be called its "manifest destiny." Those who pondered the various problems faced by the original chosen people felt that old conditions did not apply. This was a new land, a new chance.

Yet in the *Salem Gazette* on May 12, 1835, a writer—perhaps Caleb Foote—writes about a circus that has come to town and observes:

> There never was a place so filled with strange sights and sounds as was this luckless town of Salem, during the latter part of last week. . . .
>
> And all this in old Naumkeak [*sic*], "haven of comfort," as Cotton translates it; Salem, "city of peace," as it was afterwards named! What misnomers! What a haven of comfort to the poor Indians! The place in which the first settlers found that either the vengeance of stealthy and unrelenting enemies, or the pestilence which walketh in darkness, had had its perfect work. . . . And what a city of Peace it proved to those settlers, and their descendants. In the earliest periods, what contentions and groanings and strife about the cross in the standard and the long

hair of women: what wrath against the godless mummers of Mount Wollaston, and rage against the Pequods. Then what quakings and shakings about the great doings of the old roaring lion; when every old woman was a witch, and every broomstick, the devil. . . . Then what sweating with agony at the "Quaker light," which they characterized, in language less genteel than expressive, as a "stinking Vapour from Hell." The care of the Pillory was then no sinecure: the whipping post and the gallows extended their arms to all comers with drab dresses and broad brimmed hats, and secured to them that city of Peace elsewhere, which they could not find here.

Of course, all was not equitable in the little town. Citizens fought over land, over politics, over religion. When they thought about the past, they realized that Salem had not always been the city of peace. All sorts of people had come to unpeaceful ends there, including local Indians, followers of some religious beliefs, and those who had been caught up in what was later called the "witchcraft delusion." But at this particular time in history, many Americans did not want to think of that past. In Salem, the past was there, nevertheless, and its consequences lingered. It was a "[l]egend, prolonging itself," in Hawthorne's words (*CE* 2:2). This amalgamation of past and present was the Salem into which Captain Nathaniel Hathorne's son was born on July 4, 1804.

The Salem that Nathaniel Hawthorne inherited was a place of divided loyalties and fierce disputes with occasional periods of peace. When Roger Conant (1592–1679) and friends (called the Old Planters to distinguish them from the Massachusetts Bay colonists) left Cape Ann, Massachusetts, in 1626 to settle a "fruitful neck of land" the Indians called Nahum-Keike, later contracted to Naumkeag, they did so because of a fishing dispute. And when, after John Endicott's arrival, the name of the town was changed to Salem with its biblical meaning of peace, it was more of a wish than a fact.[1] The place was never peaceful for long.

John Endicott (c. 1589–1665), who arrived in the New World with his wife, Ann, on the *Abigail* in 1628, is a good example of one reason for the lack of peace. Fresh from the battles raging—metaphorically at least—in England between the Puritans and the Royalists, Endicott seems to have personified the worst of the rigidities of the Puritan faith. He was the one who cut the red cross of the Church of England from the

1. Frances Dianne Robotti, *Chronicles of Old Salem: A History in Miniature,* 13. For general histories of Salem, see Joseph Barlow Felt, *Annals of Salem from Its First Settlement,* both editions, 1827 and 1845–1849; Sidney Perley, *A History of Salem, Massachusetts,* 3 vols.; James Duncan Phillips, *Salem in the Seventeenth Century* and *Salem in the Eighteenth Century.*

flag, who led an attack upon an Indian village after its inhabitants had tortured a colonist, who gave Ann Hibbins of Boston a death sentence for witchcraft in 1656, and who urged the death penalty for Quakers. As a consequence for mutilating the flag, Endicott was banned from public office for a year. Governor John Winthrop (1587–1649) often disagreed with him, as did others.[2] One can argue that an uncompromising, principled leader is what is needed to make a new country with a new slant on religion work. Yet it is clear too that such a stance does inevitably bring dissent.

Dissent there was in early Salem, by individuals and by small groups. In 1637 Robert Moulton (d. 1655), a shipbuilder, was excommunicated from the Salem church for his Antinomian beliefs. Lady Deborah Moody (d. 1659), a church member since 1640, was admonished in 1643 because she did not believe in infant baptism. Eleanor Trusler (d. 1655) was reprimanded in July 1644 for saying that "their teacher, Mr. [Edward] Norris, taught the people lies." At her trial Cassandra Southwick, whose name was appropriated later for a poem about her daughter by John Greenleaf Whittier, testified that Eleanor "did question the government ever since she came."[3] Of course, in a town where civil and church government were the same, any person who questioned the arguments of either body was suspect.

One of the most famous dissenters of the early seventeenth century was Ann Hutchinson (1591–1643) of Boston, who claimed direct spiritual illumination from God and who taught her Antinomian beliefs to many in her home until she was banished from Massachusetts and later killed by the Indians. Hugh Peter (1599–1660), minister of Salem First Church, asserted that she had "stept out of [her] place"; he later also testified at the murder trial of Dorothy Talby, a person clearly of unsound mind, as Ann Hutchinson was not. Talby had often been in trouble with the law for mistreating her husband and for announcing that God had told her to kill her whole family. She finally did kill one child named "Difficulty," and she was hanged in 1638. Mary Oliver was another early troublemaker who said that it was a person's good life,

---

2. For Endicott, see Charles Edward Banks, *The Planters of the Commonwealth: The Study of the Emigrants and Emigration in Colonial Times: To Which Are Added Lists,* 59; Felt, *Annals,* 1st ed., 72, 77, 192; WB, "Description and History of Salem," 246; William Sewel, *The History of the Rise, Increase, and Progress of the Christian People Called Quakers,* 1:211.

3. Ernest W. Baughman, "Excommunications and Banishments from the First Church in Salem and the Town of Salem, 1629–1680," 91–92, 97; Richard P. Gildrie, *Salem, Massachusetts, 1626–1683: A Covenant Community,* 8; Felt, *Annals,* 1st ed., 60; Mrs. Henry Edwards, "Lady Deborah Moody," 97; Perley, *History of Salem,* 2:166; *Records and Files of the Quarterly Courts of Essex County, Massachusetts,* 1:68.

not church attendance, that mattered. She had a "cleft stick" put on her tongue for refusing to "own" or consent to the covenant of the Salem church.[4]

The greatest dissenter of that time perhaps was Roger Williams (1603–1682), who had been minister of Salem's church on two different occasions, but who came gradually to feel the necessity for a separation between church and state. For this opinion he was banished to Rhode Island. It was not that he tolerated all different views. He was certainly not tolerant of the Quakers, but he did intercede over and over again for the Indians.[5]

For Salem, to be sure, was not a city of peace for Indians and those who opposed them. William Bentley, clergyman of East Church, later thought that at the time of Salem's establishment the local Indians had been pretty well decimated by other tribes or by plagues (small pox and measles) brought by the Europeans, but Joseph Barlow Felt disputed that contention. He said the Naumkeags were "still lingering around this settlement" and were friendly at first. But capture or death by traveling Indians was a constant threat to the colonists, especially from the mid-1630s on. Some have felt that one reason for the witchcraft summer of 1692 was fear of the Indians, who were constantly coming closer to the area around Salem.[6]

Yet from the beginning the Indians had played a vital role in this part of the New World. Matthew Cradock, governor of the Massachusetts Bay Company, wrote Endicott that "the mayne end of our plantation [was] to bringe the Indians to the knowledge of the Gospell." John Eliot (1604–1690) took that statement seriously and founded a colony of "praying Indians." Roger Williams spent much time on the Indian question and insisted that there ought to be deeds from the Indians for Salem. This was finally accomplished with Sagamore George and others in his family in 1686.[7]

---

4. Emery John Battis, *Saints and Sectaries: Anne Hutchinson and the Antinomian Controversy in the Massachusetts Bay Colony,* 44; Amy Schraeger Lang, *Prophetic Woman: Anne Hutchinson and the Problem of Dissent in the Literature of New England,* 8, 41; Felt, *Annals,* 1st ed., 109, 117–18; Abner Cheney Goodell, "Essex County Court Records," 7:129, 187; WB, "Description and History," 252, 255.

5. See Perry Miller, *Roger Williams: His Contribution to the American Tradition,* 241–43.

6. WB, *The Diary of William Bentley, D.D.,* 2:384; Felt, *Annals,* 2d ed., 1:20–21; Charles W. Upham, *Salem Witchcraft. With an Account of Salem Village and a History of Opinions on Witchcraft and Kindred Subjects,* 1:8.

7. John Eliot, *A Biographical Dictionary Containing a Brief Account of the First Settlers and Other Eminent Characters,* 185; George Madison Bodge, *Soldiers in King Philip's War,* 10; WB, "Description and History," 6:230 (the deed is printed in Appendix, no. 1, 278); Felt, *Annals,* 1st ed., 11, 63.

But the Indians had reason to be afraid too. After the torture and killing in 1636 of a Salem colonist, John Tilly, and further disruptions by the Pequods, the tribe, according to Thomas Hutchinson (1711–1780), "was wholly extinguished." Those who were not killed were made slaves, a practice then approved of by most people. One hundred and eighty women and children "were divided between Massachusetts and Connecticut to be used as servants. Two women and fifteen boys were sent to Bermuda . . . to be sold as slaves." Hugh Peter (sometimes Peters), the Salem clergyman, wrote Governor Winthrop, asking for "some boys for Bermuda." In December 1641, certain types of slavery were legitimized in Massachusetts in the "Code of Fundamentals, or Body of Liberties," Article 91 of which stated, "There shall never be any bond slaverie, villinane, or captivitie amongst us unles it be lawful captives taken in just warres, and such strangers as willingly selle themselves or are sold to us." Emmanuel Downing of Salem wrote in 1645 that "if upon a Just warre the Lord shall deliver into our hands Indian slaves, they could be exchanged for Moores," for he reasoned, "I doe not see how wee can thrive untill wee gett into a stock of slaves sufficient to doe all our buisines."[8]

In 1675, Salem was greatly disturbed by King Philip's War. Philip (d. 1676), chief of the Narragansett tribe, was the second son of Massasoit, friend of the colonists. At the battle of Muddy Brook, later christened Bloody Brook, seventy men from Essex County under Captain Thomas Lathrop of Salem were killed. Major William Hathorne's son, Captain William Hathorne, led men from Salem against the foe. After King Philip's defeat, two hundred members of the tribe were sent to Boston to be sold as slaves. Philip was killed and his wife and son were sold into slavery.[9]

As has been indicated, there was a connection between black and Indian slavery. Nathaniel Hawthorne himself observed later in the *American Magazine of Useful and Entertaining Knowledge* that "our New England ancestors, we believe, were the only people who ever bartered one kind of slave for another." The slave trade did exist in Salem from

8. Robotti, *Chronicles,* 20; Thomas Hutchinson, *The History of the Colony and Province of Massachusetts Bay,* 1:80; Bodge, *King Philip's War,* 10, 19; George H. Moore, *Notes on the History of Slavery in Massachusetts,* 4; "The Body of Liberties," article 91, in Gildrie, *Covenant Community,* 92–93; Emmanuel Downing to John Winthrop, 1645, in Elizabeth Donnan, *Documents Illustrative of the History of the Slave Trade to America,* 3:8.

9. Felt reports that Major William Hathorne surprised 400 Indians, sent 200 to Boston, sentenced 7 or 8 to immediate death, and sold the rest as slaves (*Annals,* 1st ed., 255). See also Bodge, *King Philip's War,* 388.

the Pequod War onward, although it is difficult to document. Every mariner who sold New England rum in the Caribbean was not, ipso facto, then transporting slaves. But Salem, in common with the rest of the country in early days, possessed slaves and, for that matter, indentured servants. They wander in and out of the early records, usually with the first name only or as runaways in the early newspapers. Tituba and John English of the witchcraft period were only two such. Certain records remain. One Captain William Fairfield in the employ of Captain Joseph White (1748–1830) was murdered by the slaves he was transporting in 1789. Other persons mentioned as involved as either captains or merchants in the trade were Captain George Crowninshield, Captain Benjamin Hathorne, Joseph and Joshua Grafton, Joseph Waters, and John Sinclair. Slavery was abolished in Massachusetts in 1780, and the slave trade prohibited in 1788. The trade, however, did not stop. Elizabeth Donnan states that the most active Massachusetts port was Salem, which, "somewhat slow to enter the trade, was reluctant to relinquish it." In 1790 Bentley pointed out that Salem merchants were involved in the trade again. Joseph Barlow Felt acknowledged that "a few of our merchants, like others in various sea ports, still loved money more than the far greater riches of a good conscience, more than conformity with the demands of human rights." The slaves who were owned in Salem were gradually freed.[10]

Another dispute in Salem concerned the Quakers. The early Quakers did not conduct themselves in a way to guarantee peace. John Higginson (1616–1708), Salem's minister, had put into the covenant of the church that "The Quaker's light was a stinking vapour from hell." The Quakers were people who believed, as Arthur J. Worrall indicates, that "one did not need the preachings of a learned, salaried ministry to cultivate the Light and be saved." But in cultivating the Light, they used methods that horrified the Puritans. The Salem Quaker group was never large. It met in the woods on the west of town in the home of Nicholas and Hannah Phelps and entertained visiting missionaries. The Quakers were repeatedly fined for not attending the established church, and some were banished. Four visitors were hanged in Boston. When Charles II ascended the English throne, the order was given not to kill any more

10. [NH], "Sketch of the Fur Trade," in which the cut is of the Indian Hunter, "the aboriginal American, despised as he is" (510); William Edward Burghardt DuBois, *The Suppression of the African Slave-Trade to the United States of America, 1638–1870,* 225, 231; Donnan, *History of Slave Trade,* 3:32, 72, 80, 81, 82–83, 86, 89; Donnan, "The New England Slave Trade after the Revolution," 260; WB, *The Diary of William Bentley, D.D.,* 1:104, 384–85; Felt, *Annals,* 2d ed., 2:296, 417.

Quakers. Yet the sect continued to outrage many colonists, and beatings were decreed. The guilty were tied to a cart, stripped to the waist and whipped through town; even women were punished in this way by William Hathorne and others. Another Quaker, Thomas Maule of Salem, was whipped in May 1669 for saying, "Mr. Higginson preached lies" and "his instruction was the doctrine of devils."[11]

Nor were non-Quakers immune to controversy. Members of the Church of England found themselves in difficulty with the Puritans. Samuel and John Browne left Salem early because they were not allowed their place of worship. Philip English (1651–1736) was fined for not paying his church taxes and for not attending service in the specified meetinghouse. In 1734 he and his family sold land for five shillings for the future St. Peter's Episcopal Church. Roman Catholics had no place of worship in early Salem. Presbyterians were resisted for a time. The theology of the Presbyterians and early Congregationalists may have been almost identical, but church polity was not.[12]

Salem was certainly no city of peace for the accused witches. The story is too familiar to be retold fully here, though it should be noted that all the witches save one were hanged, not burned, as is often stated. Few of the accused were from Salem proper. Philip and Mary English, Bridget Oliver Bishop, George Jacob, Margaret Jacob, Ann Pudeater, and a few others were joined by those from neighboring towns. Much of the action took place in Salem Village, now Danvers, and later in Andover. Still, many of the trials were held in Salem, and the town is forever identified with the happenings of 1692. It is worth noting that there was almost no dissent about the existence of witchcraft, but there was gradually a great deal of disagreement about the admissibility of specter evidence.

From that dreadful summer "when madness reigned supreme," there was no peace for a long time. Eventually some restitution was made to those persons still alive or to their families. Confessions were made later by Ann Putnam, an accuser from Salem Village, and by Samuel Sewell, a judge from Boston, of their sins of commission or omission during

11. Arthur J. Worrall, *Quakers in the Colonial Northeast,* 6; Jonathan M. Chu, *Neighbors, Friends, or Madmen: The Puritan Adjustment to Quakerism in Seventeenth-Century Massachusetts Bay,* 89–90; Felt, *Annals,* 1st ed., 210; Sewel, *History of Quakers,* 1:422; Abner Cheney Goodell, "A Biographical Sketch of Thomas Maule of Salem Together with a Review of the Early Antinomians of New England," 246.

12. Perley, *History of Salem,* 1:367; George Francis Chever, "Some Remarks on the Commerce of Salem from 1626 to 1740—with a sketch of Philip English—a Merchant in Salem from About 1670 to About 1733–4," 2:162.

that time. Nicholas Noyes, minister of the church in Salem, admitted that he had been wrong to believe the testimony and tried to atone for his mistake for the rest of his life. Memories were long in Salem. Some records of the witchcraft era were deliberately lost, according to Charles W. Upham, but that did not keep Salemites, including Hawthorne, from the knowledge that their ancestors had been on both sides in a terrible time.[13]

Nor was the Revolution a time of peace for anyone. Patriots in Salem were gratified by their resistance to Lieutenant-Colonel Alexander Leslie when he tried to cross the North Bridge in Salem to seize arms. They were proud of their participation in the war and in the privateering that brought so much wealth to the town. Tea was on one occasion taken from a store and scattered on the streets, and the package that contained it was "ignominiously consigned to the public whipping post." Passions ran high. Pasted to a page of Charles M. Endicott's account of Leslie's raid is a clipping, presumably from a Salem paper, concerning Captain John Felt (1734–1785), who had participated in the opposition to Leslie and who "was a member of the Rev. Mr. Barnard's Society, and upon an occasion when Mr. B. concluded his prayer with the words 'God save the King,' he was so indignant, that he left his pew and stalked with an audible step, down the aisle, directly out of the Church, and afterwards had his pew nailed up in token of his displeasure, the marks of which it retained many years after."[14]

This was America's first civil war, as devastating in many ways as was the war of the mid–nineteenth century. The history of that time, as is usually the case, was written primarily by the victors, and for a long time the Loyalist side was barely mentioned. For these Tories the peace of 1783 was no peace, but only the final acknowledgment of their defeat. Many of Salem's wealthiest and most prominent men were Tories. Some remained during the war; others fled to Nova Scotia, Canada, or Great Britain. Most lost a good deal for their loyalty to England; others lost everything. William Browne (1737–1802), despite his handsome mansion in town and a dwelling formerly on Browne's hill, went to England and never returned. Peter Frye, whose home was burned by a

13. Felt, *Annals,* 1st ed., 303–11; C. Upham, *Salem Witchcraft,* 2:462–63; Christine Heyrman, "Specters of Subversion, Societies of Friends: Dissent and the Devil in Provincial Essex County, Massachusetts," 46. Bentley observes that "Few dared to blame other men, because few were innocent" ("Description and History," 271).

14. Phillips, *Salem in the Eighteenth Century,* 354–59, 466–67; Endicott, *Account of Leslie's Retreat at the North Bridge on Sunday, Feb'y 26, 1775,* 5. The clipping about Felt is in the Felt-White Collection.

mob in October 1774, fled to England and died there in 1820. Samuel Curwen, who lived in the house on the spot where Roger Williams had once resided and which had been the site of some of the witch trials, fled to England, always afraid for his life, but returned twice later, finally to stay. Near the Curwen residence was that of Nathaniel Ropes, who lay dying as a Salem mob hurled mud and stones at his windows and demanded he come out so that he might recant his views.[15]

Other Loyalists elected to stay during the war. Lawyer William Pynchon (c. 1721–1789) remained in Salem but had his windows smashed by a mob. Andrew Oliver (1731–1799), grandfather of Hawthorne's tutor, also stayed. So did Judge Benjamin Lynde (1700–1781), who had presided over the trial of Captain Preston of Boston Massacre fame; Dr. Edward A. Holyoke (1728–1829), a fixture on the Salem scene for a hundred years; the Rev. William McGilchrist (d. 1780), Scottish rector of St. Peter's, who was forbidden to hold service; Timothy Orne (c. 1750–1789), who was "threatened with being tarred and feathered for some expression not sufficiently anti-royal"; and Benjamin Pickman Jr. (1740–1819), who was often seen later in his old-fashioned garb. Salem indeed emerged from the war with many of its inhabitants divided over the result of the conflict.[16]

No town sports a history of pure peace and harmony. Any family in Salem could produce examples of conflicted opinions, of impassioned involvement in the past. Salem is different from many communities in that so many crucial events were played out there. We perhaps know this is true because it is one of the best-documented cities in the country. The people of Salem preserved many papers, but they also preserved many memories that were told by the fireside to their children and grandchildren.

Nathaniel Hawthorne read much about that past. He "never bought any books except at second-hand shops," wrote his sister to their cousins in 1876, but there were many sales of used books. In 1824, for example, Thorndike Deland, father of a friend of Hawthorne, published a catalogue of 39 pages listing 1,621 titles of every sort of book, including novels, biographies, poetry, 600 sheets on Salem witchcraft (this was before Charles Upham's first lectures in 1831), and textbooks.

15. Mary Beth Norton, *The British-Americans: The Loyalist Exiles in England, 1774–1789*, 97, 126, 167, 99–100, 103.

16. Phillips, *Salem in the Eighteenth Century*, 390; William Pynchon, *The Diary of William Pynchon*, 42–43. A good listing of loyalists may be found in George Atkinson Ward's *Journal and Letters of the Late Samuel Curwen, Judge of Admiralty, etc., an American Refugee from 1775*, 449–578.

Hawthorne also had not only the resources of his family's books but access to circulating libraries as well, and from 1826 on he had the fine library of the Salem Athenaeum. He could probably borrow other volumes from friends and teachers. Later he had the books at Bowdoin, and for several years he was able to use the Boston Athenaeum. Salem and Boston newspapers spoke much of the past, and it is clear from some of his stories that he read such newspapers carefully.[17]

Hawthorne's sketch, "Main-Street," illustrates his grasp of that history. One of the few pieces he wrote while he was surveyor at the Salem Custom House, it first appeared in Elizabeth Palmer Peabody's *Aesthetic Papers* in 1849 and was collected in *The Snow Image and Other Twice-Told Tales* in 1851. Hawthorne intended the tale to be one in a volume that would also include what later became *The Scarlet Letter* (*CE* 1:30). The story told in "Main-Street" is a very deft presentation of the history of Salem's first century. The teller says he wants to "call up the multiform and many-colored Past" (*CE* 11:49). On the same street will be seen that past, in more or less chronological order from the leaf-strewn path of the Indians through the boundary-making, property-buying early residents to the great snow of 1717, which "swept over each man's metes and bounds, and annihilated all the visible distinctions of human property" (*CE* 11:80). As time went on, the Conants and the Masseys and others entered and saw an Eden in what had been a wilderness. Then the whole group of Puritans arrived, built their meetinghouse and their dwellings, had their children, and made their rules. To fight off the Indians whom they had displaced, they had their musters; to chasten the rule-breakers, they had their punishments. All this can be documented in the historical record. Hawthorne had learned it from Thomas Hutchinson or William Bentley, or from Joseph Barlow Felt. His retelling of that history should not be overlooked.

In so doing, the writer does produce what the exasperated critic in the sketch accuses him of—"a bead-role of historic names"—but he also adds adjectives and facts that characterize the people: George Downing's "pliant conscience," for example, or Nathaniel Ward's "indescribable waywardness." Dorothy Talby, whose *"matronly face"* [italics mine] is shown here before she murders her child, is another historical figure. He portrays fifty historical personages and unnamed others, familiar to

17. EMH to her cousins, 1876, copy, Hawthorne-Manning Collection; Thorndike Deland, *Catalogue of Books*. As an example of Hawthorne's use of newspapers, the items in his sketch "Old News" are taken from the *Independent Chronicle and Universal Advertiser* in Boston. See Margaret B. Moore, "Hawthorne, the Tories, and Benjamin Lynde Oliver, Jr.," 214.

Salemites, such as the "Afflicted Ones" or the "flower of Essex." His facts are usually accurate, which makes one wonder all the more at his placing the minister, George Burroughs, not in the church in Salem Village but in the East Meeting House in Salem, which did not come into being until 1718—a year after the sketch ends (*CE* 11:61, 62, 66, 77, 72, 76). For the most part, however, as Hawthorne weaves in and out of time and back and forth from England to America, he depicts Salem with vivid accuracy.

In choosing to emphasize certain parts of Salem's history, moreover, Hawthorne manages to express many of his ideas about the town. The "new Eden" of a new world, a concept he uses often, he claims for Roger Conant and his wife. "How sweet it must be [he observes] for those who have an Eden in their hearts . . . to find a new world to project it into" (*CE* 11:53). The Indians also have a major part in his history from the time of stately Squaw Sachem and her second husband who rule the land, to the Indians who realize that the main street is no longer theirs, to the "drunken Indian, himself a prince of the Squaw Sachem's lineage" (*CE* 11:72). The process of civilization tramples "the wild woods, the wild wolf, and the wild Indian" (*CE* 11:55). The wolf appears repeatedly too. Once at home in the wilderness, he is pushed out, and finally becomes a bloody symbol on the meetinghouse portal.

Hawthorne expresses himself most fully on the results of Puritanism for Salem. He contrasts the simple wooden meetinghouse with the mighty cathedrals left behind in England and wonders why the settlers do not use the forest and "the awful vault of the firmament" for worship (*CE* 11:57–58). He had expressed this idea in the *American Magazine of Useful and Entertaining Knowledge* long before.[18] He speaks of the "zeal of a recovered faith" that for their children became "hard, cold, and confined" like "an iron cage" and produced the rigidity that later characterized the faith as described in a famous passage in "Main-Street": "Let us thank God," he concludes, "for having given us such ancestors; and let each successive generation thank him, not less fervently, for being one step further from them" (*CE* 11:68). "Main-Street" is interesting both for the details that Hawthorne selects and for those that he does not use. He speaks of the Indians, the Quakers, the witches. He does not mention the Africans, as Salem called them.

Grandfather's Chair, on the other hand, is more or less chronological in its telling of the history of the Massachusetts Bay Colony, more of Boston than of Salem. Using the idea that Susan Ingersoll is said to

18. [NH], "Churches and Cathedrals," 497–98.

have given him of the unifying presence of the old chair, he has a kindly old man telling his grandchildren stories of the past. Lady Arbella, John Endicott, Roger Williams, and William Hathorne are mentioned. The cutting of the red cross from the flag is detailed. The story of the Quakers appears in a wider setting. He cites the witchcraft delusion with Cotton Mather's part in it, but he also gives Mather credit for his introduction of the small-pox vaccine. He refers to the "first armed resistance" of the Revolution at Salem. Whereas "Main-Street" ends in 1717 with the great snow (although the showman refers with feigned regret to the "grand illumination" for General Taylor in 1841), *Grandfather's Chair* takes the story through the death of Samuel Adams in 1803 (one year before Hawthorne himself was born).

Hawthorne in his preface calls this volume "a ponderous tome" and adds that with "such unmalleable material" it is as difficult to interest children "as to manufacture delicate playthings out of the granite rocks on which New England is founded." But he also says, "There is certainly no method, by which the shadowy outlines of departed men and women can be made to assume the hues of life more effectually, than by connecting their images with the substantial and homely reality of a fireside chair" (*CE* 6:5). This, then, is the way Hawthorne conveys history, not as a dry recital of facts but as the story of human beings as their tales are told by the flickering light of the fire.

Hawthorne was far more than a recorder of facts, of course. In these works, and others, he examines the role of the artist who tells the story and interprets the details. He is usually accurate as to facts, but the meaning of these facts is often his own. What made the history of Salem come alive to Hawthorne was what he called "fireside tradition." Over and over again Hawthorne affirmed what was learned in the chimney-corner. In an introduction to "Main-Street," Julian Hawthorne noted that for his father the books on the history of Salem were

> supplemented by traditions and tales handed down from generation to generation, which had come to his knowledge when, as a boy, he sat by the broad hearthstone of his old-fashioned home, and listened to legends and accounts of personal experience from the mouths of the old men and women of that day, now seventy or eighty years gone by. Hawthorne was born in 1804, and the memories of those who were old when he was young, went back nearly to the beginning of the previous century, and were re-enforced by lore derived from their own forebears, which extended to the early years of the New England settlement.[19]

19. NH, *Main Street with Introduction by Julian Hawthorne*, 7.

This is not pure speculation. In 1898 another Salemite, John Felt (1815–1907), wrote his nephew in Virginia:

> I saw one day, "awhile ago" up in Essex Street near the Witch House—as I was walking down with my Mother, a man on the opposite side of the Street & Mother said "There is Doctor Holyoke over on the other side." He lived in Salem then and had lived there One Hundred (100) years. . . . Probably Dr. Holyoke had seen in his younger days men who saw the Witches hung up on Gallows Hill—in the upper part of Salem, and if I had thought of it I might have asked him to tell me about it & probably I never would have forgotten it.[20]

This was undoubtedly true of Hawthorne too, as George Parsons Lathrop suggests in recalling the "legacy of legend and shudder-rousing passages of family tradition" incorporated in his early experience.[21]

When Hawthorne grappled with Salem and its past, he put much emphasis on the telling, not just the writing, of tales. Many of his stories involved storytellers, such as those in "Alice Doane's Appeal," "The Village Uncle," and "Tales of the Province House." Sometimes the stories are embedded in a longer work, like Holgrave's story of Alice Pyncheon in *The House of the Seven Gables,* Zenobia's legend in *The Blithedale Romance,* or the two stories told by Dr. Portsoaken and Sybil Dacy in "Septimius Felton." Hawthorne planned a sort of Canterbury Tales sequence in the projected "Story-Teller" and "Seven Tales of my Native Land." *Grandfather's Chair* is a series of tales related to children. Eustace Bright is the storyteller in *A Wonder Book.* The writer actually replicated the telling of tales in each of these so that they are full of the passive voice: "it is said," or "it was whispered." Since the teller is relating something based on memory, the facts are never presented as certain; versions vary; different reports come in. Much of the ambiguity in Hawthorne stems from this approach.

One of the more pertinent storytellers for our purposes is that one in "Main-Street." Here is oral tradition in action, albeit aided by cardboard cutouts and changing light. The teller is going to relate what he knows about the history of Salem by using the main street of the town as a unifying theme. As with all such transmission of stories, the hearer must accept what the teller gives him, and must then use his own imagination. In oral history there are always two participants: the teller and the listener. Each has his role to play. If either fails, the storytelling does not work. And there is the further part that luck or machinery or light

---

20. John Felt to William Chester White, October 2, 1898, Felt-White Collection.
21. George Parsons Lathrop, *A Study of Hawthorne,* 37.

or shadow can play, which is often not under anyone's control, except, of course, the writer's. Even if the other two presences do their work well, the event of oral interpretation can fail. In the case of "Main-Street," the wire breaks and the whole story cannot be told.

Yet the tale incorporates elements of oral tradition. The showman keeps using the word "specter," a highly charged word for Salemites. The Indian woman is represented by a "spectral image" (*CE* 11:51). When the main body of Puritans come to Massachusetts, the teller says, "You shall behold their life-like images,—their spectres, if you choose so to call them" (*CE* 11:60). Governor Winthrop is shown as "our spectral representative" (*CE* 11:61). The showman wants to display "the ghosts of his forefathers" (*CE* 11:49). He hides the show behind a "mysterious curtain" (*CE* 11:49). The past and present curiously intermingle. Wappacowet would have been surprised to see the East India Marine Society building on the very spot where the white man would be surprised to see the Indians dancing and shrieking in the woods (*CE* 11:51). In "The Village Uncle," Hawthorne has his narrator say, "How strangely the past is peeping over the shoulders of the present" (*CE* 9:311). And so it is here. To him that can see, time is many-layered too. There was someone here before. Unless we see them and see what they did, we shall be like the Puritan children who have become Americans (unlike their parents who were English), whose limitation is that "nothing impresses them except their own experience" (*CE* 11:72).

This is chimney-corner history told by someone who is very aware of the impact of the advent of the Quakers; or of the witchcraft summer; or of the severity of the Puritan faith, which did not travel well in time; or of the pathos of the Indian whom "Anglo-Saxon energy" had displaced to the periphery of the settlers' lives. The narrator is not only knowledgeable but also may have a vested interest in these stories. Any Salemite, perhaps, would. Certainly someone like Hawthorne would. His original ancestor had fought the Indian; he had persecuted the Quaker; his son John had judged the witches. John Hathorne had actually died in 1717, the year of the great snow. In his sketch "Sir William Phips," Hawthorne had lamented that "[f]ew of the personages of past times (except such as have gained renown in fire-side legends as well as in written history) are anything more than mere names to their successors. They seldom stand up in our imaginations like men" (*CE* 23:59). Hawthorne does indeed have what Caleb Foote acknowledged in his review of *The Scarlet Letter:* "a peculiar power of calling up from the past not only the personages and incidents" of history but of evoking "their spirit" as well.[22] That is the task of the storyteller. The task of the audience is not to sit too close, or the spell is broken.

The whole background of *The House of the Seven Gables* is also presented as though it springs from oral tradition—something known by the family and by reports from others. Hawthorne uses the word "tradition" at least seven times; he chooses "chimney-corner" or "fireside tradition" six times; he notes "rumor" and "superstition," "gossip," and "story." The narrative is sprinkled with "it was averred"; it "was fabled"; it "was affirmed." Tradition is characterized as that "which sometimes brings down truth that history has let slip, but is oftener the wild babble of the time, such as was formerly spoken at the fireside and now congeals in newspapers" (*CE* 2:17). Moreover, there was a "hidden stream of private talk" (*CE* 2:320) of legendary aunts and grandmothers telling the stories of the past "from lip to ear in manifold repetition through a series of generations." These "ancient superstitions" "[b]y long transmission among household facts, grow to look like them, and have such a familiar way of making themselves at home, that their influence is usually greater than we suspect" (*CE* 2:124).

Much of Hawthorne's writing is informed by the oral traditions in his family and of his town. The stories told at his own fireside in Salem recur again and again in Hawthorne's writings, transmogrified and transformed by his own imagination. Salem had its share of the vicissitudes of mankind—family pride that led to tragedy, concealed wills, greed for property. All the seven deadly sins could be found there. But, in addition, Salem carried its extra burden of the fates of certain Quakers, of the hanging of the witches. It shared with the country the knowledge that the Revolutionary War was really a civil war, no matter what later historians were to say. Hawthorne recognized the tinge of the marvelous, the presence of something other or somewhere other that hedged daily life about. Sometimes these traditions and feelings strained credulity. In reviewing John Greenleaf Whittier's *The Superstitions of New England,* Hawthorne wrote about not only the legends but also the way in which the writer should treat them: "The proper tone of these legends is, of course, that of the fireside narrative . . . as simple as the babble of an old woman to her grandchild as they sit in the smoky glow of a deep chimney-corner. Above all, the narrator should have faith, for the time being" (*CE* 23:244).

In Hawthorne's youth there were many old people who could have told him much about the past. Richard and Miriam Manning had been

22. [C. Foote], review of "Main Street," *SG,* May 18, 1849.

brought up in Ipswich and could have communicated many stories of the long ago. Little Lucy Lord Sutton, grandniece of Miriam Lord Manning, visited the household several times and remembered sitting by Miriam Manning's bed and hearing "stories of my mother when she was a little girl, and the time she was nearly lost in a snow-storm in Ipswich."[23]

Doubtless, little Nathaniel was told many stories about his mother, Betsey Clarke Manning Hawthorne, and his aunts and uncles when they lived in Ipswich. His grandfather Manning lived until 1813 and his grandmother until 1826. Also in the Manning house from the time his grandfather died until her own death in 1818 was his great-aunt, Ruth Manning Rust. Aunt Rust, married late and widowed soon, would have had time on her hands.[24] Hawthorne also could have heard stories from his Grandmother Hathorne, with whom he lived his first four years and next door to whom he lived until she died in 1813. In addition to these possible purveyors of a "visitable past," there were many, many relatives in Salem who could have shared stories of yore. For instance, his aunt Ruth Hathorne could have straightened him out on one story of the time. In 1869 Rachel Forrester, daughter of John Forrester and Charlotte Story, wrote a note:

> There was a story current here that my grandfather [Simon Forrester] was a servant in Daniel Hathorne's family after he came here. My mother asked my great-aunt Ruth if it were true. She drew herself up indignantly and replied, "No, Charlotte. It is not true. Simon Forrester was not a man to work in any family. My father found that he belonged to a good family and had a good education and he brought him to our house and treated him from the first like a son. He was as much attached to him as to either of his own two sons."[25]

Surely Aunt Ruth did not keep this story from her little kinfolk so nearby. Two other relatives who we know passed on stories were his cousins Eben Hathorne and Susan Ingersoll. About Eben Hathorne, for example, Hawthorne wrote with feeling in his notebooks on August 28 [1837]. He described him as "an old bachelor, and truly forlorn. The pride of ancestry seems to be his great hobby" (*CE* 8:583). He told stories about the Hathornes, Philip English, and Susy Ingersoll.

From a story written by a member of the family we may view one legend that was probably known by Hawthorne. This was a tale written

---

23. Manning Hawthorne, "A Glimpse of Hawthorne's Boyhood," 181.
24. WB, *Diary,* 4:522; Albert D. Rust, *Record of the Rust Family,* 140.
25. Henry W. Belknap, "Simon Forrester and His Descendants," 19.

in 1869 by his cousin, Eleanor Barstow Condit, under the pseudonym of M. B., entitled *Philip English's Two Cups, "1692,"* which concerns a legacy that came to the writer from a favorite Salem spinster, Ursula Hillsworth, "hardly a relative although we might have claimed cousinship" (15), who is almost certainly modeled upon Susan Ingersoll. The legacy was composed of a brocade sofa-cover, faded yellow paper, a faded green cushion, a white silk apron, a stomacher that had been worn by Philip English on his wedding day, and a cabinet in which were two manuscripts written by Edmund Elton, to whom Ursula had been engaged. These manuscripts tell the story of the two cups.

The receipt of these papers makes the narrator remember an event in Salem when she was sixteen years old. She had been going for a walk when she passed the corner of St. Peter's Street and Brown Street. There a new building for St. Peter's Episcopal Church was being constructed (the actual new edifice was erected in 1833 with a restoration in 1845–1846).[26] The narrator stopped to look at gravestones around the church and noticed one for the Rev. William Fisher. Workmen digging to lay the foundation discovered several blackened boards on which was attached a plate with the initials P. E. A local antiquarian, Eben Saunders, urged that they tell Ursula since "she's nearer kin to the English's than any one in town" (28). When the narrator ran to tell Ursula about the cups, she was puzzled by the old lady's strange manner. Ursula wanted the cups to be reburied in Philip English's new tomb.

Ursula's manner is explained by the manuscripts, written by Edmund Elton, who wanted the reburial of the cups to be a "secret until after *everyone* had died" (12). The gold cup with a Scottish coat of arms had belonged to English's maternal ancestors, the Raeburns. Philip had left that cup in England when he fled because his older brother was to marry the woman he loved, Susannah Hollingsworth. He came to America and prospered with a combination of "Trade and Thrift." But Susannah loved him and came to America with her father, Richard Hollingsworth. Philip and Susannah married and all was well until the summer of 1691 when rumors of witchcraft began to be heard. Susannah, who was a saintly woman, sealed her fate the next year when in the silence before the communion service in the old First Church, she walked to the front of the church to sit with Goody Cloyse, accused of witchcraft and whose sister, Rebecca Nurse, was already languishing in jail for that offense. Susannah was soon accused also.

The narrator changes dates and names either from ignorance or for fictional purposes. She says later that she had neither Dr. Bentley nor the Salem Athenaeum to consult, nor does she refer to Charles W. Upham's account. She names Philip English's wife as Susannah rather than Mary; his daughter as Mary rather than Susannah. She uses William Fisher instead of Nathaniel Fisher as rector of St. Peter's, and, of course, Ursula Hillsworth instead of Susan Ingersoll. But the narrator refers directly to English, to the Hollingworth name (although she adds an "s"), to Goody Cloyse and Martha Corey, to Dr. Benjamin Lynde Oliver and his organ at the church, and most of all to Justice John Hathorne.

Condit's story takes a different turn at the arrest of Mrs. English. It is the combined work of the Mathers, the Rev. Joshua Moody, and John Hathorne that saves the Englishes. Hathorne meets with the other three when he knows he has to arrest Susannah. He says he will serve "a writ—and am I not sworn? I shall remand her to the gaol in Boston; there let her remain until you can arrange that both Philip English and herself can repair to New Amsterdam, and tarry there until this tempest be overpast" (86–87). These gentlemen so conspire and save them both. About Cotton Mather, the manuscript speaks of one "who has suffered so much for the part he took in these strange proceedings, if his mind and judgement strayed so far from what we now consider a righteous decision, surely his heart was never degraded to malignity toward the victims" (87–88). Even Sir William Phips is part of the rescue, especially after his wife recognizes Susannah as a girlhood friend from England.

When the Englishes return to Salem the next year, after sending grain to the starving populace, they are greeted by throngs of grateful Salemites. At the house of seven gables (which is the English house, not the Turner house), John Hathorne, of "composed and stately beauty" whose "devotion" has helped save them, brings them a silver cup and gives a toast: "Prosperity to our town with your blessing and forgiveness." The manuscript breaks off at this point, and the narrator says that Mary English and John Hathorne's son were married. The story ends with these words: "Certainly, the *glorious light* that ever gleamed on that notable mansion, might be traced not very indirectly to this event" (109).

In actuality, two of Philip English's granddaughters married grandsons of Justice John Hathorne. Furthermore, John Hathorne does not usually appear as the savior of the Englishes. In fact, one story is told that Philip English, on his deathbed, said he would forgive Hathorne but that if he

recovered, "be damned if I forgive him" (*CE* 8:75). Nathaniel Hawthorne
certainly does not treat Hathorne kindly. He also castigates Cotton
Mather more than once for his actions in the witchcraft proceedings. As
for Philip English's part, he observes, "Philip English, a rich merchant
of Salem, found it necessary to take flight, leaving his property and
business in confusion. But a short time afterwards, the Salem people
were glad to invite him back" (*CE* 6:78–79).

Yet, despite discrepancies in facts and points of view, Eleanor Barstow
Condit's story has many elements of oral tradition of the Hathorne,
Forrester, and English families. These legends could have been skewed
for the sake of family honor. The heroes of this story are too heroic to
reflect any reality, yet that is the way of fireside tradition. Hawthorne
has the warden in "Etherege" tell of a historian who had "too much
the habit of seeking his authorities in cottage-chimney corners. I mean
that an old woman's [stories] were just about as acceptable to him as
a recorded fact, and to say the truth, they are really apt to have ten
times the life in them" (*CE* 12:150). You do have to have faith for the
time being.

One can see how both Hawthorne and Condit probably used recorded fact as it was passed to them by word of mouth and by newsprint,
as, for example, in the *Salem Observer* on June 8, 1833:

> In digging the foundation of the new Episcopal Church in this town the
> remains of many of the old worshippers of St. Peter's were disturbed.
> Among them was the remains of Jonathan Pue Esq., "His Majesty's
> Inspector and Informer," who died in the year 1760, seventy-three years
> since. His wig was in a good state of preservation and his worsted sash
> was not entirely decayed; three silver buttons were also found in his
> grave. An old lady (now deceased of our acquaintance) informed us,
> she remembered this ancient royalist officer and that she had seen him
> frequently in his seat at Church, and instead of a box to carry his rappee,
> he had a pocket of leather, which would probably hold a pound.
>
> Sixty or seventy years ago about twenty feet was added to the
> length of the church, and directly under that part a brick grave was
> found. . . . Nothing was found by which a discovery could be made
> who the occupant was. It has been thought by some it might be Philip
> English—it is certain it was a person of some note, as six silver plated
> coffin handles were found in the grave, and some fragments of an
> ornamented plate, the bones were quite large and must have belonged
> to a large man.

Here was grist for Hawthorne's as well as Condit's imagination: the
fragments of cloth of Jonathan Pue, the silver-plated coffin handles,

and the ornamented plate that could have been Philip English's. In fact, Hawthorne reported a newspaper account of the digging up of Pue in "The Custom-House" (*CE* 1:30). Many of Hawthorne's best legends sprang from the town he so loved and hated, for the Salem world of the past was essential to his literary imagination.

2

"The Long Past"

[T]here will be a connection with the long past—a reference to forgotten events and personages, and to manners, feelings, and opinions, almost or wholly obsolete—which, if adequately translated to the reader, would serve to illustrate how much of old material goes to make up the freshest novelty of human life.
—(*CE* 2:6)

SALEM WAS like many small towns, filled with interlinked families. What Hawthorne knew of all the families who wove his tangled web is partly conjecture, yet these ancestors did play an important part in constituting his Salem world. He may not have known some stories that suited his purposes, but he probably knew more than he indicated. In "Etherege" Hawthorne described a boy growing up in a house bordering on a graveyard in a town that was surely Salem:

> And so the boy's thoughts [he said] were led to dwell on by-gone things; on matters of birth and ancestry; and connections of one family with another, and blood running in such intricate currents; sometimes sinking into the ground and disappearing forever; sometimes, after a long hidden course, reappearing, and ascending prominently like the gush of a fountain. And probably it was such meditations as these that led him to think, occasionally, what had been his own origin; whence came that blood that circled through his own veins. (*CE* 12:98)

Like that boy, Hawthorne often wondered about his own origins. He speculated most about his paternal Hathorne ancestors, and they were a fascinating lot. In "The Custom-House" he said of Major William Hathorne (c. 1606/1607–1681): "The figure of that first ancestor, invested by family tradition with a dim and dusky grandeur, was present to my boyish imagination as far back as I can remember. It still haunts me and induces a sort of home-feeling with the past" (*CE* 1:9). What Hawthorne recounts is the New England experience, as he knew it, of this "grave, bearded, sable-cloaked and steeple-crowned progenitor" who "trode the unworn street" of Salem with his "Bible and his sword" (*CE* 1:9).

Although much can be recovered now about Major William Hathorne from the English records of the time, there is much still unknown. He came from a substantial yeoman family in Berkshire, a fact that Hawthorne so longed to know and did not. The Hathornes lived in Bray and its environs, including Binfield. The emigrant's grandfather William, who died in Bray in 1626, was a church warden, a trustee of a church charity, and an owner of much land and many tenements in that vicinity. His inventory showed a sum of more than 194 pounds at his death. He owned property in Bray, East Oakley, Water Oakley, and Binfield, residences as well as many lesser buildings. When he died he left a "Bible with other Books," "one and a half dozen silver spoons," and much furniture and furnishings.[1]

His son William, Major Hathorne's father, lived in Bray until 1608, after his eldest son was born. Subsequently, this William moved with his wife, Sara, to Binfield, probably to the house that his father owned. When this Hathorne died in 1651, he too owned lands in Bray as well as Binfield. He willed money to be sent to his three children in America: one hundred pounds to William; forty pounds to daughter Elizabeth, who had married Captain Richard Davenport; and the same amount to son John, an innkeeper in Malden and Lynn, Massachusetts.[2]

Vernon Loggins thought the "yeoman" category of the family indicated a lowly status in prestige and funds. David Cressy, however, is nearer to the mark, I believe, when he remarks, "Yeomen, who were usually freeholders, had a considerable amount of wealth tied up in land." He asserts that "[r]elatively few yeomen were attracted to New England. . . . On the whole they were more literate and lived in finer style than the poorer farmers or husbandmen."[3] Furthermore, according to David Hackett Fischer, nearly three-fourths of adult Massachusetts

1. Elizabeth French, "Genealogical Research in England," 67:250–51.
2. Henry F. Waters, "Genealogical Gleanings in England," 201–2; French, "Genealogical Research in England," 67:256–57.
3. Vernon Loggins, *The Hawthornes: The Story of Seven Generations of an American Family,* 11–12, 14; David Cressy, *Coming Over: Migration and Communication between England and New England in the Seventeenth Century,* 120, 67. Also see Roger Thompson, *Mobility and Migration: East Anglian Founders of New England, 1629–1640:* "The difference between a yeoman and a gentleman was often not so much a matter of wealth as of lifestyle or 'port.' The yeoman was a working farmer" (101).

emigrants paid their own passage—"no small sum in 1630." For those who wished some comfort, the price was probably 60 or 80 pounds, and a typical English yeoman had perhaps 40 to 60 pounds as an annual income.[4]

Had he stayed in England, William, as the eldest son, would have inherited the most from his parents. He had no known financial reason to emigrate, nor was he motivated by the number in his family. Each family before had been large, and there seemed to be plenty for all. Elizabeth was the fourth child, and John the sixth. The reasons for William and Elizabeth to emigrate seem to have been primarily religious in nature. Certainly William and Elizabeth were true Puritans, insofar as we can discover their feelings. One of Elizabeth's children was named Truecross, and her husband held the banner from which the red cross was cut by Endicott.[5] Major William was constantly on call for religious as well as political summonses; of course, the two viewpoints were inseparable at the time.

There may have been some family revulsion at the extreme flexibility of the Vicar of Bray, Symon Alleyn, who retained his office from the time of Henry VIII through the reign of Elizabeth, a feat characterized in a contemporary song that maintained, "Whatsoever King does reign, / I'll still be the Vicar of Bray." Hawthorne knew of the Vicar; he mentions his cassock in "A Virtuoso's Collection" (*CE* 10:487). The very fact that William Hathorne came over with the fleet of John Winthrop in 1630 certainly leads one to believe that Puritanism played a large role in his motivation. In his will written in 1679/1680, he gives "my Soule into the hands of Jesus Christ, in whome I hope to liue for euer, & my body to the earth, in hope of a Glorious resurection with him when this vile body, shalbe [*sic*] made like unto his Glorious body." The teller of stories in *Grandfather's Chair* certainly affirmed that strong faith when he spoke of the Puritans. "They began to look around them," he affirmed, "for some spot where they might worship God, not as the king and bishops thought fit, but according to the dictates of their own consciences" (*CE* 6:12). Only John, the younger brother, left no evidence of such opinions. Fischer believes that the motivation for these early settlers was overwhelmingly religious if they joined the church upon entering the new land: "After 1635, a candidate had to stand before a highly skeptical group of elders, and satisfy them in three respects: adherence to Calvinist doctrines, achievement of a godly life, and a demonstrable

4. David Hackett Fischer, *Albion's Seed: Four British Folkways in America*, 28.
5. French, "Genealogical Research in England," 67:257; C. Upham, *Salem Witchcraft*, 1:101.

experience of spiritual conversion." William and his wife joined the Salem church in 1637.[6]

Major Hathorne, moreover, was a very solid citizen as well as Puritan. He served twenty-four terms on the Board of Selectmen (1635–1661) and eighteen years on the Court of Assistants of the Colony of Massachusetts Bay. He had first lived in Dorchester until Hugh Peter, the minister in Salem, persuaded him to move there. He was also given much property, but he repaid Salem with his work for that community and for the Massachusetts Bay Colony. He settled boundary disputes; he fought the Indians; he guarded the city and colony against blasphemers. Edward Johnson in "Wonder-Working Providence of Sion's Saviour" praised him for his "quick apprehension, strong memory, and rhetorick, volubility of speech which hath caused the people to make use of him often in publick service." Lucy Downing wrote John Winthrop in 1640 about a proposed bride for a Downing relative that she did not know whether Endicott could be trusted in her estate, "but I have heard he is not; only Mr. Hathorn and some others." Joseph Barlow Felt called him a "pillar which sustained and adorned both church and state."[7] Nathaniel Hawthorne characterizes William when he refers to the first Puritans as "stern, severe, intolerant but not superstitious, not even fanatical, and endowed, if any men of that age were, with a far-seeing worldly sagacity" (*CE* 11:68).

HAWTHORNE AND THE "STRANGE PEOPLE"

On the other hand, William Hathorne was "a bitter persecutor" who ordered the whipping of Quaker Ann Coleman through Salem and two other towns. Nathaniel Hawthorne seemed haunted by his ancestor's association with the punishment of the Quakers, the "strange people" who had the "gift of a new idea." In "The Custom-House" and in "Main-Street," Major Hathorne or "the earliest emigrant of my name" is seen as an instigator of the persecution of Quakers (*CE* 1:9; 11:68–69). In "Young Goodman Brown" that same ancestor appears by indirection (*CE* 10:77).

6. George Alexander Cooke, *Cooke's Topographical Library of Great Britain: Berkshire*, 95; Perley, *History of Salem*, 2:360; *Probate Records of Essex County*, 3:422. Eliot, *Biographical Dictionary*, said that William Hathorne was "as reputable for his piety as for his political integrity" (247); Fischer, *Albion's Seed*, 21; *Records of First Church, Salem*, 6.

7. Christine Alice Young, *From "Good Order" to Glorious Revolution, Salem, Massachusetts, 1628–1689*, 118; Arthur H. Harrington, "Hathorne Hill in Danvers with Some Account of Major William Hathorne," 104–11; Edward Johnson, "Wonder-Working Providence of Sion's Saviour," 24; Lucy Downing, "Letters of Lucy Downing [1626–1674]," *Winthrop Papers*, 3:28; Felt, *Annals*, 1st ed., 270.

Hawthorne's interest in the Quakers is evident in his frequent references to George Fox, the early English Quaker, in *Grandfather's Chair*, "Grimshawe," and "A Virtuoso's Collection," in which he calls Fox "perhaps the truest apostle that has appeared on earth for these eighteen hundred years" (*CE* 6:40; 12:395; 10:487). Yet the writer makes clear in "The Gentle Boy" his belief that Quakers also erred in their extremes of fanaticism, their neglect of family ties, and in what he saw as their omission of a rational belief dependent on something other than an inward voice (*CE* 9:69, 98).

Hawthorne had read a great deal about the period of Quaker persecution in Massachusetts. He knew not only about those who came from overseas, whom he most emphasized, but also about the homegrown variety. A well-known Salem Quaker, Thomas Maule, lends his name— inadvertently—to Matthew Maule in *The House of the Seven Gables*. If "The Haunted Quack," first printed in 1831, be truly Hawthorne's, his pseudonym of Joseph Nicholson refers to another Salem Quaker.[8] In "Young Goodman Brown" the young protagonist talks of his ancestor who commanded the constable to lash "the Quaker woman so smartly through the streets of Salem" (*CE* 10:77). Hawthorne had read this detail of the whipping of Ann Coleman in William Sewel's *The History of the People Called Quaker*, which said that Major Hathorne had once opposed "compulsion for conscience" but that his "firm warrant" for whipping had almost cost Coleman's life. In *New England Judged* (1703) George Bishop blasted William Hathorne, "Whose Name I record to rot and Stink to all Generations, unto whom this shall be left as a perpetual Record of Everlasting Shame." William Hathorne, as magistrate, was very much involved in the persecution of Quakers, but later scholars have been kinder to him than was his descendant. Arthur J. Worrall reported that Quaker Deborah Wilson, who walked naked through the streets of Salem, was lashed so leniently by William Hathorne that John Higginson saw to it that a more rigorous constable was elected. Jonathan M. Chu believes that the original Hathorne was far more easygoing than he is given credit for, that he never charged as much in the way of fines as was possible.[9]

---

8. Chu, *Neighbors, Friends or Madmen*, 49; Worrall, *Quakers in the Colonial Northeast*. This section on Quakers is only slightly changed from a paper, "Hawthorne and the 'Strange People,'" read to the Philological Association of the Carolinas at Clemson University, Clemson, South Carolina, on March 14, 1992.

9. Sewel, *History of Quakers*, 2; George Bishop, *New England Judged by the Spirit of the Lord*, 77; Worrall, *Quakers in the Colonial Northeast*, 29; Chu, *Neighbors, Friends, or Madmen*, 41–42.

Another Quaker connection involved John Hathorne, the so-called witch judge, who in 1674/1675 married Ruth Gardner, the daughter of Lieutenant George Gardner and Elizabeth Freestone Turner Gardner. Judge John Hathorne's mother-in-law, then, was the "Lieut. Gardner's wife" who was so frequently cited in the early church records of Essex County for absence from meeting and for Quaker sympathies. Born a Freestone, she was a kinswoman of the Hutchinson family of Lincolnshire, England, and came to live with William and his more noted wife, Ann Hutchinson, in Boston. Hence, she was early in contact with those who did not conform to standard Puritan practice, since the meetings of the Antinomians were held in the Hutchinson home. Elizabeth Freestone married first Robert Turner, a shoemaker of Boston, and was the mother of John Turner, who later owned a house in Salem with seven gables. She was the second wife of George Gardner. She, not George, was the convinced Quaker, but he suffered too not only by paying her fines but also by the fact that they finally had to leave Salem sometime after 1669 and go to Hartford, Connecticut, to escape persecution. His daughter Ruth Gardner Hathorne was named in her father's will as receiving a number of her father's Connecticut debts. She named her last child Freestone Hathorne, who was baptized in February 1698/1699.[10] Thus the eminent John would certainly have been aware of this Quaker connection. Would his descendant also have been?

Hawthorne's primary connection with Quaker persecution, however, was his descent from the Phelps family. His paternal grandmother was Rachel Phelps Hathorne, whose earliest known male Phelps ancestor was husbandman Henry Phelps, who came to Massachusetts in the *Hercules* in 1634. At some point Henry's mother, Eleanor Phelps Trusler, and his brothers, Nicholas and Edward Phelps, came too. We do not know whether his father came and soon died, or whether the widow Eleanor married Thomas Trusler before or after she emigrated.[11] Eleanor, a very outspoken lady, has been called a Gortonist. She and Trusler were members of First Church by 1639. In 1644 Eleanor was fined by the court for saying that "their teacher Mr. [Edward] Norris, taught the people lies,

10. George E. McCracken, "The Salem Gardners: Comments and Clues," 160–67; G. Andrews Moriarty, "The Wife of George Gardner of Salem," 105–6; Frank A. Gardner, "Thomas Gardner, Planter, and Some of His Descendants," 204–5, 210, 212.

11. Many of the facts concerning the Phelps family can be ascertained from the family genealogy (Oliver Seymour Phelps and Andrew T. Servin, *The Phelps Family of America*) with the caution that Donald Lines Jacobus gave in the *American Genealogist*, 31 (1951): 219 when he termed it "very unreliable." For other facts, see Banks, *Planters of the Commonwealth*, 108; Perley, *History of Salem*, 1:320; Merton Taylor Goodrich, "The Children of Eleanor Trusler," 15.

and that Mr. Norris and Mr. Endecott were the foundation of the church and they were unfaithful." She was also quoted as declaring that "there was no love in the church and that they were biters and devourers and that Mr. Norris said that men would change their judgment for a dish of meat." Cassandra Southwick was reported to have told the court that Eleanor "did question the government ever since she came."[12] (That is a pretty irony from one who was among the most persecuted Quakers just a little later.)

Eleanor had bought from that same Norris a lot to the west of Salem in what was called simply the Woods, and she built a house on it. When she died in 1655, she left her house and land to Henry and Nicholas. Here the story takes on a soap-opera aspect. At some point Henry had again sailed from England to America, this time on the same ship with a certain Hannah Baskell. It was later deposed that Henry and Hannah had spent entirely too much time together. The captain was quoted as saying that "it [is] not enough for yw to let Hannah lay her head in yr lapp but shee ly in yr Cabbin to." He also called Hannah a strumpet.[13] Whatever the relationship at that point, Hannah married Nicholas Phelps, not Henry, but the embers obviously smoldered.

Nicholas and Hannah Phelps became Quakers, and the meetings in Salem were held at their home in the Woods. They were repeatedly fined for absence from the Puritan meeting (the only one allowed) and for entertaining Quakers. William Hathorne had issued an order to his minions: "You are required by virtue hereof, to search in all suspicious houses for private meetings, and if they refuse to open the doors, you are to break open the door upon them, and return the names of all ye find to Ipswich Court." Finally both Hannah and Nicholas were arrested; Hannah was put into jail, and Nicholas was banished from the colony. He and Samuel Shattuck went to England in 1660 and stayed long enough to obtain from Charles II the order to the Massachusetts Bay Colony to desist from killing Quakers. In June 1661 Hannah was again presented to the court for holding that "Mr. Higginson sent abroad his wolves and his bloodhounds amongst the sheep and lambs and that priests were deceivers of the people." Perhaps it was inevitable that during Nicholas's absence Henry and Hannah would renew their relationship, whatever it was. Henry evidently bought Nicholas's half

12. Gildrie, *Covenant Community,* points out that "Gortonism seems to have been a clear precurser of Quakerism" (79). See also Phillips, *Salem in the Seventeenth Century,* 199, and *Records and Files,* 1:68.

13. *Records and Files,* 1:356; Sidney Perley, "The Woods, Salem in 1700," 188; "Ipswich Court Records and Files," 37.

of the estate, which had been deeded by law to the court in 1660, and perhaps he moved in with Hannah. At any rate, the courts were soon warning Henry not to dally with Nicholas's wife. Nicholas came back from England by 1662 and died before 1664. Meanwhile the court accused Henry of beating his son John, of making him work on the Sabbath, and of entertaining Quakers. He was again told to stay away from Hannah. John was taken away from him and put with a "religious family." At some point then in 1664/1665, Hannah, the widow of Nicholas, and Henry Phelps were married, probably at a Quaker meeting, and moved to the Perquimans District in eastern North Carolina. There they were found in 1672 by William Edmondson, an Irishman converted to Quakerism by George Fox. Edmondson wrote in his journal, "He [Phelps] and his wife had been convinced of the truth in New England, and came there to live, who not having seen a Friend for seven years they wept for joy to see us." It is intriguing to find in the North Carolina deeds and records of that area the names of Maule, Shattuck, and Nicholson, and to see a grandson of Hannah's named Jonathan Phelps, the name later given to Nathaniel Hawthorne's great-grandfather.[14]

Henry Phelps did not seem to be a Quaker while in Salem, but he appears to have become one by his time in North Carolina. His son, John, Hawthorne's ancestor, continued to live in the Woods and eventually helped determine the line between Reading and Salem. He ran the Phelps Mill, and, so far as I know, was never a Quaker. Whatever religious family he lived with or perhaps the beatings by his father may have cured him of any tendency he possibly had. His mother, Henry's first wife, is not definitely known. She has been speculated to have been a sister of Thomas Antrum or of Edmond Batter. Both have been designated as kinsmen.[15]

Another Quaker connection occurred in that Phelps line. John's son, Henry Phelps, married Rachel Guppy, daughter of John and Abigail Kitchen Guppy. Nathaniel Hawthorne's Guppy connection is a story in itself. The grandfather of Rachel, old Reuben Guppy, was part of the

14. *Records and Files,* 2:103–4, 106, 107, 118, 167; James Bowden, *The History of the Society of Friends in America,* 165–66; Perley, *History of Salem,* 2:257, 268–69; *Records and Files,* 2:220, 261–62, 314; Gwen Boyer Bjorkman, "Hannah (Baskel) Phelps Phelps Hill: A Quaker Woman and Her Offspring," 289–302, 293. The name of Phelps was often printed as Philips.

15. William P. Upham, *Town Records of Salem, 1634–1659,* 2:166, 295; Lura Woodside Watkins, "Water Mills of Middleton," 339–40; *Records and Files,* 3:277; Perley, *History of Salem,* 2:257. Perley thought Henry Phelps married Edmund Batter's sister.

Bay Colony at least by 1641 when he was accused of running away from his pregnant wife, stealing an axe, having somebody's chicken in his britches, and numerous similar crimes. Guppy is a marvelous Snopes-like creature, always on the fringes of the law, always in trouble, in the stocks, or being whipped. He told the court that he "did not go to meeting and that the parings of his nails and a chip were as acceptable to God as the day of Thanksgiving."[16]

His son, John Guppy, was not the most savory character either. He married Abigail Kitchen in 1669. Abigail's parents were John and Elizabeth Grafton Kitchen. John Kitchen was often in trouble with the Puritan authorities. He and Elizabeth were frequently fined for attending Quaker meetings and for absence from the duly constituted church. In fact, Kitchen was displaced from the office of sergeant of the foot company because of his "unworthy and malignant speeches." Elizabeth Grafton Kitchen was John's second wife, and she was also a Quaker. She received harsh treatment from Edmond Batter, the self-appointed Quaker-basher. He took her horse and said she had been "paw-wawing" and called her a "base quaking slut." For this Batter was admonished by the court, an uncommon occurrence for him.[17]

The daughter of John Guppy and Abigail Kitchen Guppy married Henry Phelps, Hawthorne's great-great grandfather. Rachel and Henry Phelps, descended as they were from Quakers in the thick of the Quaker persecution, seem to have been quiet members of the church in Salem Village, Massachusetts. Their son, Jonathan, lived in Beverly and then in Salem and showed his dissenting nature only by becoming for a short time a Presbyterian and retaining a residue of such opinion so that Dr. William Bentley of the East Church called him a man "warm in the vulgar theology of strong passions." He died before Hawthorne was born. His daughter Rachel, who married old Daniel Hathorne, the writer's grandfather, dutifully joined Daniel's church, the First Church of Salem.[18]

Thus, these Quakers were far back in Hawthorne's background, and he did not use their particular stories in his work. He often seems to

16. Perley, *History of Salem,* 2:118–19; *Records and Files,* 1:25.

17. G. Andrews Moriarty Jr., "The Kitchen Family of Salem," 126–27; *Records and Files,* 2:219, 135; 3:17.

18. *Vital Records of Reading, Massachusetts to the Year 1850,* 1:256; WB, *Diary,* 2:360; First Church of Salem Records, 312; Phelps and Servin, *Phelps Family,* 2:1581, 1593. This genealogy is incorrect in stating the second Henry Phelps's wife. She was Rachel Guppy. See Judith M. Garland on behalf of Gary Boyd Roberts to Margaret B. Moore, February 2, 1991; also see Gary Boyd Roberts, "Additions, Corrections, and Further Documentation for Previous Columns," 67.

see the Quakers as outsiders coming in to disrupt the community. He showed no reluctance to specify in the case of the first Hathorne; would he have been reluctant to use Elizabeth Gardner, the Phelpses, or the Kitchens, had he known about them? Or was the position of victim, empathetically felt, less intriguing than that of guilty victor?

On the other hand, would the old ladies of the family who sat in the chimney-corners have relayed any of these stories to the young boy? Since the tales are all on the paternal side, Rachel Phelps Hathorne would have had to do all the talking, and we do not know. There were, however, other relatives nearby in Salem of whom I am convinced the young boy was far more aware than he is generally thought to have been. He says he heard many of the witch stories; surely he heard about the Quakers as well. As he grew older, he read Joseph Barlow Felt's *Annals of Salem* and Sewel's book on Quakers, and Hutchinson's history and many another book that could have relayed these stories. Anyone as self-aware as Nathaniel Hawthorne surely did not let the Phelps name, for instance, go by in his reading without wondering about the connections. Furthermore, the very ambiguity with which he treats the Quakers may spring from his knowledge that his ancestors were not only persecutors but the persecuted as well.

What is indisputable is that Nathaniel Hawthorne had connections, whether he knew the extent of them or not. His roots were absolutely intertwined with the soil of Salem, with all the soils that make it up. Whatever he knew of his own relationships with the Quakers, he recognizes that this strange people with their gift of a new idea had touched a secret spring and were part of his mental makeup.

HAWTHORNE'S CONNECTIONS WITH WITCHES

As for Hawthorne's ties with the persecutions of the witches, they too are based partly on his paternal ancestors, in particular on John Hathorne (1641–1717), the third son of Major William and Anna Hathorne and an important merchant in Salem. Like his father, he was valuable in civic affairs. He was deputy to the General Court in 1683, an assistant to the Bay Colony in 1684, a magistrate judge of the Court of Common Pleas, and in 1702 a judge on the Superior Court. In addition, he was named commander-in-chief against the Indians in 1696.[19]

John Hathorne was also the famous "witch judge" blamed by many, such as Charles Upham, for playing a major role in the witchcraft

19. Harrington, "Hathorne Hill," 111. The following section is only slightly changed from a paper, "Hawthorne and the Summer of 1692," read to the Philological Association of the Carolinas at Elon College, Elon, North Carolina, in March 1993.

trials in Salem and Salem Village in 1692. According to his descendant, John Hathorne "inherited the persecuting spirit, and made himself so conspicuous in the martyrdom of the witches, that their blood may fairly be said to have left a stain upon him. So deep a stain, indeed, that his old dry bones, in the Charter Street burial-ground, must still retain it, if they have not crumbled utterly to dust" (CE 1:9). Even today tourists are told, as they pause by the burial ground, that the witch-judge, John Hathorne, is buried there, and his slanted slate stone can still be seen.

John Hathorne is indeed buried there. He was appointed a magistrate of the Court of Oyer and Terminer by Governor William Phips. The chief questioner of the presumed witches, he always seemed to suppose them guilty. Nathaniel Hawthorne's sister Elizabeth quoted cousin Ann Savage as saying that Charles W. Upham had "purposely and maliciously belittled" John Hathorne in his two-volume study, *Salem Witchcraft*. Hathorne's task was to query the victims about serious accusations in a time when virtually all Christians believed in witchcraft. That he was sometimes cruel in his questioning is true. When he and Justice Corwin were examining Elizabeth Cary of Charlestown, she asked to be seated. He said that she had "strength enough" and left her standing. Captain Nicholas Cary thought Hathorne and others were cruel to his wife and declared that he was "extreamly troubled at their Inhumane dealings," and hoped "[T]hat God would take vengeance on them." This curse as well as Sarah Good's threat to Nicholas Noyes may have been in Hawthorne's mind when he wrote in *The House of the Seven Gables* of Matthew Maule's prophecy that Colonel Pyncheon, who had "hunted [him] to death for his spoil" would be "given blood to drink" by God in retribution (*CE* 2:8). Chadwick Hanson believes that Hathorne was "never more brutal nor more intolerant than in the examination of Martha Cory," another accused and subsequently hanged witch.[20]

In that witchcraft year of 1692, heavy with curses, Judge John Hathorne had a son. A mariner first like his brothers, Joseph (1692–1762) eventually stayed at home. In 1715 he married Sarah Bowditch, the daughter of William Bowditch and Mary Gardner, first cousin of Ruth Gardner Hathorne. Kai Erikson speaks of "the third generation of settlers with no clear definition of the status they held as the chosen children of God." Joseph was of that generation. We do not know much about this Hathorne. He lived in the large Hathorne house and left his house in

20. JH, *Nathaniel Hawthorne and Wife,* 1:9; C. Upham, *Salem Witchcraft,* 1:187; *Salem Witchcraft Papers: Verbatim Transcripts of the Legal Documents of the Salem Witchcraft Outbreak of 1692,* 1:209; Chadwick Hanson, *Witchcraft at Salem,* 42.

town and his farm to his children when he died in 1762. Vernon Loggins observed that with Joseph the family went "back" to yeomanry. Yet his inventory showed that Joseph left more than sixteen hundred pounds as well as many possessions.

There was some sort of difficulty in Joseph's family. His will revoked an earlier document, signed by him perhaps on July 25, 1759. This will left all to his wife before a division. He left the family pew in First Church—one-half to daughters, Sarah Cheever and Ruth Ropes, and one-half to Daniel Hathorne. After Joseph's wife died, the estate was to go in four equal shares to William and Daniel, Ruth and Sarah. The most tantalizing part of the will refers to the children of his dead son John:

> I give to John Hathorne and Susannah Hathorne, the children of my son John lately deceased the sum of two hundred pounds lawful money of the Province. . . . as they respectively arrive at the age of twenty one years which sum of two hundred pounds (considering some things needless to mention here) is all that I think the said Children ought to have and it is all that they are to have out of my estate.[21]

Something had happened in the John Hathorne family that Joseph did not like. Was this a legacy somehow of the witchcraft episode?

That which delineates Joseph Hathorne for us is the fact that he left some extremely interesting children. Two of his sons married Touzels. Mary and Susannah Touzel were the daughters of John Touzel (or Tousel), a well-educated goldsmith and mariner, and Susannah English, the daughter of Jerseyman Philip English and Mary Hollingworth, two of the accused witches. English, even though he lost much after his arrest for witchcraft, was a very wealthy man. He and his family donated the land for St. Peter's Church, once an Episcopalian church was allowed in Salem in 1734. English, in fact, was so determined an Anglican that he was rowed across Salem Harbor to St. Michael's in Marblehead every Sunday. As Christine Heyrman reports, "Their Sabbath boat pilgrimages across the harbor to Marblehead were conducted in an atmosphere of unseemly festivity that raised the hackles of Salem's orthodox residents." English was also fined for not paying his church taxes to the East Meeting House.[22]

21. Kai Theodore Erikson, *Wayward Puritans: A Study in the Sociology of Deviance,* 157; Loggins, *The Hawthornes,* 160–61; Essex County Probate Court, #12875, will of Captain Joseph Hathorne, July 15, 1762.

22. Henry W. Belknap, "Philip English, Commerce Builder," 21–22; Heyrman, *Commerce and Culture: The Maritime Communities of Colonial Massachusetts, 1690–1750,* 267.

When Mary English was arrested for witchcraft, she was kept in jail in Salem for six weeks. Since Philip visited her every day, he was soon accused and seized. According to Bentley's account (received from Susannah Hathorne, granddaughter of the Englishes), friends arranged for them to be sent to the Boston jail. They stayed in that jail only at night, and were invited to church service by the Reverend Joshua Moody on the day before they were to return to Salem for trial. Moody's text was "they that are persecuted in one city, let them flee to another." They were persuaded to do just that after some conversation and fled with their eldest daughter. Their other children were boarded in Boston.

One version of the English story was held by the Forresters. Eleanor Barstow Condit used this version, as previously discussed, in *Philip English's Two Cups, "1692."* George F. Chever, who published a long article on English in 1859, obtained his "historical facts" from Nancy Forrester Barstow, Eleanor Condit's mother. In this tradition, Cotton Mather was supposed to have said that he did not believe Mary English to be guilty, that "her accusers evidently believed her to be so, but that Satan was most probably deceiving them into that belief."[23]

A slightly different tradition came from the family of Benjamin F. Browne, a friend of Hawthorne's and a descendant of the Englishes. The Browne family believed that the Englishes escaped from the church in Boston and that Philip English rode his horse with the horseshoes reversed to escape detection. That family also thought that persons in high authority helped the Englishes escape. Meanwhile in Salem, the English houses and storehouses were looted and plundered. It was conjectured that English lost more than two thousand pounds. The many-gabled English house, built in 1683, was sometimes thought to be the location of the dwelling in Hawthorne's second novel. When it was taken down, a secret room was discovered in the garret, considered to have been built after their return as a place of refuge if ever needed.[24] Hawthorne was bound to have been cognizant of these many traditions—through his own family, through Susie Ingersoll, or through Benjamin F. Browne, among others.

Nathaniel Hawthorne's two great-aunts (by marriage), then, were Touzels who married Hathornes. Their descendants were prominent in the Salem of his youth, two of whom were Susan Ingersoll and Eben Hathorne. The writer himself was not a direct descendant of

23. WB, *Diary,* 2:24–25; Eliot, *Biographical Dictionary,* 329; Belknap, "Philip English," 21–22; Chever, "Philip English," 1:163–64.
24. Chever, "Philip English," 166; Sidney Perley, "Salem in 1700. No. 21," 168.

Philip English, but many of his second cousins were. Dr. Bentley was especially interested in Susannah Touzel Hathorne, who seemed to have inherited a full share of family pride, although I am not sure whether the pride stemmed from the Hathorne or the Touzel-English side. Bentley was fascinated with some of the belongings that came down from Philip English, especially a silver goblet and table silver.[25] Later at the Essex Historical Society, Hawthorne would see "A black glass bottle, stamped with the name of Philip English" (*CE* 8:155).

Another connection with the witchcraft time was with the Proctors. John Proctor and his wife were found guilty of witchcraft. Because she was pregnant, she was not executed during that frightful summer, but he was. In "Main-Street" Hawthorne described them as an "aged couple. . . . [who] have shown their withered faces at children's bedsides, mocking, making mouths, and affrighting the poor little innocents in the night-time. They, or their spectral appearances, have stuck pins into the Afflicted Ones, and thrown them into deadly fainting-fits with a touch, or but a look" (*CE* 11:74–75). The Proctors had moved to Salem Village from Ipswich and were well known to all of Hawthorne's Ipswich forebears. According to John Wells, Proctor had a "herculean frame . . . great native force." John Proctor's great-great-great grandson, Thorndike Proctor, married Elizabeth Hathorne, daughter of Joseph Hathorne, cousin to the writer, and Elizabeth Sanders. Dr. Bentley was also interested in the interweaving of families. In his diary for May 3, 1791, he wrote, "the late Thorndike Proctor, who was guilty of suicide was a descendant of the fourth generation from a Proctor who suffered in the times of persecution for Witchcraft and that his Wife was a descendant of the same generation from Major Hathorne who was the active prosecutor."[26]

Another link with the accused witches came through the Lord family of Miriam Lord Manning, Hawthorne's maternal grandmother. The first Lord immigrant was Robert Lord, who had a daughter Sarah. She married Joseph Wilson, a cooper or a draper. She acknowledged that she had been led "into the dreadful sin of witchcraft." Her daughter Sarah confessed also. Cotton Mather himself interviewed them. Her husband added his name to a petition in October 1692, saying that the confession came from fear. And Sarah herself in 1703, in connection with others, described how she came to confess. The afflicted girls were called to Andover to try to discover the cause of the illness

25. WB, *Diary,* 1:147.
26. John A. Wells, *The Peabody Story,* 176; WB, *Diary,* 1:256.

of Joseph Ballard's wife. They were taken to the meetinghouse at Andover, and

> After Mr. Barnard had been at prayer, we were blindfolded, and our hands were laid upon the afflicted persons, they being in their fits and falling into their fits at our coming into their presence. . . . Whereupon, we were all seized, as prisoners, by a warrant from the Justice of the peace and forthwith carried to Salem. And by reason of that sudden surprizal, we knowing ourselves altogether innocent of the crime, we were all exceedingly astonished and amazed, and consternated and affrighted even out of our reason, and our nearest and dearest relations, seeing us in that dreadful condition, and knowing our great danger, apprehended there was no other way to save our lives, as the case was then circumstanced, but by our confessing ourselves.[27]

Hawthorne's extended family also included one of the "afflicted girls." His first male American Phelps ancestor was Henry Phelps, who had a brother, Edward. Edward lived in Newbury and then Andover. His granddaughter Sarah, daughter of Samuel and Sarah Chandler Phelps, was active in the Andover phase of witchcraft. She said that the two sons of Martha Carrier, that "rampant hag . . . the Queen of Hell" as Cotton Mather called her, had troubled her because their mother told them to. These were the sons who were tied from neck to heel until the blood gushed from their noses. Sarah Phelps also said that Rose Foster, Elizabeth Johnson Sr., Mary Parker, and Abigail Faulkner Sr. had afflicted her. She testified in August 1692 that she had been tormented by Abigail Faulkner "or hir apperance" and that she "veryly [do] beleve in my heart that Abigail Falkner is a wicth [sic]." Abigail was the daughter of the Rev. Francis Dane of Andover. Mary Parker was hanged on September 22, 1692; Faulkner escaped because she was pregnant. Another daughter of Francis Dane, Elizabeth Johnson Sr. of Andover, was accused of torment-ing Sarah Phelps, but she was declared not guilty and discharged. Born in October 1682, at the time of these hearings, Sarah Phelps was only nine years old. In December 1692, when Abigail Faulkner petitioned to be released from jail, she declared that her accusers (perhaps including Sarah Phelps) said that "they would not that I should have been put to death for a thousand worlds for they never would have enjoyed

27. Belknap, *Trades and Tradesmen of Essex County, Massachusetts,* 81–82; *Salem Witchcraft Papers,* 2:335, 618–20, 3:971–72, 1009; *Vital Records of Andover,* 2:220, 569. In the same petition by Sarah Wilson and others, it was stated that it was suggested to them by some gentlemen to confess, "they telling us that we were witches, and they knew it, and we knew it, which made us think that it was so" (3:971). Since it was known that Cotton Mather had talked to Sarah Wilson, he may have been one of the gentlemen.

themselves again in the world." One is curious whether Sarah Phelps did indeed enjoy herself in the long aftertime.[28]

A number of minor players in the drama were connected in some way with Hawthorne. Another direct ancestor, Andrew Eliot (d. 1703/1704) was a witness against Susannah Rootes. He later made a declaration of regret for his testimony. William Eliot, his son, was on a witchcraft jury. His granddaughter, Judith Cox, married Jonathan Phelps, Hawthorne's great-grandfather. Another relation who served on a jury in 1692 was Jacob Manning, twin brother of Hawthorne's ancestor, Thomas Manning. Jacob was also the deputy marshal. Hannah Cox, wife of Thomas Cox (c. 1664–1710) and grandmother of the Judith Cox who married Jonathan Phelps, testified against Dorcas Hoar.[29]

Two parts of the witchcraft story shed some light on the pressures on Justice John Hathorne. His sister Elizabeth married Israel Porter, son of John Porter. The Porters lived in Salem Village, but they kept their church membership in Salem. When Rebecca Nurse was accused of witchcraft, they were incensed, and Israel was the first to sign a petition to save her. Israel and Elizabeth swore to a visit they had had with Nurse in which she said that she was "as innocent as the child unborn": "But surely . . . what sin hath God found out in me unrepented of, that he should lay such an affliction upon me in my old age," she asked.[30] Colonel Hathorne may have been given pause by the firm convictions of his sister and her husband.

Another case may have strengthened his own convictions. This one concerned George Burroughs, a former minister in Salem Village. Burroughs had moved to Maine, but was brought back, convicted, and hanged. Hawthorne describes him very favorably. He speaks of his "inward light which glows through his dark countenance, and, we might almost say, glorifies his figure" (*CE* 11:76). He sees the weakness by which Satan may have tempted him—a yearning for knowledge as "he went groping onward into a world of mystery; . . . he summoned up the ghosts of his two dead wives" (*CE* 11:76).

Hawthorne suggests that this is a Christian saint going to the death

28. *Salem Witchcraft Papers,* 1:203, 331–32, 334; *Vital Records of Andover, Massachusetts, to the End of the Year 1849,* 1:303; Persis W. McMillen, *Currents of Malice: Mary Town Esty and Her Family in Salem Witchcraft,* 449.

29. *Salem Witchcraft Papers,* 3:722, 939, 2:393; Clifford K. Shipton, *New England Life in the Eighteenth Century,* 397.

30. C. Upham, *Salem Witchcraft,* 2:58–59; *Salem Witchcraft Papers,* 2:592–94, 393, 3:939; Paul S. Boyer and Stephen Nissenbaum, *Salem Possessed: The Social Origins of Witchcraft,* 116–17.

of a martyr. He has a "radiance brightening on his features as from the other world" (*CE* 11:76). In "Alice Doane's Appeal," Hawthorne again sees Burroughs as an innocent: "I watched the face of an ordained pastor, who walked onward to the same death; his lips moved in prayer, no narrow petition for himself alone, but embracing all, his fellow sufferers and the frenzied multitude: he looked to heaven and trod lightly up the hill" (*CE* 11:279). This description does not square with the testimony given at the trial. George Burroughs seems to have been a strange sort of Christian saint. He could not remember when he had last taken communion, did not have his children baptized, and he seems to have trifled with magic. Richard Gildrie holds that "there was strong evidence" that the minister had been "dabbling in the occult and that he had made claims to magical powers in order to intimidate others, particularly his wives and their friends and relatives." Charles W. Upham in his lectures on witchcraft in 1831 says of Burroughs that there was "something very dark" about him.[31] Surely Salem memories were long enough to remember the quarrels Burroughs had had with his church members.

The most telling testimony concerned the fate of his first two wives, who were known to the Salem community. His first wife died while he was minister at Salem Village. His second wife was Sarah Ruck, daughter of merchant John Ruck of Salem and widow of Captain William Hathorne, brother to Justice John. Her father-in-law, Major William Hathorne, made a special provision for her in his will. After Captain William's death (circa 1678), she married George Burroughs by 1683. One of the afflicted girls, Ann Putnam Jr., swore on April 20, 1692, that the apparition of Burroughs had appeared to her and "he tould me that his name was George Burroughs and that he had had three wives: and that he had bewitched the Two first of them to death." Later she said that the second wife "tould me that Mr. Burroughs and that wife which he hath now[,] kiled hir in the vessele as she was coming to see hir friends because they would have one another." Susannah Sheldon deposed that the two wives of George Burroughs appeared in their winding sheets to her and said that he had killed them. George Burroughs denied that he had made his wife Sarah swear that any letter to her father, John Ruck, should be examined by him before she sent it.

---

31. For Burroughs, see *Salem Witchcraft Papers,* 1:152–78; Nathaniel Ingersoll Bowditch, "The Witchcraft Papers," 31–37; Richard Gildrie, "Visions of Evil: Popular Culture, Puritanism, and the Massachusetts Witchcraft Crisis of 1692," 26. For a different slant on Burroughs, see Bernard Rosenthal's *Salem Story: Reading the Witch Trials of 1692.*

This testimony was found, according to Boyer and Nissenbaum, among Judge Hathorne's papers on August 8, 1843, which probably meant that it had special meaning for him. On August 3, 1692, Mary Walcott spoke also of seeing the first two wives in winding sheets "whom I formerly well knew; and tould me that Mr. Burroughs had murthered them."[32]

Judge Hathorne was present at all of these trials. One can imagine his feelings when he thought he was learning the fate of his former sister-in-law. Thus, both his sister's disbelief in the guilt of Rebecca Nurse and his sister-in-law's alleged fate at the hands of her accused witch husband must have made his position difficult indeed. Nathaniel Hawthorne seems to buy into Upham's thesis that the accused were all innocent when he describes the martyrs on the "blighted path" to the gallows. On the other hand, in "Young Goodman Brown," a minister is definitely among those acquainted with the Shape of Evil, and he, too, as Burroughs was accused of doing, met with the witches in the dark wood.

When the witchcraft scare had abated, a Salem Quaker, Thomas Maule, published a book, *Truth Held Forth and Maintained* (1695), which excoriated the people of Salem, especially the leaders. Maule himself believed in witches, and his wife had testified against Bridget Bishop, but he disagreed with the manner of the trials. Thomas Maule had property on Essex Street next door to a house that Philip English owned and which was inherited by John Touzel, who in turn deeded it, one-half to William Hathorne and his wife, Mary Touzel Hathorne, and one-half to widow Susannah Touzel Hathorne. It was in this house—in William's part—that the Peabodys, Sophia's family, later lived. When a descendant died in 1818, this half went out of the family. Meanwhile, Mary Hathorne, peddler extraordinaire and daughter of William, owned a house on the other side of Essex Street, just in front of the land on which First Church now stands. It stood on part of Thomas Maule's orchard. She willed this house to her sister, Ann Hathorne Savage, but the will was lost, found much later, and then stolen. So, one Hathorne house on the southern side of Essex was next door to the Maule house; the other on the northern side stood on what had been his garden.[33]

32. McMillen, *Currents of Malice,* 296–97, 299; David L. Greene, "The Third Wife of the Rev. George Burroughs," 43; *Probate Records of Essex County,* 3:422–23, will of William Hathorne, 1681; *Salem Witchcraft Papers,* 1:153, 154.

33. Goodell, "Thomas Maule of Salem," 243–53; Sidney Perley, "Part of Salem in 1700. No. 5," 166–67; "Mr. Jelly's Book," a manuscript copied and annotated by J. P. Felt, Jonathan Porter Felt Papers. William Jelly (b. 1794), a local barber, kept a book in which his patrons described current or historical events (Benjamin Frederick Browne

Maule's garden is important in *The House of the Seven Gables*. The juxtaposition of the Hathorne house on Maule land, the garden, the lost will, the witchcraft accusations: all make another possible Hawthorne connection to witchcraft.

Elizabeth Peabody once observed that Hawthorne, "having made himself thoroughly acquainted with the ancient history of Salem, and especially with the witchcraft era . . . began to write stories."[34] He was urged to write a history of witchcraft by Evert Duyckinck in 1845, to whom he replied, "I had often thought of such a work, but I should not like to throw it off too hastily. . . . such a work, if worthily written, would demand research and study, and as deep thought as any man could bring to it. . . . Perhaps it may be the work of an after time" (*CE* 16:126–27).

Such an aftertime did not come, but some of the knowledge was there. It is tantalizing to wonder what Hawthorne's interpretations and nuances would have been if he had known all of his own ties with Salem's witchcraft of 1692.

THE MANNING CONNECTION

On his maternal side, Hawthorne descended from the Mannings, who hailed from the vicinity of Dartmouth in Devonshire, England. The emigrant's father, Richard Manning (1622–1679), had been baptized in St. Petrox Church, which joined Dartmouth Castle, which in times past had protected the seaport, this "cradle of England's sea-power," as one writer termed it. The Mannings may have had mixed reasons for coming to the New World. They were mariners, as good sons of Dartmouth should be, but they were also ironmongers in the tradition of the town.[35] Possibly some of the Mannings followed the evangelistic Rev. John Flavel, a famous dissenting minister, but their father was buried at St. Petrox, not at Flavel's new church. The oldest son, Captain Nicholas Manning, whose trades were anchorsmithing and gunsmithing as well as sailing, left for America in about 1662, the year when Flavel was ejected from his church for his views. Yet Nicholas never made a strong impression as a dissenter. He became a freeman in Salem, joined the church in 1665, and was a selectman in 1675. In 1663 he had married

---

Papers). My thanks to Joyce King, Salem researcher, for helping me straighten out the deeds of the Hathornes and Maules.

34. Moncure D. Conway, *Life of Nathaniel Hawthorne*, 31.

35. Stuart Petre Brodie Mais, *Glorious Devon*, 55. Dartmouth was an iron center too. In 1663 Thomas Newcomen, an ironmonger who developed the first steam engine, was born in Dartmouth.

Elizabeth Gray, a widow, and had several children. In July 1667 he commanded the *Supply,* a ketch, sent out as a man of war to recover ketches seized by the Indians. In this he was successful. By 1679 he had done so well that he could afford to supply a ship to bring over his widowed mother and the rest of the family. But on March 29, 1681, Nicholas was accused, along with two of his sisters, of incest. The sisters suffered the punishment of sitting on high stools in the church with an "I" pinned to them, while he escaped to other parts. His mother conveyed in her testimony the deep humiliation of the family. His wife petitioned the court to ascertain what assets he had left in 1681, and in 1683 she asked for and was granted a divorce on the grounds that he was "guilty of incestuous practices."[36]

This was not the most auspicious beginning for the Manning family in the New World. They had sailed for America in the *Hannah and Elizabeth* in 1679. On the ship were Nicholas's mother Anstist [Anstiss] Manning Senr; his brothers, Jacob and Thomas; and his sisters, Anstit [*sic*], Margrett [*sic*], and Sarah. There was also a Joseph Manning, not of the immediate family but probably kin.[37] Other passengers may have had some family connections. One who probably did not was a surgeon, Dr. John Barton, who had started as an apothecary, and then gone into "physick and chirurgery." On the *Hannah and Elizabeth* he had attended, among others, Joseph Manning, who had a broken shin, and Margaret Manning, who had a "paine in her head" (which was nothing to what she would have later) that he treated with "emplaisters for her temples." The trip over must have been trying since many cuts, bruises, and broken bones were treated. For all his work, Dr. Barton had to sue later to receive his pay from Nicholas Manning. He was still in Salem at the time of the witchcraft trials and was called to treat several of the accused. He died in Barbados in 1694.[38]

After the indictment of Nicholas and his sisters for incest, Margaret, who had married Warwick Palfrey, had to endure the rumors that her expected child was not her husband's. Jacob Manning remained in Salem, married Sarah Stone, and raised a large family, from whom later came the Richard Manning so often confused with the grandfather of Nathaniel Hawthorne. The first Jacob Manning was also the deputy

36. *Records and Files,* 7:302; 8:48, 87–88, 150; Perley, *History of Salem,* 2:388–89; Philip Young, *Hawthorne's Secret: An Untold Tale,* 118; *Records of the Court of Assistants of the Colony of Massachusetts Bay, 1630–1692,* 1:240; *Records and Files,* 8:48, 87–88, 150.

37. Henry F. Waters, "More Passengers to New-England, 1679," 377, 376.

38. *Records and Files,* 7:302–4; Sidney Perley, "Salem in 1700, no. 14," 26; Benjamin F. Browne, "Youthful Recollections of Salem," 49:197.

marshal who brought Philip English before magistrates John Hathorne and Jonathan Corwin on May 31, 1692.[39]

Jacob's twin, Thomas Manning, married Mary Giddings of Ipswich in 1681, and moved there in 1683 and was accepted as citizen in 1685. He was a gunsmith and a blacksmith in the Manning tradition; his son John Manning, Nathaniel's great-grandfather, was a blacksmith. But his twin brother was a doctor who produced doctors. Had the roles of Thomas and Jacob Manning been reversed, one wonders what the consequences for Hawthorne would have been. Richard Manning, the twelfth child of John Manning and his third wife, Ruth Potter, was a blacksmith who became a stagecoach owner and a proprietor of lands in Maine.[40]

The family tradition of the Mannings pervaded Hawthorne's work. Blacksmiths and men of iron often appear in his pages. Perhaps the most pertinent example is the story, "The Artist of the Beautiful," in which Peter Hovenden, the retired watchmaker, prefers for his daughter Annie "the worker in iron . . . He spends his labor on reality" (*CE* 10:449). She indeed marries the blacksmith, Robert Danforth, who earns his "bread with the bare and brawny arm of a blacksmith" (*CE* 10:449). The artist, Owen Warfield, tries to produce beauty in the shape of a butterfly, from machinery. The story deals with the estrangement of the artist from "that order of sagacious understandings who think that life should be regulated, like clockwork, with leaden weights" (*CE* 10:455). It is hard not to believe that Hawthorne is concerned here with his own relationship with the Mannings in "an atmosphere of doubt and mockery" that he doubtless sometimes felt (*CE* 10:473). The everyday reality of that mind-set may have influenced him far more than the long-ago charge of incest against the brother of his Manning ancestor. Surely it was not only his Hathorne ancestors whose misunderstanding he sensed for his life's work.[41]

The families into which the Mannings married were, for the most part, old Ipswich families. The Giddings had been in Ipswich since

39. P. Young, *Hawthorne's Secret*, 126–31; Chever, "Philip English," 1:262; William H. Manning, *The Genealogical and Biographical History of the Manning Families of New England and Descendants*, 683.

40. Perley, *History of Salem*, 2:389–90; *Vital Records of Ipswich, Massachusetts to the End of the Year 1849*, 2:300–301; Joseph Barlow Felt, *History of Ipswich, Essex and Hamilton*, 98; Abraham Hammatt, *The Hammatt Papers: Early Inhabitants of Ipswich, Massachusetts 1633–1700*, 116, 226; Samuel G. Drake, "Early Settlers of Essex and Old Norfolk," 6:339; 7:84.

41. Hawthorne also uses the metaphor of iron to indicate the quality of Puritans, as in "May-Pole of Merry Mount" or "Endicott and the Red Cross," but the use of the blacksmith very often points to the Manning family (*CE* 9:63, 436). See Gloria Erlich, *Family Themes and Hawthorne's Fiction: The Tenacious Web*, 59.

1635; the Lords too may have come in that same year. The Goodhues, the Potters, the Days, and the Clarkes were all from old North Shore stock. Their lives often touched. Ipswich was closely connected with Salem in many ways. Two Robert Lords were marshals and sheriffs for the Essex County court. George Giddings was a deputy to the General Court in ten different years.[42] The writer's Salem roots were entwined with them all; the oral traditions he heard came from that hardy people who lived on the North Shore. Their stories became, to a large extent, his story. They all constituted his long past.

In "Grimshawe" Hawthorne has his protagonist say, "It is good to find myself here in the long past, as in a sheltered harbour" (*CE* 12:455). Yet in "Etherege" he turns from it to the present: "[t]he long past comes up, with its recollections; and yet it is not so powerful as the powerful present" (*CE* 12:261). The present for Hawthorne started in 1804.

42. Charles Henry Pope, *Pioneers of Massachusetts,* 103, 291, 192, 370, 135; Frank R. Holmes, *Directory of the Ancestral Heads of New England Families, 1620–1700,* clii, clv; David L. Greene, "The English Origin of George Giddings of Ipswich, Massachusetts," 274–86; Felt, *History of Ipswich, Essex, and Hamilton,* 116; Hammatt, *Hammatt Papers,* 21, 225–26, 70–71; Abner Cheney Goodell, "A Biographical Notice of the Officers of Probate for Essex County, from the Commencement of the Colony to the Present Time," 2:216.

3

A Tale of Two Houses

When flesh and spirit begin to fail, he remembers his birthplace and the old burial-ground, and hears a voice calling him to come home to his father and mother. —(*CE* 11:326)

WHEN NATHANIEL Hawthorne was born on the Fourth of July, 1804, in Salem, cannons roared and bells rang; processions marched; and buildings were illuminated. But all this was not in honor of the newly born writer, of course; it was the celebration of the "Glorious Fourth" as it was later called. The whole town did not participate in one splendid march; instead there were two celebrations, illustrating the divided nature of Salem.

The Federalists celebrated with a rather sedate ceremony. John Pickering (1772–1846), lawyer and linguist, made the required oration at St. Peter's Church; William Gray (1750–1825), merchant and former privateer, presided at the dinner; and they all went early to bed.[1] The Republicans, on the other hand, were more boisterous. Dr. William Bentley (1759–1819), minister of the East Church, described the day: "The number of Cannon discharged was uncommon & the roar began at 3 o'clock. . . . Precisely at eleven the procession formed at the Court House, with the Cadets & Band in front. . . . The Cannon roared till Sundown, & the Evening was illumined with Rockets & the Band gave great pleasure to the Company collected on Washington Square."[2] The divisions of politics, not to mention those of religion, were foreshadowings of the way the Hathorne son later felt about the town of Salem.

---

1. *The Saltonstall Papers, 1607–1815*, ed. Robert E. Moody, 1:206.
2. WB, *Diary*, 3:96–97.

Down near the wharves were two adjacent streets where two houses —the Hathorne house on Union Street and the Manning home on Herbert Street—backed up to each other. These two houses produced a new family and formed the stage for the writer's early Salem years.

THE HATHORNES

Nathaniel Hawthorne (he later added the "w") was born in the second story of an unpretentious house on Union Street, one block west of Herbert Street and the intersecting street between Essex (then sometimes known as Main Street) and Derby Street that fronted the wharves and the harbor. He made the ninth or possibly the tenth inhabitant of the house. His father, mother, and sister Elizabeth lived there. His grandmother, Rachel Phelps Hathorne (1734–1813), owned the house that her deceased husband, Captain Daniel Hathorne (1731–1796), had bought from her father, blacksmith Jonathan Phelps (1708–1800). In fact, it is more than possible that the Union Street house was the youthful home of Rachel. Her father had bought the house from Joshua Pickman in 1745; she had married Daniel Hathorne in 1756; and Hathorne bought the home from Phelps in 1772.[3]

The grandfather whom Nathaniel never knew was Daniel Hathorne. He was a privateer of some renown in the Revolutionary War, about whom a ballad had been written praising his courage. The account of his funeral in the *Salem Gazette* on April 26, 1796, belies the picture by Vernon Loggins of a slightly dirty, no longer heralded former privateer:

> The funeral of the late Capt. Daniel Hathorne was attended on Wednesday last with that respect which real worth inspires. The corpse was preceded by the Marine Society and the Fire Club of which he was a member. The flags of the ships in port were half mast high—and the numerous procession which attended on this melancholy occasion fully evinced the regret they felt at the departure of their worthy fellow-townsman.[4]

This "worthy fellow-townsman" and his wife were the parents of eight children. Rachel Phelps Hathorne has left few glimpses of herself. She was born in Beverly in 1734, the daughter of Jonathan and Judith Cox Phelps. The Phelpses moved to Salem, and she died there on April 16, 1813. One sister, Judith (1730–1814), married John Webb (1733–1811) and lived a short distance away on Daniel Street. Another sister,

3. Sidney Perley, "Salem in 1700. No. 25," 160; Perley, *History of Salem,* 3:193–96.
4. Loggins, *The Hawthornes,* 184; Evert A. Duyckinck and George L. Duyckinck, *Cyclopedia of American Literature,* 1:442.

Anne, married George Southward, and a third, Eunice, married Nathan Perkins.[5]

The oldest Hathorne child, Rachel, reportedly a beauty, married Simon Forrester, a man of Scotch-Irish extraction, who had been brought to America by Rachel's father. The Forresters had twelve children. He grew immensely wealthy during the Revolutionary War, but he also left a legacy of alcoholism that dimmed the family fortune and name. Nevertheless, he did leave a fortune to Rachel and his surviving children.[6] His granddaughter, Annie Meade Barstow Ashburner, said much later, probably in 1881:

> My grandfather's will at the time it was made public, caused great remark, as it was the first will ever made in the country settling property on daughters. This was in 1813! It has been in the Probate Court ever since. I have often heard my father say . . . 'Why Mr. Forrester, you have only provided for children (daughters) and their children. The will excludes your great grandchildren.' "Yes," said my grandfather, "I have provided for my daughters & their children. That is enough for a man to do. I am satisfied."[7]

That will was to cause some difficulties for the family through the years, but it also provided his daughters with interest from the trusts that could not be manipulated by their husbands.

There were all sorts of stories about Forrester: that he was of the Irish nobility; that he was a graduate of Cloyne College in Ireland.[8] His wife, Rachel, outlived him and many of their children. Her will provided for her unmarried sisters and various relatives, but not for the Hawthorne children. In their growing-up years, however, Elizabeth and Maria Louisa often went to see the Forresters. Hawthorne referred to him as "old man Simon Forrester" in "The Custom-House" (*CE* 1:28). Elizabeth Manning Hawthorne said that Hawthorne did not like Forrester because the old man had once offered him five dollars, and he refused to take it.[9] This may well have been Elizabeth's opinion of him rather than her brother's. Nathaniel wrote Elizabeth Barstow Stoddard later about a portrayal of

5. *Vital Records of Beverly, Massachusetts to the End of the Year 1849,* 1:256; Edward Stanley Waters, "Genealogical Notes of the Webb Family," 218.

6. Belknap, "Forrester and Descendants," 17–64.

7. Annie Meade Barstow Ashburner to Anne Ashburner Richards, December 28 [1881], Richards and Ashburner Papers, Mss. 20365, ff. 87–89.

8. Belknap, "Forrester and Descendants," 19; Robert L. Gale, *A Nathaniel Hawthorne Encyclopedia,* 171.

9. EMH to Una Hawthorne, November 12, 1865, Bancroft transcript, quoted in James R. Mellow, *Nathaniel Hawthorne in His Times,* 18.

Forrester in her book, *The Morgesons* (1862), that "as an old man . . . he had a very stately and high bred aspect. I can just remember him" (*CE* 18:524).

The Forrester children, Nathaniel's first cousins, married John Andrew, Charlotte Story, Gideon Barstow, Thomas Carlisle, and Thomas Coit, thus producing for young Hawthorne many interesting cousins. Other unmarried Forrester offspring died from alcoholism or suicide resulting from alcoholism.[10]

Rachel Forrester's sister, Judith Hathorne (1770–1827), married George Archer (1765–1799), a sea captain, and had four children: George (1793–1833), Sarah (b. 1794), Judith (1796–1801), and Caroline (b. 1798). Sarah married Robert H. Osgood, a former Salemite and merchant in Baltimore. Her mother and sister, Caroline, later Mrs. Wyeth, went with her to Baltimore. After Judith Archer's death, the Osgoods and the Wyeths moved to New York City to enter business there.[11] The Archers are mentioned rather frequently in the surviving letters.

Knowledge of the inhabitants of the Hathorne house is limited by the absence of correspondence from them to the Hawthornes when in Raymond. Since most of the aunts signed their wills by a mark, supposition is that they could not or did not write letters. The primary immediate family letters still extant are from Manning, not Hathorne, correspondence; thus not too many conclusions may be drawn from that silence. Grandmother Rachel, Sarah, Eunice, and Ruth lived in the Union Street house. When on shore, so did Daniel and Nathaniel.

Sarah Hathorne Crowninshield (1763–1829) is often spoken of as wealthy because she married a Crowninshield, but that is not true. Her husband, John, son of Jacob and Hannah Crowninshield and an insolvent mariner, died of dysentery at the age of twenty-four. In fact, Sarah had financial difficulties after his death because she was accused of "intermeddling" before his debts were paid. John's father had also been insolvent; in order to make ends meet, his mother took in boarders, including Dr. William Bentley, after her husband's death. By February 1820 at least, Sarah was living with her sister Rachel after Simon Forrester's death. When Sarah herself died in 1829, she left what little she had (Rachel had left her a one-thousand-dollar trust) to her sister Ruth. It is worth noting that Sarah too went back to her own family after her

10. Belknap, "Forrester and Descendants," 46–47, 26.
11. Perley, *History of Salem,* 1:214, 216; [WB], "Parish List," 15:98; 16:19; *Vital Records of Salem,* 1:45–48.

husband's death; her sister-in-law, Betsey Hawthorne, was not unique in this despite all that has been made of the latter fact.[12]

Two other Hathornes have left so little trace that it is difficult to detect any influence on the young boy. Unmarried Eunice (1766–1827) is barely mentioned in family letters. Captain Daniel (1768–1805) is another mariner lost at sea. According to William Jelly's book, Daniel "sailed from Fayal on November 4, 1805, and was never afterwards heard from."[13]

The youngest and perhaps most interesting daughter of Daniel and Rachel Hathorne was Ruth (1778–1847), also unmarried and the last occupant of the house on Union Street. Betsey Hawthorne urged her daughter Louisa to go read to her because as she noted, "it is a great misfortune to have weak eyes." She liked to be remembered by the Hawthorne children; Mary Manning often encouraged them to write to "Ruthy."[14] One niece who did communicate was Sally Archer Osgood. On February 12, 1839, she wrote her from New York:

> My dear Aunt, I hear from Ann Stone that you are enjoying tolerable good health this winter which I assure you adds much to my happiness. I cannot say how much I think of you my dear Aunt[;] sometimes feel almost tempted to set out immediately for Salem. . . . We hear much of our kinsman N Hathorne[;] his writings are beautiful. Wish we could have more of them. [H]ope that his having other pursuits will not keep him from Bestowing some of his time to the gratification of those who have had the pleasures of reading his tales.
>
> How is Aunt H and hear [sic] daughters. I should once more love to

12. Essex Probate Court, #6681, administration and inventory of John Crowninshield, mariner, November 10, 1787; Essex Probate Court, #6685, will of Sarah Crowninshield, May 19, 1829; Abbott Lowell Cummings, "The House and Its People," 88; Perley Derby, "Inscriptions from Charter Street Burial Ground, Salem, Massachusetts," 71. See, for instance, Erlich, *Family Themes*, 62–63, or T. Walter Herbert, *Dearest Beloved: The Hawthornes and the Making of the Middle-Class Family*, 65, for Betsey Hawthorne's return to the Manning family. Assumption that Sarah Crowninshield was wealthy may be found in Robert Cantwell, *Nathaniel Hawthorne: The American Years*, 8; Lou Ann Gaeddert, *A New England Love Story: Nathaniel Hawthorne and Sophia Peabody*, 25; Herbert, *Dearest Beloved*, 64.

13. *SG*, January 3, 1806; "Mr. Jelly's Book," November 4, 1805, Jonathan Porter Felt Papers.

14. Manning Hawthorne, "Nathaniel Hawthorne Prepares for College," 76; Mary Manning to ECH, November 17, 1818, Hawthorne-Manning Collection. It should be noted that the Hathorne women all had wills, save for their mother. The Hathorne house had been sold to Simon Forrester, who allowed the Hathorne sisters to continue living there. Rachel Forrester's will, probated July 6, 1824, decreed that the house was to be leased for one cent per annum during the lives of Mrs. Sarah Crowninshield, Eunice Hathorne, Ruth Hathorne, and Mrs. Judith Archer (Forrester Family Papers).

see all my kindred—wherever we go, after all we turn to the place of our nativity and feel a strong desire to visit those places again. . . .

When shall I hear from you Dear Aunt [?] [W]ish someone would write and let me know exactly how you are. . . . The children send their love[.] they often say to me Mother is your Aunt Ruth my Aunt too [?] I tell them yes all the great one [*sic*] they have [in] this world.[15]

It has been suggested that there was a certain coolness between the Hathorne sisters and the Nathaniel Hawthorne family, especially since no money was left to them. But Ruth left no money to this niece either, despite the cordial relationship. In fact, she left her estate of $2,064.74 to her nephew's wife, Charlotte Forrester, whose husband had failed in business in 1834. Ruth revoked one will and had a trust set up for Charlotte Forrester and her children that was not finalized until 1868. Ruth was attended by a cousin, Sarah Ditmore, in her last illness. An Edward Ray was also living at 21 Union, according to the 1842 Salem city directory. Sophia and Nathaniel did not seem to think of the Union Street house as a possible refuge when they came back to Salem in 1845 after they were ejected from the Manse. Perhaps one reason was the lack of room.[16]

Aunt Ruth recalled Nathaniel as "a little boy, with his rosy cheeks, and bright eyes, and his golden curls waving" as he ran about. "I believe," wrote Louisa Hawthorne to her niece Una in 1844, "she never expects to see anything so pretty again in this world, I suppose everything looked prettier to her then than now that she is old." Perhaps this letter was written to Una about the time when she was "to be dressed as sumptuously as possible to-day to visit her greataunt Ruth," according to her mother. Rose Hawthorne Lathrop identified this aunt as a Manning, but in this she was wrong.[17]

These Hathorne women may well have been partial models for some of the old women crouching in the chimney-corners or the spinsters who sometimes people Hawthorne's stories. Knowing as little individually of these women as we do, it would be hard to say. But these were Hathorne women with the pride that seemed to go with the tribe. Rose Hawthorne Lathrop said later that they had "a sense of superiority, which, I think, was the skeleton in every Hawthorne's body at that

15. Sally Archer Osgood to Ruth Hathorne, February 12, 1839, Richards and Ashburner Papers, Mss. 20368, f. 130. Ann Stone is probably Ann Osgood Stone, daughter of Robert and Rebecca Osgood Stone (Perley, *History of Salem,* 3:12).

16. Essex Probate Court, #41940, will of Ruth Hathorne, August 17, 1847.

17. MLH to Una Hawthorne, May 7, 1844, Berg Collection; RHL, *Memories,* 78–79.

time."[18] The sisters seemed to be kind to the children. Quite often the girls, particularly, went to Aunt Forrester's or wrote to "Aunt Ruthy."

THE MANNINGS

Just across the backyard from the Hathorne dwelling was a very different, taller house—the Manning home. Nathaniel's grandfather, Richard Manning Jr. (1755–1813), left his birthplace, Ipswich, Massachusetts, for Salem before 1774. He was a blacksmith and a "horseletter." According to William Bentley, he had assisted a "Mr. Coates who . . . did before the War hold a Coach with which he went to Boston once a week, and that he, Mr. Manning, assisted as a Blacksmith to repair it & that it was burnt in the Great Fire of 1774." Bentley rode to Boston in Manning's new stage for the first time on May 26, 1801. The elder Manning soon became a large landowner in Maine as well as proprietor of a profitable stage business in Salem. He was frequently away, tending to these lands. He posted in 1811 an affectionate, if miserably spelled, letter to his "Beloved Family." Hawthorne remembered his grandfather in *Our Old Home* when he mentioned "the kindly figure of my own grandfather" (*CE* 5:122). Uneducated himself, Manning saw to the education of sons Richard, John, Samuel, and Robert. Maria, Betsey, and Priscilla also benefited. William and Mary, the two oldest, do not seem to have had that privilege. Their father died suddenly away from home in April 1813, and his estate was not settled until after his wife's death in 1826.[19]

Miriam Lord Manning (1748–1826), his wife, was also from Ipswich. Her father, Thomas Lord, was a descendant of Robert Lord Sr. who had been in Ipswich as early as 1636 and served as clerk of court and the registrar of deeds. Thomas was a feltmaker and hatter who eventually moved to Boston and joined the New Brick Church. There he married an Elizabeth Clarke from London. They moved back to Ipswich, where he died in 1750.[20]

18. RHL, *Memories,* 6.

19. WB, *Diary,* 2:384, 373, 4:163; Richard Manning Jr. to William Manning, [Jan.?] 18, 1811, from Portland, Maine, Hawthorne-Manning Collection; Receipt, William Foster to Richard Manning Jr. for boarding and instructing his sons, Richard and John, May 18–July 13, 1798, Hawthorne-Manning Collection; Essex Probate Court, #17567, inventory of Richard Manning's estate, October 19, 1813, and #17562, of Miriam Manning, intestate, November 1, 1831.

20. Gideon Tibbetts Ridlon, *Saco Valley Settlements and Families,* 891; Thomas Bellows Wyman, *The Genealogies and Estates of Charlestown, Massachusetts, 1629–1818,* 630. The information in *Vital Records of Ipswich* (1:247) appears to be wrong. Miriam was the last of twelve children, as was her husband. My thanks to Janet Appleton of Beverly, Massachusetts, for sharing her knowledge of the Lord family with me.

As the twelfth child, Miriam was accustomed to living thriftily. She is characterized as parsimonious, self-righteous, and with a passion for cleanliness. Nathaniel wrote to his mother in 1819 that his grandmother did not allow fruit or jelly in the house to be eaten "for it's esteemed sacrilege . . . because she is keeping them against somebody is sick" even if the fruit spoiled in the meantime (*CE* 15:112). This penchant for giving to the sick is supported by an almost illegible note in William Manning's hand: "about 1811—I sent an adventure by My Brother In the brig Independence . . . & he brought me home two large Casks of Wine. . . . it was all Used by the family the same as if it was their own & my Mother & my Sisters sent a part of it to their friends that were at any time Sik [*sic*] at Salem or Ipswich." In *Our Old Home* Hawthorne referred to "the decorous neatness of my grandmother's kitchen," which he said was very familiar to him (*CE* 5:183). Mrs. Manning seemed to have a very strong sense of family. Her children called her "our dear mother." She was appealed to by her son Richard when he felt that William was not paying his fair share of expenses. Miriam Manning took in her husband's sister when she was old and widowed. She also gave employment (but probably with little or no wages) to her cousin Hannah Lord. From the evidence I have seen, I do not view her as tight-fisted as does Gloria Erlich or, for that matter, as did her Hathorne grandchildren. She was left a widow with money to be preserved and invested for her children and her grandchildren, and she seems to have been conscious of that responsibility.[21]

The oldest Manning child was Mary (1777–1841), born after the move to Salem. She always seemed to be the responsible one. She it was who went to Raymond, Maine, to look after her brother Richard in his last days. She encouraged the young Nathaniel, when he was probably not too easy to live with, to keep going to school and to go to college. It was Mary who looked after her mother in her old age, and reminded her sister Betsey to tell her children to write their Hathorne aunts. Mary also fed and clothed and gave advice to William, even though his money habits clearly worried her. Something of her quality is seen in an affectionate letter that her younger sister Maria wrote when Mary was visiting in Portland. "I had forgot," Maria acknowledged, "to notice your injunction 'keep grace at home' and so we shall[.] [D]id you suppose peace had vanished when your Ladyship left us?" Lucy Lord Sutton saw

---

21. William Manning note to Mary Manning, c. 1811, Hawthorne-Manning Collection; Richard Manning to Miriam Manning, October 10, 1814, Hawthorne-Manning Collection; M. Hawthorne, "A Glimpse," 30, 181; Erlich, *Family Themes,* 38.

her as the cheerful one in the family, the one whom Hawthorne loved to tease. The Manning house finally came to Mary after the estate was settled, and she lived there until her death in October 1841.[22]

Her brother William (1778–1864) is usually dismissed as a person unreliable with money and of no particular influence on the budding writer. The truth, however, is a bit more complicated than that. Born the second child and first son, William failed in many enterprises and seemed not to be scrupulous about his financial affairs with his family. His reach usually seemed to exceed his grasp, but he never ceased trying.[23] The War of 1812 found William very active commercially. He acquired shares in at least seventeen ships to be used as privateers in 1812, 1813, and 1814. He sailed himself as master of the sloop *Hunter,* the brig *Rover,* and the brig *Neutrality.* He was always active in the family stage business. On June 1, 1813, Manning horses raced to take guns to the citizens when the battle of the American *Chesapeake* and the British *Shannon* took place off Salem. The next year in April the Manning stagecoaches were especially commended when the *Constitution* was chased into Marblehead Harbor and "fast teams of horses from William Manning's stables [brought] Salemites to the scene."[24] Although he failed again in 1815, he acquired more ships after the war. He also dealt largely in real estate. He purchased the Lafayette Coffee House in 1827; the Sun Tavern, which he turned into the Bowker Block in 1830; and hired the home of Nat West, which he advertised as the Mansion House in 1832. Andrew Jackson stayed there when he visited Salem in 1833.[25]

William was the stage agent of the Salem and Boston Stage Company when it was chartered on March 3, 1829. Robert S. Rantoul comments

22. Maria Manning to Mary Manning, September 10, 1806, Hawthorne-Manning Collection; M. Hawthorne, "A Glimpse," 181.

23. William failed financially several times (See *SG,* January 6, 1809, April 23, 1811, January 6, 1815); Richard Manning Jr. to William Manning, July 1811; Richard Manning to Miriam Manning, October 10, 1814, Hawthorne-Manning Collection.

24. A. Frank Hitchings, "Ship Registers of the District of Salem and Beverly, 1789–1900," 40:234; 41:357, 160. He acquired shares in the following privateers: In 1812, the sloop *Polly,* the schooner *Regulator,* the schooner *Buckskin,* the schooner *Active,* the brigantine *Prudent,* the brig *Montgomery,* the schooner *John and George* later named the *Revenge,* the ship *Alexander,* the schooner *Diligent,* the sloop *Endeavor,* the *Grumbler,* the *Growler* later named *Frolic,* and the brig *Lion.* In 1813 he owned shares in the schooner *Rising States,* the schooner *Fame,* the brig *Neutrality,* the brig *Rover,* and the schooner *Jane.* See Hitchings, "Ship Registers," vols. 39, 40, and 41, and Belknap, "Salem Privateers in the War of 1812," vols. 78, 79, and 80. Robotti, *Chronicles,* 53–54.

25. *SG,* March 30, 1827, December 25, 1832, and January 4, 1833; William D. Dennis, "The Fire Clubs of Salem," 21.

on the "courteous management of William Manning . . . known among the 'whips' [the drivers] as 'Sir William' and to have been trusted by whom they thought enough for an epitaph." Uncle William was kind to his nephew and nieces. He employed Nathaniel as a bookkeeper for one dollar a week in 1820, although he may well have thought he was merely training the next generation to run the stagecoaches. He also gave his nephew a new suit of clothes on one occasion, and before he went to college, William gave him five dollars and sent another five dollars to him at Bowdoin. He urged Louisa to go to dancing school and bought Elizabeth a Leghorn bonnet (*CE* 15:130, 124, 155, 150). Later the Hawthorne children may have regarded him with a less indulgent or more amused eye. Louisa wrote of him to Sophia that "if anyone wants anything of his, it is sure to acquire a new value in his eyes, and he finds out that he wants it himself." When Hawthorne was appointed consul in Liverpool in 1853, Uncle William pestered him for a recommendation until he wrote Democratic officials and the new president himself. On November 4, 1853, it was reported that William Manning was to be the superintendent of repairs at the Salem Custom House.[26]

William always dreamed big dreams. His niece Elizabeth epitomized him later when she compared her landlady to him. Mrs. Cole, she said, "was a little like Uncle William in a propensity to boast of the great things she meant to do." William H. Foster, the clerk for the Stage Company, remarked, "Sir William Manning was then an oldish man but now that some seven or eight and thirty years have passed—gone, he is a young man, thus reversing the order of nature." Again, in speaking of a cousin, Daniel C. Manning, Foster called him "a true Manning, that is, as he grows older in years, he becomes young."[27] Perhaps in "Peter Goldthwaite's Treasure" Hawthorne was thinking of that quality in his Uncle William as well as his eternal optimism when he describes Peter: "It was his nature to be always young, and the tendency of his mode of life to keep him so. . . . [T]he true, essential Peter, was a young man of high hopes, just entering out on the world. At the kindling of each new fire, his burnt-out youth rose afresh from the old embers and ashes" (*CE* 9:392).

26. Robert S. Rantoul, "Some Notes on Old Modes of Travel," 60; MLH to SPH, September 3, 1845, Berg Collection, as quoted in Mellow, *Hawthorne in His Times,* 262; Arlin Turner, *Nathaniel Hawthorne: A Biography,* 257.

27. EMH to cousins [Sat. 1881?], copy, Hawthorne-Manning Collection; W. H. Foster, "Days of Stage Coaches," in the *Salem Observer,* May 1860, as found in The Salem and Boston Stage Company Records.

William's younger brother Richard (1782–1830) went to live in Maine after his father's death to manage the family's affairs there. Sickly and later crippled, he had very little to do with the stagecoach lines after the first years. He often resented William's cavalier treatment of money matters, and he also felt ill-used by Robert, who so often said he wanted to move to Maine but never seemed to do it until 1821, and then the move did not last. He was disappointed too in Samuel, who worked at the Manning store in Raymond for only a very short time. Still, Richard made a name for himself in Raymond, married a Raymond girl, and managed the family's affairs there scrupulously. He was fond of books and often asked that they be sent to him. He would seem to be an ideal correspondent for Nathaniel, but I have seen references to early letters only between the two. In letters to his brother Robert, Richard inquired several times during Nathaniel's lameness, thanked him once for a present, and told him that he would give him a good "Fowling Piece" that had once belonged to Nathaniel's father. As time went on, Nathaniel's relationship with this uncle seems to have cooled. In July 1825 he wrote his sister Elizabeth that he "received but little pleasure from my visit to Raymond, and do not desire to go there again. Uncle Richard seemed to care nothing about us, and Mrs. Manning was as cold and freezing as a December morning" (*CE* 15:194). He did go back in 1826, but that may have been the last time.[28]

Robert Manning (1784–1842), on the other hand, was the uncle most often present in the Manning home. He is the one who took charge of the children's education and to whom Betsey looked for advice. It may be, as Gloria Erlich says, that he was too domineering, too much of an authority figure for Nathaniel. But since he was the main male authority who actually stayed in the house for great periods of time, he was naturally the one on whom Nathaniel could lay his resentment. The fact that they shared a bed may sound strange to our twentieth-century ears, having become accustomed to thinking too much in sexual terms, but in those times of large families, it was not uncommon. As Jane C. Nylander, director of the Society for the Preservation of New England Antiquities, remarks in her thorough study, *Our Own Snug Fireside,* "New Englanders were used to sharing beds. . . . So unused were many people to sleeping alone that they often sought out sleeping partners."

28. Richard Manning to his mother, Miriam Manning, October 10, 1814; Richard Manning to Robert Manning, November 15, 1814; Richard Manning to Robert Manning, September 11, 1815, Hawthorne-Manning Collection. Also see Richard Manning to NH, August 8, 1813, Manning Hawthorne Papers, and Edwin Haviland Miller, *Salem Is My Dwelling Place,* 50.

And she cites an example in 1844.[29] Dominating older men do show up in various of Hawthorne's sketches and tales who may well be reflections of the child's view of his uncle, but he described himself often later as his "affectionate nephew," and as an adult he helped Uncle Robert with the writing of his articles and a book on horticulture (*CE* 15:209). Robert was also the uncle to whom, from those letters preserved, Nathaniel wrote the most. These two, though unlike, do seem to connect, whereas Hawthorne and his uncle Richard do not, despite similar interests. Of course, the distance between them would make a difference.[30]

Robert may have influenced Nathaniel in another way. He recorded over and over again to Richard his dislike for Salem, "this worst of towns," and his determination to leave the salt water and old Salem behind. He may well have talked as he wrote. Richard Manning's disappointment that the family had not made good its decision to move to Maine eventuated in a long letter on December 18, 1820, from Richard to Robert in which he quoted excerpts from Robert's letters from 1814 to 1819 expressing his feelings about Salem. In January 1814 Robert remarked that he wanted to leave. In July 1815 he wrote "I should rather live in the Woods poor than in the City rich." In September 1815 he wished he were "clear of this odious Town." He wanted to be "released from this plague (Stages and Horses I mean). I am tired of this place and long to live in the Woods" (October 21, 1815). He hoped in August 1816 that by January 1817, "(if I Live) I shall say farewell Old Salem never more to return." In December 1817 he noted, "the third year of my captivity is nearly gone." In July 1818 he admitted that despite Samuel's decision not to live in Raymond, he and his mother "remain stedfast & immovable." But by April 13, 1819, he owned that "Raymond will not do for Nathaniel."[31] From the time Nathaniel was nine until he was just short of being fifteen, he heard this constant refrain of the disadvantages of the town on the North Shore as contrasted with the glories of the woods in Maine. The continuous talk may well have contributed to Nathaniel's ambivalence about his town. Robert does not sound so discontented in later life. He married his cousin, Rebecca Dodge Burnham; they had three children; and he turned to his passion, the growing of fruit trees,

29. Erlich, *Family Themes,* 49, 116, 118; Jane C. Nylander, *Our Own Snug Fireside: Images of the New England Home, 1760–1860,* 95.

30. Erlich, however, thinks that Nathaniel much admired his plucky Uncle Richard (*Family Themes,* 41).

31. Richard Manning to Robert Manning, December 18, 1820, Hawthorne-Manning Collection.

and became known for his knowledge of pear trees. He published with John M. Ives in 1838 his *Book of Fruits*. But all of this was later.[32]

Another Manning aunt, Maria Miriam (1786–1814), had auburn hair and was intelligent and talented, as Elizabeth M. Hawthorne affirmed in 1880. She said Maria was a "very good judge of books" and "the most intellectual of the family." It was rumored that Joseph Emerson Worcester came to tutor Nathaniel at home when he was lame because he was attracted to Maria. Whatever the truth of that, it is a fact that Dr. Samuel Worcester, his uncle, came to see Maria. After their father's death, she and Priscilla left the family's East Church and went to the Tabernacle where Samuel Worcester preached. Priscilla actually joined that church in 1814. Maria probably would have joined, had she lived. In the files at the Peabody Essex Museum is a warm and helpful letter to Maria from Worcester, whom she had consulted about the state of her soul. At her death, Maria left money to various good causes in Salem. Her mother did not distribute these bequests until 1823, a delay that Erlich attributes to Mrs. Manning's parsimonious nature, but it seems to me that it could indicate prudence on her part. Since the money was to come from the undivided estate, she could have waited to be sure that the money was still there. There was so often only a step between success and failure in the precarious early nineteenth century.[33]

John Manning (b. 1788) was the uncle who went to sea and never came back again, a fate not rare in Salem. He had almost drowned as a lad. In fact, his father had asked Dr. Bentley to make an address to praise George Crowninshield Jr., who had saved him in 1800. This near fatal event may have contributed to Nathaniel's mother's fear of water or swimming for her son. John was sick enough once to prompt William to write his absent father about it. But very little else is known about John. It is his absence that was discussed in family letters, not memories of his presence. His mother grieved and looked for him all the rest of her life. Many stories were told about his whereabouts. In the Manning genealogy, a letter from Joseph Lakeman to Nathaniel Wells dated February 25, 1814, states, "I have the pleasure to inform you that I saw John Manning about six months ago in the city of New York. He informed me that he was going to the lakes to work at his trade." It is also recorded in the genealogy that "the belief of the survivors of the

32. Felt, *Annals,* 2d ed., 2:148–49.

33. EMH to niece Maria Manning, February 5, 1880, copy, Hawthorne-Manning Collection; Samuel Worcester to Maria Manning, April 26, 1814; Tabernacle Church of Salem Records; Priscilla Manning to Richard Manning, May 10 [1814], expense accounts, Hawthorne-Manning Collection; Erlich, *Family Themes,* 39.

family [was] that he had gone down on a lake with a man of the name of Manning at the helm."[34] The mystery of it all haunted Mrs. Manning. Yet it was such a common occurrence. Just next door the same lot had been Daniel Hathorne's. We do not know the private thoughts of Rachel Hathorne, but surely her loss was just as great.

The youngest daughter, Priscilla Miriam Manning (1790–1873), married in 1817 a widower, John Dike, with two children. She had no children of her own, but she exerted a fair amount of influence on the Hawthorne as well as the Dike children. She lived with the Mannings until sometime after 1817. Elizabeth ended up with a strong distaste for her. She thought Priscilla too puritanical, that she did not read because she thought a book might contain evil. "She never thought it good to be too comfortable," wrote Elizabeth to her cousins. A different view of Priscilla Dike was that of Rose Hawthorne Lathrop: "How serene she always seemed, how kind always," she observed. Ingrained in her aunt's character was her Calvinist theology. Whatever made her turn away from her father's church, we do not know, but she was steadfast in her conservative beliefs the rest of her life.

Her influence on young Nathaniel is seen in her encouragement for his writing a diary, whether the one reportedly found in Maine was his or not. She found a place for him in Mr. Archer's school. She may well have helped him to appreciate some of what he saw. For instance, her description of an ice storm in March 1820 is very similar to the ice storm depicted by Hawthorne in "Alice Doane's Appeal": "The trees were hung with diamonds and many-colored gems" (*CE* 11:274). Priscilla expressed it this way: "The trees have the last week [she reported] exhibited the most beautiful appearance, the branches were covered with ice, and bent almost to the ground with the weight of it. Some hung in such a manner as to resemble the most elegant chandeliers."[35] On the other hand, the description in the *Salem Gazette* (March 14, 1820) may have been influential as well: "The bright sun of Saturday morning exhibited a scene like enchantment, in particular the trees seemed decked in a profusion of ornaments, as for a great gala. Nothing could be more splendid than their crystallizations glistening in the rays of the sun or more graceful than their branches drooping toward the ground."

34. WB, *Diary,* 2:358; William Manning to Richard Manning Jr., September 16, 1806, Hawthorne-Manning Collection; W. Manning, *Manning Families of New England,* 715, 716.
35. EMH to Rebecca Manning, February 22 [1869], copy; RHL to Rebecca Manning, October 22 [1873], Hawthorne-Manning Collection; Priscilla M. Dike to ECH, March 14, 1820, Hawthorne-Manning Collection.

John Dike, Priscilla's husband, always seemed kind and helpful to Nathaniel. He believed the best of him. That Nathaniel was fond of him is evident, I believe, in his letters to John S. Dike, Dike's son by a previous marriage. After the elder Dike failed in business in 1829, Nathaniel wrote John S. Dike, "I often go in to see him and your mother, and find them quite contented and comfortable. He appears to be in excellent spirits and looks younger than when you were here" (*CE* 15:201). The Dikes's favorite of the three Hawthorne children was Louisa, and she reciprocated the feeling. She became another child to the Dikes and lived with them for a short time after the death of Dike's daughter Mary. After her mother died, Louisa went to live with them; in fact, she was traveling with John Dike on her last fatal journey when their steamship burned. Elizabeth, however, was not charitable about John Dike. She thought him too exacting and declared she would rather be in charge of an orphan asylum as to be in charge of him.[36]

The youngest Manning child was Samuel (1791–1833). He had enrolled in Atkinson Academy in 1805. By 1809 in Salem he was sending in ships what were called "adventures" (that is, some sort of goods that the mariner would try to sell abroad for the profit of the one who sent them). In 1813 he took over the family firm of stagecoaches with Holten Dale and Henry Cross. That firm failed at the end of 1814. Priscilla had written Richard in October 1815 about Samuel's embarrassments, which "have been very painful to his feelings." In 1816 he went to Raymond to operate the store that Richard had built, but in two years he was back in Salem. He had written Robert from Raymond on April 22, 1817, that he had been "constantly employed in retailing out Rum, Molasses & Tobacco to a set of drunken, noisy, quarrelsome, ignorant people."[37]

Later Samuel was in charge of the horses for the stage lines. He often took trips to buy more animals, and sometimes he took Nathaniel with him. In 1820 and 1821 he visited the south (whether for health or horse trading is not clear), but seems to have gone no farther than Washington and Baltimore. In 1828, according to a reminiscence of Horace Conolly, Nathaniel went with his uncle Samuel to New Haven, Connecticut. They went again in 1829, according to a letter written at that time to Louisa (*CE* 15:198). In 1831, Samuel and Nathaniel went to Concord and Canterbury, New Hampshire. In Guilford, Nathaniel wrote to Louisa

36. JH, *Hawthorne and Wife,* 1:454; EMH to Robert Manning, March 6 [1870?], copy, Hawthorne-Manning Collection. For more on John Dike, see Margaret B. Moore, "Hawthorne's Uncle John Dike," 325–30.

37. Priscilla Manning to Richard Manning, October 23, 1815; Samuel Manning to Robert Manning, April 22, 1817, Hawthorne-Manning Collection.

that "the news of your Uncle Sam's arrival spread all over the country, and every man that had a horse mounted him and came galloping to the tavern door, hoping to make a trade or swap; so that they fairly hunted us out of town. . . . Your Uncle Sam complains that his lungs are seriously injured by the immense deal of talking he was forced to do" (*CE* 15:212, 213).

Samuel did have trouble with his lungs, although not, one presumes, from talking. A constant problem to him, he died from lung congestion in 1833. He was listed as a gentleman in his will written on November 13, 1833, in which he left to his sister Mary his title to a pew in First Church. Among other bequests, he left one hundred dollars each to the three Hawthorne children. Perhaps because he was younger, Samuel seemed to have none of the seriousness characteristic of most of his brothers and sisters. Nathaniel always felt particularly at ease with him.[38]

Aside from servants who came and went and who did not always live in the house, there was one other resident in the Herbert Street home from 1813 to 1818: Nathaniel's great-aunt, his grandfather's sister. Ruth Manning (1740–1818) married late, against her family's wishes, as the third wife of Francis Rust, a widower of Ipswich who died in 1799. After the death of Richard Manning Jr., she came to live with the Manning family and was an added complication to the Manning move to Maine. In August 1816 Elizabeth queried her Aunt Mary Manning, "Can you reconcile Aunt Rust to spend her life in this cold, unfruitful country? Can you be reconciled yourself?" After Aunt Rust died of "cramps in her stomach as she sat in her chair," Richard Manning wrote his brother Robert about her death: "we could not expect (from her great age) that she would stay with us a long while, but I had anticipated the time when I should have seen her in Raymond . . . we have this consolation that we endeavored to have her (in her old age) live as comfortable & easy as possible & that she should not want for anything necessary."[39]

Thus in Hawthorne's childhood there were in close proximity Grandmother Manning and Great-Aunt Rust. Before 1813 there were also Grandfather Manning and Grandmother Hathorne. Each could have told him family traditions that he later incorporated into his stories.

38. M. Hawthorne, "Hawthorne and the Man of God," 262; Essex Probate Court, #17569, will of Samuel Manning, gentleman, November 13, 1833; William B. Upton, "List of Deaths Recorded by the Rev. John Prince LL.D.," 110.

39. *Vital Records of Ipswich,* 1:262, 2:301, 379, 668; *SG,* May 19, 1818; Manning Hawthorne, "Aunt Ebe—Some Letters of Elizabeth M. Hawthorne," 211; Rust, *Record of the Rust Family,* 140; Richard Manning to Robert Manning, May 26, 1818, Hawthorne-Manning Collection.

Each must have given him a feeling for the reality of the past that is so evident in his work.

There were two other persons who were mentioned as being in the Manning home. Hannah Lord (1788–1869) was a kinswoman of Miriam Manning who seemed to function as a servant the way many "poor relations" did then. She died on July 14, 1869, at the age of eighty-one. On her tombstone was written, "She lived unmarried and for forty years was content to spend her wealth of love and thought and bodily strength as a family servant. Her Lord she served from birth." She appears in Hawthorne's first extant letter more than forty years before in which she is said to have carried him out of the house when he was lame (*CE* 15:105). Hannah was the daughter of Captain Richard Lord, a brother of Miriam Manning, and of Hepsibah Lakeman, whose first name Nathaniel may have appropriated for use in *The House of the Seven Gables*. In 1827 Hannah Lord was paid $52.10, but that is the only sum I have found in the Manning Papers at the Peabody Essex Museum.[40] A "poor relation" she may have been, but she was clearly valued by the Mannings. She may well have served as a model for the various servants in Hawthorne's abortive last novels, one of whom he called "Hannah."

A helper named Jane also lived with the Mannings at times. She in fact went to Raymond with them in November 1818 and again in 1821. Whether eventually Jane stayed in Maine or came back to Salem is not known.[41] It is too bad that no one seems to have interviewed Hannah Lord or Jane for their impressions of Hawthorne. They could probably have added many fascinating details. Interviewing retainers, however, may be a more modern custom.

There have been many characterizations of the Manning home. Some felt it was cheerless or filled with those who kept to themselves. A fair reading of the various letters through the years, however, gives a picture of many visitors, mostly relatives, especially in the early years. Not only Manning relatives but Hathorne families came to the two houses. Rebecca B. Manning wrote in retrospect, "There was a large family connection on both sides—both in Salem and in other towns, cousins on the Hawthorne side, & cousins & other relatives near & far removed on the Manning side who were constantly coming and

40. "Family record," Hawthorne-Manning Collection; "Estate of Richard Manning, Jr.," Hawthorne-Manning Collection.
41. Mary Manning to ECH, November 17, 1818, Hawthorne-Manning Collection; EMH to Priscilla M. Dike, December 15, 1818, Manning Hawthorne Papers; M. Hawthorne, "A Glimpse," 183; Robert Manning to John Dike, October 23, 1821; Mary Manning to ECH, April 7, 1822, Hawthorne-Manning Collection.

going from this busy bustling hospitable home."[42] Not all visitors were welcome, however. Miriam Manning seems to have been particularly troubled by the family of Daniel Giddings, whose wife, Sarah Lord (1738–1797), had been her sister. Some of the daughters were evidently trying to take as much advantage of the Richard Mannings in Raymond as they had of the Manning family in Salem. Mrs. Manning was quite irritated. She asked her daughter Mary to request Elizabeth to write and warn those in Maine about this "artful, designing set of people." Furthermore, she was reported as saying "that she hopes none of her children will be troubled as she has been with the company of distant relations, and that if Mr. Giddings' children are in want, let them work as she did at his father's, and if they cannot maintain themselves let them go to the poorhouse."[43] There is more than a hint here of buried resentment and reasons for thriftiness on Mrs. Manning's part.

THE NATHANIEL HATHORNE (HAWTHORNE) FAMILY

From the Hathorne and Manning homes a new family emerged. The last son of Daniel and Rachel Hathorne was Captain Nathaniel Hathorne (1776–1808). He was known to be reserved but fond of children. He rarely saw his own children and little Maria Louisa (1808–1852) not at all. Like his brother Daniel, he was away at sea most of the time. He had brought his bride, Elizabeth Clarke Manning, to live at his mother's house on Union Street, just behind the Manning home. George P. Lathrop, who had not known him but later married his granddaughter Rose, said Captain Hathorne was considered by tradition to be "inclined to melancholy, and very reticent." He also had a vigorous appetite for reading and took many books along with him on his journeys. A sailor long afterward recognized a likeness to him in his son.

George B. Loring maintained that

> There was never a more intense Hathorne than the father of Nathaniel Hawthorne, the silent, sombre sailor, who represented all the courage and power of the family, with a busy and thoughtful mind which dwelt upon that curious and interesting family-record with a sort of superstitious awe and deep admiration. So far as any inheritance of faculties from his father's line is concerned, Hawthorne had a right to be a powerful, thoughtful, reticent, dreamy, brooding, sensible, unambitious, retiring man—and he was.[44]

42. Rebecca B. Manning, "Some Facts," Hawthorne-Manning Collection.
43. EMH to Richard Manning, March 30, 1826, Manning Hawthorne Papers.
44. Hubert J. Hoeltje, "Captain Nathaniel Hathorne," 329–56; G. Lathrop, *A Study of Hawthorne,* 61; Loring, "Nathaniel Hawthorne," in Cameron, *Hawthorne among His Contemporaries,* 214.

Loring seems to have learned what he knew about Hawthorne's father
from hearsay, but somehow all the legends of the silent, stern man have
survived, primarily through oral transmission.

There were other more tangible reminders of Captain Hathorne: a
ship's log into which he had scribbled poetry about Betsey's charms; a
set of china that he brought home with his initials "N.H." on the pieces;
an oval tray "that came from beyond the sea" which Rose Hawthorne
Lathrop remembered. She also recalled "[o]n my father's side of the
family there had been a distinct trait of material elegance, appearing
in such evidences as an exquisite tea-service, brought from China by
my grandfather, with the intricate monogram and dainty shapes and
decoration of a hundred years ago; and in a few chairs and tables that
could not be surpassed for graceful design and finish." There was also
"the beautiful India box, and the superb . . . bowl and pitcher, which
Mr. Hawthorne's father had made in India for himself." All of these
objects must have elicited conversation in the family about the man who
owned them. I cannot believe that the father was never talked about
by the Hathornes or the Mannings, or that such curious children would
not have enquired and been answered about their father. Hawthorne
later gave "a most interesting account of his father" to James T. Fields,
but aside from the fact that the sea captain had died in Surinam in
1808, Fields tells us nothing more. The Captain left little money: his
personal estate was $338.66; the sum collected on notes was $940.89.
He also left a gold watch, a silver watch, gold buttons, and a number
of books, appraised at $10.[45] In July Betsey moved her family to the
Manning household on Herbert Street. It was not a long move, but she
left a manless house for one with her father and her brothers as well as
sisters and her mother. The houses in that section are crowded together.
One given to a solitary way would have been hard put to it to find much
seclusion.

Hawthorne's mother was the second daughter of Richard and Miriam
Manning. She was born in 1780, married Captain Nathaniel Hawthorne
in 1801, and was the mother of the three Hawthorne children. In a
letter to Thomas Wentworth Higginson in the 1880s, Elizabeth Palmer
Peabody wrote: "She was poetical [by?] temperament with great good
sense and highly cultivated by reading. . . . She was lovely in person

45. E. Manning, "The Boyhood of Hawthorne," in Cameron, *Hawthorne among His
Contemporaries,* 355; RHL, *Memories,* 263; JH, *Hawthorne and Wife,* 1:368; James T.
Fields, *Yesterdays with Authors,* 54; Essex County Probate #12882, inventory of Captain
Nathaniel Hathorne, April 19, 1808.

even to her dying day & I used to think she looked as if she had walked out of an old picture as she preserved the ancient costume." Elizabeth Peabody also referred to Mrs. Hawthorne's reading in a letter to Francis Henry Lee, collector in the 1880s of facts and impressions of Salem. Louisa asked her mother in 1844 if she "had read anything new since [she] went away," as though she expected her to be reading much of the time.[46]

Hawthorne's mother, it seems to me, has been badly misrepresented through the years, not least perhaps, as Nina Baym has suggested, by the writer himself. The figure of the recluse who hid herself away after the death of her husband seems unlikely to me. It was the Peabodys who promulgated the recluse idea with a lot of help from Nathaniel, who was attempting to show his intended bride that she had brought him out into the sunlight again. The facts we have simply do not show Elizabeth Clarke Hawthorne as room-bound. Family letters repeatedly mention her health, which had either kept her in her room or had allowed her to come out of her room. When she was well, she was no longer confined. The fact that she was so often ill can be documented too. Over the early years her illnesses were referred to in 1816, 1818, 1819, 1820, 1826, 1828, 1829, and 1831. Mary Manning wrote her brother Richard and his wife on February 9, 1829, that Elizabeth was "very sick . . . but is now recovered so as to go out of her room." Richard Manning informed his brother Robert from Raymond on November 10, 1816, that "Sister Hathorne has had a relapse and has been confined to her Chamber most of the time till yesterday." Priscilla Manning Dike notified the Mannings in Raymond on October 17, 1828, that "Mrs. Hathorne is quite indisposed and not able to leave her chamber at present."[47]

Also, there were activities in which Elizabeth Hawthorne participated. She joined First Church in 1806. Had she never gone to meeting after her husband's death, surely there would be a mention somewhere. She was very active in Raymond with establishing a Sunday school. She managed to move to Raymond and to supervise a household there. Moreover, she went to Dearborn Street to oversee that home, although she was ill for a

---

46. EPP, *Letters of Elizabeth Palmer Peabody: American Renaissance Woman,* 451, 419; MLH to ECH, August 12, 1827, Berg Collection.

47. Nina Baym, "Nathaniel Hawthorne and His Mother: A Biographical Speculation," 16–17. For her illnesses, see the letters in the Hawthorne-Manning Collection: Mary Manning to her father, November 4, 1806; Richard Manning to Robert Manning, November 10, 1816; Priscilla Dike to Richard and Susan Manning, October 17, 1828; Mary Manning to Richard and Susan Manning, February 9, 1829; MLH to Mary Manning, March 3, 1831; Mary Manning to Susan Manning, May 18, 1831.

while as a consequence of moving. Sophia, after repeating all the words about her mother-in-law's reclusiveness early in her marriage, observed after they were all in the Mall Street home in 1848 that Mrs. Hawthorne was "so uninterfering" (which is quite different from reclusiveness), and that she had "kindness, sense, and spirit." She also said that she will be a "great resource in emergencies." This does not sound like the woman described years later by Elizabeth Peabody. Another memory of Peabody's, however, seems more likely. She remarked that her mother had characterized Mrs. Hawthorne as "a most intelligent, well-read, and lively woman."[48]

She was called beautiful with "deep dark eyes" and "powerful brows." She was tall. Horatio Bridge recalled that she had "quiet and refined manners." Her niece Rebecca B. Manning reported that Betsey was known to be warm and cordial and that many visitors came and went from the Manning house, almost as though it were a tavern. Yet Betsey also seemed to be very reserved. That is not to say that she was entirely normal, if there is such a thing. Rebecca Manning reported that both the Hawthorne and the Manning families "possessed deep, strong, passionate affections & natures, but were very undemonstrative with a real inability to express their deeper emotions." Julian Hawthorne showed some perspicacity when he noted "that strange New England shyness masking in visible ice the underlying emotion," which could be true of both mother and son.[49]

Nathaniel Hawthorne's relationship with his parents has been characterized in many ways. He himself recognized as his mother lay dying in 1849 that his relationship with her was not quite natural: "I love my mother, but there has been, ever since my boyhood, a sort of coldness of intercourse between us, such as is apt to come between persons of strong feelings, if they are not managed rightly. . . . I shook with sobs. For a long time, I knelt there, holding her hand; and surely it is the darkest hour I ever lived" (*CE* 8:429). Gloria C. Erlich asserts that the Manning influence (that is, the influence from that whole family, rather than the Hathorne family) was paramount, since his mother lost her independence when she went back to live in their home. Edwin Haviland Miller believes Hawthorne spent his life searching for his absent father, that that was his dominant motivation, that his

48. SPH to EPP Sr., September 10, 1847, in JH, *Hawthorne and Wife,* 1:314; EPP, *Letters,* 418–20.

49. Horatio Bridge, *Personal Recollections of Nathaniel Hawthorne,* 38; Rebecca B. Manning, "Some Facts," Hawthorne-Manning Collection; JH, *Hawthorne and His Circle,* 6.

mother was cold, non-nurturing, almost absent, and his father was ever present to his mind. Nina Baym, on the other hand, thinks that his father never meant much to Nathaniel. He had died too early, and his uncles immediately took his place. His mother was the dominant figure in his life, was almost too present, and had sinned in bringing Elizabeth early into the world. Therefore, the Hathornes did not like her, and she herself always felt estranged. T. Walter Herbert holds that Hawthorne felt that he and his mother and sisters were in a "circle of shared bereavement" in opposition to the Mannings. He also says that "comparatively few boys lost their fathers in boyhood," which is demonstrably untrue in Salem. It happened frequently; for instance, it was true of Caleb Foote, Jones Very, and Hawthorne's cousin George Archer, among others.[50]

Many scholars assume the Hathornes liked neither Betsey nor her children. They base this on the fact that they did not leave them any money. There are no affectionate letters, it is true, nor any evidence to say they were close. But, of course, they lived nearby; there was no need usually to write. Perhaps, too, there were no letters because the Hathornes could not write (at least the women left in the house after Captain Nathaniel died). They all signed their wills with their marks. Ruth Hathorne had poor eyesight also. Still, they did seem to enquire about the children, according to extant Manning letters. Furthermore, Aunt Ruth had a fond memory of Nathaniel as a child; Sally Archer Osgood wrote with pride about "our kinsman"; the Barstows all seemed aware of him; and Eleanor Condit was especially his friend.

One must balance against these assumptions of estrangement the facts that many young Salem widows went back to live with their own families after the deaths of their husbands. Sarah Crowninshield was one such. On the other hand, there were numerous instances of young widows opening shops, taking in boarders, sewing or nursing in order to care for their children. Death, in fact, was a constant, brooding presence in Salem. There were deaths not only at sea but also of sickness, of suicide, of accident. It is a truism to say that the nineteenth century was reticent about sex but open about death, whereas we of the present time are just the opposite. When we judge these people in terms of our own inhibitions and obsessions, we get it wrong. This is not to say, however, that Salemites were not grieved seriously by death nor unaware of sexual tensions. It is to say that their priorities were somewhat different

---

50. Erlich, *Family Themes,* 37; Miller, *Salem Is My Dwelling Place,* 28, 36, 120; Baym, "Hawthorne and Mother," 3,13, 10; Herbert, *Dearest Beloved,* 68, 60.

from those of the late twentieth century, and we should try at least to judge them on their own terms.

Also part of this Hawthorne family were two sisters. Nathaniel's older sister, Elizabeth Manning Hawthorne (1802–1883), was a sharply edged individual who seemed almost the twin of her brother. Born two years before the writer, Elizabeth was not long alone with her mother in the house on Union Street before she was joined by a brother and then four years later by a sister.

All that is known of her education is that she went for a short time with her brother to Elizabeth Carlton's Dame School. Mrs. Elizabeth Palmer Peabody offered to educate her after her father died. Later she was taught by William P. Cranch in 1812 and by Mrs. Peabody's sister, Amelia Palmer Curtis, from 1812 to 1815. In October 1814, Elizabeth received a certificate from Mrs. Curtis, who commended her "amiable manners" but urged her to more industry.[51] Even then she did not work hard at what did not interest her.

Elizabeth, called Ebe, was a beautiful girl, and she must have retained that beauty. Her youngest niece, Rose, remembered her in 1897 with her "dark brown, long lashes and broadly sweeping eyebrows" against "the pallor of her skin, which was so delicately clear, yet vigorous." She thought she "fascinated like a wood-creature." Annie Fields described her in 1865 as "a small woman with small fine features, round full face, fresh-looking in spite of years, brilliant eyes, nervous brow which twists as she speaks, and very nervous fingers. . . . She is a woman of no common mould." She also said that Lucy Larcom "calls her a hamadryad, and she says she belongs in the woods and should be seen there."[52]

Elizabeth was very like her brother. They both enjoyed walking, although she perhaps relished the woods more than he (forests, except perhaps in Maine, often represent a domain of evil in Hawthorne's work). They each took long walks by the sea. She too loved reading books and newspapers, and she wrote beautifully and helped Nathaniel with the articles for the *American Magazine of Useful and Entertaining Knowledge,* although he often had to urge her to completion. She and he later collaborated on the two-volume *Peter Parley's Universal History on the Basis of Geography.* He seems to have read many of his tales to her for her opinions, although he often feared them. She did not like household chores, or church, or the demands of Salem. She wrote her

51. Certificate of merit for EMH, October 1814, Berg Collection. For an expanded version of Elizabeth, see M. Moore, "Elizabeth Manning Hawthorne," 1–9.
52. RHL, *Memories of Hawthorne,* 475; M. Howe, *Memories of a Hostess,* 69.

brother in September 1852 that "[i]n Beverly I can do exactly as I choose, and even appear to be what I am, in a great degree."[53]

It was rumored that she was once in love, and many were the speculations. A Mr. L., Jeremiah Briggs, Dr. Winthrop Brown, and someone in Newburyport were mentioned.[54] Whatever the truth of these rumors, she seems to have kept her own counsel. She was so individualistic that she would have found it difficult to fit into a conventional marriage. She was witty, intelligent, and prickly.

After their mother's death, Elizabeth went to live in Montserrat in Beverly, and spent her time reading, walking in the woods, writing letters, and translating Cervantes. She was not averse to company; in fact, she often begged her Manning cousins to come see her. Elizabeth wrote her cousin Robert that she felt "the want of conversation, which is the great want of my life." She also saw her cousins, Eleanor Barstow Condit and Ann Savage. Her nieces, Una and Rose, came to visit, as did Julian and her brother. She observed, too, various people in the neighborhood. Occasionally she went to Salem, and she visited Concord, but never after her brother's death. She spent a lot of time correcting what Elizabeth Peabody and others had to say about Nathaniel.[55]

In 1854 Elizabeth showed Hawthorne's portrait to Charlotte Forten, a young black woman who had been sent from her Philadelphia home to be educated in the nonsegregated schools of Salem. Forten was impressed not only by the portrait but also by Elizabeth herself. She thought her "singular-looking" with an "eerie, spectral look," but soon found her "pleasant" and "cordial." Nine days later Forten walked with Elizabeth, some of her classmates, and her teacher on Marblehead beach. They sat under the shadow of rocks and watched the waves, and then strolled along the beach. "Miss Hawthorne," she recounted, "gave me a singular stone to remember the place by." Ever after Charlotte Forten designated particularly memorable days as "white stone days," possibly a thought initiated on this day. This is a picture of Elizabeth slightly different from that of the isolated spinster often recalled.[56]

The younger sister, Maria Louisa (1808–1852) was, in many ways, the

53. JH, *Hawthorne and Wife,* 1:465.

54. Manning Hawthorne, "Maria Louisa Hawthorne," 120; Norman Holmes Pearson, "Elizabeth Peabody on Hawthorne," 263; John Dike to Robert Manning, August 4, 1818, Hawthorne-Manning Collection; EMH to Robert Manning, August 18, 1818, Manning Hawthorne Papers.

55. EMH to her Manning cousins [1870s and 1880s], copies; EMH to her Manning cousin, copy [1861], Hawthorne-Manning Collection.

56. Charlotte Forten Grimké, *The Journals of Charlotte Forten Grimké,* 84, 87–88, 162.

most normal member of the family. She was openly friendly, outgoing, and amenable, which one could hardly say about her sister. She never saw her father, and she was very attached to her mother. In fact, Sophia Hawthorne said that "she was always inconsolable for her mother, and never could be happy away from her," but one must make allowance for Sophia's habit of overstatement on such matters.[57]

Her letters reveal a sprightly, outspoken person with opinions of her own. One to her mother in 1827 when Louisa was visiting her Lunt cousins in Newburyport reflects her personality:

> I do not know that I ever spent so dull an evening in my life, it seemed at least ten hours long and yet we were home before nine-o'clock, such a party I never saw, the women looked as if they had dropped from the moon, ready dressed for the occasion, and had got a little tumbled by the fall, as for the men, I cannot imagine where they could have come from; there was the reverend and learned Dr. Dana, looking as stiff as a stake, and talking about "this interesting and joyful occasion" I [torn] did not like the man and he has not advanced in my good graces, as to the bride I presume Miss Manning [Mary] has given you a description of her at least, such a round-shouldered, crooked looking figure I have not seen this many a day.

The "interesting and joyful occasion" was the wedding of Micajah Lunt to his second wife. His children by his first wife, Sarah Giddings Lunt, were cousins.[58]

Maria Louisa's health was not good. Whether she suffered primarily from respiratory problems, like her mother, we do not know, but she was often spoken of as "ailing." She was gentle, but she had a sharp wit. She was a great favorite with the children. She was good at sewing and often made clothes for them. Sophia wrote about the children to Louisa, never Elizabeth. Julian Hawthorne later called her "commonplace" (by which I am sure he meant only that she was more normal than her sister), but Rebecca B. Manning, her first cousin, maintained that she was not at all commonplace, that she was an "acknowledged authority on all matters of custom and etiquette." She was, like her mother, tall, pale, fragile, and feminine, and, according to Julian, "a delightful person to have in the house," with "a playful humor" but "not very effective." Still, he was only five years old when she died.[59] Since it was she, after her Aunt Mary's death, who seemed to keep the household going and

57. JH, *Hawthorne and Wife,* 1:456.

58. MLH to ECH, August 12, 1827, Berg Collection; John J. Currier, *History of Newburyport, Mass. 1764–1905,* 2:250–51.

59. JH, *Hawthorne and Wife,* 1:5; Rebecca B. Manning, "Some Facts," Hawthorne-Manning Collection; JH, *Hawthorne and His Circle,* 16.

who wrote many of the letters to Nathaniel that are extant, Julian may not have known how effective she really was. She was never dependent on her brother, primarily because she lived with the Dikes and probably kept their household going too. She was the one who had helped Nathaniel with the "Spectator" when they were young, even writing a poem for it. She sent him Salem papers when he was away and kept him abreast of Salem gossip. It has been thought that she published poems. Perhaps one does not need another writer in the family. Somebody has to be, in Elizabeth Peabody's phrase, "more like ordinary people."[60]

These two families—the Hathornes and the Mannings—or members of them, have been accused at various times and by sundry critics of child neglect and mental child abuse, of fornication, of homosexuality, and of incest. If such had been the case, a small town like Salem would have known it or some of it, I believe. There would have been rumors, intimations. But it is late-twentieth-century critics who attribute retroactively. Both families had their faults and probably some guilty secrets, but I fail to find any evidence of more heinous behavior.

Whatever the future would bring for young Nathaniel, I think his childhood was happier than do many critics. Erlich sees him as especially hating his domineering uncle even though he tried to be fair to his motives. Miller sees him like little Ilbrihim, always longing for the father he could barely remember. T. Walter Herbert thinks of him as submissive and unsure of his manliness.[61] Yet he is remembered by those who actually knew him as a little golden-haired boy who ran around playing with other children. He asserted his independence with such sayings as "I'm going to run away to sea and never come back again." He enjoyed dancing and roaming the area around Salem. He especially enjoyed the freedom of Maine, but that does not mean he was always unhappy in Salem. When he wrote in "Grimshawe" that little Ned "continued that sad, fatal habit of growing out of childhood," the implication is that childhood is a good time, a time of innocence, from which all people must go to sterner realities, but which in itself is a time for irresponsibility, for books, for dreams (*CE* 12:424). In these two homes (and three families) young Nathaniel grew out of childhood to sterner realities.

60. EPP, *Letters,* 420.
61. This may be overstating the case, but see Erlich, *Family Themes;* Miller, *Salem Is My Dwelling Place;* Herbert, *Dearest Beloved.* Also see Frederick C. Crews, *The Sins of the Fathers: Hawthorne's Psychological Themes* (although since partially recanted); Mellow, *Hawthorne in His Times;* P. Young, *Hawthorne's Secret;* and the theme of subversion is still at the flood.

4

A Salem Education

Were boys created merely to study Latin and Arithmetic? —(*CE* 6:85)

I F, A S Wordsworth says, the child is father to the man, then it is vital that those of us who want to understand a writer know as much as we can about that child and his education. This is particularly true of Nathaniel Hawthorne, whose childhood is ill-documented and about whom there are often wrong assumptions. Not that it is easy to fill in the gaps in our knowledge. Records are poor; Hawthorne barely mentioned his early education; and those who might remember, such as his sister Elizabeth, were not always specific. "We were the victims of no educational pedantry," she wrote her niece Una later. "We always had plenty of books, and our minds and sensibilities were not unduly stimulated." That made it sound as though Hawthorne, like Topsy, just "grow'd." Elizabeth added, "[a]t the time our father died, Uncle Manning had assumed the entire charge of my brother's education, sending him to the best schools and to college. It was much more expensive than it would be to do the same things now, because the public schools were not good then, and of course he never went to them."[1]

When in 1853 Nathaniel Hawthorne sent to Richard Henry Stoddard a few paragraphs on his life, he observed, "One of the peculiarities of my

1. JH, *Hawthorne and Wife,* 1:99, 1:100. Perhaps Robert Manning did not pay all the expenses: the receipts from Elizabeth Carlton, Francis Moore, and Joseph Worcester still extant were written to Nathaniel's mother; Mary Manning in February 1820 offered to "put down 100 Dollars" for his college expenses (Mary Manning to ECH, February 29, 1820, Manning Hawthorne Papers); and there is notice of a contract signed on September 28, 1823, by Robert Manning, John Dike, and Samuel Manning for Nathaniel's expenses at Bowdoin (Nathaniel Hawthorne Papers).

boyhood was a grievous disinclination to go to school, and (Providence favoring me in this natural repugnance) I never did go half as much as other boys, partly owing to delicate health (which I made the most of for the purpose), and partly because, much of the time, there were no schools within reach."[2] It is clear that Hawthorne did have "this natural repugnance" to formal schooling, but it can also be established that he went to school perhaps more than he remembered and that there were schools often within reach. He was thinking, of course, of the time when he was lame and either could not or would not go to school or of his time in Maine when he had to be sent away to board with Reverend Caleb Bradley in Stroudwater because there were no proper schools in Raymond.[3]

The town of Salem, Massachusetts, took education seriously. By the time young Nathaniel was born in 1804 there were six public schools and innumerable private schools. Joseph Barlow Felt reported that in 1812 there were four public schools for English with 465 boys and 295 girls, a grammar school with 40 pupils, and seven women's schools. A perusal of the Salem papers in 1812 shows private schools taught by such people as Mrs. Elizabeth Peabody, John Southwick, Robert Crowell, John Hoitt, and others. There were also dancing schools conducted by William Turner and a Mr. Kingsbury in Lynn. George Dean kept a writing school. In addition, beginning in 1813, there were Sabbath schools for indigent souls who could not read or write, taught by earnest young ladies such as Sarah Savage, the half sister of Hawthorne's second cousins, who were determined that the education of their scholars would also include knowledge of the Bible.[4]

ELIZABETH CARLTON

Hawthorne began his formal education early. Three months before he was four years old and several days after the family learned of his father's death, Nathaniel and Elizabeth were sent to school to Elizabeth Carlton (sometimes spelled Carleton), who lived on Union Street either in her own family's home or with her sister, Eunice Barr, who also lived on the street. As Arlin Turner points out, it was probably done to "relieve

2. Richard Henry Stoddard, "Nathaniel Hawthorne," cited in JH, *Hawthorne and Wife,* 1:95.

3. Since Hawthorne did not like Caleb Bradley, perhaps he had him in mind when he wrote the unflattering piece on Hannah Duston for *AMUEK.* Bradley was her great-grandson ("Obituary" [of Caleb Bradley], 358).

4. Felt, *Annals,* 2d ed., 1:459, 499; *SG,* March 3, 10, 20, and 31, 1812. For Sarah Savage and Sabbath schools, see Margaret B. Moore, "Sarah Savage of Salem," 243–44. Later these Sunday schools expanded to nearly all Protestant churches.

his mother in her distress" and in her care of little Maria Louisa, only a month old. Nathaniel stayed with Miss Carlton for two years (from April 11, 1808, to May 1810). In this Dame School the children would have begun to learn the rudiments: the alphabet and beginning reading. Values were also communicated.[5]

The ties seemed to last with Betsy Carlton. The family requested her to ask her brother John to try to discover some intelligence about the missing John Manning, but that search was unsuccessful. In 1841, Maria Louisa, in complimenting Hawthorne on his portrait by Charles Osgood, remarked that Miss Carlton says it "only wants to speak." In 1852 Elizabeth Hawthorne wrote her sister, "I am sorry Miss Betsy Carlton has been so sick; it seems as if I should never have an opportunity to go to see her." Subsequently, Ebe wrote her Manning cousins to ascertain the proper address for Eunice and Elizabeth Carlton. Some years later the Peabody Essex Museum (then the Essex Institute) possessed a copy of a photograph of Nathaniel Hawthorne given them by Miss Carlton, but it can no longer be identified.[6]

Schools like Carlton's, taught by maiden ladies, are mentioned often in Hawthorne's works. Hepzibah Pyncheon had thought about teaching a school; Mr. Higginbotham's niece was a schoolteacher; Martha in "The Shaker Bridal" was sometimes schoolmistress of the village children (*CE* 2:38, 39; 9:115, 421). Phoebe Pyncheon had been an instructor in her native village (*CE* 2:77).

FRANCIS MOORE

In May of 1810 Nathaniel was almost six years old, and it was time for him to be taught by a Master. Elizabeth C. Hawthorne paid Francis Moore for instruction from May 21 to August 21, 1810; he continued to teach Hawthorne through July 20, 1811. He used the schoolhouse on Herbert Street, a convenient place for young Nathaniel.[7]

Francis Moore remains a somewhat shadowy figure. He was born in Cambridge, Massachusetts, on March 30, 1782, the son of a baker, Francis Moore Jr., and his second wife, Phebe Preston. His father had been a participant in the Boston Tea Party. After the war, the Moores moved to Lynn, Massachusetts. There in 1805 young Francis married

---

5. Turner, *Hawthorne,* 19; receipts in Hawthorne-Manning Collection.
6. Priscilla Manning to Robert Manning, February 12, 1816, Hawthorne-Manning Collection; Rita K. Gollin, *Portraits of Nathaniel Hawthorne: An Iconography,* 20; EMH to MLH, [1852], typescript, Hawthorne-Manning Collection; EMH to cousins, November 22 [1880?], copy, Hawthorne-Manning Collection; Jane E. Ward, Curator of Manuscripts, Peabody Essex Museum, to Margaret B. Moore, March 11, 1993.
7. Receipts, Hawthorne-Manning Collection; *ER,* April 10 and June 15, 1811.

Sarah Cheever, daughter of Abner and Mercy Newhall Cheever. In that same year he was a preceptor in the newly established Lynn Academy. On May 11, 1810, an ad appeared in the *Salem Gazette* that read, "Gentleman opening school for instruction of lads in schoolhouse lately improved by Mr. Stone." The first notice of Moore's school on Herbert Street was an advertisement in the *Salem Gazette* on April 9, 1811. On June 15, 1811, in the *Essex Register,* under the heading of "School Near the Common," Moore announced, "The subscriber respectfully informs the inhabitants of Salem that he continues his school in Herbert Street where the strictest attention will be paid to the moral and literary improvement of those committed to his care. . . . The number of pupils is limited to thirty." In 1812 Moore received his M.D. from Harvard. He had evidently been teaching school to finance his education, with no intention of continuing as a schoolteacher. Dr. Moore then moved to Brighton, Massachusetts, to Eaton, New York, in 1825, and eventually to Texas.[8]

His stay in Salem, then, was a brief one, and his influence on Hawthorne may have been slight. We would be unaware of his existence were it not for the receipts Moore gave to Mrs. Hawthorne for the boy's schooling. Elizabeth C. Hawthorne's name, not that of Robert Manning, is on the receipts both for education and for wood to burn, but that may have only been a courtesy. Francis Moore died, presumably in Texas, in 1856.

JOSEPH EMERSON WORCESTER
Nathaniel's early schooling under Joseph Emerson Worcester, only briefly alluded to by scholars, may well be significant in understanding the man and writer: Worcester was one of his most important teachers. He was the one who was remembered by the family. He was born in 1784 in New Hampshire in a family of fifteen children, fourteen of whom taught at one time or another in their lives. His father also taught and wrote for the press. Two of his uncles were well known. Noah Worcester wrote *Bible News* and became editor of the *Christian Disciple,* which later became the *Christian Examiner,* an influential Unitarian newspaper. His uncle Samuel, on the other hand, was a fiercely orthodox Salem minister who engaged in written skirmishes with William Ellery Channing and verbal battles with all who entered the fray, including

8. Lucius R. Paige, *History of Cambridge, Massachusetts, 1630–1877,* 612. He may have been the editor of *The Telegraph and Texas Register* in 1840 (*Travels in the Old South,* 3:165–66); *Quinquennial Catalogue of the Officers and Graduates of Harvard University,* 350.

his brother Noah. Perhaps it was Samuel Worcester's presence that prompted Joseph Worcester to go to Salem after graduating from Phillips Academy and, in 1811, from Yale. He first advertised his Salem school in March 1812; he gave up the building in the fall of 1815.[9]

After two years in Andover during which time his *Geographical Dictionary* (1817) and *A Gazetteer of the United States* (1818) appeared, he moved to Cambridge, where he lived the rest of his life, producing many textbooks, atlases, and histories. He turned in 1828 to lexicography and compiled a number of pronouncing and critical dictionaries, culminating in his *Universal and Critical Dictionary of the English Language* (1846), which led to the famous War of the Dictionaries with Noah Webster and Webster's publishers, the Merriams. His ultimate work was his *Dictionary of the English Language* (1860), which had illustrations as well as his own conservative definitions. He also edited, anonymously for twelve years (1831–1843), *The American Almanac and Repository of Useful Knowledge,* a magazine crammed with facts and lists of all kinds, including an early list of American writers in 1840 that does not include the name of Hawthorne.[10]

Worcester was a good friend of Henry Wadsworth Longfellow. In fact, they both rented rooms at the Craigie House in Cambridge and shared the house after Mrs. Craigie's death. When his father-in-law bought the property for Longfellow, Worcester built a home next door. In 1841 Worcester had married Amy Elizabeth McKean, daughter of Rev. Joseph McKean, a professor of rhetoric and oratory at Harvard.[11] Longfellow, writing about the event to his brother Stephen, said, "In the meantime my friend and fellow lodger Mr. Worcester is making a rush into the Elysian Fields of matrimony; thereby illustrating the great doctrine of the Perseverance of the Saints. He has been for six years looking over that fence with longing eyes; and has at last cleared the ditch at a leap, and to all appearances is revelling in clover."[12]

To get some idea of what this early teacher of Hawthorne's was like, one need only read the various biographical sketches. Certain words stand out: industrious, persistent, careful, and kind. Thomas Wentworth Higginson gives a vignette of the man in *Old Cambridge* (1900):

9. *DAB,* 20:526–28; William Newell, "Memoir of Joseph E. Worcester, LL.D.," 169–73. The section on Joseph Worcester is based largely on a paper read at the Philological Association of the Carolinas (Carolina Coastal College, University of South Carolina) at Myrtle Beach, South Carolina, in March 1990.

10. For the War of the Dictionaries, see Ronald A. Wells, *Dictionaries and the Authoritarian Tradition,* 67–68.

11. Newell, "Worcester," 172.

12. *The Letters of Henry Wadsworth Longfellow,* ed. Andrew Hilen, 2:42*n*, 293; 3:33.

Among the various academic guests who used to gather in my mother's hospitable parlor on Sunday evenings, no figure is more vivid in my memory than one . . . Dr. Joseph E. Worcester . . . who was wont to sit silent, literally by the hour, a slumbering volcano of facts and statistics, while others talked. He was tall, stiff, gentle, and benignant, wearing blue spectacles, and with his head as it were engulfed in the high coat collar of other days. He rocked to and fro, placidly listening to what was said, and might perhaps have been suspected of a gentle slumber, when the casual mention of some city in the West, then dimly known, would rouse him to action. He would then cease rocking, would lean forward and say in his peaceful voice: "Chillicothe? or Columbus? What is the population of Columbus?" and then putting away the item in some appropriate pigeon-hole of his vast memory, would relapse into his rocking-chair once more.[13]

The building that Worcester took in April of 1812 had been the one used by Jacob Knapp from 1803 to 1811. The school itself, after several locations, came to rest near the spot on which John Andrew was to build his great house in 1818 and which today is the Andrew-Safford house owned by the Peabody Essex Museum.[14] The institute was private, funded by proprietors who wanted only the best, and was limited to thirty pupils. I think we may assume that Hawthorne studied with Worcester from April 13, 1812, although the only receipt preserved from Worcester is one from 1813.

Hawthorne's years at Worcester's school fell into three parts: the period before the injury to his foot (April 1812 to November 1813); the interval spent at home (November 1813 to January 1815); and the time in which he may have sometimes attended the school (January–September 1815), which may also have been concurrent with his mysterious second illness.

The approximately nineteen months before the injury was a time of great excitement. The War of 1812, unpopular as it was in Salem, changed the town. Sailors and shipowners were full of tales of the forty privateers that Salem sent to sea. Uncle William Manning began his speculation by buying shares in ships and privateers; Uncle Robert participated in a minor way in such dealings and also sold guns. Home guards were formed and drilled. On June 1, 1813, Hawthorne watched with other townspeople the battle fought offshore between the *Chesapeake* and the *Shannon*. He followed the ceremonies when the bodies of Captain James Lawrence of "Don't Give up the Ship" fame and that

13. Thomas Wentworth Higginson, *Old Cambridge,* 51–52.
14. Felt, *Annals,* 2d ed., 1:458–59; Browne, "Youthful Recollections," 289. See also Gerald W. R. Ward, "The Andrew-Safford House," 59–88.

of his lieutenant were brought to Salem. The funeral procession moved solemnly through the streets as bells were tolled and guns fired in salute. "People poured into the town in torrents," wrote one correspondent, "all the taverns were completely filled. . . . the whole of Union Street [immediately behind Hawthorne's home] was a stable, horses champing from one end to the other."[15] This first period was also one of loss. The deaths of Hawthorne's grandfather Manning and his grandmother Hathorne were announced in the *Salem Gazette* on the same day in April 1813.

In the midst of such high emotions, Hawthorne emerges in the only account we have as rather normal, with the typical little boy's disgust for the company of girls, who found excitement in the relics of old chaises stored nearby and in declaiming from the steep roof of the Manning house. But he also showed some of what he was learning in his discussions with his cousin Lucy Lord Sutton on the poet Byron, witches, and, above all, Shakespeare.[16]

His injury, caused by being hit on the foot by a ball at school, and from which he had to be carried home, marked the period from November 1813 to January 1815. His earliest extant letter dates from this time: in December 1813 he wrote his Uncle Robert in Raymond that his foot was no better and that "it is now 4 weeks Yesterday, since I have been to school and I dont know but it will be 4 weeks longer before I go again I have been out of the office two or three times and have set down on the step of the door and once I hopped out into the street" (*CE* 15:105). During this time Joseph Worcester came to hear his lessons at home. James T. Fields said that it was rumored that Worcester did so because he favored Hawthorne's Aunt Maria, but Maria died in May 1814 and had lost her voice a year earlier.[17] Moreover, Joseph Worcester did not marry until he was fifty-seven. Whatever the truth of that family tradition, it was exactly like the conscientious, kind schoolmaster to see to it that his disabled pupil did not lose his educational opportunities.

Hawthorne indeed seems to have been genuinely handicapped, at least for some of his convalescence. Priscilla Manning, his aunt, wrote

15. James Duncan Phillips, *Salem and the Indies,* 405, 379, 383; Hitchings, "Ship Registers," 40:50; 41:327; *SG,* June 27, 1812; "Salem Social Life in the Nineteenth Century," 113.

16. M. Hawthorne, "A Glimpse," 180–81, 182.

17. Fields, *Yesterdays with Authors,* 43; WB, "Parish List," 23. Dr. Jocelyn Neufeld of Athens, Georgia, upon hearing what little we know of Hawthorne's symptoms, suggested he could have had osteomyelitis, a bone infection that antibiotics, not then available, might have helped.

Robert in Maine on July 13, 1814, that Nathaniel "realized the severity of his confinement more on *Independent day* than he ever had done before, William was engaged, I was at Andover, and he could not even ride out to witness the *celebration of that event* in which he has ever taken *such delight.*" By the end of August she informed her brothers that there was some alteration in his foot, that he was playing around the yard and in Herbert Street all day, and she urged Robert to advise him to attend to his writing and lessons. "Far be it from me," she wrote, "to complain of him, at his age, he cannot be expected to have consideration enough, to do this, except it be required of him." On behalf of the young student, however, it might be said that the family was continually talking about moving to Maine, although Richard wrote Mary Manning that he never wanted to see the family move unless the "War should drive the Family from Salem."[18] All in all, it was an unsettled time, not conducive to concentration on study.

During the first nine months of 1815, Nathaniel seemed to recover and then to relapse. Elizabeth Hawthorne and Richard Manning are our chief sources of information. Hawthorne's mother wrote Richard on January 20, 1815, that Nathaniel had entirely recovered the use of his foot, that he was joyful he could walk without crutches, and that "he was lame fourteen months." One could surmise, I think, that that was the period in which Hawthorne used his former illness to advantage, as he confessed later to Richard Henry Stoddard. Even when he had been well, Lucy Lord Sutton had noticed that he did not talk at all about school or seem to have any playmates.[19] Since his lameness coincided with the time of his schooling under Worcester, one may draw some tentative conclusions that he was unhappy with that particular schoolmaster, who may have insisted on a persistence and industry to match his own. On the other hand, few children aged seven to ten are naturally anxious to do meticulous work, no matter how kindly the master.

It is possible to speculate about what Hawthorne derived from this particular part of his education. Surely he gained an appreciation for the subject of geography, which Worcester was emphasizing in his own studies just then. Along with that may have been added an

18. Priscilla Manning to Robert Manning, July 13, 1814; Priscilla Manning to Robert and Richard Manning, August 29, 1814; Richard Manning to Mary Manning, August 30, 1814, Hawthorne-Manning Collection.

19. ECH to Richard Manning, January 20, 1815, Manning Hawthorne Papers; Mellow, *Hawthorne in His Times,* 20; JH, *Hawthorne and Wife,* 1:95; M. Hawthorne, "A Glimpse," 183.

appreciation for concrete details, which Hawthorne used later so skill-fully in his writings. He was also probably encouraged in his love of reading, a taste that was powerfully enhanced when lameness forced his physical inactivity. George Parsons Lathrop suggests that he may have then read *The Speaker,* by William Enfield, whose rules for elo-cution may have prompted Hawthorne's later rooftop declamations. Frank Preston Stearns says that Worcester taught the boy Latin, "the single study of which he was fond."[20] Perhaps, however, the study of Latin commenced only later with Benjamin Lynde Oliver Jr. During his childhood Hawthorne read many writers: Bunyan, Milton, Spenser, the Newgate Calendar, Froissart, Clarendon, the Waverley novels, Rousseau, and Shakespeare. It is difficult to assign them to specific years, but Worcester's own wide reading was bound to have an effect on the boy. Above all, Hawthorne must have learned from Worcester the importance of words.

Years later when Worcester compiled his great dictionary and sent it to Hawthorne, whom he recalled "as a very pleasant and interesting young pupil," Hawthorne replied:

> . . . of all Lexicographers, you seem to me best to combine a sense of the *sacredness* of language with a recognition of the changes which time and human vicissitude inevitably work upon it. . . .
> I well remember your kindness, my dear Sir, in my early days; and I have seen with the greatest pleasure the growth of that solid and indestructible reputation which you have since built up. (*CE* 18:377, 376)

Surely the kindly, erstwhile schoolmaster felt gratified and rewarded for his exertions so long ago in behalf of the little boy who had not particularly liked school.

THE OBSCURE YEARS, 1815–1818

We know little of Hawthorne's education during the period from the fall of 1815 to the fall of 1818. By June 1815 he had been pronounced to be recovering from his second illness. By October his Aunt Priscilla said he was entirely well. In February 1816 she noted that he was going

---

20. G. Lathrop, *A Study of Hawthorne,* 68; Frank Preston Stearns, *The Life and Genius of Nathaniel Hawthorne,* 54–55. Hawthorne's familiarity with many writers could have sprung from the passages included in Enfield. On March 13, 1854, Hawthorne wrote of a visit to a graveyard in Liverpool, where he saw the gravestone of William Enfield, "whose name has a classical sound in my ears, because, when a little boy, I used to read his 'Speaker' at school (NH, *Our Old Home and English Note-Books,* 1:483). Lathrop also suggests that Worcester may have acquainted Hawthorne with Boswell's *Life of Johnson.*

to school regularly.[21] Yet no word of which I am aware remains of his schooling then. One can only surmise.

One possibility is that he went to the school that had opened in October 1814 and was taught by Joseph Barlow Felt, the annalist of Salem, in the vestry of the new South Meeting House. Such a possibility would help explain Nathaniel's later interest in Salem history. Felt was of an old New England family that had been in Massachusetts since at least 1633 and in Salem since the late seventeenth century. He had financed his theological education by becoming a merchant in Salem and then by teaching school until December 17, 1819, while he studied with Dr. Samuel Worcester. Felt had married Abigail Adams Shaw, niece of Abigail Adams, in September 1816 and doubtless needed a source of income.[22]

There were many other private schools in Salem during this period. Another one that seems possible to me, because of proximity, was that of John Southwick (d. 1833) where earlier Benjamin F. Browne had gone for instruction. His school was on Southwick's Alley, which ran from Essex Street to Forrester (Bath) Street. He "went to Quaker meetings on Thursday," says Browne, so that the scholars received that afternoon off rather than Wednesdays like other schools.[23] Had Hawthorne attended Southwick's school, he was very likely to have received some of his ideas on Quakers there.

A better possibility, I believe, is that his teacher was Harvey or Hervey Brown (1784–1860) who began an evening school in October 1814 and moved into the schoolhouse "lately occupied by Joseph Worcester" in September 1815. His classes were to commence there on October 1, 1815. He again advertised his evening school on October 11, 1816, and on November 11, 1817, he announced his school now open for both sexes "for English Literature at the corner of Newbury and Brown streets where he continues his Day School for the instruction of young masters."[24]

Harvey Brown was one of triplets born to John and Mary Brown of Beverly and Hamilton, Massachusetts. His school was spoken of by Benjamin F. Browne and by Edmund B. Willson in his memorial to

21. Richard Manning to Robert Manning, June 8, 1815; Priscilla Manning to Richard Manning, October 23, 1815; Priscilla Manning to Robert Manning, February 3, 1816, Hawthorne-Manning Collection.

22. John E. Morris, *The Felt Genealogy: A Record of the Descendants of George Felt of Casco Bay,* 289–94; *SG,* September 2, 1814.

23. Browne, "Youthful Recollections," 51:53; *SG,* November 21, 1817.

24. *SG,* September 12 and October 1, 1815, October 11, 1816, and November 11, 1817.

Charles T. Brooks. It was subsequently moved to his residence on Bath Street, later designated Washington Square. The schoolhouse where he and Worcester taught was taken down in 1818 to make room for the Andrew-Safford barn.[25]

A major reason for surmising that Harvey Brown was Hawthorne's teacher during much of the period from October 1815 to October 1818 is that one of his triplet brothers was Dr. Winthrop Brown, who seemed to have a rather close relationship with the Mannings. Winthrop studied with Dr. Oliver Hubbard in Salem, moved to Raymond, and was the Manning doctor. He practiced in Cumberland County, Maine, from 1819 to 1835. Robert Manning in writing to his mother from Raymond on March 9, 1819, said "if Doct. Brown can come we should be glad. Tell Mr. Dike to tell Doct. Hubbard that we have no Doctor." Hawthorne in the September 25, 1820, issue of his little newspaper, the "Spectator," announced that the "celebrated Dr. Winthrop Brown" was to marry "the beautiful and accomplished Miss Sophia Longley, both of Raymond" (*CE* 23:42). A later issue of the "Spectator" reported the birth of "a son and heir" (*CE* 23:47). When Richard Manning was ill in 1821, Mary Manning wrote Priscilla, "Dr. Brown is here now and says if any of our friends wish to see Brother, he thinks they had better come as soon as they can." In 1830 Mary Manning again informed Priscilla that Doctor Brown had visited Richard almost every day. He is mentioned also in other letters during Richard's last illness. Much later in November 1850 when Rev. John W. Ellingwood, brother-in-law of Priscilla Dike, was pursuing her wish to provide financial help to the church in Raymond, he found there Brown's widow, about forty and "of very respectable appearance," who said that her husband had been clerk of the church and that she had the records. Despite the church's much diminished membership, he told the Sabbath school teacher "that there was a lady in Salem, who felt a great desire for their spiritual improvement & had offered to pay 100 dolls. for the support of preaching, for their benefit."[26] This connection

25. *Vital Records of Salem*, 1:124; 3:146; Browne, "Youthful Recollections," 51:298; E. B. Willson, "Memorial of Charles T. Brooks: Birth and Beyond," 4; G. Ward, "Andrew-Safford House," 60*n*.

26. *Vital Records of Beverly*, 1:54; [John Brown Descendants], *EA*, 13:45; [W. Woodford Clayton], *History of Cumberland County, Maine*, 358; Robert Manning to Mrs. Miriam Manning, March 9, 1819; Mary Manning to Priscilla M. Dike, March 4, 1821, August 30, 1830, October 19, 1830, and January 11, 1831; John T. Ellingwood to Priscilla M. Dike, November 29, 1850, Hawthorne-Manning Collection. For Sophia Longley, see Henry P. Warren et al., *The History of Waterford, Oxford County, Maine, Comprising Historical Address by Henry P. Warren, Record of Families by Rev. William Warren, and Centennial Proceedings by Samuel Warren*, under Longley Family. This must have been a later wife.

with the Brown family seems to me to suggest that Harvey Brown might well have been Hawthorne's teacher.

Wherever Hawthorne went to school, he was living in an intensely interesting time. Salem was beginning to lose its position as a premier city of the seas, although probably not many Salemites then realized it. Her harbors were still crammed with ships. Yet the *Gazette* reported on March 31, 1816, that before the War of 1812 Salem had owned 225 vessels; after the "war, the ruinous war," she owned only 57. Many foreigners walked her streets. The air was filled with the aroma of spices. But there were also failures. The year had begun with the failure of William and Samuel Manning in the stagecoach business, which Robert had to hold together.

There was a respite from school in the summer of 1816 when the Hawthorne family went to Raymond for a glorious period of freedom for the boy. In late summer Mrs. Manning and her daughter Mary joined them. In October Nathaniel returned to Salem, leaving his mother and sisters behind. Richard Manning wrote Robert on November 10, 1816, that Elizabeth (Betsey) Hawthorne "now wishes she had gone home with Mother and Sister Mary. I thought at first she was worried about Nath as she was very lothe [*sic*] to part with him."[27] So far as I know, Nathaniel then remained in Salem until November 1818.

During this period there were weddings: Uncle Richard Manning to Susan Dingley in 1815; cousin Sally Archer to Robert H. Osgood, formerly of Salem then of Baltimore, in 1816; and George Archer to Eliza Osborne in 1817. There were deaths: Ruth Manning Rust in 1818 who had lived with the Mannings for five years, and Simon Forrester in July 1817. There was a sea serpent reported to have been observed off Cape Ann and Nahant, which even Dr. Bentley claimed to have seen on September 30, 1817. A new steamship plied the waters between Boston and Salem; it had a short-lived existence but produced much excitement. George Crowninshield sailed away in his splendid ship, *Cleopatra's Barge,* on March 31, 1817, and sailed back again on October 3, 1817. When Crowninshield died in November, it was discovered that his unknown mistress had a will signed by him, and it was judged by the court that his natural child was to benefit by that will, something "humbling to the family pride" as Bentley wrote in his diary. There were fires, which Elizabeth later said Nathaniel loved to watch, at Dr. Benjamin Lynde Oliver's and at Reverend Thomas Carlisle's. Carlisle, it

27. Richard Manning to Robert Manning, November 10, 1816, Hawthorne-Manning Collection.

should be noted, had married Hawthorne's cousin, Eleanor Forrester.
William Manning introduced two Indians to Dr. Bentley and possibly to
Nathaniel. The cashier of Essex Bank, Sheppard Gray, and his endorser,
James King, made off with the bank's money to the consternation
and loss of many Salemites. A long-time driver for the Manning stage
lines, Holten Dale, hanged himself in October 1818. It was probably
during this period that Hawthorne went to his schoolhouse to declaim,
according to the recollection of his friend Horatio Bridge, and was
overheard by some older boys who taunted him. He was always loath
after that to speak in public.[28] In sum, it was an educational time to be
alive in Salem.

The family thought all through these years about moving to Maine,
and finally moved there in October 1818, but Nathaniel was not free of
school for very long. He was sent to board with and learn from Rev.
Caleb Bradley in Stroudwater. He was not at all happy there and came
back to Raymond, and returned soon thereafter to Salem to resume his
studies.

DANCING SCHOOL

Dancing always seemed to be a part of the education of a Salemite. In
1810 Madame Martelly offered to teach French Dancing. In 1816 Pierre
Guigon, a pupil of the Royal Academy of Dancing at Paris and lately
the first dancer at the Great Theater of Bordeaux, offered to lend his
expertise. An amazing number of Frenchmen arrived in Salem with the
same object in view. In 1818 Mr. G. Grand De Val, who had been rec-
ommended by Monsieur De Val, French consul to Boston, announced
that he could teach "Dancing, French, Drawing, and Fencing."[29] In
"Grimshawe," Hawthorne speaks of a Frenchman, "an M de Grand
but secretly calling himself a Count—who taught the little people, and,
indeed, some of their elders, the Parisian pronunciation of his own
language and likewise dancing, (in which he was more an adept and
more successful than in the former branch) and fencing" (*CE* 12:373).

There were many dances at Hamilton Hall. Mrs. Eben Putnam remembered the old Assemblies when dancing "commenced at six and
finished precisely at twelve"—even if in the middle of a dance. At the
end of the dancing school season there were balls and exhibitions. After

28. *SG,* June 6, November 28, December 2, and April 15, 1817; WB, *Diary,* 4:481, 489,
496, 508, 446, 499–502, 542. There was also another illegitimate daughter not mentioned
by Bentley (Crowninshield Family Papers); *ER,* October 24, 1818; Bridge, *Recollections,*
33–34.
29. *SG,* March 16, 1810, December 27, 1816, and April 21, 1818.

the pupils danced, "the old folks took the floor, much to the amusement of the younger, who thought their Grandfathers and Grandmothers were poor dancers."[30]

Hawthorne's dancing teacher was William Turner, who taught the subject for nearly forty years. The style proposed was far more acrobatic than was true of later years. He instructed his pupils to "jump high, cross the feet, and avoid sliding. . . . The lesson included the minuet. Hornpipe and jig for the boys." Julian Hawthorne recalled in *Hawthorne and His Circle* that his father "could stand and leap as high as his shoulder," a feat that the dancing had probably helped. Each year there was an exhibition by the pupils. Israel P. Williams remembered that girls lined up on one side, the boys on the other, and that just as they neared each other, the boys dropped "fine bird shot on the hard pine floor and as the girls sashaed, they went on their beam ends fast." In 1818 when Hawthorne took dancing from Turner, the fee was five dollars at entrance and nine dollars for the twelve-week quarter. Maria Louisa came back from Raymond with her Uncle Robert in June 1820, and both children took dancing with Mr. Turner. In October they were preparing for the annual ball, which Uncle Robert felt would consume "much time & money lost to no good purpose I fear."[31] Mr. Turner described the ball in the *Salem Gazette* (October 24, 1820) as "the closing scene of my professional life." Both youngsters thoroughly enjoyed themselves.

Hawthorne's next dancing instructor was John M. Boisseaux, who had opened his school in Salem in 1820. On October 31 of that year, Boisseaux advertised that he had "practiced the art in Paris and other large cities," and continued:

> His method does not merely teach jumping . . . the object in teaching young people to dance, does not consist wholly in the amusement which it yields them, but is intended to give a polish to their manners and grace to their carriage and movements; it is also calculated to prevent or correct a stoop in most young people, whereby many contract diseases in the chest, frequently ending in consumption.

He also announced that "he will correct those young persons who walk crooked with their feet turned in, and will be very particular in forming their gestures easy and genteel." In the following December, Robert

30. Mrs. Eben Putnam to Lee, April 26, 1884; Scrapbook, 1:31–32, copy, Francis Henry Lee Papers.

31. Francis Henry Lee, "Notes on Old Times in Salem," 366; Scrapbook, 1:92, Francis Henry Lee Papers; JH, *Hawthorne and His Circle,* 14; Israel P. Williams to Lee, December 12, 1884, Scrapbook, 3:205, copy, Francis Henry Lee Papers; *SG,* March 10, 1818; Robert Manning to ECH, October 24, 1820, Hawthorne-Manning Collection.

Manning wrote that Nathaniel was going to dancing school to "Monsieur Bosseaux [*sic*]." In January 1821 he reported that Nathaniel "continues to Mr. Olivers & to dancing."[32] Perhaps Boisseaux appealed to the young Hawthorne or to the Mannings in the light of the boy's past lameness.

SAMUEL H. ARCHER JR.

With initial reluctance, Nathaniel Hawthorne spent the first eight months of his fifteenth year in Mr. Archer's school on Marlboro Street. It was there that he was encouraged to use his mind sub specie aeternitatis. Subsequently, Archer was apparently instrumental in persuading Hawthorne and his family that the lad should go to college.

Samuel Haraden Archer, born in Salem in 1798, was a descendant of a family as ancient in Salem as the Hathornes. He was a graduate of the Dartmouth class of 1818; among his fellow graduates was Thomas P. Upham, later to be Hawthorne's teacher in his senior year at Bowdoin. Archer came back to Salem in the fall of 1818 and announced that his school would open on the first Monday in February 1819. He continued his school until the spring of the panic year of 1837, when he and his brother, bookstore owner John Woodwell Archer, moved west to look for better lives for their families. Illness, precipitated by the strenuous journey and conditions in the West, forced his return in 1838 to Salem, where he died on December 28 at the age of forty. According to his obituary notice in the *Salem Observer,* "a large number of the personal friends and former pupils of Mr. Archer attended the funeral service," among whom may well have been Nathaniel Hawthorne himself.[33]

Unlike the usual bare-bones announcement of death in the Salem papers of the time, the *Observer*'s notice was placed on the first page of the *Essex Register* and gave some idea of the character of the man:

> While he was not deficient in any of the qualifications of the school teacher it was in the moral influence he exerted upon those under his care, that he was truly wonderful—among the hundreds that have received their education in his school, during a period of almost twenty

32. Scrapbook, 1:111, clipping from *SG,* Francis Henry Lee Papers; Robert Manning to ECH, December 19, 1820; Robert Manning to "sister," February 13, 1821, Hawthorne-Manning Collection.

33. Facts on Samuel Archer are found in a reminiscence of him and his "Temple of Learning" in the *Salem Daily Gazette* of June 8, 1895. The piece was attributed to Dr. George A. Perkins by John Felt of Salem in a letter to his sister, Mary Felt White, June 10 [1895], Felt-White Collection. Information may also be found in Archer's obituary in the *SG,* December 28, including a description of the funeral, January 1, 1839, and in the *Salem Observer,* January 5, 1839. My section on Archer is taken, only slightly changed, from its appearance in "Hawthorne and the Five-Dollar School," 1–9.

years, not more than six or eight have failed to become respectable men. . . . He convinced all under his care that to every act and thought there was a right and a wrong, and that their own self-respect, their safety and happiness, as well as the favor of God, could only be promoted and secured by choosing the right.[34]

Perhaps we can fill in the outline of the sort of teacher Archer was by looking at contemporaneous accounts. Margaret Heussler Felt wrote her mariner husband on March 21, 1826, about the progress of their sons, Porter and John, in the Archer School. Porter was there at least by the fall of 1820 and may have been there at the first of the year when young Nathaniel attended. Felt was nine years younger, having been born in 1813, but the school was not so big that methods would have varied much. Mrs. Felt reported:

> Yesterday afternoon Mr. Archer called on me, and he said so many good things of our Sons that I hardly know how to begin to tell them [.] Porter he said was one of his very best Boys, and one of his very best scholars. . . . industrious, ambitious, and attentive in everything, and bids fair to become an ornament and an honor to the school . . . [N]ow for John—he says it is with great pleasure and great satisfaction that he can say, that a great change has taken place in John, he has become attentive, and studious, and has learned to keep a bridle on his tongue and to mind the Rules of the school.

Archer is revealed in this and other letters to be a dedicated teacher, encouraging the best in his boys; but he was also strict, demanding good behavior as well as studiousness.

The Archer School itself was vividly described in a reminiscence printed in the *Salem Daily Gazette* on June 8, 1895, attributed to Dr. George A. Perkins. The school was on Federal Street (that part then called Marlboro) in a two-story wooden building next to the Baptist Meeting House. The churchyard was the playground, beyond which the boys were forbidden to trespass. The school was "heated with wood, burned in one of those large, tall, square old-fashioned stoves in vogue at the time. The water used had to be drawn from a neighboring pump or from wooden pipes of the old Salem aqueduct. The sanitary equipment were of the most primitive, meagre, and inconvenient description."

When Archer first advertised in the papers, he proposed offering instruction in the following branches of education: reading and writing; English grammar; geography and astronomy; bookkeeping; rhetoric and composition; chemistry; natural and moral philosophy; mathematics;

---

34. *Salem Observer,* January 5, 1839, taken from the *ER.*

and Latin and Greek. Eight-year-old Porter Felt mentioned Adams' geography, spelling, writing, reading and "cyphering" in a letter to his
father in 1821. By 1823 he was studying "Ancient Geography." In 1825
Margaret Felt reported ten-year-old John's uneasiness that once he went
into "fine hand" or "spirall Hand," Master would make him "keep a text-
book and get references." Evidently there was a progression of study,
and one could take certain branches of learning later, an arrangement
very similar to present-day required and elective courses. Presumably
the choice of elective would determine either the five- or six-dollar fee
that Archer specified in his ads. Archer also opened a school for the
"Instruction of Young Ladies" that would meet from 5 to 7 A.M. and
would cost only three dollars a quarter.[35] Whether he continued that
school or, indeed, whether enough young ladies showed up at the first
5 A.M. session is not known.

The Archer's usual routine, according to Perkins's account, was that "the
school was opened with prayer by the Master, the Bible was regularly
read, and great care was exercised over the morals and deportment of
pupils, both in and out of school." It is probably important to note
the influence of Priscilla Dike in gaining for her nephew a teacher
of views more orthodox than the prevailing views at the East or First
Churches, where the Mannings and the Hathornes worshiped. Also the
care exercised out of school may well have influenced Hawthorne's
fairly mild rebellions at Bowdoin later, not unusual for those free, to
a certain extent, from strict supervision. The hours of the school may
have been similar to those of the public town schools of the time: from
8 A.M. to 1:30 P.M. and from 2 to 4:30 P.M.[36]

The end of the school quarter was marked by an oral examination of
the scholars by eminent men of the town. Public school examinations
at this time were noticed in the press, but those of the private schools
apparently were not. Among Archer's students were Charles Osgood
(1809–1890), the painter of the most engaging of Hawthorne's portraits,
and John S. Dike (1807–1891), stepson to Hawthorne's Aunt Priscilla
and to whom Nathaniel described himself as "Your affectionate Cousin"
in later years (*CE* 15:209). George Perkins recalled at least 122 names

35. *ER,* January 23 and April 14, 1819; Jonathan Porter Felt Jr. to his father, October
23, 1821, and November 7, 1823; Margaret Heussler Felt to Jonathan Porter Felt, March
21, 1826, and November [1825]. The letters of Margaret Heussler Felt (1787–1863) to
her husband, Jonathan Porter Felt (1785–1860), and the letters of Jonathan Porter Felt
Jr. (1813–1840) are all in the Felt-White Collection. John Felt lived from 1815 to 1907.
These letters are corrected only when clarity is needed.
36. *ER,* June 26, 1819.

of boys who had been Archer's students in the eighteen years the school operated. Dike was certainly there, and Osgood probably, when Nathaniel was present.

Like Shakespeare's schoolboy, Hawthorne went unwillingly to school in July 1819. After he had spent a miserable period in Caleb Bradley's school in Stroudwater, Maine, in early 1819, his Uncle Robert told his own mother, Miriam Manning, on March 9, 1819, that he was thinking "of sending N to Salem," though six weeks later, on April 28, Richard Manning informed Robert that Nathaniel was unwilling to go to Salem. Nathaniel himself wrote Uncle Robert on May 16, "I am sorry you intend to send me to school again. Mother says she can hardly spare me" (*CE* 15:111). But by June 25 (in a letter misdated 1818) Mary Manning mentioned to her brother Robert in Raymond that "Sister Priscilla, after particular enquiry has engaged a place for Nathaniel at Mr. Archer's School in Marlboro St. [H]e is to begin after the fourth of July." Nathaniel came to Salem with his Uncle Samuel, but still delayed. He finally went to school on July 7, as Arlin Turner has noted, although many scholars have given the date as the fifth. Mary Manning informed Elizabeth Clarke Hathorne that "Nathaniel [had] a solitary Independence and birth day this year [;] he requested that he might not begin going to school until after the 5th of July. . . . He sighs for the woods of Raymond, and yet he seems to be convinced of the necessity of prepairing to do something." She also observed that he went the day after her last letter to Robert, which was dated July 6. She used that time to make him some clothes for school, and he stayed there until sometime before March 7, 1820, when he wrote his mother that he had left school and was fitting for college under Benjamin Lynde Oliver (*CE* 15:117).[37]

Hawthorne's letters written during the Archer School period sound a despondent note. One (July 26, 1819) was directed to his Uncle Robert in Maine:

> I have begun to go to school and can find no fault with it except it's not being dear enough only 5 dollars a quarter and not near enough for it is up by the Baptist Meeting House. I am as well contented here as I expected to be, but sometimes I do have very bad fits of home sickness. but I know that it is best for me to be up here as I have no time to lose in getting my schooling. (*CE* 15:112)

37. Robert Manning to Mrs. Miriam Manning, March 9, 1819; Richard Manning to Robert Manning, April 25, 1819; Mary Manning to Robert Manning, June 25, 1818 [1819], Hawthorne-Manning Collection; Turner, *Hawthorne*, 24; Mellow, *Hawthorne in His Times*, 22.

In his only other extant letter of that time (September 28, 1819), to his sister Louisa, he wrote, "I do not know what to do with myself here. I shall never be contented here I am sure. I now go to a 5 dollar school, I, that have been to a 10 dollar one. 'Oh Lucifer, son of the morning, how art thou fallen!'" (*CE* 15:114).

Yet one can also detect rising spirits and less reluctance in the youth. Priscilla Dike notified her sister Betsey on October 25 that Nathaniel was pleased with the school and that "Mr. Archer says he improves in the branches of education he is attending to."[38] Mary Manning had written Betsey even earlier on August 3 that "since he went to school his health and spirits appear much better. . . . this morning he got up before six o'clock to study his lesson" (*CE* 15:115). Unfortunately, we do not know what branches of education he did attend to. He probably studied Latin, and possibly Greek, although his study of language is not mentioned until he was under the tutelage of Mr. Oliver. He may well have taken bookkeeping since, as Arlin Turner points out, he inscribed a book, B. Shey's *The American Book-Keeper*, on October 25, 1819.[39] He certainly did a lot of writing and was inspired to do much reading, presumably on his own. He mentioned to Louisa that he had read Scott and Ann Radcliffe, Smollett and the *Arabian Nights*. He also quoted from Thomas Moore (*CE* 15:114).

The Archer period seemed to be the beginning of his brief time as a poet. He told Louisa that he was "full of scraps of poetry," and asked her to tell his sister Elizabeth that she was "not the only one of the family whose works have appeared in the papers" (*CE* 15:115). Some of the poetical mood spilled over that summer into the "Spectator" after he had left the Archer school. Perhaps those poems had been written while he was a student at Archer's. The set prose pieces on wealth or industry or benevolence may well have originated as school assignments (*CE* 23:34, 26, 29–30).

But whatever Hawthorne's course of study in Archer's School, we know that he heard the Bible read daily, had his deportment carefully monitored, and was encouraged to go to college. In his first year of teaching it must have been satisfying to Samuel Archer to have a student like young Hawthorne. Robert Manning had written Louisa, perhaps teasingly, on February 8, 1820: "Nathaniel's last Quarter will be out in 8 or 10 days & I have no employment ready for him indeed in the present situation of Business a choice is not readily made however as

38. Priscilla M. Dike to ECH, October 25, 1819, Hawthorne-Manning Collection.
39. Turner, *Hawthorne,* 24.

a last resort we can bind him for 7 years to turn a Cutlass Wheel & perhaps better."[40] The latter statement was a jest, but Robert's vision of another merchant Hawthorne was surely being countered by Samuel Archer, who saw other possibilities. Mary Manning wrote Nathaniel's mother on February 29, 1820, that "we must not have our expectations too much raised about him, but his Master speaks encourageingly [*sic*] respecting his talents etc. and is solicitous to have him to go to College" (*CE* 15:118). Archer, as encouraging about Hawthorne as he had been in other ways about the Felt boys, was strongly suggesting the prospect of college to a family that did not normally think in those terms.

Although Nathaniel left school at the end of February, he may have gone back at the end of August to take part in the end-of-the-year examination. Louisa told her mother that she went to hear John S. Dike and Nathaniel give orations at Archer's school.[41] So it was probably his own graduation that he described with dry wit and special meaning to his family in the "Spectator," Monday, September 4, 1820:

> On Monday last was an examination at Mr. Archer's School. The Schol-ars displayed all the abilities and good qualifications, which, from the high character of their Instructor, we were led to expect. Questions in all Branches in which they were examined, were answered with the greatest promptness. The Speeches, Dialogues, Etc. were delivered with an ease and Spirit which we have never seen excelled by Performers so young and inexperienced. No embarrassment was evinced, but they spoke with as little constraint as if exhibiting only before their Playfel-lows. . . . In short, every thing was conducted with the greatest order and regularity, much to the honour of the School, and the pleasure of the Spectators. (*CE* 23:29)

And so concluded Nathaniel Hawthorne's direct experience with his five-dollar school. It was a place that gave his life structure, imparted a strong sense of morality, and widened his intellectual horizons. The en-couragement that Samuel Archer gave him alone made it far more than a five-dollar school. Throughout all his writing Hawthorne exhibited a strong sense of morality. Such an influence on him surely would have come from the Archer School.

BENJAMIN LYNDE OLIVER JR.

On March 7, 1820, Nathaniel wrote to his mother that he had left school and had "begun to fit for College under Benjm L. Oliver, Lawyer. So you are in great danger of having one learned man in your family"

40. M. Hawthorne, "Maria Louisa Hawthorne," 111.
41. Ibid., 117.

(*CE* 15:117). From then until September 1821 he studied under Oliver's instruction. Very little is known of Oliver. He is often confused with his uncle of the same name, and sometimes he is passed over in silence.[42] Yet he was bound to have been an important person to Hawthorne, who spent eighteen months of his most impressionable years seeing him every weekday morning.

Oliver was descended from a famous family in Massachusetts that was Loyalist during the Revolution. He was the great grandson of Andrew Oliver, lieutenant governor of Massachusetts under Governor Thomas Hutchinson, whom Hawthorne depicts in *The Whole History of Grandfather's Chair* (*CE* 6:152,159–60). His great uncle was Peter Oliver, the chief justice of Massachusetts, who was impeached during the Revolution and forced to flee the country. His grandfather, Andrew Oliver Jr., was the only member of the family not forced to leave during that time. The Olivers were connected to the Hutchinsons, the Lyndes, the Pynchons, and other Tories. His father, Thomas Fitch Oliver, an Episcopal clergyman, and his mother, Sarah Pynchon, were living in Marblehead when he was born in 1788.[43]

Benjamin Lynde Oliver Jr. was not able to go to Harvard, as had most of the Olivers before him, but he studied law with Joseph Story, his brother-in-law, and Samuel K. Putnam, and he was admitted to the Essex Bar in 1809. He advertised a school in 1813, but he probably tutored privately, for the most part, as he seems to have done in Hawthorne's case. In 1818 he published a philosophical and moral treatise, *Hints for an Essay on the Pursuit of Happiness*. Among the principles he enunciated were the following: "Man as a rational creature is free to determine and act, according to his nature and constitution but not in a manner incompatible with them. Our passions and anxieties etc. were given us for our protection, improvement, and preservation, and for the continuance of the human race." Man, Oliver continued, should "form no habits but what are absolutely virtuous." He should "keep within proper bounds, all passion, propensities, and appetites." And he "should consider every sin [he] commit[s] as a trial of [his] virtue, and a proof of its feebleness." These principles he may well have imparted

42. See Turner, *Hawthorne,* 33; Mellow, *Hawthorne in His Times,* 23–24; Miller, *Salem Is My Dwelling Place,* 53. For those who replace Oliver with his uncle, see Hubert H. Hoeltje, *Inward Sky: The Mind and Heart of Nathaniel Hawthorne,* 9, 35–36, 59; Cantwell, *Nathaniel Hawthorne,* x, 54–55; Jean Normand, *Nathaniel Hawthorne: An Approach to an Analysis of Artistic Creation,* 22; Melinda M. Ponder, *Hawthorne's Early Narrative Art,* 67. She mixes uncle and nephew.

43. For information on the Oliver family see William Henry Whitmore, *A Brief Genealogy of Descendants of William Hutchinson and Thomas Oliver.* Also see M. Moore, "Hawthorne, the Tories, and Oliver," 213–14.

to his young scholar two years later. A brilliant conversationalist and chess player, according to George B. Loring, he practiced law and also wrote words and music for hymns, and published them in a book and in *Oliver's Magazine.*[44]

In 1818 he had proposed the creation of a literary paper for Salem called the *Observer,* which finally appeared in 1823 with Oliver as its first editor. In the opening issue he explained his purpose: "We think these reflections reflect ample reason why literature in the *Observer* should take the place of party politics. Without denying any of the advantages which may be supposed to arise from encouraging the latter, we exclude them."[45] This was a vain hope. He spent his year answering angry letters espousing the airing of party politics in the paper. At the end of the year the publishers decided that the paper should be more commercial and another editor succeeded him.

In 1830 Oliver moved to Malden, Massachusetts, to practice law in Boston and to write books. In a book entitled *The Rights of an American Citizen with a Commentary on State Rights and on the Constitution and Policy of the United States* (1832), he spelled out his views on revolution, views that probably had been simmering for a long time and would be interesting to many in Massachusetts who had considered secession from the Union during the period of the Embargo and the War of 1812 and who would ponder it again during the war with Mexico. He quotes from a "profound historian" who has said that overthrowing the government "unhinges many of those principles which bind individuals to each other." Oliver continues:

> the right of the people to resist their rulers, when invading their liberties, forms the corner stone of American Republics. This principle, though just in itself, is not favorable to the tranquility of present establishments. . . . To overthrow a monarchy is one thing; to establish a permanent, free, popular government is another. . . . Well-disposed men therefore will hesitate long before they join in any attempt to overthrow or revolutionize their government, under any pretext whatever.

He further inveighs against mobs of unruly men who see themselves as "the people" and riot to get what they want. Oliver thought that it is the "duty . . . of every conscientious citizen and the interest of

---

44. *History of Essex County,* 1:xxxvi; Benjamin Lynde Oliver Jr., *Hints for an Essay on the Pursuit of Happiness (Designed for Common Use),* 14, 17, 24, 26, 27; George Bailey Loring, "Literature," in *History of Essex County,* 1:141–42.

45. Harriet S. Tapley, *Salem Imprints, 1768–1825: A History of the First Fifty Years of Printing in Salem, Massachusetts,* 450; *Observer,* January 6, 1823. The paper became the *Salem Observer* in 1824. See also Claude Moore Fuess, ed., *The Story of Essex County,* 2:923–24.

every peaceable one to discountenance as much as possible all party distinction."[46]

In 1841 he put out *Oliver's Magazine,* another try. This time he observed in his prospectus:

> Its object is to be a vehicle of useful information and innocent enter-tainment . . . [and] its pages will be open to . . . Religious, Moral and Literary subjects. . . .
>
> Though the Editor takes no side in politics, with which he disclaims all connection, not having ever voted at any election, for twelve or fifteen years, even when a single vote was of the highest consequence in deciding an election, yet it is one of the principal objects of the magazine to discuss political measures and consider their bearing on the interests of Society.[47]

That was the only issue of the magazine to appear, and it is not clear how Oliver dealt with political subjects on which he took no stand himself. The very fact of his neutrality and even distaste for political commitment may have sprung from his individual personality, or it may have come from his family's unfortunate involvement in a time when passions ran high and consequences were great. At any rate, the position of detached observer, which Oliver seemed to assume, may have rubbed off on Hawthorne. On the other hand, his eschewing of all political views may have rubbed Nathaniel the wrong way.

Oliver was a conservative in religion. He thought it best in 1818 "to rest satisfied with being saved as a Christian, without engaging ourselves to any particular sect," although in the 1841 issue of *Oliver's Magazine,* he furiously castigated Theodore Parker. "Mr. Parker believes," he wrote, "that if there had been no Jesus Christ, Christianity would be equally true. Here we are tempted to leave him. . . . We look upon Mr. Parker's sermon as an infidel discourse."[48]

Hawthorne went to Oliver's home at 7 A.M. each day to recite his Latin or Greek. His family seemed gratified with his diligence. Aunt Priscilla wrote Betsey on March 14, 1820, that "N seems to be pleased with attending to the languages, and I believe—intends to puzzle M L with latin later." On May 16, 1820, she informed Mary Manning, who had gone to Raymond for a visit, that "Nathaniel is very well and applies

46. Benjamin Lynde Oliver Jr., *The Rights of an American Citizen with a Commentary on State Rights. . . . ,* 55, 56, 64, 398.
47. *Oliver's Magazine* (October 1841), the only issue, was published in Boston by Moses A. Dow.
48. *Oliver's Magazine,* October 1841.

himself to study with exemplary diligence."[49] Nathaniel himself mentions having to parse and translate ten to fourteen pages of Latin, and he wrote a brief note to his mother in that language. Later he spoke of studying Greek in the morning while he worked for Uncle William as a bookkeeper in the afternoon (*CE* 15:122, 127, 130).

If the requirements for Bowdoin were unchanged from those published in 1816, a prospective student was informed that he must know "the four fundamental rules of Arithmetic, the Latin Grammar, the Greek Grammar, the *Aenead* of Virgil, the Select Orations of Cicero, the Greek Testament together with the ability to make grammatical translation of English into Latin."[50] This statement was made by Jesse Appleton, a former president of Bowdoin, but it may have suited the similarly precise William Allen, president in Hawthorne's time. Mr. Oliver must have succeeded well with his pupil; indeed he thought that Hawthorne could have gone to Bowdoin in the fall of 1820.[51] When he did go in the fall of 1821, he passed the admissions test handily.

It is clear, I think, that Oliver would not have undertaken Hawthorne's college preparation lightly. In his book, *Hints for an Essay on the Pursuit of Happiness,* which he published two years before he tutored the lad, he declared, "But parents may be assured that if their sons, at the age of fifteen, with the usual advantages, have not made a figure in school, they will be more likely to prove a disgrace than an ornament to any of the professions. They should therefore be sent to learn a trade" (123). Oliver thought Hawthorne both intelligent and energetic enough to prove capable of the work. His portrait in the privately printed book *Faces of a Family* looks intelligent and kind. His writings depict a man moderate in his views, conservative in religion and politics, and comfortable in the stance of disinterested bystander. Hawthorne may have picked up this position in narrative point of view as well as the knowledge of conjugating Latin verbs.

Thus, at long last, Hawthorne had completed his formal Salem education and was ready to go to college. For the most part, he seems to have been fortunate in his schooling. Robert Manning did, as Elizabeth had said, procure some of the best teachers and schools for him. Worcester, Archer, and Oliver each had strengths to communicate to Hawthorne. Carlton, Moore, and the unknown teacher may have also contributed

49. Priscilla M. Dike to ECH, March 14, 1820, Priscilla M. Dike to Mary Manning, May 16, 1820 (enclosed with a letter from John Dike to Robert Manning), Hawthorne-Manning Collection.

50. *Boston Recorder,* February 7, 1816.

51. Turner, *Hawthorne,* 26.

a great deal to him. Our lack of knowledge keeps us from definite conclusions there. But for that time and for a family that was not wealthy nor even particularly cultivated, Nathaniel was well served.

This was not, of course, the sum of his education in his early years in Salem. He learned much on his own in his voracious reading. He went to the theater and to concerts. He learned from others. But from his schools he seems to have gained a respect for words, enhanced by his study of Greek and Latin. Henry Fairbanks mentioned his "preference for Latinate synonyms over Anglo-Saxon monosyllables."[52] From Worcester he surely had his geographical boundaries widened. From most of his teachers he would have heard Bible readings and vigorous Christian teachings on morality.

When Hawthorne was considering his life's work, he never mentioned the possibility of teaching. Nor did he teach in his college vacations as did so many bright young men. Perhaps he was too shy, but the profession probably just did not appeal to him. He mentioned schoolteachers often in an offhand sort of way in his works, but he drew few pictures of them. In "Little Daffydowndilly" he portrayed a Mr. Toil, a "very strict schoolmaster," who seemed to think "that little boys were created only to get lessons" (*CE* 11:200–201). But since the narrator discovers that every line of work involved toil, schoolteaching was not singled out. In his picture of Ezekiel Cheever, teacher in Boston, in *Grandfather's Chair,* Hawthorne stressed the use of the rod of birch placed over the fireplace and the heavy ferule on the master's desk, but he mentioned those boys who were "whipt into eminence by Master Cheever" (*CE* 6:92). Whipping was often used in Salem schools long after Cheever's time.

A schoolmaster in "The Village Uncle" with his "green spectacles and solemn phiz" was viewed as the object of dread by the teller of this tale. He did not want to trust his children to learn even the alphabet. "It was the key to a fatal Treasure" (*CE* 9:318). But here it seems to be the acquisition of knowledge rather than the conduit through whom it comes, which could be fatal.

Toward the end of his life, Hawthorne wrote in "Grimshawe" about the education of little Ned who lived with the stern, gruff old man and little Elsie. Grimshawe was "no inadequate instructor. . . . [He] proved himself a far more thorough scholar in the classics and mathematics than was ever after to be found in our country." Grimshawe taught the

52. Henry G. Fairbanks, *The Lasting Loneliness of Nathaniel Hawthorne: A Study of the Sources of Alienation in Modern Man,* 135.

boy manners. He also sent him to a Frenchman for lessons in dancing, French, and fencing. Grimshawe even tried "to speak of man's spiritual nature and its demands, and the emptiness of everything which a sense of these demands did not pervade, and condense and weighten into realities" (*CE* 12:371, 372, 373, 375). It was all the more strange, then, that a schoolmaster, Seymour, entered the children's lives, who was "a thin, mild looking man, with a peculiar look of delicacy and natural refinement about him" (*CE* 12:386–87). He had come to the aid of Dr. Grimshawe, who was being attacked by irate townsmen. There is something slightly reminiscent of "Billy Budd" in this portrait of a man who takes the blows aimed at Grimshawe. He is several times called a "milksop" or "milky." He undertakes Ned's and Elsie's education, and "touched springs and elements in the nature of both, that had never been touched till now, and that sometimes made a sweet high music" (*CE* 12:393). When he disappears from their home, the children had the "sense that he was something that had been lost out of their life too soon." Ned is sent to an Academy, where he feels that "the world is cold." Much later when Ned, now become Edward, meets Seymour, now become Colcord, he calls him "[m]y old kindly instructor" (*CE* 12:456). There is something powerful hinted at in this powerless man who does not believe in the rod and who is more than once denounced as passionless (*CE* 12:393, 401). Yet he is delineated by Grimshawe as a "dangerous fellow [because] he would have taken the beef out of you" (*CE* 12:408). Hawthorne intended to use this teacher as a way of bringing in the story of the English castle with the bloody footprint, but his depiction of him may have been based on some one or several of his instructors in Salem.

~5~

Hawthorne's Instinct of Faith

Doubts may flit around me . . . but so long as I imagine that the earth is hallowed, and the light of heaven retains its sanctity, on the Sabbath . . . never can my soul have lost the instinct of its faith. —(*CE* 9:21)

NATHANIEL HAWTHORNE'S early religious comprehension may have had rather precocious beginnings, since one family story has it that he, as a child, upturned a tinted bust of John Wesley, complete with clerical garb, filled it with water, and left it outside in the freezing cold to explode. It did not, to his disgust, reported his sister Elizabeth to his daughter Rose years later.[1] Surely this antipathy to Wesley, if the story be accurate, was based on aesthetic rather than doctrinal reasons. Yet the lad did grow up at a time of fierce theological argument in Salem, and his own religious proclivities have been much debated through the years. Was he a Calvinist who had lost his creed, or Calvin's ironic stepchild? Was he a partial convert to the Unitarianism then prevalent in Salem, or an amused bystander?[2] Surely the religious ambiance of his childhood played a vital part in his life and is worth serious consideration. This chapter attempts to examine the possible religious opinions brought to bear on the youth and the varying religious trends in Salem after he returned from college.

1. RHL, *Memories,* 453–54. The first part of this chapter is an enlarged version of a paper read at the 1990 Hawthorne Conference in North Adams, Massachusetts.
2. See, among others, Samuel M. Crothers, "Address," 12; Agnes McNeill Donohue, *Hawthorne: Calvin's Ironic Stepchild;* Michael J. Colacurcio, *The Province of Piety: Moral History in Hawthorne's Early Tales;* Leonard J. Fick, *The Light Beyond: A Study of Hawthorne's Theology.*

The single meetinghouse of the first Puritans in Salem had grown to six congregations by Hawthorne's time: three orthodox meetings (Tabernacle, South, and Howard Street) and three of a more liberal bent (First, East, and North). In addition, Salem contained an Episcopal church; a Baptist Society and its offspring, the Free-Will Baptists; the Quaker meeting; the Roman Catholic faithful; the Methodists' forerunners; and the Universalists.[3] The meetings that had the most direct connection with the budding writer were Salem's First, the East or Second Society, and the conservative Tabernacle.

It should be emphasized that the years of Hawthorne's youth were the very time of the most decided and heated controversy between the orthodox Congregationalists, called Trinitarians because they upheld the Trinity of God and tenaciously maintained conservative positions, and the emerging Unitarians, some of whom thought that Christ was less than God, albeit still a splendid example of what a man could be. They also differed decidedly on the question of whether mortals were basically good or intrinsically evil. The battle was fiercely waged, and in the end the Unitarians won, only to become the conservatives of another day when the Transcendentalists parted from them. That dichotomy has been stated too simply in that there were varying shades of thought on both sides, but this was part of the essential battle that raged until and after the separation of church and state in Massachusetts in 1833.

First Church, which claimed to be the original society (although that was fiercely debated), was the church, for the most part, of the Hathornes. Nathaniel's grandfather, "Bold Daniel," had been a member, and his grandmother, Rachel Hathorne, had joined soon after their marriage. His father had been baptized there. His mother, along with his aunt, Mary Manning, joined in 1806. The minister of First Church during the writer's youth was the Reverend John Prince (1751–1836). Prince was rumored to have been one of the "Indians" at the Boston Tea Party, a charge he denied. He became famous not for his sermons but for his exceedingly skillful making of scientific instruments. Although sometimes assumed to be a Unitarian, and probably Arian in his thinking, he was, nevertheless, not combative in his views. In fact, one biographer said that he "never preached distinctively upon any of the points of controversy which in his day, agitated the New England

3. Felt, *Annals,* 2d ed., 2:606–16; George Willis Cooke, *Unitarianism in America: A History of Its Origin and Development,* 70–72; J. P. Felt, "Ecclesiastical Chronology of Salem," Ms., Felt-White Collection; James F. Almy, "A History of Methodism in Salem," 275–301; James Robinson Newhall, *The Essex Memorial for 1836: Embracing a Register of the County,* 237–38.

churches." Yet one wonders if First Church was Unitarian at all at that time, since as late as 1827, members joining First Church were required to sign an agreement that they believed in Jesus Christ as the Messiah. At the same time, however, the document calls for improvement of "the imperfections of our past service," which was a thought somewhat distant from the conception of total depravity of the Orthodox. Yet to say, as do some, that it does not matter whether Hawthorne went to First or East meeting is to overlook the very real differences between them.[4]

For East was very definitely liberal and Unitarian. Since their removal from Ipswich to Salem, this was the church of the Manning grandparents. Dr. William Bentley, who presided over East from 1783 to 1819, was an always combative leader. His voluminous diary is a delight to read; he is never guilty of humble opinions. For his flock he compiled his own collection of hymns in 1788 (which reflected, of course, his liberal views), and he used Joseph Priestley's Unitarian catechism rather than the *Westminster Confession,* dear to Calvinists.[5] He spoke frequently of the Trinitarians as "the fanatics" or "the vulgar." He was intensely interested in politics, science, and gossip (and not necessarily in that order). His preaching was considered by some to be erratic and to lack reverence in manner and clarity in style; "less serious and scriptural than could have been desired," said Joseph E. Sprague in a biographical notice.[6]

The Tabernacle, on the other hand, was a bastion of orthodoxy. Founded as the Third Congregational meeting in 1743, it was rebuilt after a fire as a building modeled on George Whitefield's sanctuary in London. In Hawthorne's childhood the minister was Dr. Samuel Worcester (1770–1821), who was installed in 1803. He came from an extraordinary family and was the uncle of one of Hawthorne's teachers, Joseph Emerson Worcester. Samuel Worcester was one of the primary spokesmen in New England for conservative positions. He battled William Ellery Channing in the press and won that fight, according to Conrad Wright. In a letter to Channing in 1815, Worcester wrote, "The God whom you worship is different from ours; the Saviour whom

4. First Church of Salem Records; WB, *Diary,* 1:341; Harold D. Burstyn, "Salem Philosophical Library: Its History and Importance for American Science," 179–80; *SG,* September 24, 1833; William Ward to Lee, January 22, 1884, Scrapbook, 1:152–54, Francis Henry Lee Papers; William Buell Sprague, *Annals of the American Pulpit,* 8:131; [John Stone], "Notes from the Memorandum Book of John Stone, Deacon, First Church, Salem," 111; Colacurcio, *Province of Piety,* 22. Colacurcio does say that it was not in the doctrine of the Trinity but in Arminianism that the churches were alike.

5. Joseph E. Waters, "A Biographical Sketch of Rev. William Bentley," 242, 244.

6. Sprague, *Annals,* 8:156.

you acknowledge is infinitely inferiour to ours; the salvation which you preach is immensely diverse from that which we preach." His sermons were thought excellent. Leverett Saltonstall, a leading Unitarian lawyer in Salem, liked them because they combined emotion with reason even though he was aware that Worcester was a "sound calvinist."[7]

One cannot always tell exact doctrinal opinions of individuals just by knowing their church membership. People then as now were born into churches (or more precisely into families that went to certain churches), or they sometimes changed memberships for reasons other than theological. Yet it is fair to say, I think, that the people of Salem in the early nineteenth century took church membership or lack thereof more seriously than do most today. Signing a covenant with others of like mind usually showed a commitment to certain principles, not just family loyalty or a feeling that it was the expected thing to do. Thus, these memberships may well tell us something about the general religious atmosphere of Nathaniel's youth. Furthermore, church membership was usually restricted to those who made open confession of their conversion and upon this depended the permission to take communion or receive baptism. Salemite John Pickering in *A Vocabulary; or Collection of Words and Phrases Which Have Been Supposed to Be Peculiar to the United States of America* (1816) makes the following distinction:

> A Church, as a body of persons . . . is distinguished in New England from a Congregation, by the privileges which the former in general reserve to themselves of receiving exclusively in that church the sacrament of baptism; in consequence of their having publicly declared their assent to the creed which that church maintains. Marriage, burial, and public worship are open to the members of the congregation at large, according to the forms and methods employed in each church; as are also catechizing for children and visits to the sick.[8]

Paying the pew tax or attending the service was not the same thing as membership in the church.

The writer's mother, Elizabeth Clarke Manning Hawthorne, was reared in Bentley's East society. She had been a member of his singing school in 1792. She obtained full communion, however, in First Church in 1806 and had her children baptized in that faith. It has been suggested that she switched her allegiance in order to join her husband, but he

7. Phillips, *Salem in Eighteenth Century,* 164; Conrad Edick Wright, "Institutional Reconstruction in the Unitarian Controversy," 20; Sprague, *Annals,* 2:405; *Saltonstall Papers, 1607–1815,* 2:408, 414.

8. John Pickering, *A Vocabulary; or Collection of Words and Phrases Which Have Been Supposed to be Peculiar to the United States of America,* 60.

was seldom home, and, in fact, died just two years later in 1808. She seemed to be fairly orthodox. She wrote her brother Richard in Maine on January 20, 1815, that "one thing only is needfull, an interest in Jesus Christ, secure that, and you will have treasure in Heaven where neither moth nor rust can corrupt nor thieves break through and steal."[9]

Her daughter Elizabeth reported that "we were required to pay some regard to Sunday, which was a day of amusement to most people. On Sundays, my mother was unwilling to have us read any but religious books." Mrs. Hawthorne was remembered by a neighbor in Maine "as a pious woman, and a minute observer of religious festivals, fasts, feasts and Sabbath days." She organized and ran a Sabbath school in Raymond. The very use of the term "Sabbath school," rather than Sunday school, was often a sign in those days of Orthodoxy rather than of Unitarianism. In 1887 a writer to the *Salem Gazette* (designated as O.M.) said that Mrs. Hawthorne remained in First Church all her life and was buried by the minister of that Church.[10] Her religious influence on her son was probably lessened, however, by the facts that she was away from him at crucial periods of his life and that she was known to be not very strict as a mother.

Even more interesting is the fact that Mary Manning joined First Church with Elizabeth Hawthorne in 1806, even before her sister and her children moved to the Manning household. Mary does not seem at all the sort of person who would sign a covenant just to be companionable. One wonders if she found the "less serious and scriptural" preaching of Bentley not adequate for her needs. Her letters reveal her innate conservatism. She urged her brother Richard in Maine to pay strict regard to the Sabbath, to repent and "to be daly [sic] more and more reformed and conformed to the precious example and precepts of our dear Saviour." She subscribed to a conservative paper to give as rewards to the Sabbath school scholars in Maine.[11] Both Elizabeth and Mary were interested in those aspects of the Christian life which at that time sometimes marked off the Orthodox from the Unitarians—Sabbath schools and missions. When Hawthorne wrote his mother on May 15, 1821, that he went to meeting constantly, he was speaking of Mary

9. WB, *Diary*, 1:3; First Church of Salem Records; ECH to Richard Manning, January 20, 1815, Manning Hawthorne Papers.

10. Stewart, "Recollections of Hawthorne," 319; Manning Hawthorne, "Parental and Family Influences on Hawthorne," 3; *SG*, March 29, 1887. Thomas T. Stone succeeded Upham at First Church. It was he who buried Mrs. Hawthorne.

11. Mary Manning to Richard Manning, November 8, 1813, and December 14, 1814, Hawthorne-Manning Collection; Mary Manning to ECH, June 3 [1819] (misdated 1818), Hawthorne-Manning Collection.

Manning's directives to him, not those of his Uncle Robert, who was in Maine at the time (*CE* 15:144). Furthermore, when Hawthorne wrote in "Septimius Norton" of the "habitual obedience that young men pay to old Aunts," he was no doubt thinking of her. He knew the power of such aunts even when young men's "lawless speculations set them free from all authority" (*CE* 13:205).

Uncle Robert, who has been called the "most-nearly-Puritan member" of the family, did not seem ardent in his religious life. He wrote about ministers from time to time, and paid the Manning pew tax once, but I have found no record that he actually joined a church. In fact, he seems to be in the company of the other Manning brothers about whom Mary Manning wrote Priscilla after Brother Richard's death in 1831. "I hope Brother William and Robert and Samuel and Brother John and Nathaniel will all improve this loud call to improve the present time, to attend to the one thing needfull, to secure their best interest, a Treasure in Heaven which faileth not."[12] This is language often used to denote a person who had not had the "call" or joined the church. Uncle Robert's work ethic may have impressed his nephew, but his religious influence seems much more tentative to me.

Only Uncle Richard of the Manning brothers has left evidence in his letters of strong religious belief, and he lived in Maine. The others paid their pew taxes and probably went to church. Samuel Manning, the carefree youngest brother, was buried by the minister of First Church, and he held a pew in that church which he willed to Mary at his death. Robert Manning's wife and children joined the Tabernacle much later, and by 1861 so had Uncle William Manning.[13] What seems to have been a lack of strong religious convictions of the Manning men who remained in Salem during Nathaniel's youth may have had its own influence on the boy. It appears evident, however, that the Manning women were more committed to the churches and the principles taught therein. Bentley's East Church and hence its Unitarianism may have had less place in Hawthorne's life than is sometimes supposed.

On the other hand, influence from the Tabernacle, the conservative society, may have been greater than we have known. Another aunt who

12. Colacurcio, *Province of Piety,* 25. Robert Manning, son of Robert Manning, is the one who joined an orthodox church in 1858 (Tabernacle Church of Salem Records); East Church Records; First Church of Salem Records, 176, 312; WB, *Diary,* 4:257; Mary Manning to Priscilla M. Dike, March 17, 1831, Hawthorne-Manning Collection.

13. W. Upton, "List of Deaths by Prince," 9, 2:110; Essex Probate Court, #17569, will of Samuel Manning, November 13, 1833; *Articles and Covenant,* 13; "Membership of Tabernacle Church in 1861," Tabernacle Church of Salem Records.

contributed to his views on religion was Priscilla Manning Dike, who became a member of Tabernacle in 1814, three years before she married John Dike, who joined later. Priscilla was ever active in its service, even to the giving to a church in Maine after the Mannings were no longer there. It was she who obtained a place for Nathaniel in Samuel Archer's school in 1819, where conservative religion was emphasized.[14]

When Nathaniel was ten, his aunt Maria Manning died during the time when he was more or less confined to the house by his lameness. Her last months were bound to have made an impression on him. She consulted Dr. Worcester of the Tabernacle about the state of her soul. One letter from him to her shows perhaps her own orthodoxy as well as his sincere concern for her:

> The heart, my amiable friend, is deceitful. The adversary of your soul is subtle and malignant; both the one & the other would fain make you believe that you ought not to impart your feelings. . . . let me intreat you firmly to resist the temptation, to summon up your resolution, & make an open & free disclosure of the whole state of your mind to some friend. . . . Look tenderly to that glorious Saviour, believe in him—believe in yourself: & you shall find peace.[15]

Maria evidently did disclose her feelings to her sister Priscilla, if not to others, so that when she died the next month, Priscilla was able to write to Richard that Maria, as she lay dying, was "enabled to give evidence to the truth of religion, and that God is the support of those who put their trust in him [.] Her dying words were it is the will of God. . . . God is good and I am his own child."[16] The nine-year-old boy was not privy to all this discussion, but he could not have missed the seriousness of that time, and Priscilla would not have been reluctant to discuss its import afterward.

Perhaps also his Grandmother Hathorne may have had some influence. It is often forgotten that she only married a Hathorne; she was born a Phelps and was baptized in Beverly. Her father, Jonathan Phelps, was evidently a man of strong Calvinist opinions. He had been a member of the Third Church, as the Tabernacle was then called, when it was for eleven years Presbyterian. He was, in fact, one of the twenty or so of the brethren who petitioned to be admitted to Presbytery. Bentley in

14. *Articles and Covenant,* 13; M. Moore, "Hawthorne and the Five-Dollar School," 1.
15. Samuel Worcester to Maria Manning, April 26, 1814, Hawthorne-Manning Collection.
16. Priscilla Manning to Richard Manning, May 20 [1814], Hawthorne-Manning Collection.

noting his death said that he was "warm in the vulgar theology of strong passions," which was one of Bentley's ways of describing Calvinists.[17] Some of those stern beliefs may have rubbed off on Rachel Hathorne, who in turn may have imparted the "feeling" of them to her grandson. It was after all in her house on Sunday afternoons that Nathaniel read *Pilgrim's Progress.* And though he is recorded as not speaking, she may have done so.

Surrounded by family with differing opinions, Nathaniel Hawthorne attended the venerable church of the Hathorne fathers. What he remembered later was "the good old silver-headed clergyman" and "the old wooden meeting-house in Salem which used, on wintry Sabbaths, to be the frozen purgatory of my childhood" (*CE* 5:28, 63). The white hair of Prince and the cold at First Church were also recollected by Marianne Silsbee, a contemporary. They both remember the "hardly suppressed laughter [by the children] in the middle of long sermons" (*CE* 5:563, 225). The seats were made to turn up at prayer time, when the congregation stood. Perhaps Nathaniel, like the other boys, "used to enjoy the clattering fusilade made when they were shut down." Hawthorne may have gone occasionally to other churches as a lad, but it is Prince's church he remembers.[18]

Another reminder of the importance of religion may have been the use of the bakehouse for Sunday meals. Joseph Hodges Choate, who also went to First Church, recalls that

> all work on Sunday was prohibited, even the necessary cooking for the family. There were public bakehouses to which private families on Saturday afternoon sent their pots of pork and beans, or Indian pudding, and brown bread, which were ready for them hot on Sunday morning at the entrance of each of the bakehouses. Sunday began on Saturday, and nothing but good books were allowed to be read by children until the sun had set on Sunday afternoon.[19]

Despite the tilt toward religious conservatism by the female members of the family and the detachment of the males, religion in the Manning household was not all gloom. In this family children were seen and heard. Discussion of churches and of ministers, not all of it favorable, was allowed. The issues of the "Spectator" that Hawthorne produced

17. William P. Upham, "Beverly First Church Records," 38:358; Felt, *Annals,* 2:602–3; WB, *Diary,* 2:360.

18. Marianne C. D. Silsbee, *A Half-Century in Salem,* 34, 37; *SG,* January 31, 1890.

19. Edward Sandford Martin, *The Life of Joseph Hodges Choate as Gathered Chiefly from His Letters,* 1:52.

primarily for his family are replete with such references. He suggests that some of the ministers may have had financial motives in responding to certain calls from churches. He teased his Aunt Mary about Charles W. Upham, newly installed as associate pastor with Prince (*CE* 23:25, 27, 31, 41; 15:190). He also twitted his cousin, Lucy Lord Sutton, about her very conservative minister.[20] The "sombre spirit" of his ancestors in this family had more than rose-gold threads; it was interwoven with humor as well.

However he conducted his life or voiced his beliefs subsequently, Hawthorne gained in this family and in the church a knowledge of the Bible that later was to permeate his work. He also received an intimate knowledge of conflicting opinions about religion. Later he observed in his notebook, "The conversation of the steeples of a city, when the bells are ringing on Sunday—Calvinist, Episcopalian, Unitarian etc." (*CE* 8:242). Though he stopped listening to sermons as soon as he could dictate his own actions, he "never quite passed beyond the limits of a Christian imagination," as Michael Colacurcio says.[21] And that imagination was nurtured in the Salem of his boyhood.

RELIGION AFTER COLLEGE

When Hawthorne returned to Salem after his four-year stay at Bowdoin, he found that some attitudes toward Christianity had changed. Perhaps he had not been aware of these changes in a college that, to his dislike, had "red-hot Calvinist Sermons" and ministers from the "Andover Mill" to speak to the students (*CE* 15:159, 160). And of course he had changed also. For one thing, he could follow his own convictions about the institutional church. In 1825 he found that many of the clergymen in Salem were different from his precollege days. New intellectual beliefs had come with some; new emotional urgency had come with others. The outside world was impinging on the town.

Hawthorne wrote later in *Our Old Home* that only his fond memories of John Prince of First Church helped him retain "a devout, though not intact nor unwavering respect for the entire fraternity" of ministers (*CE* 5:28). Indeed he had never looked upon them with blinkered eyes. "Through all these darkening years," he affirmed, he "much needed whatever fragments of broken reverence (broken, not as concerned religion, but its earthly institutions and professors) remained" (*CE* 5:28). When as an adult he grew to know more about the very human men who were ministers in Salem, he developed even more skepticism.

20. Turner, *Hawthorne,* 32; M. Hawthorne, "A Glimpse," 180–81.
21. Colacurcio, *Province of Piety,* 26.

Many Salem churches had different ministers after his return from college. Charles W. Upham came as colleague pastor to John Prince at First Church in 1824, and after Prince's death in 1836 became the pastor. James Flint, brother of itinerant minister and writer Timothy Flint, was the clergyman of the East Church after Bentley's death in 1819. John Brazer was at the North Church, and Brown Emerson was still at South Church. A new church, sometimes called the Independent and sometimes the Barton Square Church, asked Henry Colman in 1825 to be its leader. Tabernacle Congregational Church kept Elias Cornelius as colleague pastor until 1826 when he became Secretary to the American Education Society. The former minister, Samuel Worcester, had died in 1821 on a trip south to visit the Indian work of his denomination. In 1827 the church called John P. Cleaveland, who stayed until the spring of 1834. Another conservative church, the Howard Street or Branch, retained William Williams until 1832, when Williams became the minister of the new Crombie Street Church. In 1833 George B. Cheever, a classmate of Hawthorne's at Bowdoin, began a stormy pastorate at the Howard Street Church.[22] The battle between the Trinitarians and Unitarians continued to rage. Salem became decidedly more Unitarian as successors to the pulpits of First and North Churches were installed. When the Unitarians became an official body in 1825 the fight continued with renewed vigor.

Hawthorne's almost cousin, the half sister of his second cousins Ann, Mary, and John Savage, was typical of the shifting opinions. Sarah Savage (1784–1837) was a teacher, a writer, and a battler for good causes. She seemed not to have joined any church, but she began her work with the Sabbath school at the Tabernacle. She was also a moving force in the Clarkson Society, which aided blacks to read, write, and learn the Bible. She may have been connected with the Tabernacle simply because it was early in Sunday school work. Her writings, published anonymously, evidence an increasing tendency toward Unitarian thought. One of her children's books, *James Talbot,* was the first production of the Publishing Fund, founded by Unitarians in 1821 to oppose the American Tract Society. She also published with that fund a self-help manual, *Advice to Young Women at Service,* in

22. James W. Thompson, "Tribute to the Memory of Rev. Henry Colman," states that Colman had also been called by North, East, and First Churches; Felt, *Annals,* 2d ed., 2:627; *SG,* September 26, 1826. For G. B. Cheever see Alfred H. Marks, "Hawthorne, G.B. Cheever and Salem's Pump," 260–77, or Margaret B. Moore, "Hawthorne and the Lord's Anointed," 27–36. For the Howard Street Church, see Charles Cotesworth Beaman, "The Branch or Howard Street Church," 281.

1823, and *The Suspected Boy* in 1824. When the Publishing Fund ceased to function, Savage published several other books with the *Christian Register,* a Unitarian paper. She was chosen in 1835 to write the first book in a series overseen by Henry Ware Jr., *Scenes and Characters Illustrating Christian Truth*—a volume titled *Trial and Self-Discipline.* She died suddenly in 1837, cutting short a promising career.[23]

The two sides of the controversy joined battle in the war of the tracts. The New England Tract Society, which later became part of the American Tract Society, flooded the country with evangelical and Calvinist pamphlets. The Unitarians countered with the Publishing Fund. They did not wish to issue mere doctrinal disquisitions but wanted "stories of a didactic character, in which the writers assumed the broad principles of Christian theology and ethics which are common to all followers of Christ, without meddling with sectarian prejudice or party views." As David Reynolds has pointed out in *Beneath the American Renaissance* (1988), "the mainstream churches knowing they had to compete with novels for the public's attention, began issuing thousands of tracts which increasingly featured moral stories . . . [and] what was once the province of theologians became largely the business of creative writers."[24] The fund continued until 1827–1828 when it was felt that too many children's books were being published to compete.

Perhaps the peak of the controversy came when George Barrell Cheever moved to town in 1833 as pastor of the Howard Street Church. Cheever was a strong temperance advocate and a vigorous opponent of Unitarianism. He alienated many Salemites when he carried on a long correspondence with Charles Upham, through the auspices of the *Salem Gazette,* on the issue of Unitarianism. He managed to ignite the controversy thoroughly when he wrote a tract entitled "Inquire at Amos Giles's Distillery," purportedly dealing with temperance but which was generally understood to be aimed at Unitarians, especially at a Unitarian distiller, John Stone, who was a member of Charles Upham's church. Cheever was "cowhided" on the street by the foreman of Stone's distillery and was taken to court for libel, convicted, and remanded to Salem jail for thirty days.[25]

Hawthorne had known Cheever at Bowdoin only slightly, but he was said by his sister Elizabeth to have gone to visit him in prison. A

23. For Savage, see M. Moore, "Sarah Savage," 240–59.

24. Cooke, *Unitarianism in America,* 107–8; David S. Reynolds, *Beneath the American Renaissance: The Subversive Imagination in the Age of Emerson and Melville,* 15. For discussion of more orthodox tracts, see Jane Tompkins, *Sensational Designs: The Cultural Work of American Fiction, 1790–1860,* 149–59.

25. M. Moore, "The Lord's Anointed," 28, 31.

classmate at Bowdoin maintained that Cheever had encouraged a despondent Hawthorne to write for publication. Hawthorne was certainly
aware of Cheever's views. He poked gentle fun at him, I believe, in "A
Rill from the Town Pump" for his views on temperance. Cheever was
later an opponent of capital punishment, and Hawthorne seemed to
have him in mind in one section of "Earth's Holocaust."[26] Hawthorne's
temperament and views were quite different from Cheever's, although
they both loved Bunyan's *Pilgrim's Progress* and both saw human beings in something of the same light.

There was a greater variety of churches in Salem now. St. Peter's
Episcopal Church served a flock of modest size during this period. St.
Mary's Catholic Church had been erected in 1821 at Mall and Bridge
on "land deeded for the purpose by Simon Forrester to be used only
for Catholic religious services forever." Catholics had been meeting,
however, for some time in private houses. The Methodists had some
itinerant preachers but were not a force until 1822 when Jesse Filmore
came. They bought land on Sewall Street and dedicated the church
in 1824. The popularity of camp meetings or "protracted meetings" in
this time aided the Methodists as well as the Baptist meetinghouse,
where Rufus Babcock succeeded Lucius Bolles in 1826. A second Baptist
church also had a minister, George Leonard, in 1826. The Free Will
Baptists who previously had worshiped in English Street had a church
on Herbert Street in 1828, very close to the Manning home.[27]

SOPHIA AND UNITARIANISM

Although Hawthorne had been conscious of Unitarianism for a long
time, he probably had not been confronted with its force until the
end of the 1830s, when he came to know the Peabodys and their
friends. He knew various people at First Church, including his mother
and his Aunt Mary, but they were not Unitarian in outlook. He also
knew Caleb and Mary Foote, the Barstows and the Savages, and others
who went to Unitarian North Church.[28] He was aware, too, of the
interminable discussions in the newspapers and the magazines about
the fight between the Trinitarians and the Unitarians. Yet the difference
would not have become real until he conversed with such true believers
as Elizabeth Palmer Peabody. It would not take long for him to realize

26. Stewart, "Recollections of Hawthorne," 328; Turner, *Hawthorne,* 404*n19.* For possible references to Cheever in Hawthorne's work, see M. Moore, "The Lord's Anointed."
27. Charles S. Osgood and Henry M. Batchelder, *Historical Sketch of Salem, 1626–
1879,* 96; Almy, "Methodism in Salem," 278; Felt, *Annals,* 2d ed., 2:615, 628.
28. *The First Centenary of the North Church and Society in Salem, Massachusetts,*
161, 162, 56.

that all the Peabody women at least were ardent converts. Through them he met Susan Burley, also an attendant of North Church.

In a long instructive letter to Sophia on March 31, 1823, her sister Elizabeth wrote, "You have now no system; but undoubtedly a strong bias toward Unitarianism." She proceeded to tell her what to read and how to think about religious matters. Elizabeth had said that she considered herself Sophia's religious guardian and was determined that "she should never hear of any of the terrible doctrines of Calvinism."[29] Sophia's earlier experiences, however, had brought her in contact (she believed) with those Calvinists, and she did not need to be warned. When she was four or five years old, she had been sent to visit her grandmother. As she described this experience for her children years later, she gave one reason for that bias: "I was subjected to grandmamma's unenlightened religious zeal, and taken to church elaborately dressed in very tight frocks, and made to sit still; and after infinite weariness in the long church service, I was led into the sacristy, and, with other unfortunate babies, tortured with catechism, of which I understood not a word."

But even without that early experience, Sophia would have been Unitarian. Her temperament would have demanded it, and her mother and sisters would have seen to it. In contrast to Calvinists, Unitarians believed, for the most part, in the individual goodness of man "with the simple creed that everything that can happen to a human being is either for enjoyment in the present or instruction for the future." Sophia saw her invalidism that way and tried to enjoy each day, or when the headaches were too bad, to see them as building character. She always wrote the name of God as GOD, and for a while, Nathaniel copied her example, but not for long. She believed very much in a loving God and in immortality. The more she read the English and German Romantics and the homegrown variety, the more she picked up their vocabulary, which made her sound inexplicable at times. She admired Ralph Waldo Emerson, "the greatest man that ever lived," she informed Elizabeth Peabody.[30] She felt close to most of the Transcendental group as her husband did not, but she had none of the reforming zeal some of them had. She and her husband were content, as with slavery, to leave such problems to God.

Nathaniel never altogether followed her lead. He knew the same people, but it is clear that his views differed. He believed in sin, for example, or the ineradicable evil that seemed to persist in man. He did

29. EPP, *Letters,* 60, 15.
30. JH, *Hawthorne and Wife,* 1:56, 61, 186.

not go to hear the Reverend Edward Taylor (1793–1871), the famous Methodist preacher to the seamen, because he felt "somewhat afraid to hear this divine Father Taylor, lest my sympathy with thy admiration of him be colder and feebler than thou lookest for" (*CE* 15:431). He added that he was "a most unmalleable man," and indeed he was. Had he known what Taylor said to Cyrus Bartol on one occasion, he might have changed his mind. Taylor had defined Transcendentalism by saying it was "like a gull—long wings, lean body, poor feathers, and miserable meat."[31] The Unitarians seemed to Hawthorne too rational, too little inclined to see the vast mysteries of life, I think. The Transcendentalists were too much inclined to soar into the ethereal. The wonder is that Nathaniel and Sophia, who were led in opposite directions, got along so well. Some would say that was because Sophia was not assertive. I believe that the bond between them was too strong to be broken, and that Nathaniel, especially in the Manse years, began to see more sunshine than shadow in the affairs of men.

"THAT MARVELOUS LIGHT"

Another cause for religious friction in this period was the prevalence of revivals or camp meetings. George Whitefield (1714–1770), the English revivalist, had preached to about six thousand people on Salem Common in 1740, an event long remembered there. Dr. Bentley had been vigorously opposed to those he called "fanatics" who were of conservative bent but were also revivalists. Sarah Savage had written in *Filial Affection* (1820) of the "ranting visionaries" who roamed the countryside preaching their own conception of the gospel. These were often Baptists or Methodists who in that day did not require their clergy to be educated. Hawthorne had written of revivals with distaste at Bowdoin (*CE* 15:189). In August 1824 the *Gazette* spoke of a revival in Salem. The editor remarked that more than two hundred people attended the meetings, and "[a] much greater number than this are known to be anxious in the town." It was announced in July 1825 that a revival had added "about 85 souls each to Mr. [Brown] Emerson's church and to the Tabernacle, 35 to the Presbyterian [the Branch church under William Williams] and that Baptists and Methodists shared in the blessing." The papers and magazines continued to be full of stories either in favor of or in opposition to revivals or protracted meetings. Hawthorne's own family was not immune to such experience, for his uncle, John Dike,

31. Austin Warren, *New England Saints,* 111; Reynolds points out that Taylor called himself "a Unitarian graft on the Methodist stock" (*Beneath the American Renaissance,* 20).

later came to a state of "religious solicitude," according to a letter written by Hawthorne to Dike's son in 1831 (*CE* 15:216). Leverett Saltonstall also noted those who had come to the "marvelous light," and he mentioned Dike among others. These meetings were opposed by most Unitarians and many Trinitarians as appeals to emotion by unlettered ministers. It seems to me that Frank Shuffelton's view that Hawthorne's story "Young Goodman Brown" was very possibly a reflection of a nineteenth-century revival with all its unrestrained enthusiasm as well as a seventeenth-century Witches' Sabbath is worth considering.[32]

It is clear that Hawthorne was not particularly fond of the approach of Methodists. He writes in "Sir William Pepperell" of "the Methodistical principles with which he was slightly tinctured." He associates George Whitefield with this approach in that same story:

> . . . we turn . . . to the dark enthusiast . . . a preacher of the new sect, in every wrinkled line of whose visage we can read the stormy passions that have chosen religion for their outlet. Wo to the wretch that shall seek mercy there! At his back is slung an axe, wherewith he goes to hew down the carved altars and idolatrous images in the Popish Churches; and over his head he rears a banner which displays the motto given by Whitefield—CHRISTO DUCE—in letters red as blood. (*CE* 23:88)

In "The Toll-Gatherer's Day" he describes a person who seems to be a Methodist: "Now paces slowly from timber to timber a horseman clad in black, with a meditative brow, as of one who whithersoever his steed might bear him, would still journey through a mist of brooding thought. He is a country preacher, going to labor at a protracted meeting" (*CE* 9:208). In "The Seven Vagabonds" Hawthorne describes seven very different people who intend to go to a camp meeting at Stamford. They are stopped when they see a man "sticking up in his saddle with rigid perpendicularity, a tall, thin figure in rusty black . . . a travelling preacher of great fame among the Methodists" who informs the assembled group that "the camp meeting is broke up" (*CE* 9:368–69). These descriptions sound very much like the one given by James F. Almy of Jesse Fillmore, who was the first Methodist minister in Salem. He depicts him as "tall, spare, and erect," "clad in well-brushed garments of faded black" with a "tall black hat of pattern old" and a face of "the

---

32. Felt, *Annals,* 2d ed., 2:597; [Sarah Savage], *Filial Affection: or, The Clergyman's Granddaughter. A Moral Tale,* 93, 104; *SG* as cited in the *Boston Recorder,* August 21, 1824; *Boston Recorder,* July 8, 1825; Leverett Saltonstall, *The Papers of Leverett Saltonstall, 1816–1845,* 2:23; Frank Shuffelton, "Nathaniel Hawthorne and the Revival Movement," 311, 318.

Andrew Jackson type."[33] Perhaps when the young Nathaniel first hoped to break the plaster head of John Wesley, he forecast his more mature reaction to the preachers somewhat like the Methodists.

THE SOCIETY OF FREE ENQUIRERS
At the opposite extreme from the revivalists (although borrowing some of their techniques) were those who preached freedom from religious doctrines and put in their place free love, human reason, and atheism. One very evident practitioner of this point of view was Abner Kneeland (1774–1844). Kneeland was a New Englander, "a former clergyman," as Roderick S. French says, "who over a period of years had worked his way cautiously out of an orthodox Protestant orientation under the successive influences of Hosea Ballou, Joseph Priestley, the elder Robert Owen, Thomas Cooper, and finally Frances Wright." Kneeland in August 1829 delivered six lectures in New York on his reasons for abandoning Christianity, published in a popular book entitled *A Review of the Evidences of Christianity*. He was elected president of the Association for the Protection of Industry and the Promotion of National Education, an organization which advocated that all children be fed, clothed, and educated at state expense. He soon moved to Boston with "his fully supportive wife" to be the lecturer to the Society of Free Enquirers, which had been founded after Frances Wright's Boston lectures in 1829.[34]

In Boston, Kneeland published a weekly paper, the *Boston Investigator,* which advocated "the existence of no being, beings, or things, whether angelic, infernal, or divine, of which the senses of man can take no cognizance." He also urged the abolition of slavery, repeal of unjust laws, the cause of the laboring people, and the rights of women, birth control, pantheism, and Jacksonian democracy. He conducted Sunday services, often to thousands, at the Federal Street Theater in Boston. At one time or other Kneeland had been Baptist, Congregationalist, Universalist, and pantheist. By 1834 he was attacked by Samuel Gridley Howe in an article in the *New England Magazine* entitled "Atheism in New England" for his "base hypocrisy and low cunning" and for sermons whose general tenor was "to ridicule the Christian religion, to persuade the congregation that there is no God, no future state, and no soul; in short, to preach the doctrines of the French infidels. . . . by bold assertion, impudent assumption, unblushing falsehood, coarse

33. Almy, "Methodism in Salem," 285–86.
34. Roderick S. French, "Liberation from Man and God in Boston: Abner Kneeland's Free-Thought Campaign, 1830–1839," 203; Kneeland, *Kneeland Family,* 218.

ridicule and profane jests." In an article reprinted in the *Investigator* in December 1833, someone authorized by Kneeland had compared Andrew Jackson with God, "an unpardonable offense in Boston," observed Henry Steele Commager. Another associated article written by Kneeland declared he did not believe in God. Kneeland was charged under a 1782 Massachusetts law with blasphemy, defined as "denying, cursing, or contemeliously [*sic*] reproaching God." He had four trials and an appeal and finally went to jail on June 18, 1838, for sixty days. He left Boston in 1839 and died in 1844.[35]

Hawthorne would have known about Kneeland, since the news of his opinions and trials was in all the newspapers. He would also have been interested because of his political leanings. John Barton Derby, a former Salemite and a grandson of Elias Haskett Derby, said that "nineteen-twentieths of the followers of Abner Kneeland were or are now Jacksonmen." Ralph Waldo Emerson wrote in April 1834 in his journal, "Don't despise the Kneelands & Andrew Jackson." Later he signed a petition saying that Kneeland should be released from jail. Furthermore, Andrew Dunlap, a Jackson follower and a Salemite, was Kneeland's counsel for several of his trials.[36]

But Hawthorne had an even closer connection than his admiration for Jackson. Abner Kneeland's third wife was Elizabeth Daland Osborne, whose daughter, Eliza Osborne, was married to George Archer (1793–1833), Hawthorne's cousin. Earlier on, the Kneelands had lived in Salem. They had been married in 1813 and opened a dry-goods store in Salem in 1814. According to one source, Kneeland went back to preaching in 1816, whereas his wife sold feathers and beds in a store in Salem in 1817. Benjamin Herbert Hathorne wrote his sister, Elizabeth Ranney, in March 1817 that "the two Mrs. Felts have left the brick house & shops & Mrs. Kneeland formerly Eliza Osborne has the house and some of the shops." Eliza Kneeland died in 1834, and Kneeland remarried that same year.[37]

There is no evidence at all that Hawthorne was influenced by the opinions of Kneeland, but it is safe to say that he must have been aware

35. R. French, "Kneeland's Free-Thought Campaign," 204, and Samuel Gridley Howe, "Atheism in New England," 500–509, 53–62; Henry Steele Commager, "The Blasphemy of Abner Kneeland," 31–32.

36. John Barton Derby, *Political Reminiscences Including a Sketch of the Origin and History of the 'Statesman Party' of Boston,* 135, 145; Robert E. Burkholder, "Emerson, Kneeland, and the Divinity School Address," 11.

37. Perley, *History of Salem,* 1:216; *Vital Records of Salem,* 3:56; *SG,* April 19, 1814; Russell Leigh Jackson, "Additions to the Catalogue of Portraits in the Essex Institute," 59; Benjamin Herbert Hathorne Papers in English/Touzel/Hathorne Papers; *Salem Observer,* June 7, 1834.

of the man and his views. Some of his attitude toward reformers may have come from this knowledge.

JONES VERY'S REVELATIONS

Another approach to religion in Salem (although limited perhaps to one man) was that of Jones Very (1813–1880), a member of North Church. He was also one of the group that met at Miss Burley's along with Hawthorne and the Peabodys. A graduate of Harvard, he was tutoring in Greek at the college when he began to exhibit signs of what some called insanity. He took a vital interest in his students and used much classroom time to preach to them. He was also studying in the Divinity School, where Unitarianism, the order of the day, was beginning to be attacked by Transcendentalists as too rational and dry. Influenced by Henry Ware Jr. and by his voracious reading, Very felt that he had had a "new birth" and eventually that he had subdued his own identity totally to the ruling of God. From thence he progressed to a feeling that he represented the Spirit of God.

One morning in class he told his students to "flee to the mountains, for the end of all things is at hand." This, when reported to the higher authorities, was too much for them, and Very was replaced and sent home. In Salem he went around telling people—including the ministers John Brazer and Charles Upham—that they should reform, that he was speaking as the messenger of God. They felt that he was out of his mind, perhaps naturally enough, and he was sent for a month to McLean Asylum for the Insane in Charlestown. When he returned to Salem, he remained so full of his visions that Elizabeth Peabody thought he was still insane, but she also helped him become acquainted with Emerson and others. Very kept going to see Brazer and Upham, who felt that the asylum was the place for him. Fortunately for him, his family did not.[38]

Very has been characterized as a Quietist, a Transcendentalist, a mystic, or as a fanatic. He had a genuine experience and during the years in which this emotion gripped him, he wrote his most notable poetry. The Transcendentalists were very interested in him as was he in their philosophy, yet he remained a Unitarian minister all his life. Helen Deese believes that he was accepted by both groups, but that he also fits very well the criteria set up by William James for mysticism.[39] One can understand that his spiritual tribulations would intrigue Hawthorne; but one can also understand that the latter would not be converted by him.

38. For information about Jones Very see Helen R. Deese's introduction to *The Complete Poems,* and Edwin Gittleman, *Jones Very: The Effective Years, 1833–1840.*
39. *The Complete Poems,* ed. Deese, xxix.

There were other permutations of religion with which Hawthorne came into contact in his Salem years. His friend William Baker Pike progressed from Methodist to Episcopal to Swedenborgian views. William Miller of Second Advent fame had been making predictions in the 1830s, and his disciples had a camp meeting in Salem in 1842. Hawthorne alluded to him in "The Hall of Fantasy," "The New Adam and Eve," and "The Christmas Banquet" (*CE* 10:183, 185, 247, 302). The Second Advent Church was built on Herbert Street in 1848, after the disappointment that the Second Coming did not occur in March 1843 when prophesied.[40] The Shakers Hawthorne left town to see in his summer excursions, and he recorded his impressions both during his Salem years and later (*CE* 15:213, 218, 220). By the end of his time in the seaport, he knew of spiritualism too. But most of these sects were curiosities to him.

Hawthorne's own connection with churches was broken in later Salem years. He knew about them, and mentioned their ministers just as he had in an earlier day in the "Spectator." As he had observed then, he suspected that a minister's new "call" was motivated as much by money as by a distinct mission from God. He seems to have been friends with Charles Upham, although he did not attend his church. The two did exchange books, and Upham was mentioned in a favorable light for his talents as a historian. Hawthorne's views, of course, changed later when Upham became a politician and was instrumental in removing him from the Custom House. His attitude toward John Brazer of North Church could not have been favorable after Brazer treated Jones Very badly. He mentioned John Cleaveland of the Tabernacle to John S. Dike in telling of an instance of loose talk by the minister's wife in that church (*CE* 15:216–17). He took out a book of Henry Colman's Sermons from the Athenaeum in 1827; and earlier he had praised a sermon of Colman's before he went to Bowdoin (*CE* 23:31). Colman's actions during the White murder trial, however, could not have endeared him to Nathaniel.[41]

It is clear that Hawthorne did not attend church in Salem after college. His sister Elizabeth recalled that Eleanor Condit (little Annie) "once . . . came to him, crying, because somebody had told her that he was an

---

40. Emmanuel Swedenborg (1688–1772) through his mysticism had a tremendous influence on transcendentalism; William Miller (1782–1849), a leader in the nineteenth-century Adventist movement, proclaimed that the second coming of Christ would be "on or around" March 1843.

41. Thomas Woodson, "Hawthorne, Upham, and *The Scarlet Letter,*" 187; EPP, *Letters,* 216, 219; Marion L. Kesselring, "Hawthorne's Reading, 1828–1850: A Transcription and Identification of Titles Recorded in the Charge-Books of the Salem Athenaeum," 116.

infidel—he must be, as he never went to church." He denied being an "infidel," and told her that he "did go to church whenever he happened to be elsewhere than in Salem, on a Sunday."[42] He did not go often elsewhere either. He resisted Sophia's plea to go hear Father Taylor, who is presumed to have been used by Herman Melville in *Moby Dick* (*CE* 15:420–21). He did go to see the Shakers, and perhaps he did go to a Bible class in Farmington, Massachusetts, when he was on a trip with his Uncle Samuel (*CE* 15:211–13, 198). But for the most part he seemed to live by his remarks in his essay "Sunday at Home," where he wrote, "though my form be absent, my inner man goes constantly to church." He also said that he did not often "fructify . . . by any but printed sermons" (*CE* 9:21, 24). He or his Aunt Mary or Elizabeth Hawthorne took a great many books of sermons from the Salem Athenaeum, especially in 1828 and 1829. It is hard to visualize either Mary Manning or Ebe poring over such sermons as those for Election, Thanksgiving, Fast, Ordination, or even Occasional sermons, although Aunt Mary's faith and practice were genuine.

Julian said of his father many years later, "His reverence for the holy of holies was so profound that I never recall hearing him speak the name of the Almighty except in reading. . . . As for the mysteries of Christ, they were never touched on; and the 'One God and Three Persons' was left unchallenged." Julian was not even sure which denomination the family may have claimed. He said at another time that his father " 'believed' in God, but never sought to define him." Two years after Hawthorne's death, Sophia wrote about her husband's belief in Christ to General Ethan A. Hitchcock: "I remember my husband saying once that he could not do without the warmth of this best image of His Father. He would not have it explained away from existence—as distinguished from Being." David Lyttle says that when Emerson told Hawthorne that they must get rid of Christ, Hawthorne replied, "No, Mr. Emerson, we cannot do without Christ."[43] Hawthorne jostles the pagan and the Christian worlds in *The Marble Faun*. He mentions Christianity, God, and the Savior, but the general mood is that of a nondoctrinal but still sensitive awareness of mystery.

---

42. Stewart, "Recollections of Hawthorne," 330.

43. Kesselring, "Hawthorne's Reading," 121–27; JH, "Nathaniel Hawthorne's Blue Cloak, a Son's Reminiscences," 503–4; *Memoirs of Julian Hawthorne,* 16; SPH to General Ethan Hitchcock, February 14, 1866, Nathaniel Hawthorne Collection (#6249), Clifton Waller Barrett Library; David Lyttle, *Studies in Religion in Early American Literature: Edwards, Poe, Channing, Emerson, Some Minor Transcendentalists, Hawthorne and Thoreau,* 167.

Ever since the sea of faith began its melancholy, long, withdrawing roar, the importance of the Christian religion has been debated or ignored. Scholars have drawn many conclusions as to Hawthorne's religious faith, and few seem to agree.[44] What seems to me to be clear is that in the Salem he knew he inhaled a great many doctrines, but found little meaning in such precise formulations. In this he agreed with Job, who finally admitted that he was finite and had uttered things "too wonderful for me" (42:3). But Hawthorne also absorbed the conviction that religion was significant. Secular Hawthorne's writings are not; they exude an "instinct of faith" that may be fractured, but that retains a vitality reacting to or drawn from the very air of Salem.

44. Hyatt Howe Waggoner in *The Presence of Hawthorne* writes, "Surely there must be something about Hawthorne and his works that permits—or even encourages such disagreements" (44). With which statement, considering the multiplicity of published interpretations through the years, surely all could agree.

~6~

Salem after College

Old Salem now wears a much livelier expression than when I first beheld her.
—(*CE* 9:338)

ALTHOUGH LEVERETT Saltonstall wrote Joseph Story on March 16, 1825, that "there is nothing new in old Salem," the town to which Hawthorne returned the following September was for him in the process of change. Mrs. Hawthorne had moved back to Salem from Raymond for good in May 1822. Uncle Robert had married Rebecca Dodge Burnham from Ipswich in December 1824 and was living on Dearborn Street. Gideon Barstow had been in Washington in the House of Representatives from 1821 to 1823; Rachel Hathorne Forrester had died, leaving money to her sisters but not to her brother's widow. General Lafayette had visited Salem in 1824, and cousin Sarah Savage had written a tale, *The Badge,* about it. Hawthorne's former teacher, Samuel Archer, had married Fidelia Worcester, daughter of the late Dr. Samuel Worcester. Two new arrivals of eventual importance to Hawthorne had settled in town: Charles W. Upham had come as associate pastor of Salem's First Church and Dr. Malthus Ward, whom Hawthorne had known at Bowdoin, had succeeded Seth Bass as superintendent of the East India Marine Society.[1]

Hawthorne's Salem was in transition. In 1828 Hawthorne, his mother, and his sisters moved into a house on Dearborn Street that Robert

---

1. Saltonstall, *Papers, 1816–1845,* 1:164; *SG,* December 24, 1824, September 1, 1824, October 24, 1823, and March 11, 1825; *Biographical Directory of the American Congress, 1774–1971,* 559; *New England Galaxy,* July 4, 1823; [Sarah Savage], *The Badge* (1824); "Salem Social Life," 239.

Manning had built next to his own. The Hawthornes were to live there until 1832. Several relatives died after Hawthorne's return from Bowdoin, including his grandmother Manning in December 1826; his aunts Eunice Hathorne and Judith Archer in 1827; and Aunt Sarah Crowninshield in January 1829. Mary Manning stayed in Raymond from October 1827 to March 1828 and then kept house for her sister-in-law Rebecca Manning, who was visiting in Ipswich, in the summer of 1828. She wrote her brother Richard and his wife in Raymond in February 1829 that she had visited for about two years before moving back to the Herbert Street house. So, dull old Salem was not without change in the late 1820s.[2]

There was a restlessness in the town. Many of its younger and energetic citizens were moving away, as Margaret Huessler Felt informed her husband in 1827.[3] On July 30, 1830, the editor of the *Salem Gazette* was moved to remark, "Young men, especially, of good families and enterprising dispositions, have been led off in crowds, in search of some fancied Eldorado—some barren gold mine, in the sickly South—some fertile farm in the boundless West—or some colliery or canal route in the great Middle States."

LOOKING FOR GOLD

The reference to "some barren gold mine in the sickly South" was not plucked out of thin air. Many were the comments on the gold found in the South, sickly or otherwise. The *Salem Observer* announced the finding of gold in Anson County, North Carolina, on June 21, 1823. The *Salem Gazette* quoted the *Boston Patriot* on April 17, 1829, that "new gold mines in North Carolina are said to be discovered daily." The news about the strikes in North Carolina led to the formation of the Anson Gold Mine Company in 1828 by certain Salem sea captains: Jonathan Porter Felt, Andrew Watkins, William Duncan, William Brown, Edward Barnard for Judith Barnard, and Benjamin Blanchard. Watkins and Felt spent much time in Anson County, searching for gold on Richardson's Creek. Even Eben Hathorne, Hawthorne's cousin, considered joining them at one point. But the company went broke, and the men returned home. Gold fever does not go away so quickly, however. In 1830 Felt, with his brother-in-law, William K. Smith, and Benjamin and Nathaniel

2. Mary Manning to Richard and Susan Manning, February 9, 1829; Richard Manning to Robert Manning, December 26, 1826, Hawthorne-Manning Collection; *SG*, May 15, 1827, and January 14, 1829; W. Upton, "List of Deaths by Prince," 9, 2:107, 108.

3. Margaret Heussler Felt to Jonathan Porter Felt [incomplete], June [16? 1827], Felt-White Collection.

Chamberlain, all of Salem, went to Spotsylvania County, Virginia, just outside of Fredericksburg, to seek again for gold. Quite a Salem colony moved there in that search. Felt, after an exhausting period, returned to Salem. The Chamberlains moved west, but Smith stayed in Fredericksburg and was successful for a time.[4]

These adventures were probably in Hawthorne's mind when the narrator remarks in "Peter Goldthwaite's Treasure" that "[o]nce, he had gone on a gold-gathering expedition, somewhere to the South, and ingeniously contrived to empty his pockets more thoroughly than ever" (*CE* 9:384). In his piece on "April Fools" in the *American Magazine of Useful and Entertaining Knowledge* (April 1836), he mentions as one fool "he who has been heaping up gold." He also lists as fools the farmer who "left a good homestead in New England, to migrate to the Mississippi Valley or anywhere else"; the "fresh-cheeked youth who has gone to find his grave at New Orleans"; or the Yankees enlisted for Texas. His cousin, John Touzel Savage, moved to Natchez, Mississippi, in 1821 and became a professor at a college near there. Eben Hathorne moved out west in 1819 and visited his sister Elizabeth Ranney and her husband in Wisconsin. He was a merchant for a while in Cincinnati before he returned east.[5] Salem was changing all through the period when Hawthorne first began to write in earnest.

TRANSPORTATION

Concurrently, a revolution in transportation took place. The Mannings' stage line had many permutations, but it had kept on going. When Nathaniel came back from Bowdoin, he took various trips with his Uncle Samuel on the stagecoach. Although Samuel had once in 1816 shifted to storekeeping in Raymond, he had settled into his true vocation— that of buying horses for the stages. Uncle Robert was trying to get out of the business and to concentrate solely on his horticultural interests. Robert, Samuel, and William kept what was now called the Salem and Boston Stage Company going, but they had competition from various other firms. On March 10, 1829, the shareholders were asked to meet to incorporate. They were listed in the *Salem Gazette* as Robert Manning, John Dike, James Potter, J. S. Leavitt, William Manning, Benjamin Bray,

4. For an account of the Anson Gold Mine Company venture, see Margaret B. Moore, "Salem Sea Captains and Carolina Gold," 69–89; for the Virginia story, see Margaret B. Moore, "Gold-Gathering Expedition[s]: Three Possible Sources for 'Peter Goldthwaite's Treasure,'" 14.

5. [NH], "April Fools," 339; Lawrence Park, "Old Boston Families, No. 3: The Savage Family," 324; Stephen Ranney to Benjamin H. Hathorne, January 23, 1819, English/Touzel/Hathorne Papers.

and Albert Knight. In the meantime, Samuel Manning was advertising a new stage to Lowell, and in August 1833 he announced that the stage office and books would move to West Place. He died a few months later. From 1834 on, the stage seemed to have periodic difficulties. The firm sold off coaches in 1834. In September 1836 the Salem and Boston Stage Company announced that it had not failed for $600,000; that its liabilities were only $20,000, its stock was worth $45,000, and that "service would resume in several days." By 1837, however, the company seemed to go out not with a bang but with a long dying moan. Over and over its stock, carriages, and horses were advertised for sale, first by auction, then by sheriff's sale, then by mortgagee's sale. Even then it had not entirely given up. On June 8, 1838, "A New Arrangement for Salem and Boston Stages" appeared. The fare was reduced to seventy-five cents. The books were still kept at the Lafayette Coffee House and at the Stage Office, West Place. On September 7, 1838, however, George Peabody addressed a crowd at the opening of the Eastern Railroad. A week later, the stage company tried one more time, informing the public that coaches would be at West Place to take people to the railroad station or anywhere in the city for twelve and one-half cents. The stage line was remembered fondly as late as 1884.[6]

The advent of the railroad was a mighty happening for Salem. Joseph Hodges Choate (1832–1917) remembered the time his father took him to the top of Castle Hill to see the first railroad train come in from Boston, a spectacle he recorded: "Compared with any railroad-train now known, it was a very petty and puny affair, a little engine with two small-sized passenger cars and what was called a "nigger car" attached for colored people to ride in. . . . The town was dead before this first railroad-train arrived, and from that moment it really began to wake up."[7] The *Observer* reported in every autumn issue of 1838 the number of passengers on each train. In "The Sister Years" Hawthorne speaks of the alteration that had come with the railroad when he personifies the year 1838:

> I have opened the Rail-Road. . . . But a more important change awaits
> the venerable town. An immense accumulation of musty prejudices will

6. Mellow, *Hawthorne in His Times,* 16; *SG,* February 6, 1827, August 27 and November 19, 1833, August 26, 1834, September 16, 1836, January 31, April 28, May 30, July 28, and August 8, 1837, and June 8, September 7, and September 14, 1838; Hawthorne-Manning Collection; W. Ward to Lee, February 13, 1884, Scrapbook, 1:141–42, Francis Henry Lee Papers.

7. Martin, *Life of Joseph Hodges Choate,* 1:42.

> be carried off by the free circulation of society. A peculiarity of char-
> acter, of which the inhabitants themselves are hardly sensible, will be
> rubbed down and worn away by the attrition of foreign substances. . . .
> [T]here will be a probable diminution of the moral influence of wealth,
> and the sway of the aristocratic class, which from an era far beyond
> my memory, has held firmer dominion here than in any other New
> England town. (*CE* 9:338–39)

This resembles Clifford's talk in *The House of the Seven Gables:* "[T]his admirable invention of the railroad—with the vast and inevitable im-provements to be looked for, both as to speed and convenience—is destined to do away with those stale ideas of home and fireside, and substitute something better" (*CE* 2:259).

SWAY OF CLASS
As to class structure in Salem, there was some disagreement with Haw-thorne's remarks in "The Sister Years." Elizabeth Hawthorne, for exam-ple, later heatedly denied that there was such a thing. In a letter to her cousin, Maria Manning, she asserted, "[George Parsons] Lathrop wrote of wealthy families maintaining vigorously the distinction of class etc. . . . by which he betrays his inability to discern the reality of anything, for who would apply the terms 'magnificent and splendid' to Salem, whose best praise is that nothing of the kind is ever aimed at, and whose richest men at the period he is describing rose from poverty."[8] Elizabeth, of course, never felt inferior to anybody and probably would not have recognized an aristocratic snub if one were directed at her. Others, however, thought that certain distinctions were present in Salem. John B. Chisholm wrote on February 4 [1885?] to Francis Lee that there was an "aristocratic element by no means insolent but socially conservative from about 1805 to 1830 or 35. . . . It was quite marked then, and Hamilton Hall with its Assemblies was the touchstone or dividing line." Previously, the Rev. Stephen P. Hill observed to the same Francis Lee on March 3, 1884, that "society in my boyhood was divided into two classes which might not be inappropriately characterized by *caste* called the first and second classes," and William Driver, formerly of Salem and the originator of the phrase "Old Glory," informed Lee that "a sort of gulf lay *perhaps imaginary* between me or my Father's house and those named in your note of enquiry."[9] In Hawthorne's youth, the *Salem*

8. EMH to cousin Maria Manning, December 22 [1876], copy, Hawthorne-Manning Collection.
9. Chisholm to Lee, February 4 [1885?], Scrapbook, 2:100–103; Hill to Lee, March 3, 1884, Scrapbook, 1:211–14; Driver to Lee, December 1884, Scrapbook, 3:37–41, in Francis Henry Lee Papers.

Gazette always distinguished between "yeoman" and "gentleman" in legal notices.

Vernon Loggins and Edwin Haviland Miller both stress the inferior social status of the Hathornes after the first two generations. Nathaniel certainly was aware that there were class distinctions in Salem, although the effect on him could be debated.[10] In *The House of the Seven Gables,* the narrator refers to an ancestor of the Pyncheons who "had the blood of a petty huckster in his veins" and who was "an unworthy ancestor." Holgrave in the same book never "lost his identity" despite the fact that he was not of the first class (*CE* 2:177). The Hathorne family was said by Dr. Bentley to have a great deal of family pride. Elizabeth Barstow Stoddard, cousin to Hawthorne's cousins, the Barstows, wrote tellingly of Salem's oppressive class structure in *The Morgesons* (1862). Caroline King observed that "there was a decidedly aristocratic element in Salem society then, but I must say, in spite of Mrs. [Elizabeth] Stoddard's accusations that if a candidate for its favor could show an undoubted ancestry, no question was asked as to his or her wealth." That feeling of superiority is epitomized, perhaps, by the fact that the Leverett Saltonstalls thought that Charles Barstow, son of Gideon and Nancy, was not the social equal to their daughter and would not let them marry. This feeling can be seen too in Richard Manning's letter to his brother Robert when he says that Rebecca Dodge Burnham was a greater treasure than any of the "proud and haughty heiresses of Salem."[11] Class was a factor in Salem, but events in Salem and perhaps particularly the opening of the railroad conspired to loosen the strictures of lineage.

OTHER ISSUES: INDIANS

The first few years after Hawthorne's Bowdoin career also saw many other issues come to the fore or become hotter than ever. Salemites began to talk about the plight of the Indians and the role of women, and to question somewhat faintly the status of the black portion of the population.

Nineteenth-century Salem was far enough removed from the Indian wars to allow a more dispassionate perspective on what had happened to the original settlers. Occasionally some Indians came through town.

---

10. For instance, see Loggins, *The Hawthornes,* 213–14, or Miller, *Salem Is My Dwelling Place,* 88.

11. Elizabeth Barstow Stoddard, *The Morgesons and Other Writings, Published and Unpublished,* 161–201; King, *When I Lived in Salem,* 22; Saltonstall, *Papers, 1816–1845,* 3:59, 62, 134, 135*n*, 141; Richard Manning to Robert Manning, June 19, 1829, Hawthorne-Manning Papers.

Two chiefs of the Penobscot tribe were present in February 1818. William Manning introduced them to Dr. Bentley, who said that "they had none of the tinsel about them that the other company had, of whom they complained they were too noisy."[12] Perhaps Nathaniel met them too; at least he would have heard about them.

There had long been some concern for the Indian in Salem. Dr. Samuel Worcester was corresponding secretary of the Prudential Committee of the American Board of Commissioners for Foreign Missions from 1812 to 1821 and had directed its work from his church. He died on a visit to the board's Cherokee Mission in 1821. His associate minister, Elias Cornelius, wrote a book entitled *The Little Osage Captive* in 1822. Lucius Bolles with Thomas Baldwin of Boston formed in 1813 a Baptist Society for Propagating the Gospel in India and Other Foreign Parts, which later concentrated on American Indians. During Hawthorne's so-called solitary years, much was written and done about the Indian. In 1826 an article in the *Boston Monthly,* "The Aborigines of New England," was copied by the *Salem Gazette*. "Indians had no historians to tell the story of their wrongs," asserted Elizabeth Elkins Sanders, the mother-in-law of Leverett Saltonstall, so she composed articles constantly but anonymously on the subject. Lydia Child had published a novel, *Hobomok* (1824), about an Indian in Salem. Sarah Savage wrote in 1827 a history for young people about King Philip in which she described him as a "penetrating statesman, a great warrior, a noble, disinterested, self-denying patriot." On December 25, 1829, there was declared a day of fasting for the Cherokees who were "to be driven from their homes and torn from their heritage." On February 12, 1830, Leverett Saltonstall read from Indian treaties at a meeting in Salem. In January 1831 a meeting on the plight of the Indians at the Tabernacle church was interrupted when the large crowd in the balcony caused it to break loose and fall. B. L. Oliver Jr. pleaded passionately for justice to Indians in 1832.[13]

Hawthorne made more use of the Indians than is generally acknowledged, even by him. In "Our Evening Party Among the Mountains," he

12. WB, *Diary,* 4:502.
13. William Gerald McLoughlin, *The Cherokees and Christianity, 1794–1870,* 57–58; *SG,* February 15, 1831; [Elizabeth Elkins Sanders], "The Aborigines of New England," *Boston Monthly* (1826) as noticed in the *SG,* February 28, 1826 (which later became a book, *Conversations*); Lydia Maria Child, *Hobomok;* [Sarah Savage], *Philip the Indian Chief; SG,* December 25, 1829, February 26, 1830, and February 15, 1831; Benjamin Lynde Oliver Jr., *The Rights of an American Citizen with a Commentary on State Rights,* 406–11.

observed, "It has often been a matter of regret to me, that I was shut out from the most peculiar field of American fiction, by an inability to see any romance, or poetry, or grandeur, or beauty in the Indian character, at least, till such traits were pointed out by others. I do abhor an Indian story" (*CE* 10:428–29). He particularly mentioned King Philip in "Young Goodman Brown," "The Gray Champion," "A Virtuoso's Collection," *Grandfather's Chair*, and "Main-Street," among others (*CE* 9:11; 10:77, 483; 6:50; 11:72). In *Fanshawe* he somewhat dismisses the Indian when he says that at college there were a "few young descendants of aborigines to whom an impracticable philanthropy was endeavoring to impart the benefits of civilization" (*CE* 3:336).

In truth, Hawthorne never seemed to see the Indian as yet civilized, an opinion he shared with most of his countrymen. In some of the early stories he refers to Indian savagery. In "An Old Woman's Tale" one character has the scar of a tomahawk on his head (*CE* 11:246). In "Alice Doane's Appeal" an Indian massacre deprives young Alice and Walter of their parents (*CE* 11:271, 273). He refers to the war cry in "The Seven Vagabonds" and in "Young Goodman Brown" (*CE* 9:367; 10:83). At times he indicates the early view of some of the settlers that the Indian was with the Black Man or the Devil in the forest as in "The Haunted Quack" or "Young Goodman Brown" (*CE* 11:261; 10:85). The fear of captivity plays a part in "Roger Malvin's Burial" and "Etherege" (*CE* 10:342, 344; 12:223). He even attempts to portray Indian characters such as the "son of the wilderness" in "The Seven Vagabonds" or "Crusty Hannah," who has mixed Indian and Negro blood, in "Grimshawe" (*CE* 9:363; 12:344). Septimius Felton is part Indian, as is his Aunt Keziah (*CE* 13:72). Septimius Norton is descended from an Indian sagamore. Hawthorne describes the potency of this Indian blood at great length (*CE* 13:256–67).

But he also shows the Indians to be dignified and stately in "Endicott and the Red Cross," or in "Main-Street" (*CE* 9:436; 11:50–51). He regrets the introduction of alcohol to the Indians in "A Rill from the Town Pump," or "Old Ticonderoga" (*CE* 9:144; 11:190). His fiercest remarks are reserved for what the white man has done to the Indian. In "The Gray Champion," for example, he acknowledges "the veterans of King Philip's war, who had burnt villages and slaughtered young and old, with pious fierceness, while the godly souls throughout the land were helping them with prayer" (*CE* 9:11). And in "Young Goodman Brown" the devil confirms that "it was I that brought your father a pitch-pine knot, kindled at my own hearth, to set fire to an Indian village, in King Philip's war" (*CE* 10:77). In "Main-Street" he comments rather sadly that "the Indians, coming from their distant wigwams to view the white man's settlement, marvel at the deep track which he makes, and perhaps are saddened by a flitting presentiment, that this heavy tread will find its way over all the land; and that the wild woods, the wild wolf, and the wild Indian, will alike be trampled beneath it. Even so shall it be. The pavements of the Main-street must be laid over the red man's grave" (*CE* 11:55). He seemed to feel sadness rather than guilt, a sort of "survival of the fittest" idea. The disappearance of the Indian may have been inevitable, but he deplored the sometime cruelty of the white man— or woman. In "The Duston Family" it is Mrs. Duston, not the Indian, who is seen as the most cruel.[14] Hawthorne's portrayal of the Indian as savage and wild, even though sometimes surpassed by the cruelty of the settlers, especially women, was in contrast to some of the writings of that time, such as those of Lydia Maria Child.

THE ROLE OF WOMEN

As the role of Mrs. Duston might suggest, another issue of the day was that of the place of women, and particularly the proper education they should have. "Constantia," in an article "On Female Education" in the 1825 *Portfolio,* asks, "What is the end of education? It is to qualify us to act with propriety the part assigned to us by Providence." It was precisely the question of what role Providence intended for women that was at issue. Sarah Savage in *Filial Affection* (1820) asserts that women were capable of doing far more than "household occupations."[15]

The situation of women will be discussed in chapter 10, but perhaps an example of one side of the issue will suffice here. At the center of the controversy of woman's place in the late 1820s and early 1830s was Frances Wright of Scotland, who, after a first journey to this country, came back to reform it.[16] She set up what she believed to be a utopian plantation near Memphis, Tennessee, called Nashoba. Frances and her

14. [NH], "The Duston Family," 395–97. Hawthorne obviously learned much about Indians in order to edit *AMUEK.* See, for example, in vol. 2, pieces on the Boston Tea Party, 317–19; Flat Head Indians, 327–28; Indian Hieroglyphics, 356; Indian Totem, 384; Wild Horseman, 432; Indian Superstitions, 476; the Antiquity of Scalping, 510; and many others.

15. Constantia [pseudonym], "On Female Education," 414; [Savage], *Filial Affection,* 127.

16. For Fanny Wright D'Arusmont, see her *Biography, Notes and Political Letters.* Another book, *Views of Society and Manners in America* (1821), which praised America, was in the Salem Athenaeum, although there is no proof that Hawthorne read it (*Catalogue of Books Belonging to the Salem Athenaeum.* Salem: Warwick Palfrey Jr., 1826, 88).

sister and a few others tried to prove that slaves whom she had purchased would gladly work for their freedom and dignity.

Everything went wrong. The land outside Memphis was swampy,
hot, and mosquito-infested. Wright and her sister worked hard, but the
slaves did not. Rumors of free love spread abroad. Wright moved to
New Harmony, Indiana, an experiment begun by Robert Owen, the
owner of New Lanark in Scotland, a planned mill village of utopian
propensities. Wright then became a public lecturer. In Cincinnati, Mrs.
Frances Trollope, who had come to America with her, wrote of the reaction to her as a speaker: "That a lady of fortune, family, and education,
whose youth had been passed in the most refined circles of private
life, should present herself to the people as a public lecturer, would
naturally excite surprise anywhere. . . . but in America, where women
are guarded by a seven-fold shield of habitual insignificance, it caused
an effect that can hardly be described."[17] After finally sailing her Nashoba
blacks to Haiti where she freed them, Wright began to write and to edit
(with Owen's son, Robert Dale Owen) the *New-Harmony Gazette.* She
continued to lecture on her beliefs. Having moved to New York, where
she and Robert Dale Owen started another paper, the *Free Enquirer,*
she bought an old church, named it the Hall of Science, and lectured
there. Her fame spreading before her, she appeared in Boston in the
summer of 1829. If Hawthorne had somehow missed the furor over her
speaking before, he could not have missed it now. The *Salem Observer*
of August 1, 1829, reported that Miss Wright's visit was "the subject
of conversation in almost every circle," but the author conceded that
"her head was good for a female," and that "she is not like some blues
perpetually wearying you with quotation or dazzling you with display."
The *Salem Gazette,* however, quoted on July 31 an article from the
Boston Courier which stated that she had "not a single novel doctrine,"
and that the "task does not belong to her sex." The writer continued,
"For the same reason we cannot but withhold our approbation from
ladies who are conducting newspapers or magazines, and assuming
the prerogatives which naturally belong to their husbands." The *Boston
Gazette* (July 22, 1829) was quoted as admitting that "we do not feel
predisposed to relish the masculine eloquence of this bold and forcible
female." The next year the *Salem Gazette* published in full on June
15, 1830, a story from the *New York Courier,* entitled "Miss Wright's
Parting Address": "The parting address of Miss Wright at the Bowery
Theatre on Wednesday evening was a singular melange of politics and

17. Frances Trollope, *Domestic Manners of the Americans,* 69–70.

impiety—eloquence and irreligion—bold invective and electioneering slang. . . . Nearly the whole newspaper press of this city maintains a death-like silence while the great Red Harlot of Infidelity is madly and triumphantly stalking over the city."

This whole discussion of the role of women and, in the case of Fanny Wright, the example of a woman breaking out of the mold and advocating so much more than education for women, was bound to have been noticed by Nathaniel Hawthorne. In addition, Abner Kneeland had affiliated himself with Wright in New York and Boston. The use of "Nashoba," the Chickasaw word for wolf, may also have stuck in Hawthorne's mind when he toyed with a name for the old aunt in "Septimius Norton," as well as the name for a village of John Eliot's "praying Indians" (*CE* 13:567*n*).

There has been much written on Hawthorne's conflicting views of the woman writer. Perhaps it is worth noticing that not long after Miss Wright's lectures, Hawthorne composed his piece on Mrs. Hutchinson. The anger and trepidation one feels in the first part of that sketch may very well have been influenced by these events, particularly when he says that he will not "look for a living resemblance," but recognizes "portentous" signs that "threaten our posterity." He continues, "As yet, the great body of American women are a domestic race; but when a continuance of ill-judged incitements shall have turned their hearts away from the fire-side, there are obvious circumstances which will render female pens more numerous and more prolific than those of men. [T]he ink-stained Amazons will expel their rivals by actual pressure, and petticoats wave triumphant over all the field" (*CE* 23:66–67). Joel Pfister seems to share my long-held view that Fanny Wright's orations in 1829 and 1830 set off Hawthorne in the first part of the sketch of Mrs. Hutchinson. Pfister suggests "It is possible that this notorious orator, who refused to see her 'sisters' dwarfed by 'mental imbecility,' was the antinomian 'monster' of the 1820's who agitated young Hawthorne to judge women with a 'stricter, instead of more indulgent eye.' "[18]

HAWTHORNE AND SALEM BLACKS

Attracting more of Salem's attention during this period was another group whose members were usually called the Africans, both slave and free. Among the many characters who people *The House of the Seven Gables*, there is one who seems almost invisible: Scipio in the story-within-a-story told by Holgrave. He takes in young Matthew Maule,

18. Joel Pfister, *The Production of Personal Life: Class, Gender, and the Psychological in Hawthorne's Fiction*, 72–73.

the carpenter who has been sent for by "the worshipful Gervayse Pyncheon." The slave is revealed as frightened of old Colonel Pyncheon, who still seems to haunt the house; he shows the whites of his eyes when Maule comes to the front rather than the tradesman's door; and he speaks a dialect that shows him to be the white man's image of a slave (*CE* 2:187). This image is all we see in fleeting glimpses. Having performed his function, he disappears from the story.

Other instances of Hawthorne's idea of the black man appear in his short pieces. In "Sir William Phips," he balances two footmen: "one an African slave of shining ebony, the other an English bond servant" (*CE* 23:61). In "Mr. Higginbotham's Catastrophe," a "nigger" is accused of Higginbotham's murder, but the mulatto, with "a deep tinge of negro blood," appears and proves that he is not a murderer (*CE* 9:110). In "Sunday at Home," the writer portrays a black couple who are the last to leave the church, their "faces as glossy as black satin," and his patronizing remark is "Poor souls! To them, the most captivating picture of bliss in Heaven is—'There we shall be white'" (*CE* 9:25).

In reading old Boston newspapers, which he did with great care, Hawthorne digressed in "Old News" (1835) with the following remarks on slaves and "their lot":

> [W]e confess our opinion that Caesar, Pompey, Scipio, and all such great Roman namesakes, would have been better advised had they staid at home, foddering the cattle, cleaning dishes—in fine, performing their moderate share of the labors of life without being harassed by its cares . . . It must have contributed to reconcile them to their lot, that they saw white men and women imported from Europe, as they had been from Africa, and sold, though only for a term of years, yet as actual slaves to the highest bidder. (*CE* 11:139)

On August 15, 1838, while visiting a tavern five miles from Williams College, Hawthorne noticed many blacks among the crowd. He detailed the mistreatment of one who reacted with "ridiculous antics" and talked about the whippings he used to get as a slave. Hawthorne noted that he was "without any of the foppery of the race in our parts." There was another black who talked of the rights of his race, yet who ended with "a merry retort, a leap in the air, and a negro's laugh." Other blacks present were ashamed of his actions. Hawthorne ends this report by noting, "On the whole, I find myself rather more of an abolitionist in feeling than in principle" (*CE* 8:112). The lack of specificity keeps the reader from knowing in the next paragraph whether he is still talking of the blacks or of the people in that section of Massachusetts in general. He writes, "The people here show out their character much more strongly than they do with us:—there was not the quiet, silent, dull decency as in our public assemblages—but mirth, anger, eccentricity, all showing themselves freely" (*CE* 8:112). On his way home in September 1838, he described a black in Hartford, Connecticut, as being "like any other Christian," and confessed to a queer feeling when someone talked of the black as property to be owned, since "the negro was really so human" (*CE* 8:151).

All this seems to say that Hawthorne was a white man of his time—in North or South—in his stereotypical image of blacks. Yet he professes to a certain unease in the situation. When he edited Horatio Bridge's *Journal of an African Cruiser,* he learned a great deal about blacks and slavery. Bridge had sailed on the USS *Saratoga,* the flagship of Commodore Matthew Perry, with the mission to stop and search all American ships on the west coast of Africa that might be carrying slaves. That mission was fruitless (they saw none), but Bridge's comments on the efforts of the American Colonization Society in Liberia and on Africa in general were vivid. Of course, much of the imagery may have come from Hawthorne's "trimmings and varnishing," but he insisted that the facts were Bridge's (*CE* 16:127). For instance, Bridge remarked that "more vessels came to the coast of Africa from Salem than from any other port." He later noticed the *Vintage* from Salem.

Bridge discussed the fate of the *Mary Carver* of Salem two years before. That schooner, commanded by Captain Farwell of Vassalboro, had gone to Half Berebee to trade with the natives, but they had overpowered Farwell, tortured him by sticking thorns in his flesh for three hours before they killed him, killed the mate and crew, and plundered the ship. These natives were ruled by King Ben Krako. To make the point that this could not be done to an American ship or crew, the U.S. Navy held a "palaver" with the king, which ended in a wild melee. Krako was captured and killed; villages were burned and some natives killed. This was in accord with African custom, according to Bridge, and would be long remembered. Patrick Brancaccio thought that Hawthorne had softened Bridge's remarks about the whole affair. Bridge added, however, that "one would fain hope that civilized man, in his controversies with the barbarian, will at length cease to descend to the barbarian level, and may adopt some other method of proving his superiority than by the greater power to inflict suffering."[19] Hawthorne,

19. [Horatio Bridge], *Journal of an African Cruiser, by an Officer of the United States Navy. . . . ,* 75–84; Patrick Brancaccio, "The Black Man's Paradise: Hawthorne's Editing of the 'Journal of an African Cruiser,'" 34–35.

in response to a letter from Bridge about this fight, replied on April 1, 1844, "In the sight of God, one life may be as valuable as another; but in our view, the stakes are very unequal. Besides, I really do consider the shooting of these niggers a matter of very questionable propriety; and am glad, upon the whole, that you bagged no game on either of those days" (*CE* 16:26). To both Bridge and Hawthorne, there was a contrast between the civilized and the barbarian, yet the methods used made them both uncomfortable. Much later in "Chiefly About War Matters" (1862) Hawthorne describes what he saw in a visit to Virginia from the war capitol of Washington. A party of contrabands from "Secessia" caught his eye. He was interested in their lack of speed, in their rather rude attire, in their "crust of primeval simplicity (which is quite polished away from the northern black man)." He opined that the benefits of the war would not help the present generation of blacks. After viewing some Confederate prisoners, most of whom he described as "peasants, and of a very low order," he felt that these Southern whites would be freed by the victory of the Northern troops, and remarked that "so far as the education of the heart is concerned, the negroes have apparently the advantage of them" (*CE* 23:420, 429, 430–31).

Many of the views expressed by Hawthorne can be taken to be those of someone who had no intimate knowledge of blacks, yet had swallowed the simplistic assumptions of others. It makes one wonder about his Salem experience and the views derived therefrom. Was all this knowledge derived only from books or newspapers written by whites who knew no more than he? How were slavery and the slave trade viewed in Salem? Just how prominent were the blacks there? Did his own family have any intimate ties with slaves?

Few Salemites discussed the traffic in slaves, and it was thought that those families engaged in the trade had destroyed their records. Nevertheless, rumors persisted about Captain Joseph White, the Fairfields, and others. William Bentley was unhappy about such trade. Louise Chipley says that he wrote that the schooner *Felicity,* under the command of William Fairfield and partly owned by Joseph White, was supposedly being used for the slave trade and was "giving great pain to thinking men."[20] Both men were Bentley's parishioners.

20. WB, *Diary,* 1:104; Louise Chipley, "The Financial Anxieties of New England's Congregational Clergy during the Early National Era: The Case of William Bentley, 1783–1819," 285; Browne said that Bentley "was ahead of the vast majority of the people of his day" in "Youthful Recollections," 50:295.

The Essex County Court Records had shown the presence of slaves in the seventeenth century. Tituba, although probably not a Negro but an Amerindian, had been the slave of Samuel Parris, minister at Salem Village, as had Indian John. On the other hand, according to Ralph D. Paine, slaves captured in British privateers during the Revolution were not permitted to be sold as property, but were treated as prisoners of war. Elias H. Derby refused to let the *Grand Turk* board slaves on its first voyage to the Gold Coast. For the most part, Salem did not seem to be heavily involved in slavery; at the same time the town did not seem overly aware of any problem with it. James Pope-Hennessy remarked in 1968, "Yet it was from Salem, as well as from Boston and from Newport that the slaving ships set sail for the coast of Guinea. One of the grievances of white Southerners in the nineteenth century— probably even a covert grievance still today—was that the Yankees who had become so vociferously humanitarian over the evils of slavery were the direct descendants of the chief American traders in slaves." Arthur O. White details the treatment to which blacks were subjected before Hawthorne's time and during it. Forced to be separate and unequal in matters of pay, jobs, and justice, their lot was not, on the whole, a happy one.[21]

During Hawthorne's lifetime a sizable colony of blacks inhabited Salem. They lived in the "Huts" on the turnpike near Buffum's Corner, in the rear of High Street, on the lower part of St. Peter's Street, or on the Neck Lands, according to Oliver Thayer. The High Street area was what Hawthorne later called New Guinea in "The Custom-House." Dr. Bentley indicated that the blacks lived on what was "vulgarly called Roast Meat Hill" between Mill Street, High Street, and Pickering Hill burying grounds (Broad Street Cemetery). He said that there were about one hundred huts or houses there.[22]

Many interesting figures were among them. One named Mumford, "well fitted to be chief of the tribe," was mentioned in a poem by Charles T. Brooks. Mumford was called by Mrs. Lydia Nichols "the giant of Negroes whom we children looked upon with fear." There was Portsmouth (a cook), Newport, and Tom Piper. Oliver Thayer described

21. See Elaine G. Breslaw, "The Salem Witch from Barbados: In Search of Tituba's Roots," 217–38; Ralph D. Paine, *The Ships and Sailors of Old Salem,* 192; James Pope-Hennessy, *Sins of the Fathers,* 229; Arthur O. White, "Salem's Antebellum Black Community: Seedbed of the School Integration Movement," 99–118.
22. Oliver Thayer to Francis H. Lee, January 28, 1885, Scrapbook, 3:22–28, Francis Henry Lee Papers; H. Brooks, "Localities about Salem," 114–15, 117; WB, *Diary,* 4:382.

another: "Prince Savage, an intelligent black man, highly respected, and probably well remembered by many of our older citizens. He was a native of Africa and once a slave." He listed also George Dickinson, "a burley black man [who] had a fondness for old Medford" [rum] and who had three sons: Obed, Robert, and William, who were all educated at Hacker School, a local institution recognized for its teaching of writing.[23] Bentley mentioned Deacon Robert Freeman, whose slave name was Mingo, and who had been brought to the United States by Captain Jacob Crowninshield. Known for his devotional aids to the blacks, Freeman was appointed by the Rev. Joshua Spaulding as overseer of the blacks at the Howard Street Church. An early servant of the Joseph Whites, Patience Whipple, whose father was Plato Whipple of Hamilton, was "remarkable for her Cake and pastry." She later married Robert Freeman. Lemon Shillaber was a member of the First Baptist Church. When he died at forty-eight, the *Salem Gazette* (September 30, 1825) called him a "respectable black man—universally lamented." Bentley also referred to Primus Manning, "a worthy free black," whose wife was Dinah, the widow of Jack Deland alias John Black. He also described as "worthy" Abraham Williams and his wife and Cato Ransom and his wife, who may have been the "Member" Ransom listed as running a boardinghouse in the *Salem Directory* of 1842. Peter Green, the servant of General Nathanael Greene, came to Salem and married Flora Gerrish. He died there at the age of eighty on November 17, 1815. The Ruloff family had a son who was either a cook or steward on the *George.* In fact, many of the blacks listed in the 1842 *Directory* as mariners were probably either cooks or stewards on board ships. Caroline King remembered a black cook on the Crowninshield's *Cleopatra's Barge* "who had formerly sailed with Bowditch [and] was said to be as capable of keeping the ship's reckoning as any of its officers." Marianne Silsbee recalled "coalblack" Johnny Geer. Not of Salem, but often in Salem, was "Black Harry," the fiddler for William Turner, the dancing master, who knew the tunes so well that he often went to sleep as he fiddled. Pompey Nolegs was a veteran of the Revolutionary War, in which he had lost his legs. In 1820 the *Salem Gazette* noticed that the aged black man, Cuffee Gardiner, "the laughing philosopher," had died. Was the

23. Charles Timothy Brooks, "Poem" in "An Account of the Commemoration, by the Essex Institute, of the Fifth Half-Century of the Landing of John Endicott in Salem, Massachusetts," 200; Oliver Thayer, "Early Recollections of the Upper Portion of Essex Street," 211; Lydia Nichols to Lee, May 6, 1884, Scrapbook, 3:100–112 and Thayer to Lee, January 28, 1885, Scrapbook, 3:24, Francis Henry Lee Papers; Alonzo Lewis and James R. Newhall, *The History of Lynn, Including Nahant,* 181.

book with Cuffy's name found later in a secret staircase at the house with seven gables his? A Turner had married a Gardner at one point, and he could have been their slave.[24]

John and Nancy Remond were one of the most noted black couples in Salem. John Remond, a free black always called Mr. Remond, had come to Salem at the age of ten in 1798 on the ship *Six Brothers*. John Needham, the ship's master, obtained work for him with his brother, Isaac Needham, a baker. Remond married Nancy Lenox, another free black, whose father had fought in the Revolutionary War and who herself was an excellent maker of cakes. The pair was genuinely respected. Remond was the caterer at Hamilton Hall where the various assemblies were held. He catered the receptions for Lafayette in 1824 and for Joseph Story in 1829. In these duties he was greatly helped by his wife. Marianne Silsbee said that Nancy Remond was known for her "charming manners and good cooking," especially her "mock-turtle soup, venison or alamode beef, and roast chickens with perhaps ducks, and light, not flaky, pastry." The couple was given an apartment on the ground floor of Hamilton Hall and one of the two stores in that building, from which Remond sold oysters, eggs, poultry, and livestock. But the Remonds were more than cooks. They raised ten children, two of whom were extremely important in the Abolition movement: Charles Lenox Remond (1810–1873) and Sarah Parker Remond (1824–1873).[25]

Another person admired by Bentley was Mrs. Chloe Minns, a schoolteacher who married Schuyler Laurence on February 6, 1817. Bentley, who had performed the ceremony, observed:

> He is a man of good person & of good manners, attending on the best families in Marblehead & these are the first grade of Africans in all our New England towns. Chloe enters upon her third marriage, & has two children & is a Mulattoe. She was introduced while I was in the Salem School Committee as a Preceptress in the Salem African School then

24. WB, *Diary,* 4:54, 435; First Baptist Church Records; WB, *Diary,* 4:594, 435–36, 361; *Salem Directory and City Register,* 1837 and 1842 (in which there are separate listings for people of color); King, *When I Lived in Salem,* 46; M. C. D. Silsbee, *A Half-Century,* 116; Putnam to Lee, April 26, 1884, Scrapbook, 1:91–93, Francis Henry Lee Papers; *SG,* February 29, 1820.

25. Mrs. Georgie A. Hill, "Passenger Arrivals at Salem and Beverly, Massachusetts, 1798–1800," 207; M. C. D. Silsbee, *A Half-Century,* 94; Dorothy Burnett Porter, "The Remonds of Salem, Massachusetts: A Nineteenth-Century Family Revisited," 262–64, 269–70, 273, 280; Miriam L. Usrey, "Charles Lenox Remond: Garrison's Ebony Echo World Anti-Slavery Convention, 1840," 112–25; Ruth Bogin, "Sarah Parker Remond: Black Abolitionist from Salem," 120–50.

first established & has acquitted herself with great honour, as to her manners & as to her instructions.[26]

Bentley had long been interested in education for blacks. He had worked with John Hathorne Jr. (1775–1829) and Joshua Spaulding, minister of the Howard Street Church, to aid black instruction. He had encouraged the blacks to go to that church, and he was irritated, to say the least, when "[c]ertain devout women of the straitest sect have undertaken to change our plan & have actually opened a place of worship on the high land in the southern part of town, in a place to which the Africans formerly resorted for pleasure. . . . The Negroes have such a mixture of teachers as makes their instruction useless. They would have been content in their former state if left to proper direction." These ladies had also started an African Sunday School, "its object being the improvement of the religious and moral character of the coloured people." The organization soon took the name of the Clarkson Society after the British organizer of antislavery societies. Adults were taught to read the Bible, and children were encouraged to memorize certain portions of Scripture. The Society hired a large room that had once been a dancing hall and announced, "The Clarkson Society are aware that a people, whose prevalent characteristic is the love of amusement, cannot at once be made to submit to the restraints of well ordered society, but it is to be hoped that they have in some instances been the means, if not of subduing, at least of making that propensity subservient to useful instruction." One of the devout ladies and a prominent member of the Clarkson Society was Sarah Savage. At the point of the Clarkson Society's origin, she was working at Tabernacle Church. Later she was to write a book, *Trial and Self-Discipline,* which has a black character who comes close to being a major figure. The *Salem Gazette* remarked rather skeptically that "the character of Phillis will perhaps seem to many an unusual one; but as the author assures us it was drawn from life, we cannot justly call it unnatural."[27]

In the James Duncan Phillips Library of the Peabody Essex Museum, there is an unsigned list of the members of the African School on January 1826. These children range in age from perhaps three (Eliza Ann Arnold) and certainly four (Ann Morson) to nineteen (Mrs. Eliza Reed). Their addresses are given as High Street, North Fields, Neck

26. WB, *Diary,* 4:435.
27. WB, *Diary,* 4:621; *ER,* July 21, 1819; [Caleb Foote], review of *Trial and Self-Discipline, SG,* March 31, 1835.

Gate, the Turnpike, back of the Courthouse, and Fish Street. Some are merely listed as "at service." No teacher is recorded.[28]

According to Oliver Thayer, the blacks were "all apparently happy in their humble sphere, especially on Election Week." It is, of course, not easy to read the moods of others, but in an age that was perhaps not so aware of victimization as our own, there may be a modicum of truth in the statement. Nevertheless, as Arthur White has indicated, " 'Lection,' the last days of May following Election Day, included free dancing, fiddling, eating, drinking, and parades with drums, swords, and banners. Though established in prerevolutionary days to 'alleviate the depressed condition' of slaves, local townsmen disapproved of the proceedings and only the restlessness of otherwise industrious loyal servants secured them leave to attend the festivities." Thayer also said that the blacks did not seem to have particular callings, "but were ready for any little job." He perhaps did not realize that it would have been difficult for blacks to have fulfilled their higher callings. Blacks were listed in the 1837 and 1842 city directories as mariners, barbers, chimney sweeps, gardeners, and cooks. Thayer noted, too, that they were "a church-going people." The South Congregational Church had a semicircular gallery for them; other churches set apart black pews. He added that they seemed to have no ambition to obtain seats in the white section and that they had later dropped away from the white churches. On June 22, 1827, the *Salem Gazette* mentioned a Union Bethel Church for blacks.[29]

What seems to have been operating was a strict pattern of segregation, with the whites assuming that blacks agreed with that pattern. The *Salem Observer* printed a letter on July 12, 1834, from an outraged citizen who declared that black girls had been introduced into Eastern Female School and were *"promiscuously seated with the white children."* A town meeting was held in which the principal issue was whether to have a separate school for blacks. It was carried by a large majority. John Remond moved to Newport, Rhode Island, from 1835 to 1841 so that his daughters could obtain an adequate education. According to a writer in an 1850 letter in the *Salem Register,* blacks were also not allowed to enter the East India Marine Society.[30]

28. Family Ms., "List of Scholars that have attended African School, January 1826," Peabody Essex Museum.

29. Thayer, "Early Recollections," 211; White, "Salem's Antebellum Black Community," 102–3; Thayer to Lee, January 28, 1885, Scrapbook, 3:24, 25, Francis Henry Lee Papers.

30. *Salem Observer,* July 12 and 19, 1834; Barbara M. Solomon, "The Growth of the Population in Essex County, 1850–1860," 98.

Surely Hawthorne was not unaware of many of these people or developments. Elizabeth Peabody wrote years later to Horatio Bridge that Hawthorne "knew *nothing* about slavery—He had never been at the South." But Elizabeth with that particular myopia, or "squint" as Hawthorne called it, thought that you had to go south to know anything about slavery. Hawthorne never knew his grandfather, Jonathan Phelps, who had died in 1799, but surely he had heard that in 1774 Phelps, "to be consistent with his professions of liberty, has released a valuable slave." Also, according to his Aunt Ruth Hathorne, his grandfather Hathorne had had two "servants," which was the usual euphemism for slaves. Nathaniel did not seem to grow up with black servants, unless the unsurnamed Jane was such. But in 1819 after Robert Manning sent a youth to his brother Richard when Hawthorne was still in Raymond, Richard wrote Robert that "The pickaninny of a boy that you brought from Salem will never answer." Also the William Symms who was a Maine playmate in the disputed first diary was at least partly black. In college one of Hawthorne's classmates, John B. Russworm, was black and established one of the first "Negro newspapers in the United States, *Freedom's Journal*, in 1827." He was later governor of the Maryland colony in Liberia at Cape Palmas and was visited by Horatio Bridge in 1843.[31]

Elizabeth Hawthorne was familiar with one black girl: on at least three different occasions she was with Charlotte Forten, a young female sent to Salem in 1854 to secure a good education. On one August day in 1856, they toured the Hugh Peters House and then went to Marblehead Beach where "we took our dinner [Forten wrote] in a delightful old barn; and passed a pleasant afternoon, lying on the straw, and listening to the music of 'the swallows song in the eaves'; or to the deeper, wilder music of the waves, which we could see dashing furiously against the rocks." Charlotte also visited Hawthorne's cousins, Maria and Rebecca Manning, several times and admired their house with its "beautiful books, plants, and fine engravings."[32] Hawthorne's family seemed to welcome this young black girl.

The papers and magazines were full of antislavery matter from about the 1830s on. Salem had its own antislavery societies by 1834, both male and female. The year 1835 was called the "mob year" because

31. EPP, *Letters*, 445; Felt, *Annals*, 2d ed., 2:417; Belknap, "Forrester and Descendants," 18; Richard Manning to Robert Manning, April 6, 1819, Hawthorne-Manning Collection; Turner, *Hawthorne*, 399, 41.

32. Grimké, *Journals*, 162, 84, 87–88, 197, 202.

there were race riots in New York, Philadelphia, Hartford, and other places. A group called the "Friends of Order" was formed in Salem, which, while against slavery, was also against abolitionism. The *Salem Gazette* reported on October 27, 1835, that it had been "rumored that Thompson [George Thompson, the English abolitionist and friend of Whittier's] was going to lecture at the Anti-Slavery meeting at Howard Street. Young men and boys assembled—broke a lantern in the hands of the sheriff who put one in jail, but he escaped." Only the deaf and blind could have been unaware of certain tensions regarding the black community.[33]

We are guilty of presentism, I believe, when we try to make the Hawthorne of that time conform to present views. Elizabeth Peabody especially attempted to change his mind, to no avail. We may wonder about his stance before and during the Civil War, but we must remember that he was in Europe for most of the 1850s when abolitionism became more tolerable for many New Englanders. Hawthorne's support of and friendship for Franklin Pierce and his determination to dedicate *Our Old Home* to him, despite Pierce's unpopularity, made the writer not acceptable in many New England circles. In fact, according to Howard Mansfield, at Hawthorne's funeral, Pierce was not allowed to be a pallbearer and was "made to sit by himself in the balcony." Hawthorne was against slavery, but he thought abolitionists would produce misery, not freedom. He was by no means alone in his attitudes. Many of Salem's worthies were antagonistic to the abolitionists.[34] We may wish his blacks were not so much in the background in his work. Yet the truth of the matter is, I think, that they *were* in the background for many whites, sometimes almost unseen in Salem and elsewhere in the early part of the nineteenth century, and Hawthorne only reflected that.

Hawthorne incorporated many new ideas or factors in Salem life in his writing. He often mentions those who gather gold in whatever way, as in "Sir William Pepperell" or "The Great Stone Face." His interest in alchemy is kin to this. The railroad plays a vital part in "The Celestial Rail-road" or *The House of the Seven Gables*. Class differences occur in "Lady Eleanore's Mantle" or *The Blithedale Romance*. Perhaps the most interesting comparisons may be made between Hawthorne's use of the Indians and the blacks. Hawthorne's Black Man, meaning the

33. *SG,* March 21, 1834, June 13, 1837, and January 22, June 16, June 30, July 28, and November 3, 1835.

34. Howard Mansfield, *In the Memory House,* 70; Saltonstall, *Papers, 1816–1845,* 5:68; Lydia Maria Child, *Lydia Maria Child: Selected Letters, 1817–1880*. See p. 375 for the opinions of Nathaniel Silsbee Jr. and his wife, Marianne.

devil, is connected to the Indian, not the African. Despite Hawthorne's disclaimers about his ability to depict Indians, they show up again and again in his stories—often at a short distance, usually motionless—but still there. When the Indian in "The Seven Vagabonds" chooses to go with the storyteller to Stamford, the narrator muses, "Wandering down through the waste of ages, the woods had vanished around his path; his arm had lost somewhat of its strength, his foot of its fleetness, his mien of its wild regality, his heart and mind of their savage virtue and uncultured force; but here, untameable to the routine of artificial life, roving now along the dusty road, as of old over the forest leaves, here was the Indian still" (*CE* 9:365). The black also is at the periphery occasionally— a Scipio in "Lady Eleanore's Mantle" or a Caesar in "The White Old Maid," but blacks are not nearly so omnipresent as the Indian. The fact that they did not appear to be as real to the writer as the Indian probably suggests some clue to his attitudes during the Civil War. Nevertheless, these issues were coming gradually to the foreground in the period after Hawthorne's return from college.

7

Dull Old Salem

There is a peculiar dulness [*sic*] about Salem—a heavy atmosphere which no literary man can breathe.—Horatio Bridge to Nathaniel Hawthorne, January 19, 1830, in Julian Hawthorne, *Nathaniel Hawthorne and Wife*

M ANY PEOPLE, including Hawthorne, complained at times of the dullness of Salem. Elizabeth Palmer Peabody lamented in 1836 after moving back to Salem from Boston that "[t]he people here care about nothing stirring—& read every species & form of transcendentalism as if it were Evil Lore." Leverett Saltonstall informed his daughter Anne in 1843 that Salem "is *dull, dull, dull* & yet it is a good, comfortable old place after all." Octavius Brooks Frothingham, minister of North Church, wrote in 1852 to George E. Ellis, editor of the *Christian Examiner,* that "in this clam bed of Salem, I may be relapsing into a condition of perilous inertness [and] mental rust."[1] Yet the town was no provincial backwater; its port brought people and newspapers from all over the world. A glance at the papers of Hawthorne's time shows it to be a lively place with many diversions. This was especially true of the Salem that faced outward to the sea.

THE SEA
The sea that lapped Salem round provided a salty tang for the town. Even constant comings and goings on the water could not pall. "Hawthorne's love for the sea amounted to a passionate worship," wrote James T. Fields when they were returning by ship from England, "and

---

1. EPP, *Letters,* 190; Saltonstall, *Papers, 1816–1845,* 5:80; J. Wade Caruthers, *Octavius Brooks Frothingham, Gentle Radical,* 21.

while I . . . was longing . . . to reach land as soon as possible, Hawthorne was constantly saying in his quiet, earnest way, 'I should like to
sail on and on forever, and never touch the shore again.' " As a boy,
Nathaniel had informed his mother that he would make the sea his
career as had his father before him; though he did not, the sea was in
his blood. Richard Stoddard recalled that in 1853 he and Hawthorne "fell
to talking about the sea, and the influence it had had in the childhood
of both."[2]

And how could it not have had? Hawthorne lived just a short block
from the wharves. He could smell the sea from his home, and he
could presumably see the sparkling waters from his third-story room on
Herbert Street. He could certainly see it from other eminences around
town. In his early "Sights from a Steeple," he has the narrator say, "On
the fourth side is the sea, stretching away towards a viewless boundary,
blue and calm, except where the passing anger of a shadow flits across
its surface and is gone" (*CE* 9:192).

The air was fragrant with not only salt spray but also cinnamon,
sandalwood, pepper, and ginger, and all the freight which its seamen
brought home. Shipowners thronged the streets, as did sea captains
(proudly called master mariners) and ordinary sailors. The lovely homes
of Salem, designed by Samuel McIntyre and others, on Federal, Chestnut, and Essex Streets contained porcelain from China, leather from
Brazil, and cashmere shawls from India. The Custom House had a new
building in 1818/1819 on Derby Street. Salem was a town known in
every port, and every port was known to Salemites. Her museum was
beginning to be filled with artifacts from all over the world.

Yet, the dangers of the sea were ever-present also. Not only were
family members and fellow townsmen often lost at sea but also constant
reminders abounded. In his boyhood, Nathaniel had to go to church.
One of the customs of the time was to send up requests for prayer
for the loved ones of parishioners, especially those who were at sea.
Hawthorne indicated that he was familiar with the practice when he
recorded in his notebook in 1840 that "a man . . . puts up a note in
church desiring the prayers of the congregation" (*CE* 23:222). In a town
so aware of the perils of the sea, it was universally done.

Jonathan Porter Felt (1785–1860) was told by William Gavett (1766–
1856) that "the inhabitants of Salem previous to the Revolution possessed but little property" and that they were "generally engaged in

2. Fields, *Yesterdays with Authors,* 92; Richard Henry Stoddard, *Recollections, Personal
and Literary,* 125.

fishing, some few going to the West Indies with cargoes of fish for sale and return[ing] with sugar, molasses, coffee, and rum for return cargoes."[3] The Revolution changed that. Salem privateers made the city wealthy. After the war, Salem had its moment of renown when its use of the sea was preeminent. Then the town was hurt by the Embargo of 1807–1809 and the War of 1812. Forty privateers went out in this war, but such ventures were not so productive as before. When the harbor began to silt up, custom gradually went to Boston or New York. The advantage of access to the sea was subsequently never as remunerative, but it remained a way of life for many.

Beyond its uses, however, the ocean was there—a potent symbol. Hawthorne's first known published work was a poem, "The Ocean," which appeared without his name, but with the initials C.W., in 1825 (*CE* 23:6–7). Two of his poems in "The Spectator" referred to the water (*CE* 23:32, 44). He was always aware of it. His notebooks are full of walks along the shore in which he noticed every plant or shell. He observed the reflections in its stream, swam in the protective inlets, noted the blue of its color, the white of its breaking waves. He describes in "Foot-prints on the Sea-shore" his welcome from that body: "the great sea has been my companion, and the little sea-birds my friends, and the wind has told me his secrets" (*CE* 9:461). He always felt better physically near the sea. He wrote to William Pike on July 24, 1851, that he would like to find a home on the seacoast or "at all events with easy access to the sea" (*CE* 16:465). At the end of his life, Sophia apprised Horatio Bridge on April 5, 1864, that "he needs the damp sea-air for health, comfort and enjoyment. I wish . . . that he could wander on sea-beaches all the rest of his days." Julian Hawthorne considered that his father might have lived twenty more years if he had resided within sight of the Atlantic.[4] There was something in the sea's very air that energized him.

Yet only rarely did he use the ocean in his works. He did observe in *The Scarlet Letter* that "the sea, in those old times, heaved, swelled, and foamed, very much at its own will, or subject only to the tempestuous wind, with hardly any attempts at regulation by human law" (*CE* 1:233). Aside from one skeptical paragraph in the "Spectator," and a remark in "Foot-prints on the Sea-shore" that he "can never rid myself of the idea, that a monster endowed with life and fierce energy, is striving to burst his way through the narrow pass," he did not make use of one possible subject for a story (*CE* 23:22; 9:456). In 1817, 1818, and

3. Felt Family Collection.
4. Bridge, *Recollections,* 187–88; JH, *Hawthorne and His Circle,* 20.

1819, a sea serpent was seen off Nahant or Gloucester. It was described as a huge serpent with humps or coils on its back. The reports made Dr. Bentley very curious. One had been observed as early as 1638 by Dr. John Josselyn, who told of a "sea serpent or snake that lay coiled up, like a cable upon the rock of Cape Ann." In 1819 the Reverend Cheever Felch saw it from the longboat of the USS *Independence* and wrote a Boston newspaper that "we had a good view of him." Colonel Thomas Handasyd Perkins of Boston had also seen it and, according to one report, Daniel Webster had been with him. Through his spyglass Perkins vowed that he had seen an "undulating, chocolate-colored sea serpent, some forty feet in length, whose flat head, raised a yard or so above the water, was equipped with a single horn in the shape of a marlinspike." The *American Magazine of Useful and Entertaining Knowledge* had a story about a serpent noticed in or near Penobscot Bay in Maine by reputable people. Even so important a scientist as Louis Agassiz remarked in a lecture in Philadelphia in 1849, "I still consider it probable that it will be the good fortune of some person on the coast of Norway or North America to find a living representative of this type of reptile . . . which is thought to have died out."[5]

Despite his failure to use the serpent in his fiction, Hawthorne was aware of it. The descriptions of the unconquerable sea creature must have made him think of his favorite Book of Job: "Canst thou draw out leviathan with an hook? or his tongue with a cord which thou lettest down?" (41:1). On August 21, 1820, in the first number of the "Spectator," Hawthorne wrote under domestic news the following: "The great Sea Serpent still continues to cause much effusion of ink among the Editors of Newspapers. His appearance is extremely useful to this wise fraternity. . . . He seems to possess a strange and We think rather unusual faculty of appearing in different shapes to different eyes, so that where one person sees a shark, another beholds a measureless dragon" (*CE* 23:22). He foreshadows here his feeling about the use of specter evidence against the witches. It is not strange that he did not believe in the sea serpent, but it is odd that he did not use the story in his work. Moreover, he did not really make use of the sea itself in any major way in his creative pieces. There is far more mention of the sea in his notebooks than in his fiction. Of course, such fictional work may have been lost.

5. WB, *Diary*, 4:473, 481; Fred A. Wilson, *Some Annals of Nahant, Massachusetts,* 160–67; Joseph E. Garland, *Boston's North Shore,* 26–27, 28; Herbert A. Kenny, *Cape Ann: Cape America,* 188–89; Carl Seaburg and Stanley Paterson, *Merchant Prince of Boston: Colonel Thomas Handasyd Perkins, 1764–1854,* 278–80, 289, 402; "The Sea Serpent," 2:122–23.

Elizabeth Hawthorne said that her brother showed her in the summer of 1825 the tales that would have made up his projected "Seven Tales of My Native Land" which "dealt with witchcraft and the sea. . . . One tale contained some verses, only one line of which has been preserved. 'The rovers of the sea, they were a fearful race.'" Joseph Flibbert points out, however, that the minutely detailed picture of the seven-gabled house, thought to be the Turner house, never mentions its "sea-side location."[6]

Hawthorne simply did not write the kind of sea stories that Melville did, where you can hear the surf and feel the heat of the midday sun on the blue water. This is natural in that Hawthorne did not go to sea as an occupation and Melville did, and when Hawthorne pictured the sea, he stood on the shore. But in "The Village Uncle," although he still views the ocean from the land, he shows his intimate knowledge of it when he describes the homecoming of the fisherman: "When the wind was high; when the whale boats, anchored off the Point, nodded their slender masts at each other, and the dories pitched and tossed in the surf; when Nahant Beach was thundering three miles off, and the spray broke a hundred feet in air, round the distant base of Egg Rock; when the brimful and boisterous sea threatened to tumble over the street of our village; then I made a holiday on shore" (*CE* 9:314). The whole story of the uncle is told with an authentic feel of the sea, of men who "have all been christened in salt water, and know more than men ever learn in the bushes" (*CE* 9:315). Yet even in the last incomplete novels, when he had crossed the ocean and the English Channel, the sea plays no great part. The characters are either in America or in England, as though magic carpets had whisked them here or there.

LIFE ON SHORE

The sea was full of interest, but so was the shore. Salem was certainly not isolated from the great events of the day. Presidents and notables visited the town, as had George Washington before young Nathaniel's time. A visit by President James Monroe was reported in the *Salem Gazette* on June 13, 1817. When President James Madison also stopped in 1817, he stayed with Benjamin Crowninshield. John Quincy Adams came often, either in a public or private capacity since his first cousin was married to Joseph Barlow Felt. In 1825 Adams dined with the East India Marine Society. The Marquis de Lafayette had come on November 2, 1784; he appeared again on August 31, 1824, and passed

6. G. Lathrop, *Study of Hawthorne,* 134; Joseph Flibbert, "Hawthorne, Salem, and the Sea," believes that Hawthorne's neglect of sea stories sprang from the loss of his father to the sea (or across the sea) and his own unresolved conflicts about that painful fact (2–9).

in the pouring rain between rows of schoolchildren wearing ribbons with his picture. Andrew Jackson made his northern tour on June 28, 1833, and was met by Major Charles Amburger Andrew, a cousin of Hawthorne; by the selectmen of Salem; and by "a cavalcade of about 200 horsemen." Jackson became ill, however, and retired to the mansion of Nathaniel West. The *Salem Observer* (June 29, 1833) described the look of Beckford Street, through which Jackson was to have gone. An arch was surmounted by an eagle with the inscription "The Union, it must be preserved." Portraits of Washington and Jackson and an "elegant" copy of the Declaration of Independence were all attached to the arch. In 1818, on October 25, Henry Clay arrived for a visit.[7]

Salem also had special days to look forward to. In addition to the Fourth of July, Thanksgiving was the big day in Salem, not Christmas. In fact, the whole of Thanksgiving week was a holiday. Hawthorne called it "New England's Festival" in "John Inglefield's Thanksgiving" (*CE* 11:179). He wrote his Aunt Mary Manning from college, "I wish that I could be at home . . . Thanksgiving, as I really think that your puddings and pies and turkies are superior to anybody's else" (*CE* 15:190). Marianne Silsbee (1812–1899), sister-in-law of Mary Crowninshield Silsbee (1809–1887), described the Thanksgiving dinner of her youth: "First in order was a huge turkey, roasted before a wood fire, vegetables of the season, cranberry sauce at discretion; next roast ducks; plum pudding, mince pie, apple pie, and squash pie; nuts, raisins, figs, and apples. There was no preliminary soup, and as for ice cream, I doubt if a spoonful could have been had in Salem for love or money." But Thanksgiving was not only commemorated by food. It was a day to give thanks at church with a donation to the poor. Dr. Bentley was often unhappy about the paucity of the congregation and the slimness of the offering.[8]

Christmas, on the other hand, was not universally celebrated by Salem in Hawthorne's youth. The children may have had the day off from school (as an item in the *Salem Gazette* reported), but it was not a general holiday. Caroline King, in fact, noted that "no schools or shops were closed." The lack of celebration was a result of the Puritan feeling that the festivities came from not only the church at Rome but also pagan celebrations. Dr. Bentley was very exercised by the fact

7. Robotti, *Chronicles,* 46, 44, 49, 56, 57, 60; Mary H. Northend, "Historic Salem," 512; WB, *Diary,* 4:548; Paul C. Nagel, *The Adams Women: Abigail and Louisa Adams,* 152; *SG,* November 2, 1784, and June 28, 1833; WB, *Diary,* 4:557.

8. M. C. D. Silsbee, *A Half-Century,* 40–41; WB, *Diary,* 4:216–17, 300, 363, 424.

that the Episcopalians and the Universalists did celebrate the day with pine boughs and special church services. The day was also kept, he observed, in "the Catholic private place of worship." When Hawthorne later wrote in "The Christmas Banquet" about the holiday replete "with glad and solemn worship in the churches, and sports, games, festivals, and everywhere the bright face of Joy beside the household fire," he was scarcely describing a Salem Christmas (*CE* 10:293). There was a long custom there of marking New Year's Day, not Christmas, with gifts. And much later when he commented on a Christmas in England, Hawthorne's feeling that he was then "happier this Christmas than ever before" reflected not only his genuine joy in his family that year, but also the fact that his previous Christmases had hardly been celebrated at all.[9] Hawthorne touched on the meaning of the day in a letter to Sophia on December 24, 1839, when he mentioned "the holiest of holydays—the day that brought ransom to all other sinners" which that year kept them in slavery because they could not be together (*CE* 15:391).

Training Day was another exciting time in Salem. The military companies came to Salem to be reviewed on the Common. The sounds of the bands, or the drums and fifes, and the costumes of the troops were memorable to Caroline King. Observed William Driver to Francis Lee, "I am sorry to say those meetings and musters were usually graced with a little tub filled with New England Rum, molasses and water."[10]

Election Day, in the last week of May, was celebrated particularly by blacks with dancing and merriment, much like the celebration of Christmas by Southern blacks. Silsbee remembered that children were taught on that occasion that they should assure the happiness of others, and were sent to take cake to "some old dependent or reduced gentlewomen."[11]

ENTERTAINMENTS AND CIRCUSES

Not only were there special days for amusement, as well as for benevolence, but Salem had entertainments of many kinds. There were circuses and displays of animals almost every year. An elephant and a bear were being shown at Barton's Hotel in 1825. In 1826 one hundred living rattlesnakes were exhibited at the Lafayette Coffee House. Elephants were particularly favored; they had been special ever since 1797 when

9. King, *When I Lived in Salem,* 114–15; WB, *Diary,* 4:223, 429; NH, *Our Old Home and English Note-Books,* 1:549.

10. King, *When I Lived in Salem,* 74–76; Driver to Lee, Scrapbook, 3:37–41, copy, Francis Henry Lee Papers.

11. M. C. D. Silsbee, *A Half-Century,* 19–20.

an elephant was brought back on the *America* from India, and was constantly given rum because the sailors were afraid she would drink all their water. Ever since the Salemites have called her the "stoned elephant." There was an Elephant Caravan in March 1827. Captain Samuel Kennedy brought an elephant home on his ship *Rome* in January 1832. The tradition lingered. In June 1857 Jonathan Porter Felt wrote his daughter, Mary Porter Felt White of Virginia, that he saw from the Franklin Building a large body of people. "I asked what the ruckus was about [and] received for reply that the Circus of five elephants had just gone down Essex Street. Understand they turned down toward Derby Street. . . . I was told the Elephants were attached to carriages and went as fast as a horse on a canter, that People had to keep on a run to keep up with them."[12]

In May 1838 the *Essex Register* announced the coming of the "Grand Menagerie with strange animals never seen before in the United States." Frances Robotti reported that the newspaper used a pen-and-ink drawing which spread over a fourth of its space to invite young and old to see the entertainment. Caroline King recalled the day the circus

> made its annual entrance into the town. And a great day that was, not only for the children, but for grown people as well. The schools were adjourned until the parade was over, and the tradesmen refused to work on "Circus Day." There being no railroad in those days, the Circus had to travel on the high roads, and usually came to Salem over the turnpike, stopping just after passing the Toll-House to marshall its clans, and arrange the great entering show.[13]

In "The Toll-Gatherer's Day," Hawthorne depicts "a train of wagons, conveying all the wild beasts of a caravan" waiting to pass over the bridge (*CE* 9:211).

In 1810 John Roulstone, who had been in the circus, offered a riding school to Salemites. The earlier name of Hathorne Street was Circus Street since that was the area in which circuses set up; formerly it had been the Hathorne pasture. "The Riding School and Circus was built nearly opposite Mr. Savage's house" on Broad Street. Hawthorne describes a circus in his *American Notebooks* for May 28, 1835. Almost twenty years later in England, he notes that an American circus in Liverpool had made him feel somewhat patriotic, but he observed, "As

12. *SG,* August 19, 1825, February 2 and March 30, 1827, and January 3, 1832; WB, *Diary,* 2:235; Jonathan Porter Felt to Mary Porter Felt White, June 1857, Felt-White Collection.

13. Robotti, *Chronicles,* 61; King, *When I Lived in Salem,* 19.

for the circus, I never was fond of that species of entertainment, nor do I find in this one the flash and glitter and whirl which I remember in other American exhibitions" (*CE* 23:123).[14]

Marvelous demonstrations of all sorts entertained Salem. Wax exhibitions of figures were brought to town in 1809, 1812, 1817, and 1820. Hawthorne remembered these also in his description of the Village-Hall in *The Blithedale Romance* (*CE* 3:196). In addition, Miss Honeywell ("Deformed" with "no hands" and "three toes") cut watch papers for the populace in February 1809. In 1811 Day Francis, "emperor of the Conjurers," entertained. Performances on the tightrope, ventriloquists, and the Siamese Twins Chang and Eng were also available. In October 1834 a "Mysterious Lady" appeared at the Mansion House. The *Observer* said that she was "thought to be gifted with a peculiar and strange facility and to possess a 'secret' which she inviolably 'kept.'" By December 1835, she had been exposed as a fraud in Buffalo, New York. She and the ventriloquist with her then fled. That lady is perhaps shown later, with modifications, in *The Blithedale Romance* (*CE* 3:201–2). Matthias the Prophet came in 1835, but he too was exposed as an imposter and jumped into the river and escaped. An apparatus composed of iron, copper, and brass for the purpose of walking on water was shown in 1837. A machine that could even teach grammar was exhibited by Joseph Knowlton in 1820. A Temple of Industry with "36 moving figures each working at different occupations" arrived in 1820, and Louisa Hawthorne attended (*CE* 15:128).[15]

On November 30, 1833, the *Salem Observer* advertised "Maelzel's Conflagration of Moscow with a Bass Fiddler, Automaton Speaking Figures and Slack Rope Dancers" at Franklin Hall. Mr. Maelzel had been in Vienna, Austria, when the French army penetrated the interior of Russia. Someone had ridden by him saying, "Moscow is in Flames!" This stirred him to write his production, which was a great hit. On December 14 the *Observer* noted that the show still commanded "closely wedged houses." Despite a threat to close the performance on December 21, it

14. *SG,* April 2, 1810; "Oliver Thayer's Reminiscences of Broad Street," copy, Francis Henry Lee Papers; NH, *Our Old Home and English Note-Books,* 2:422.

15. *SG,* March 25, 1817, January 24 and February 10, 1809, August 2, 1811, October 12, 1810, June 15, 1820, December 1 and September 5, 1835, August 17, 1838, September 8, 1835, and May 16, 1820; *Observer,* November 15, 1834; *SG,* October 31, 1834; WB, *Diary,* 4:402. For "the veiled lady" as an embodiment of mid–nineteenth-century trends, see Brodhead, "Veiled Ladies," 273–94; *ER,* April 5, 1820. Although the letter in which we learn that Louisa was going to the Temple of Industry is dated August 15, 1820 (*CE* 15:128), that particular entertainment is advertised in the *SG* only in April 1820. The last show was April 26.

was announced on December 28 that the exhibit was to be shown for one more week. In 1838 the *Observer* reported sadly that after Maelzel's death, the "Conflagration of Moscow" was sold in Philadelphia for only nine hundred dollars.[16]

Animal magnetism also interested Salemites. Monsieur Charles Poyen, famous practitioner, had lectured in Salem on mesmerism in September 1837. Dr. Robert H. Collyer had also spoken on the subject on August 10, 1841. Joshua H. Ward wrote Leverett Saltonstall in Washington on August 9, 1841, "We are all wide awake here about *Animal Magnetism.* We have had a course of lectures and experiments and great numbers have become converts." Elizabeth Elkins Sanders informed her daughter Mary Saltonstall on June 7, 1842, "Our Caroline who is not easily deceived you know, is in part a believer in this delusion, & was invited with the children to pass an evening at Dr. Barstows, where they were entertained with some experiments in magnetism."[17] Both Matthew Maule's hold over Alice Pyncheon in *The House of the Seven Gables* and the magical doings in *The Blithedale Romance* had plenty of stimulus in Salem.

Perhaps on a more elevated level were the many concerts and literary readings in Salem. Dr. Bentley had a singing school at East Church that Hawthorne's mother and his Aunt Mary had attended in 1792. There was a Handel Society and a Mozart Society, to say nothing of concerts by many traveling artists (most of them from Europe), and a Shaker Concert by the Chase Family. There were also various literary programs, including readings from Walter Scott, Shakespeare, and Annie Barbauld.[18]

LECTURES

In fact, there was no dearth of intellectual stimulation in the town. Long before the advent of the renowned Salem Lyceum, other lectures had been given. In 1812, Dr. Reuben Mussey and Dr. Daniel Oliver, brother of Hawthorne's tutor, had lectured on "Light" and "Chemistry." Various talks were given in the churches on such topics as temperance, horticulture, and botany. The Salem Charitable Merchants Association was organized in 1817, gathered a library, and had weekly lectures

16. *Observer,* November 30 and December 6, 14, 21, and 28, 1833, and August 25 and September 22, 1838.

17. WB, *Diary,* 2:40; Taylor Stoehr, *Hawthorne's Mad Scientists: Pseudoscience and Social Science in Nineteenth-Century Life and Letters,* 38; Saltonstall, *Papers, 1816–1845,* 3:164–65, 4:153–54.

18. See among others WB, *Diary,* 1:341; *ER,* January 14, 1818, and March 30, 1829; *SG,* March 13 and June 15, 1810, and February 24, 1826; *Salem Advertiser,* March 27, 1847.

during the winter season for about thirty-eight years. Conway Felton discussed the Acadians in 1828 under its auspices, and Hawthorne went to hear his lecture. Longfellow had been urging him to write a history of the Acadians (*CE* 16:220–21). On January 3, 1840, Rev. George E. Ellis, editor of the *Christian Examiner,* spoke on "Witches and Quakers." Salem's Quakers were incensed and demanded he not give his second lecture. Ellis won their favor, however, when he made it clear he was not categorizing the Salem Quakers of the 1840s, but of the 1650s.[19]

The Salem Lyceum was officially incorporated on March 4, 1830, "for the purpose of mutual instruction and rational entertainment by means of lectures etc." Daniel Appleton White, the father of Mary White Foote, was the first president and speaker. Nearly one thousand lectures were given. By 1832 there were twelve hundred members of the Lyceum, and others could buy tickets at the door. Women, however, had to be "introduced by a gentleman" before buying a ticket. Alfred Rosa asserts that the Lyceum "attracted almost every important lecturer to its platform." A look at the titles and orators certainly substantiates that claim. At first the Lyceum used Salemites for its programs, but very quickly it attracted others. There were talks on phrenology, Transcendentalism, temperance, Christianity, Salem witchcraft, and the leaders of New England (the latter two by Charles W. Upham). For the most part, all the lectures were successful.[20] The Lyceum was called "the theatre of New England," according to the October 6, 1838, issue of the *Observer.*

Hawthorne's presence at the lectures is difficult to document. In an undated letter to her mother, Sophia announced with excitement that her husband was actually going with her to a lecture, and she discussed the social activities involved.[21] Sophia, however, was sometimes inclined to be too optimistic. One account of Hawthorne's reaction to the lyceum hall may be found in *The Blithedale Romance.* The hall was "dedicated to that sober and pallid, or, rather, drab-colored, mode of winter evening entertainment, the Lecture" (*CE* 3:196). In "The Celestial Rail-road," he mentions "innumerable lecturers, who diffuse such a various profundity, in all subjects of human or celestial science, that any man may acquire an omnigenous erudition without the trouble of ever learning to read" (*CE* 10:198). These remarks sound as though Hawthorne had more

19. *SG,* October 8 and April 6, 1813, and February 13, 1827, and January 3, 7, 14, and 17, 1840; *Observer,* May 31, 1823; *ER,* June 14, 1830; Felt, *Annals,* 2d. ed., 2:38–39; Alfred Rosa, *Salem, Transcendentalism, and Hawthorne,* 28.

20. *History of Essex County,* 1:179–80; Rosa, *Salem, Transcendentalism and Hawthorne,* 12. Also see *Historical Sketch of the Salem Lyceum . . .*

21. RHL, *Memories,* 92.

of an acquaintance with the lectures than merely reading about them in the newspapers. Furthermore, in late 1848–1849 Hawthorne was the corresponding secretary of the Salem Lyceum, almost the only civic responsibility he ever undertook, even though George Holden maintained he was appointed "without his knowledge or consent."[22] He arranged for lectures with Thoreau (twice), E. P. Whipple, Emerson, Horace Mann, James T. Fields, and Bronson Alcott. Other lectures seem to have been prearranged, such as those by Louis Agassiz, or John S. Holmes, or Henry Colman. Hawthorne handled the correspondence whether he invited the speakers or not (*CE* 16:243–61).

THEATER

The history of the theater in Salem in Hawthorne's years in the town seems to be, like Gaul, divided into three parts. A performance of *Fortune's Frolic* was announced in the *Salem Gazette* on April 19, 1811. Then the *Essex Register* (May 3, 1820) reported that "after a lapse of 15–20 years we have again an opportunity of witnessing a Theatrical performance." Some members of the Boston Company appeared at Washington Hall, identified as the Washington Theater at the Essex Coffee House. Starting in April the actors performed twenty plays, including not only several Shakespeare plays, such as *Catherine and Petruchio or The Taming of the Shrew, Richard the Third, Romeo and Juliet,* and *MacBeth,* but also *Killing No Murder* and *Poor Soldier* in June. In May 1821 they produced *Honeymoon, or How to Rule a Wife.* Perhaps some of these were the plays that Hawthorne remembered years later in Liverpool when he spoke of "the mysterious glory that has surrounded theatrical representation, ever since my childhood."[23]

In November 1827, Salem tried again in a new theater on Crombie Street. Joseph G. Waters offered fifty dollars for the best poem written for the opening of the Salem Theater. In May *Isabella* was performed, and was reviewed by someone known only as "H." Several other plays were produced, but in February 1829 a negative vote to incorporate the Salem Theater was announced. In August 1829 the *Camden Journal* (South Carolina) reported that the Salem Theater Address was never used, "owing to some conscientious scruples on the part of the committee," but that "our readers will recognize in it the hand which has before

22. Holden, "Hawthorne among Friends," 264.
23. *ER,* June 17, 23, and 28, 1820; *SG,* May 18 and 29, July 11, and August 1 and 4, 1820; NH, *Our Old Home and English Note-Books,* 1:575. Also see Pat M. Ryan Jr., "Young Hawthorne at the Salem Theater," *EIHC* 94 (1958): 243–55.

amused them in similar straits." The first stanza was then given, a part of which follows:

> When first Moll Pitcher from her magic cell
> Around her votaries threw a magic spell. . . .
> Taste hung its head, Apollo feared to shine
> Our only stage was then, the Salem line.[24]

In that last line a connection was made, if only in punning, between the theater and the Manning family business. Perhaps the theater continued a little longer. The *New England Galaxy* reported in March 1831 that Master Burke at the Salem Theatre had had "good houses." But Orthodox Crombie Street Church bought the building that had housed the Salem Theater and dedicated it to religious service on November 22, 1832.[25]

In the late 1840s when Hawthorne was again in Salem, a semblance of theater had revived there. But from past experience, Hawthorne was skeptical, as indicated in his review in the *Salem Advertiser,* May 10, 1848: "But, it is hardly possible that a city of the size of Salem should support a theatre worthy of the name. . . . If we choose to have a theatre we must be content with melo drama instead of tragedy, and farce instead of comedy . . . the question occurs . . . whether it were not better to dispense with the Theatre altogether" (*CE* 23:255).

PAINTINGS, PANORAMAS, AND BOOKS
The showing of paintings and panoramas also kept Salem from being boring. Paintings by Rembrandt Peale, Colonel Henry Sargent, and Benjamin West were exhibited. West's "Christ Rejected" and "Death on a Pale Horse" were displayed in 1839. Hawthorne later penned a sketch of West for his *Biographical Stories for Children,* but in London, because of a "dreary picture of Lear," he remarked "(though it pains me to say it of so respectable a countryman) [West] had a gift of frigidity, a knack of grinding ice into his paint, a power of stupefying the spectator's perceptions and quelling his sympathy, beyond any other limner that ever handled a brush" (*CE* 5:230). The importance of paintings to Hawthorne has been amply shown in a recent book by Rita Gollin and John L. Idol Jr. Although much of Hawthorne's knowledge came

24. *SG,* November 29, 1827, and February 8, 1828; *ER,* February 9, 1829; *Camden Journal* [S.C.], August 22, 1829.
25. *New England Galaxy,* March 11, 1831; Irving Kinsman Annable, "Historical Notes of the Crombie Street Congregational Church, Salem, Massachusetts," 206.

after he met Sophia Peabody and especially during his European travels, the writers point out the opportunities in Salem during his youth: the collections of the East India Marine Society and in the homes of Salem that had been enriched by the wares brought back by her many sea captains.[26]

Salem harbored many artists who depicted people or scenes in the town. Hometown artist George Ropes painted pictures of the many ships in Salem Harbor. Various panoramas were presented, including several of the famous sea serpent in 1817. Many local citizens sat for portraits or miniatures by such artists as John Brewster, John Bache, J. Joye, Mrs. Antoine Mathieux, James Frothingham, A. Meucci, J. A. Cleveland, Sarah Lockheart Allen, and Manasseh Cutler Torrey. Of particular importance to Hawthorne were Charles Osgood (1809–1890), who painted his portrait, and perhaps painter George Southward (1803–1876), who was his cousin. In addition, there was the talent of Sophia Peabody, which became very important to him and which he used when she illustrated "The Gentle Boy." Her ability was evidenced all through their marriage: she painted their furniture, she decorated lamp shades, and she copied or painted pictures. Furthermore, she taught him the importance of art.[27]

Books also provided amusement and education. Henry Whipple, John Dabney, Thomas Porter, Samuel West, John D. Wilson, and Thomas Carey all had stores at various times in Hawthorne's youth. John W. Archer, brother of Hawthorne's teacher, opened his store in 1820. In 1826 John M. Ives had five thousand volumes in his Circulating Library. In August 1827 Louisa Hawthorne complained about the lack of literary knowledge of a Newburyport friend in a letter to her mother: "I don't believe she ever read John M. Ive's [sic] catalogues. Don't you think they ought to be distributed as tracts?" The Salem Athenaeum was made up of the pooled holdings of the Philosophical and Social libraries, which merged in 1810. In 1837 the Athenaeum had eight thousand volumes. William Manning owned a share from 1820–1827; Mary Manning was a member from 1826, a share which she later gave to Hawthorne. An added bonus may have been the presence of Edwin P. Whipple as librarian of the Athenaeum in some of these years. The

26. *SG*, July 6, 1821, and March 2, 1827; *Observer*, January 5, 1839; Rita K. Gollin and John L. Idol Jr., *Prophetic Pictures: Nathaniel Hawthorne's Knowledge and Uses of the Visual Arts*, 12–13.

27. For artists, see *SG*, May 4 and July 10, 1810, November 11, 1817, October 11, 1831, and October 23, 1835; Theodore Bolton, "New England Portrait Painters in Miniature: A Checklist," 131; Frederick Alan Sharf, "Charles Osgood: The Life and Times of a Salem Portrait Painter," 203–12; William Leavitt, "Notice of the Southward Family in Salem," 79.

Essex Historical Society (1821) and the Essex County Natural History Society (1833) eventually became the Essex Institute, which had fine holdings of books.[28]

In addition, various schools and instructors were available. Many teachers of French, especially Peter C. Louvrier, advertised their services. Teachers of navigation, military training, music, dancing, and sparring offered their specialties.[29] Many of these schools were for children, but adults could extend their learning if they chose.

CHURCHES AND GOOD CAUSES

The churches too afforded events of interest. There was a revival in Salem in 1824 when more than two hundred people "attended an inquiry meeting" that included both Baptists and Methodists. In the 1830s there were protracted services at churches that had all the trappings of revivals. Howard Street, Crombie Street, the Tabernacle meetinghouses, and the Methodist chapel all had such sessions. St. Peter's Episcopal Church raised a new building, as did North and East Churches. And the Mormons had a meeting in town.[30]

Salem also had many benevolent societies. A long list of such societies filled a page of the *Salem Gazette* on August 2, 1816. Many of these societies were the work of Salem women: the Female Auxiliary Education Society; the Salem Female Society on Educating Heathen Children; and the Clarkson Society. In addition, there was also the Salem Society for Moral and Religious Instruction of the Poor, and the Marine Bible Society. No cause escaped notice. The work being done for the education of the blind in Boston prompted the ladies of Salem to have a fair in April 1833. Nancy Forrester Barstow collected $2,957 for the New England Institute for the Blind from the proceeds of the Salem Fair. Sarah Savage wrote a children's book, *Blind Miriam* (1833), which was sold for the cause. The Salem Anti-Slavery Society was begun in 1834, just a year after the Essex Society was started by fellow Essex Countian William Lloyd Garrison. The Essex County Temperance Society began in July 1835. William Manning bought the Lafayette Coffee House, which was "well calculated for a temperance tavern." This had not always been

28. *SG,* October 26, 1810, May 9, 1820, and February 28, 1826; *ER,* August 5, 1818, March 11, 1820, and June 26, 1819; C. Deidre Phelps, "Printing, Publishing, and Bookselling in Salem, Massachusetts, 1825–1900," 265–95; LMH to ECH, August 12, 1827, Berg Collection; Edwin M. Bacon, *Literary Pilgrimages in New England,* 215.

29. *SG,* May 8, 1810, February 15, 1810, March 2, 1810, March 16, 1810, and May 15, 1835.

30. *Boston Recorder,* August 21, 1824; Tolles with Tolles, *Architecture in Salem,* 113, 178–79, 13–14; *SG,* August 23, 1836.

the mood of Salem. On December 9, 1817, the *Gazette* had listed "six-score" different ways of saying that you or someone else was drunk.[31]

CRIMINAL TRIALS

One of the most absorbing occupations during Hawthorne's residence was attendance at or reading about criminal trials. The trial and execution of Stephen Clark of Newburyport in 1821, "the last public hanging for arson," was noticed by Hawthorne, even though he did not attend (*CE* 15:141). Richard and George Crowninshield were brought up on petit larceny charges in 1827 and acquitted. In 1833 George Barrell Cheever was tried for libel by Deacon John Stone, a distiller, and imprisoned for thirty days. Caroline L. Smith wrote Francis Lee in 1884 about her memory of that long-ago time:

> My father was of course Dr. Cheever's jailer-in-chief. . . . When the thirty days of his sentence were expired . . . father went down at midnight to liberate him. It was a beautiful night and as Doctor C came out, thoughts of the quiet hours of soul-communion when he was shut in alone with God in his cell, rushed over him and he was so affected that he requested the privilege of one more midnight hour there alone, which, of course, was granted.[32]

Cheever's experience was certainly in Hawthorne's mind, but a far more important event during Hawthorne's apprenticeship as a writer was the murder of Captain Joseph White of Salem and the ensuing litigation. Some scholars have mentioned these events as influential in the formation of *The House of the Seven Gables.* Robert Cantwell made it extremely important and saw Hawthorne as some sort of government agent, leaving town during the trial in order to escape scrutiny. Subsequently, Alfred Rosa followed this lead. Others such as Arlin Turner and James R. Mellow give the trial little or no space. More recently Brook Thomas in his bid to make Judge Joseph Story one of the villains satirized in *The House of the Seven Gables* makes much provocative use of the trial.[33]

---

31. *ER,* September 16, 1818, and April 21, 1819; *SG,* March 28 and June 22, 1819, November 3, 1826, and November 18, 1836; [Sarah Savage], *Blind Miriam, Restored to Sight.* My thanks to Laura E. Wasowicz, Senior Cataloguer of American Children's Books at the American Antiquarian Society, for helping me identify this book as Savage's.

32. Robert Ellis Cahill, *New England's Cruel and Unusual Punishments,* 67; Caroline L. Smith to Lee, March 3, 1884, Scrapbook, 1:206–11, copy, Francis Henry Lee Papers. Nehemiah Brown, the jailor in 1830, was also the Tyler-appointed surveyor of the Custom House whom Hawthorne replaced.

33. Cantwell, *Nathaniel Hawthorne,* 149; Rosa, *Salem, Transcendentalism, and Hawthorne,* 34; Mellow, *Hawthorne in His Times,* 291; Brook Thomas, *Cross-Examinations*

The murder electrified every citizen of the vicinity. Joseph Story wrote Daniel Webster that he never knew "such a universal panic. It is not confined to Salem, or Boston, but seems to pervade the whole community. We are all astounded & looking to know from what corner the next blow will come—There is a universal dread & sense of insecurity, as if we lived in the midst of a Banditti." Caroline King wrote of her French teacher "coming in great terror to my mother. . . . saying, 'Oh, this horrible America where people murder each other not for cause! I have had a bolt put on my chamber door, but sleep I shall not tonight.'" King continued, "I remember that the same kind of unreasoning terror spread through the whole community in the first bewilderment of that fearful news which shook our peaceful little town to its centre. . . . Nobody could guess at first the why and wherefore of the murder nor knew who would be the next victim." According to Louisa L. Dressel, a cousin and writer of the preface of her book, King shortly before her death had destroyed a chapter in the book on the White murder because she felt it "to be indiscreet." Leverett Saltonstall Jr., son of the lawyer and representative to Congress, described in his reminiscences in 1885 the shock in his family in learning the news. He added, "Who that was then living can forget the Committee of Vigilance, the proscribed list of prominent men which was reported and believed to exist."[34]

The victim, Captain Joseph White (1748–1830), was a very wealthy merchant, shipowner, and former slaver, who lived in the eastern part of Salem, not far from the Manning house. He and his late wife had no children, but he was good to many of his relatives. He employed Mrs. Mary Beckford, the daughter of his deceased brother, as his housekeeper. She was, as remembered by former Salemite William Driver in 1884, "a fine looking woman of about forty or forty-five . . . a truly clever woman, not too old to love or be loved." According to Driver, White was not on good terms with either Stephen or Jack White, his nephews, and made a new will leaving his money to Mrs. Beckford. The actions of her son-in-law, Joseph Knapp, led him to make yet another will, leaving only a small legacy to Mrs. Beckford. The will now benefited his nephew, Stephen, a lawyer who lived in Tremont House in Boston. Not so lucky

---

of *Law and Literature: Cooper, Hawthorne, Stowe, and Melville,* 56–63. The following do not mention the trial: G. Lathrop, *Study of Hawthorne;* Turner, *Hawthorne;* Miller, *Salem Is My Dwelling Place;* and Herbert, *Dearest Beloved.*

34. Daniel Webster, *The Papers of Daniel Webster,* 3:310; King, *When I Lived in Salem,* 163–64, 9; Leverett Saltonstall [Jr.], "Leverett Saltonstall's Reminiscences of Salem Written in 1885," 62. His own father was one of them.

was his nephew John or "Jack" who complained of his treatment by his uncle, especially in his "strange, unexpected . . . cruel will."[35]

Captain White was eighty-two years old when he was bludgeoned and stabbed thirteen times on the night of April 6, 1830. The event was so horrifying that immediately a Committee of Vigilance with twenty-seven members was formed. The head of the committee was Hawthorne's relative by marriage, Dr. Gideon Barstow. This committee was given the "power to search the house and interrogate any person." The ensuing events reminded many of the witchcraft days. It is perhaps no coincidence that Charles W. Upham delivered his first lectures on witchcraft the next January. He was probably working on them during that fateful summer.[36]

Among the villains of the case were two Knapp brothers, Joseph Jenkins (1804–1831) and John Francis (1811–1830), sons of a respectable Salem family. Joseph, the husband of Mrs. Beckford's daughter, was supposedly the instigator of the plot. The Knapps labored under a common delusion that the childless White had by law to leave his money at death equally divided among his possible heirs if no will was found. The plan was to find and destroy the will and to murder the old man. Joseph did find and destroy a will, but not the right one. Frank Knapp hired Richard Crowninshield Jr. to do the murder. Richard's brother, George, was also in the conspiracy.

Henry Colman, minister of the new Barton Square Independent Church, went to see Joseph Knapp in jail and obtained a confession from him that Joseph later nullified by refusing to testify. Colman's action caused the wrath of many, including the father of the Knapps and their brother Phippen, a young lawyer. Colman and Phippen Knapp gave directly opposite testimony about Colman's role in the case. The attorney general of Massachusetts said that he had given Colman authority to try to get confessions from both Knapps and to offer them immunity if they did confess. If Phippen was lying to save his brothers, he was another victim of the trials. The minister's role throughout the affair was ambiguous; he left Salem and the ministry the next year.[37]

The Knapp family belonged to the society of the East Church, now

35. William Driver to Lee, December 22, 1884, Scrapbook, 3:42–46, copy, Francis Henry Lee Papers; John White to Andrew Dunlap, May 11, 1830, Andrew Dunlap Papers. For summaries of the case, see George Ticknor Curtis, *Life of Daniel Webster*, 1:378–80, or Thomas J. Allen, *The Accomplice: The Truth on Vigilanti Salem: Hawthorne, Melville, Robert Rantoul, Jr., and the Captain White Murder Case*.

36. *SG*, April 13, 1830.

37. *SG*, August 31, September 3, and November 12, 1830.

under the ministry of James Flint. He testified that "he had once visited F. Knapp in his cell, about two or three weeks after his arrest—had known him for eight years—but had known little of him for the last 5 years. About 5 years ago, when a school boy, he was enticed away and ran off, causing great distress to his family. . . . He was soon after sent to sea." The Crowninshield boys were among the last of the illustrious family in Salem that had succeeded the Derbys in importance in the town. The elder George Crowninshield had left sons. One of them, Benjamin W. Crowninshild, had been secretary of the navy and a representative in Congress. Another son, George, had built the ship *Cleopatra's Barge* and had been an illustrious privateer in the War of 1812. Brother Jacob had also served in Washington. Another brother still was Richard, who broke the pattern by moving to New York, marrying an Irish lady, and eventually returning to Danvers, where he opened a cloth factory. In April 1819 William Bentley had commented on the Richard Crowninshields, "The tales of this family exhibit something yet unknown in this part of the country for want of domestic economy, education of children, management of affairs & conduct among their servants & neighbours." Richard's two sons, Richard Jr. and George, were machinists and ne'er-do-wells. The two Crowninshield boys were first cousins to Sarah Hathorne Crowninshield's long-dead husband. She at least was spared any disgrace, since she had died in 1829.[38]

The trials of the conspirators lasted from August to December 1830. The Knapps were suspected of conspiracy when their respectable sea-captain father received an anonymous letter that seemed to be about the murder. He turned it over to the Committee of Vigilance, only to have the letter implicate his own children. A special session of the Supreme Court of Massachusetts was called to hear the evidence. Three judges, including Salem's Samuel Putnam, presided over the first trial, which ended in a hung jury. Richard Crowninshield in June had committed suicide in his jail cell, after learning that the trials had to have a principal before accessories could be convicted. He evidently thought that his death would spare the others. Frank was then tried as a principal, after legal maneuvering by Daniel Webster. Webster proved that there had been a conspiracy and that Frank's presence in a nearby street during the murder somehow made him a principal. Rufus Choate later said that Webster had established "the truth of his own: inferring a conspiracy to which the prisoner was a party, from

38. *SG,* August 20, 1830; William T. Whitney Jr., "The Crowninshields of Salem, 1800–1808," 103; WB, *Diary,* 4:586; *Ladies' Miscellany,* January 20, 1829.

circumstances acutely ridiculed by the able counsel opposing him as 'Stuff'—but woven by him into strong and uniform tissue." At the trial Webster, who had been brought in as a friend to the prosecution, made a speech that Claude Moore Fuess observed "has become part of the tradition of the American Bar."[39]

Webster's speech is powerful. Parts of it may well have influenced Hawthorne in his later writing. F. O. Matthiessen suggested in *American Renaissance* that one should compare Webster's speech with Hawthorne's piece on the death of Judge Pyncheon. Webster said, "The assassin enters, through the window already prepared, into an unoccupied apartment. With noiseless foot he paces the lonely hall, half lighted by the moon. . . . The room was uncommonly open to the admission of light. The face of the innocent sleeper was turned from the murderer, and the beams of the moon, resting on the locks of his aged temple, showed him where to strike." The emphasis on the moonlight and the dead man reminds one forcefully of Hawthorne's picture of the dead Judge Pyncheon. Brook Thomas sees influence of the trial not only in *The House of the Seven Gables* but also in "Mr. Higginbotham's Catastrophe," which seems less likely to me.[40] But it does appear that parts of *The Scarlet Letter,* especially the passage where Arthur Dimmesdale feels the urge to confess his guilt, may have had some connection to this passage in Webster's speech:

> He feels it beating at his heart, rising to his throat, and demanding disclosure. He thinks the whole world sees it in his face, reads it in his eyes, and almost hears its workings in the very silence of his thoughts. It has become his master. It betrays his discretion, it breaks down his courage, it conquers his prudence . . . the fatal secret struggles with still greater violence to burst forth. It must be confessed, *it will be confessed;* there is no refuge from confession but suicide, and suicide is confession.[41]

When Hester heard Dimmesdale's last sermon, she could "detect the same cry of pain. What was it? The complaint of the human heart, sorrow-laden, perchance guilty, telling its secret, whether of guilt or sorrow, to the great heart of mankind; beseeching its sympathy or

---

39. Rufus Choate, *A Discourse Delivered before the Faculty, Students, and Alumni of Dartmouth College on the Day Preceding Commencement, July 27, 1853, Commemorative of Daniel Webster,* 30; Claude Moore Fuess, *Daniel Webster,* 2:292; *SG,* June 18, 1830.

40. Francis Otto Matthiessen, *American Renaissance: Art and Expression in the Age of Emerson and Whitman,* 214; Allan L. Benson, *Daniel Webster,* 197–99; Thomas, *Cross-Examinations,* 264n3.

41. Benson, *Daniel Webster,* 193–99.

forgiveness,—at every moment,—in each accent,—and never in vain!" (*CE* 1:243–44).

That Hawthorne followed these judicial events is sure. He wrote his cousin John S. Dike on September 1, 1830, about the trials:

> The town now begins to grow rather more quiet than it has been since the murder of Mr. White. . . . Frank Knapp's situation seems to make little or no impression on his mind. The night after his sentence, he joked and laughed with the men who watched him, with as much apparent gaiety as if he had been acquitted, instead of condemned. . . . It is reported also that he declares that he will not go to the gallows, unless two women go with him. . . . Perhaps you have not heard that many people suspect Mrs. Beckford and her daughter, Joe Knapp's wife, of being privy to the whole affair before the murder was committed. (*CE* 15:207)

Frank Knapp was executed on September 28 and his brother on December 31, 1830. Joseph Barlow Felt reported that "more than 4000 spectators witnessed each of their melancholy exits."[42]

George Crowninshield was acquitted because he had an alibi, since he was with two prostitutes on the night in question. That he knew about the murder was never in doubt, and he was not popular afterward with his fellow townfolk. Hawthorne observed to John S. Dike in September 1831 that "George Crowninshield . . . seems not at all cast down by what has taken place. I saw him walk by our house, arm-in-arm with a girl about a month since" (*CE* 15:217). In December 1830 Margaret Heussler Felt wrote to her husband in Virginia that "[George] Crowninshield, they say is everyday seen with his old companions, he was over in Northfields on thanksgiving day afternoon, playing keel with vile fellows. Mr Shillaber [Ebenezer Shillaber, Crowninshield's attorney] says he trembles for George, for he hoped a full and thorough refformation [*sic*] would have followed his acquittal, but fears it will not." Joseph A. Willard in his recollections (1895) remarked that George lived a long time and that he saw him as a witness in a case "many years later" in which a lawyer kept asking him where he had lived, and that George kept avoiding the name of Salem until directly asked. He was then dismissed as a witness.[43]

Hawthorne was living on Dearborn Street in North Salem during 1830, but he could well have been a spectator of the trials and executions. A

---

42. Felt, *Annals,* 2d ed., 2:466; *SG,* September 28, 1830, and January 4, 1831.
43. Margaret Heussler Felt to Jonathan Porter Felt, December [13] 1830, Felt-White Collection; Joseph A. Willard, *Half a Century with Judges and Lawyers,* 149.

writer in the *Salem Gazette* of August 20, 1830 (one presumes it was Caleb Foote), observed, "While Mr. Webster was closing the cause [*sic*] we observed that the windows of the houses near the Court House were filled with attentive listeners. Hundreds of individuals were also gathered around the house, being enabled by the powerful voice and distinct enunciation of Mr. W. to hear the greater part of his address to the Jury, from the street."

Hawthorne had other connections with the case. The Knapps had once lived at the corner of Derby and Herbert Streets. Not only was Gideon Barstow, father of "Little Annie," the head of the Committee of Vigilance, but Ann Savage's father, Ezekiel Savage, had been the magistrate before whom the Crowninshields were first arraigned. Another witness, John R. C. Palmer Jr., had stayed for two weeks at the Lafayette Coffee House, which William Manning owned and where he presumably boarded. John Forrester Jr., a cousin, had testified on behalf of Frank Knapp; so had Zachariah Burchmore Jr. The *Salem Gazette* on August 6 and 13, 1830, pointed out that Webster accused Hawthorne's later friend of lying: "This witness stands in a much worse plight than . . . the others. It is difficult to reconcile all he has said with any belief in the accuracy of his recollections." Still another witness was John Felt Webb, a cousin through the Phelpses. Webb was the counting room clerk to John Forrester, the father of John Forrester Jr. and cousin to Hawthorne.[44]

Forrester was a Democrat. So was Robert Rantoul Jr. who helped with the defense and who always felt that one of the defendants did not get a fair trial. He was convinced that his political leanings were held against him. Although admitted to the bar in 1829, Rantoul was not yet a member of the court, and he was replaced by William H. Gardiner, who said, according to the press, that the prosecution was conducted with the "asperity of private hostility." Webster, of course, was a leading Federalist or National Republican. So was Gideon Barstow. There is just enough evidence to make one wonder about the political ramifications of this trial.[45] There were other mystifying circumstances. Just after Joseph Knapp was convicted, in December 1830, the *Salem Gazette* published a long editorial maintaining that the facts had not been fully ascertained. The writer felt that the prime mover behind the Knapps

44. "Murder of Mr. White," *Ladies' Miscellany* 2 (1830): 35, taken from the *ER*, April 12, 1830.

45. See Thomas, *Cross-Examinations,* for a cogent explanation of the politics involved in the trial.

had not been caught, that people had tried to make sure that the Knapps did not tell all they knew. The December 21 *Gazette* continued, "Further prosecutions will undoubtedly take place, whatever may be the condition in life of the offender, whether high or low, rich or poor, if the prosecuting officers obtain sufficient evidence."

But no other prosecution followed, and the end of the trials left unanswered questions. This is what Hawthorne had suggested earlier. In December also Stephen White wrote to Daniel Webster that

> the wretched woman Mrs. . . . Beckford had sent him a private message intimating her wish that I should not interfere to obtain a commutation for J J Knapp Jr. The message said she thought it better he should be hung! . . . She seeks his life to smother further investigation. . . . This I know will not take you by surprise for I have long seen where your suspicians pointed but it horrifies me who have always thought her very weak but not very wicked. She must be a very devil.[46]

Fearful of libel, the editor of the *Gazette* did not give names to his suspicions. This editorial occurred in the same issue of the *Gazette* as "An Old Woman's Tale." Indeed, just at the end of the trials there was a whole outpouring of Hawthorne's first essays and stories: "The Battle Omen" on November 2; "The Hollow of the Three Hills" on November 12; "Sir William Phips" on November 23; "Mrs. Hutchinson" on December 7; "An Old Woman's Tale" on December 21; and "Dr. Bullivant" on January 11, 1831. If one reads them, as did the people of Salem, in conjunction with or just after the events of that year, another dimension is seen in these tales.

In addition to the use he made of this murder in *The House of the Seven Gables,* Hawthorne kept mulling over other connected ideas. In 1840 he recorded in his journal, "A Coroner's inquest on a murdered man—the gathering of the jury to be described, and the characters of the members; some with secret guilt upon their souls" (*CE* 8:185). In November 1847, when Hawthorne was living again in Salem, he wrote in his notebook that the Committee of Vigilance would be "good as the machinery for a sketch or story" (*CE* 8:279). In 1852 when he was examining the records of the church at Gosport on the Isle of Shoals, he noted the baptism of Joseph White, "murdered more than fourscore years afterwards in Salem" (*CE* 8:550). It was not an event easily forgotten.

The quality of life in Salem was certainly not dull, although many of its citizens seemed to think so. Even the constantly optimistic Leverett Saltonstall repeatedly called it so in his letters. Perhaps any town of the

46. Webster, *Papers,* 3:90.

time may have had similar characteristics, but one of Salem's citizens had the imagination to take this raw stuff and make it live. Hawthorne did not have to participate in all these activities to know something about them. He spoke often of his preference for being a spectator of rather than a participant in events. But these happenings were available, and bits and pieces of them surface in his works. "Dull old Salem" had its uses after all.

8

Politics
"THE ITCH OF FACTION"

Ever since he was of capacity to read a newspaper, this person had prided himself on his consistent adherence to one political party, but, in the confusion of these latter days, had got bewildered and knew not whereabouts his party was. (*CE* 10:303)

NATHANIEL HAWTHORNE was once asked why he was a Democrat. He replied disingenuously, "Because I live in a democratic country," which was, of course, no answer at all.[1] In such a Federalist town as Salem it does seem strange at first glance that he was a steadfast member of the party called Republican and then Democrat. Yet he was employed as a Democrat by the Boston Custom House and the Salem Custom House, and was given the consulate in Liverpool not only with the help of friends (not all Democrats) but also because of his political leanings, despite his frequent disclaimers. He also wrote for Democratic periodicals and he often spoke of politics in his writings, even though he and others frequently said he was not interested in public affairs.[2]

It is the origin of his particular orientation that interests me. Why was he a Democrat and possibly a Locofoco to boot, despite Sophia's remark

---

1. Stearns, *Nathaniel Hawthorne,* 130.
2. For instance, EPP wrote to Elizabeth Davis Bliss Bancroft, November 6, 1838, that "Mr. Bancroft asked me if he was 'interested in politics' & I thought looked disappointed when I said I thought not . . ." (EPP, *Letters,* 218). In a letter written by EMH to EPP in 1840 or 1841, she urged, "Do not tell him you hope the *Whigs* will do something for him. He might think himself bound in honour to make some demonstration of his Zeal for democracy" (C. E. Frazer Clark Jr., "New Light on the Editing of the 1842 Edition of *Twice-Told Tales* . . ." 95).

to her mother in the summer of 1849, "my husband supposed he was removed [from the Custom House] because he was a Democrat (and you know very well how he has always been a Democrat, not a Locofoco—if that means a lucifer match.)" The term "loco-foco" came into existence in the 1830s when the machine politicians of New York turned off the gas lights "and forced the radicals to use 'loco foco' matches so they could continue their meeting and declare their principles." Hawthorne used that term about Eben Hathorne when he said that Eben gave "vent to the most arrant democracy and locofocoism, that I have happened to hear; saying that nobody ought to possess wealth longer than his own life" (*CE* 8:75). Henry Longfellow in a letter to George Washington Greene on July 23, 1839, declared, "The *Loco-focos* are organizing a new politico-literary system. They shout Hosanna to every *loco-foco* authorling, and speak coolly of, if they do not abuse, every other. They puff Bryant loud and long; likewise my good friend *Hawthorne* of *Twice-Told Tales.*"[3]

I contend that, though he may not have been a Locofoco (and that term was time-bound anyway), he became a Democrat for at least three reasons: the friends and events of his early life in Salem, including Andrew Jackson's part in the War of 1812; an identification with or reaction to many of his larger family; and his ideological bent. Hawthorne first seems to have indicated a political preference by joining the Athenaeum Club at Bowdoin College, in which were his friends Horatio Bridge, Jonathan Cilley, and Franklin Pierce, all Democrats. In his 1852 biography of Franklin Pierce he acknowledged, "My sympathies and opinions, it is true—so far as I had any in public affairs,—had, from the first been enlisted on the same side with his own." In the same book he asserted that in 1827, 1828, and 1829 "the contest for the presidency had been fought with a fervor that drew almost everybody into it, on one side or the other and had terminated in the triumph of Andrew Jackson" (*CE* 23:287).

Although political contests were usually rife with fervor, each party had many factions, a fact that makes the whole matter confusing at times. The Federalist party in Massachusetts fell apart in 1824, went through a period from 1829 to 1834 when it called itself the National Republicans, and finally in 1834 coalesced into the Whig party. The Republicans at the turn of the nineteenth century became the Jackson party in the late 1820s and 1830s, even called itself the Liberal party at one point, were

3. RHL, *Memories*, 98; Arthur B. Darling, *Political Changes in Massachusetts 1824–1848: A Study of Liberal Movements in Politics*, 189n34; *Letters of Longfellow*, ed. Hilen, 2:162.

the Locofocos for a while, and finally became Democrats. In Boston, particularly, there was a Statesman party in 1821 and a Workingmen's party in the late 1830s that was allied eventually with the Democrats.[4]

But it was in Salem, I suggest, that Hawthorne received his initial impetus. The town into which he was born was fiercely divided politically. For a time after the conclusion of the Revolution there was surface unanimity. Tories were forgotten or remained elsewhere; George Washington was venerated; John Adams was one of their own. The Derby family was supreme. By 1800, however, the Crowninshields, who by all the signs should have been Federalists but were not, were challenging the Federalist Derbys. Elias Haskett Derby had died in 1799, and his expensive mansion on Essex Street was lived in briefly by a son but for the most part lay empty until it was torn down in 1815. As the Derbys' power, for various reasons, declined, the Crowninshields, as William T. Whitney Jr. says, filled the void.[5]

The Crowninshields were descended from the German physician Johannes Kasper von Kroninshieldt. Salem's primary citizens in the early nineteenth century were George Crowninshield and his sons. When Federalist Timothy Pickering lost an election to Jacob Crowninshield in 1802, the *Gazette* cried foul, and concluded, "It is now proved, we confess, that 'our family' can do what they please in this town." "Our family" was the Crowninshield family, a member of which had made just this statement on October 29, 1802. This perceived arrogance was remembered in 1819 when young George Crowninshield was found, after his death, to have had a mistress and an illegitimate daughter, Clara, who became later a friend of Longfellow's.[6] It was also remembered in 1830 when members of the family, albeit the black sheep, were very much involved in the White murder trial.

Some of the family fierceness is illustrated in the *Salem Gazette* when Benjamin W. Crowninshield went to Thomas C. Cushing, editor, and complained about treatment given Joseph Story in the paper:

> Capt. B[enjamin] . . . Crowninshield laboured to impress upon me [Cushing observed], that many of my publications had been highly improper and injurious. . . . His father, he said, was a man of strong passions; and he apprehended that had he met with me on a former occasion, when a writer in my paper called him the leader of the

4. Darling, *Political Changes,* 3, 52, 178, 42, 99; *ER,* March 9, 1811; *SG,* May 15, 1829, and April 24, 1835.

5. Whitney, "Crowninshields," 15.

6. [Clara Crowninshield], *The Diary of Clara Crowninshield: A European Tour with Longfellow, 1835–1836,* xv-xvii.

Jacobin party, the consequences would have been serious to me. He said that his brother George had thought I came near attacking his private character—that he was very powerful, and that if I should do anything of the kind, I should repent it. (November 11, 1802)

The "family" lived in the eastern end of Salem; in fact, it was George Crowninshield's house that was later torn down to make way for the present Custom House. The Crowninshields were allied with Nathaniel Silsbee, Colonel John Hathorne, and Dr. William Bentley. In 1800 the Republicans started a newspaper, the *Register,* then called the *Impartial Register,* to reflect their views. In 1803 Salem began marking the Fourth of July with two distinct celebrations: each faction, the Federalists and the Republicans, usually had a speaker, a military muster, and a dinner. The Federalists ejected the Republicans from their "Court Balls"; hence, the Crowninshields, the Storys, the Silsbees, and the Hathornes could no longer go. These bitter divisions were primarily local in origin. As Whitney says, "Salem politics, then, had at stake supremacy in Salem itself."[7] Most of these Salem Republicans were not for Jefferson; they did not all celebrate Jefferson's second inaugural.

Closely allied at first with the Crowninshields was Joseph Story (1779–1845). Story was a Republican (but evidently not always trusted as such) in his early law practice. He was a state senator and member and Speaker of the U.S. House of Representatives. He gave the oration at the memorial service for Captain James Lawrence and Lieutenant Augustus Ludlow, which the Federalists mostly ignored, in 1813, but he bitterly opposed the Embargo by President Jefferson and composed the first formal protest, which caused the president to say that he "ascribe[d] all this to one pseudo-Republican Story." That was not the only time he was out of step with his party, and that fierce Republican, William Bentley, said that he had "brainless ambition and deficient principles."[8]

Story was appointed in 1811 at a very young age to the U.S. Supreme Court, where he became a fast friend of Chief Justice John Marshall. He was also appointed to the Dane Professorship of Law at Harvard and, according to Brook Thomas, appeared to be a man who used his connections with the powerful Crowninshield family to his own advantage and eventually to their disadvantage. Story succeeded Benjamin W. Crowninshield as president of the Salem Merchants' Bank, rose over Crowninshield in the Massachusetts legislature, and maneuvered him

---

7. Whitney, "Crowninshields," 34.
8. Priscilla Sawyer Lord and Virginia Clegg Gamage, *Marblehead: The Spirit of '76 Lives Here,* 148; WB, *Diary,* 4:307.

out of a seat in Congress. He was very much involved in the legislation arising from the Yazoo affair (the *Fletcher v. Peck* case) in which New England speculators were somewhat protected from ruin. As Thomas says, Story's views began to change after he reached the Supreme Court. He became very conservative and knew how to manipulate the system to further his own ends.[9]

The *Salem Gazette* published a poem on November 5, 1802, that Benjamin F. Browne said concerned Story, who is referred to as Josey S. . . . the L. . . . r. The subject of the lyric is said to hide "with smiles the venom'd heart." He "glibly moves the oily tongue." He "seems so humble, though so proud." The ballad ends:

> Long may his health and power abound,
> For Satan's self was never found
> To spread the itch of faction round
> Like Josey S. . . . the L. . . . r.

For those who believe that Hawthorne based his picture of Judge Pyncheon on Story, the whole poem illustrates the likenesses. What it does not do is to give the writer a strong enough motive to use Story in that way. This poem is copied in Benjamin F. Browne's papers, and Hawthorne could have learned of it through him or through his reading of the *Gazette*.[10]

The political battle was fiercely waged by the town's newspapers. The *Gazette* promoted the Federalists. The editor of the Republican *Register,* William Carlton, had been jailed for printing libelous material on Timothy Pickering in a supplement to the *Salem Register* (October 28, 1802). He did not reveal the author of the libel, but his identity has been guessed to be William Bentley. When Carlton died in 1805, the paper was edited for two years by Dr. Bentley for the proprietors, Jacob Crowninshield, John Hathorne Jr., and Joshua Ward. The feud between the Derbys and the Crowninshields ended in 1806, but the struggle between the factions continued. The fight now seemed to be between the Crowninshields and those whom Bentley called the "Pickeronians." Timothy Pickering (1745–1829) and his son John (1777–1846) were often castigated by Bentley in his diary and in his column in the *Register.* Hawthorne too was aware of the Pickerings. In his sketch "The Book of Autographs" he characterized Pickering as "upright" and "sternly

9. Thomas, *Cross-Examinations,* 62.
10. Poem to "ridicule Justice Story," vol. 3, Browne's book, Benjamin F. Browne Papers.

inflexible," and recalled, "In our boyhood we used to see a thin, severe figure of an ancient man, time-worn, but apparently indestructible, moving with a step of vigorous decay along the street, and knew him as 'Old Tim Pickering'" (*CE* 11:372). He noted too Timothy Pickering's "Easy Plan of Discipline for a Militia" in the *American Magazine of Useful and Entertaining Knowledge*.[11] In "Grimshawe" the narrator speaks of John Pickering (Timothy's son) as "a lawyer of the town, a man of classical and antiquarian tastes, as well as legal acquirement" (*CE* 12:435). Later in Rome, he knew Mary Orne Pickering (1805–1886), the daughter of John Pickering (*CE* 14:139).

One reason that Hawthorne became a Democrat in the first place was, I suspect, a reaction to the fierce political battles in the Salem of his youth, particularly in what must have been a pivotal event in his early life: the War of 1812. The Embargo and the war proved decisive in the split of parties. The Federalist *Gazette* contemptuously called it "Mr. Madison's War." The partisans not only did not attend the same assemblies nor use the same halls but also did not even attend the same churches. The Federalists for the most part attended North and First Churches, and the Republicans attended East and Howard Street Churches. The military units were also divided politically. The Salem Light Infantry was Federalist and helped its party celebrate on the Fourth. In 1814, William Orne, a Federalist merchant, wrote his friend and captain, Jonathan P. Felt, "The 4th July we had an important and excellent oration delivered by Saltonstall and the largest procession we ever had. [T]he dem^{ct} had *none.* . . . [T]he Demos I found kept cussing and damning the Tory bells for ringing in the procession. . . . [T]he Officers of the British Cartell walked and went to the Meetinghouse to hear the oration."[12] The degree of partisanship extended even to the view of the enemy. The Federalists were against France, not England, and it was *British* officers who attended their Fourth of July celebration!

When the *Chesapeake* and the *Shannon* fought offshore in June 1813, a Salem ship, captained by George Crowninshield, was sent to Halifax to bring back the bodies of Lawrence and Ludlow, killed in the

11. James Duncan Phillips, "Political Fights and Local Squabbles in Salem 1800–1806," 6–8; WB, *Diary,* 4:158 and 4:14, comments, "T. Pickering's Letters as they issue, are read and praised by one party, & they are read and ridiculed by the other. . . . A greater Egotist never existed." The *Salem Register* became the *Essex Register* in 1807; [NH], "Revolutionary Sentiments," 496.

12. William Dismore Chapple, "Salem and the War of 1812," 296, 297; Charles Cotesworth Beaman, "The Branch or Howard Street Church," 273; M. C. D. Silsbee, *A Half-Century,* 76; William Orne to Jonathan P. Felt, July 6, 1814, Felt-White Collection.

battle. The bodies "were placed in barges and [were] preceded by a long procession of boats filled with seamen uniformed in blue jackets and trousers, with a blue ribbon on their hats bearing the motto of 'Free Trade and Sailors' Rights.'" There was a fierce dispute about the location for a memorial service. North Church refused to have it; East Church was too small. The ceremony finally took place on August 23, 1813, at the Branch Church on Howard Street, which was decorated with cypress and evergreen. The procession moved up Union Street from the wharf; bells tolled; crowds gathered. Afterward a party was given by Susan Ingersoll.[13] Prominent Federalists did not attend these events, although many other Salemites did.

The guns of a war that was fought, in part at least, in the young artist's harbor could be expected to reverberate in his later work. Julian Hawthorne subsequently pointed out that his father's "imagination . . . was . . . nourished by tales of the War of 1812 . . . related to him by his elders." Involved with the war Salem certainly was, albeit ambivalently. Verbal battle lines were fiercely drawn, and opinions were divided, but the war engulfed the town nonetheless. Forty privateers were sent to sea by Salem; some came back with prizes, but twenty-six never came back at all. Cartels bringing captured, repatriated Americans arrived from Halifax or Barbados. On the other hand, a prison ship for captured British sailors was anchored in Salem harbor. Merchantmen with goods for barricaded ports eluded the lurking enemy.[14] As is the way with war and the sea, men vanished, never to be seen again. Hawthorne's uncle, John Manning, was one such.

On shore, home guards were drilled. Robert and Samuel Manning joined the Salem Light Infantry in 1812 and 1810 respectively, and their nephew must have watched the military exercises with great interest. His brief vignette of such an event in "Sights from a Steeple" could very likely be a memory from that time: "it stirs my heart; their regular advance, their nodding plumes, the sun-flash on their bayonets and musket-barrels, the roll of their drums ascending past me, and the fife ever and anon piercing through—these things have wakened a warlike fire, peaceful though I be" (*CE* 9:195). Review of the troops often took place in Union Street. Arms were eagerly collected. Robert Manning advertised "muskets, pistols, blunderbusses, swords, bayonets,

13. Charles Edward Trow, *The Old Shipmasters of Salem*, 106–8, 110; WB, *Diary*, 4:187, 189, 191–92, 195; Gilbert L. Streeter, "Some Historic Streets and Colonial Houses of Salem," 208.

14. JH, *Hawthorne and Wife*, 1:6; *History of Essex County*, 1:15; WB, *Diary*, 4:317, 319; Phillips, *Salem and the Indies*, 405–6, 381.

gun locks" for sale in July 1812. Robert and especially William Manning owned shares in many of the privateers.[15]

In April 1814 the boy Hawthorne was lame and could not run to watch another battle, but he must have known that Manning stage horses were requisitioned to hurry cannon to protect the *Constitution*, which had been chased by the British into Marblehead Harbor. When the enemy seemed sure to invade a nervous Salem in the late summer of 1814, Hawthorne told his mother, who wanted to retreat temporarily to Ipswich, that he would rather stay and see the British.[16]

Caleb Foote remembered that time:

> The Infantry did its duty bravely, taking its turn in marching to the [Salem] Neck with spade and pickaxe on shoulder, digging and delving to build the forts which were thought necessary for defense, and flying to arms in the dreary alarums, when, in the dead of the night, the glare of beacon lights, the dreadful alarm bells, and the outcries as one armed man after another rushed from his house, shouting, "an alarm! an alarm! the British have come!" struck terror to the hearts of the timid. Every house facing the street had a candle in the window; and it had a solemnizing effect upon the women and children to see armed men hastening singly in that ghastly light to their rendezvous. Few minutes sufficed to bring the men into marching order, and in a surprisingly short time they were moving in solid bodies down to the Neck, or toward Beverly, or Marblehead, or wherever the alarm came from.[17]

The fighting ended with the victory of Andrew Jackson at the Battle of New Orleans in 1815, and the Republican/Democrats had a new hero. "I clearly remember [wrote William Ward to Francis H. Lee in 1884] seeing a man on a white horse bearing a small white flag with Peace on it, driving furiously through the town on a cold February day and the shouting of the people."[18] It was an exciting, frightening, and ultimately crucial time for Salem, since she never recovered her prewar dominance. It was also a defining moment for a young boy, and the rhetoric of that time would remain in his memory. Hawthorne lived on the eastern side of the town, which was predominantly Democratic. He was aware of the heroism of his cousin Joseph Ropes, captain of the *America* and a valued Democrat. Perhaps conscious of the conflicts of

15. George M. Whipple, "History of the Salem Light Infantry," 260–61; *SG,* June 30, 1812.

16. Turner, *Hawthorne,* 19; WB, *Diary,* 4:246–47; M. C. D. Silsbee, *A Half-Century,* 73–74.

17. Whipple, "Salem Light Infantry," 260–61.

18. William Ward to Lee, January 16, 1884, Scrapbook, 1:133–35, 138, copy, Francis Henry Lee Papers.

the period, he was ready to see life from the Democratic side. Add to that the fact of a genuine hero like Andrew Jackson who engaged the public consciousness at just the time that a hero was needed, and the grounds of opinion seem visible.

Hawthorne's admiration of Andrew Jackson was lifelong. He called Jackson "the greatest man we ever had" in the *French and Italian Notebooks* (*CE* 14:367). He described a "fierce and terrible bust" of Jackson in *Our Old Home* (*CE* 5:8). In the "Book of Autographs" he remarked, "But of all hands that can still grasp a pen, we know not the one belonging to a soldier or statesman, which could interest us more than the hand" of Jackson (*CE* 11:374). He praised the Jackson administration as "the most splendid and powerful that ever adorned the annals of our country" in his biography of Franklin Pierce (*CE* 23:287). In May 1836, Hawthorne, as editor of *The American Magazine of Useful and Entertaining Knowledge,* contributed an article on John C. Calhoun in which he spoke of his admiration of Jackson: "The strong character of the new President, his tenacious grasp of his own opinions, and energetic action upon them made it difficult for a man himself of so decided principles as Mr. Calhoun, to remain in perfect harmony with him." But, he added, "our narrative has now brought us to forbidden ground where the embers of faction are still smouldering and may scorch our feet, if we venture farther." His sister Elizabeth remembered that when Jackson visited Salem in 1833, Hawthorne "walked out to the boundary of the town to meet him,—not to speak to him, but only to look at him. When he came home at night he said he found only a few men and boys collected, not enough people without the assistance he rendered, to welcome the General with a good cheer." One of those men was no doubt his cousin Eben Hathorne, who "prided himself on having been the first 'Jackson man' in Salem." In 1861, Elizabeth Hawthorne, after a visit in Concord, remarked on Old Hickory in the context of the Civil War in a letter to her cousin Robert Manning: "Nathaniel says that wherever he is, he [Jackson] would undoubtedly rather be on earth at this crisis. I think so too."[19]

Unity of political thought was not achieved even by the emergence of a hero; certainly it was not in many families. The Manning relatives, so far as is known, were Federalists. Richard Manning Jr., Hawthorne's grandfather, was listed as a Federalist in 1808, as was his uncle William

19. [NH], "John C. Calhoun," 360; Fields, *Yesterdays with Authors,* 66; H. Brooks, "Localities about Salem," 108; EMH to Robert Manning, December 31, 1861, copy, Hawthorne-Manning Collection.

Manning in 1810. Another uncle, Richard Manning, showed his displeasure with Andrew Jackson in a letter in 1828 to his brother Robert: "But I hope we shall live to see the end of the Chieftain's [*sic*] reign. . . . I hope his Sucessor [*sic*] will be a better man." Hawthorne's uncle-in-law, John Dike, was a Federalist, as was Nathaniel's sister Elizabeth. A cousin on his grandmother Manning's side, lawyer Nathaniel James Lord, however, was a Democrat. Nancy Forrester's husband, Gideon Barstow, started as a Republican/Democrat and was a member of Congress from 1821 to 1823, but he switched to the Federalist/Whig side. It was recorded in the Forrester family Bible that Simon Forrester was "in politics an undeviating and discriminating Federalist."[20]

Yet, on the Democratic side were many Hathorne relatives also. Colonel John Hathorne, his father's first cousin, was a vigorous Democrat, an elector for Jefferson, and he was accused of rigging the local elections in 1812. Also in the Democratic party were his cousins John Forrester and George Archer. Democrats in Salem seemed to pass on the faith to the family. Joseph Ropes and John Hathorne Jr., both sturdy Democrats, were married to two of Zachariah Burchmore's aunts, Captain Stephen Burchmore's sisters. Colonel John Hathorne's children were Democrats: John Jr., Ellen Hathorne Bailey, and Eben were definitely such. Ellen's husband, Adams Bailey (1789–1862), was appointed to the Boston Custom House in 1815. He was deputy collector in 1841; removed by Collector Lincoln; reinstated by Collector Rantoul. He was depicted in his obituary as "politically opposed but amiable." Eben also was a political appointee at the Boston Custom House. Only Benjamin Herbert Hathorne of the children seemed to lack interest. He was a merchant in Salem and once wrote Ellen that Eben had come to him for money "after spending a number of his best years devoted to politics and other unproductive pursuits."[21]

20. M. Hawthorne, "Aunt Ebe," 218; *SG,* May 13, 1808, March 20, 1810, May 12 and 15, 1829, April 24, 1835, and March 25, 1828; Richard Manning to Robert Manning, November 24, 1828, Hawthorne-Manning Collection; *ER,* May 8, 1813; *Salem Advertiser,* November 6, 1847; Mellow, *Hawthorne in His Times,* 38. On January 9, 1821, the *SG* reported, "Dr. Barstow the Republican candidate was the only gentleman in nomination who stood any chance for this election." By November 1, 1833, the *Gazette* stated that "the chief virulence of the *Advertiser* [the Democratic paper] has lately been directed against Dr. Barstow. The vainest man need desire no higher compliment"; Belknap, "Forrester and Descendants," 28.

21. *SG,* December 23, 1834, March 13 and 27, 1805, May 12, 1810, and May 7, 1816; *CE* 8:75. John Forrester seemed to switch from the Federalists to the Jackson Democrats (*SG,* February 23, 1809, and May 15, 1829); B. B. Crowninshield, "An Account of the Private Armed Ship 'America' of Salem," 50, 51; David Augustus Neal, "Salem Men in the Early Nineteenth-Century," 14; *CE* 15:66–67; "Obituary" [of Adams Bailey], 85; Benjamin Herbert Hathorne to Ellen H. Bailey, February 1820, English/Touzel/Hathorne

Thus, a large element of the family was interested in politics, and sometimes politics came before family. One of the two inspectors fired from the Salem Custom House by Hawthorne was William Webb (1773–1848), his father's first cousin. Webb's mother had been Rachel Hathorne's sister.[22] Hawthorne seems a bit callous when he remarks that after "abbreviating the official breath" of the old inspectors, they soon died (*CE* 1:13). Surely he was not unaware of the family relationship with Webb, but perhaps he did not care. The Webbs lived, however, very nearby.

Another important Democratic connection was that of the Dunlaps. Hawthorne said later that he recognized the Dunlaps in Elizabeth Barstow Stoddard's 1862 book, The *Morgesons* (*CE* 18:531). Sarah Stone Dunlap was the mother of Anstis Dunlap Barstow, mother of Benjamin Barstow, Gideon Barstow's nephew, but she was also connected with the Osgoods, one of whom married Sally Archer, daughter of Judith Hathorne Archer. Mrs. Dunlap was also the mother of Andrew Dunlap, a young lawyer tutored by William Bentley before he went to Harvard, the attorney for Abner Kneeland in his blasphemy trial, and U.S. attorney until shortly before his death. His mother visited Washington in 1830 and had a long interview with President Jackson, which she wrote up in her reminiscences found after her death. Her great admiration for Jackson was probably conveyed to all who would listen.[23]

In addition to the events in Salem and the political leanings of various friends and relations, Hawthorne's personal beliefs also tilted toward the Democratic side. His idea of the inequity of property was vigorously expressed by Holgrave in *The House of the Seven Gables*. Judge Pyncheon is satirized for "enjoyment of his real estate in town and country, his railroad, bank, and insurance shares, his United States stock" (*CE* 2:270). Brook Thomas maintains that in that novel "Hawthorne uses the history of Salem to present an allegory about national politics." Sarah I. Davis links Judge Pyncheon with Nicholas Biddle, president of the Second United States Bank, and a favorite target of Democrats.[24] Hawthorne writes in "The Ancestral Footstep" of a man of "the Nicholas Biddle stamp, a mighty speculator, the ruin of whose schemes had crushed hundreds of people" (*CE* 12:52).

Collection. I believe that the Mary Otis Bailey to whom Hawthorne wrote of "the claims of kindred" on December 11, 1860, was related to Ellen and Adams Bailey (*CE* 18:344–45).

22. E. Waters, "Genealogical Notes of the Webb Family," 228.

23. WB, *Diary,* 4:418; Thomas C. Amory Jr., "Reminiscences," 228–30.

24. Thomas, *Cross-Examinations,* 47; S. Davis, "The Bank and the Old Pynchon Family," 150–65.

Ideologically, Hawthorne probably most identified with the Democrats on the possibility of financial ruin, produced by the greed of banks and moneyed men. From a very early age, he was acutely aware of business failures due to speculation in property of various kinds. "In this republican country, amid the fluctuating waves of our social life," he asserts, "somebody is always at the drowningpoint" (*CE* 2:38). William Manning overspeculated during the War of 1812 and was "ruined." Yet he persevered in acquiring property. Samuel Manning became insolvent in his acquisition of the family stage business. John Dike failed several times. A cousin, John Forrester, went bankrupt in 1834. John Andrew, Catherine Forrester's husband, was ruined and went to Russia to recoup.[25]

The Salem papers were full of such losses, especially in those hard times that seemed to come around with regularity. Jackson's removal of the deposits of the banks enormously increased factional bitterness and the possibility of ruin. Stephen C. Philips, who succeeded Rufus Choate as the representative to Congress, was a stalwart Whig, as was his clerk, Porter Felt Jr. On January 26, 1834, Felt informed his father, then on a voyage for Phillips, "The Bank has been obliged to call in 8 or 9 millions of money, and to stop discounting, which you will perceive has obliged the state banks to do the same, and this has produced a great scarcity of money. Failures in great numbers have taken place." He then goes on to detail the insolvency of John Forrester and others in Salem, Boston, and New York.[26]

Hawthorne often commented on the idea of ruin in his notebooks. He spoke of "the various guises under which Ruin makes his approaches to his victims: i.e. to the merchant, in the guise of a merchant offering speculations" (*CE* 8:23). He also suggested to himself that he might write an article on the various kinds of ruin, including that "as regards property" (*CE* 8:30). He wrote mightily on the whole subject in *The House of the Seven Gables*. Of course, he never confined that term to a connection with property only. He used that same expression later in a plaintive letter to his friend Horatio Bridge on November 5, 1860, when he mentioned "the ruin and dismemberment of the party to which I have been attached" (*CE* 18:336).

His views fit with the party of that time in part, but in part only. Ambiguous as ever, he accepted positions offered by the Democrats,

---

25. *SG,* August 3, 1810, April 23, 1811, October 9 and July 14, 1812, January 11, 1814, December 8, 1829, January 5, 1830, and April 8, 1834; G. Ward, "Andrew-Safford House," 70.

26. Porter Felt Jr. to Jonathan Porter Felt, January 26, 1834, Felt-White Collection.

but many of his remarks seem to reflect a desire for status rather than ideology. He was also quite aware of the toll any political stance took. In "Etherege" he speaks of a young man who was a member of Congress and later was defeated. He remembers also "the virulence of party animosity, the abusiveness of the press" (*CE* 12:147). On the other hand, however, he seemed genuinely committed to the idea of personal liberty. As George Dekker affirms, his political belief "was the result not only of friendships, family connections, and prospects of patronage, but also of the deep appeal of that party's tradition of Jeffersonian-Jacksonian liberalism." I tend to agree with James M. Cox's view that "political life was somehow as essential for him as the life of literature, although he veiled its importance for him."[27]

Hawthorne's political leanings surely cost him dearly in Salem. George Holden in writing about Hawthorne and his friends for *Harper's New Monthly Magazine* spoke of "the muck-heaps of local prejudice" that persisted about his figure in his native town. This was due partly, he thought, to the writer's aloofness, which was seen as rudeness. But he also averred, "Hawthorne was a Democrat in politics at a time when, by these unfriendly people, themselves of Whiggish proclivities, grave doubts were entertained whether a Democrat might by any possibility be admitted to heaven."[28] Hawthorne, as well as Joseph Story, was thought to be possessed of the "itch of faction" by both his political friends and foes.

It was probably in the Salem Custom House that the writer most felt the power of politics. Neither the Boston Custom House nor the position in Liverpool impressed him in the same way. In Boston he had a job to do, and he did it well. In Liverpool he was enough removed from his own country so that he did not see his work altogether in purely political terms. But in Salem, in "his dear old native town," he was able to see the seamier side exemplified in the people he knew. He also probably saw his own shameful side, for he allowed kick-backs and retired two venerable gentlemen who might have been content to sit in the custom house until retirement.

He met all kinds of men there: General James Miller, who did not take kindly to a change of habits, but was esteemed for his service in the War of 1812; Miller's son Ephraim, whom Hawthorne was later criticized for promoting as collector; the naval officer, John D. Howard, "an excellent fellow" who talked about Napoleon and Shakespeare; the collector's

27. George Dekker, *The American Historical Romance,* 130; James M. Cox, "Reflections on Hawthorne's Nature," 155.
28. G. Holden, "Hawthorne among Friends," 263.

junior clerk, J. Linton Waters, who wrote poetry; and the permanent inspector, William Lee, whose daughters never forgave Hawthorne for trivializing him. His sketch of Lee was caustic, and he later regretted having written it when he remembered the old man's kindness to him.[29]

When he wrote the "Custom-House" sketch, he may have had in mind a book, *Political Reminiscences,* published in 1835 by a grandson of Elias Haskett Derby. John Barton Derby (1792–1867) had been a Democratic employee in the Boston Custom House, but had turned against the Statesman party, one wing of the Jackson party. This is a vitriolic, scathing work about a party that hated Boston merchants, made its employees pay "kick-backs" from their own salaries, and "decapitated" its opponents: "In a few days, [Derby wrote] the area of the [Boston] Custom House was strewed with the heads of decapitated public officers. . . . As the victim was led to execution, he exclaimed 'am I not an American citizen,—a republican, a faithful officer?' The fatal nod was given, and his head rolled upon the pavement." One section of one chapter is entitled "The Custom House," in which he describes the inequities between the greater offices (the collector, the surveyor, and the naval officer) and all the lesser minions.[30]

Surely Hawthorne knew of or had read this book. It skewered his own party; it particularly knifed Andrew Dunlap; and it was written by a former Salemite with all sorts of Salem connections. It must have been in his mind when he wrote his own sketch, and it may account for his partial surprise that what must have seemed to him the much kinder approach of his own was greeted so harshly by his fellow townsmen. Later he would write of a character's disgust with the "fierceness of political contests in our country" (*CE* 12:51). He ridiculed corrupt politicians in *The House of the Seven Gables.* When his friend Franklin Pierce failed to solve the nation's problems as president and was hated by everyone he knew, Hawthorne got his back up and dedicated *Our Old Home* to him despite pleadings by James T. Fields and Elizabeth P. Peabody (*CE* 18:567, 589–92).

His support of Pierce probably contributed to his stance during the Civil War. He was also only too aware of the abiding animosity the Revolutionary War had left in its aftermath. In addition, his experience affected his attitude toward abolitionism. He was against slavery,

29. David Mason Little, "Documentary History of the Salem Custom-House," 265; R. Holden, "General James Miller," 283–302; *CE* 8:287–92; Thomas Amory Lee, "The Lee Family of Marblehead," 267–69. John D. Howard was praised by Benjamin F. Browne as "a vigorous and able political writer" (Turner, *Hawthorne,* 171).

30. J. B. Derby, *Political Reminiscences,* 71, 120–32.

but the reforming zeal of the abolitionists had always intensified his ambivalence. He had missed, by being in Europe in the 1850s, the progressively harsher attacks on the institution of slavery. He informed George M. Sanders, who opposed abolition, that he wished Louis Kossuth had made "a sturdier condemnation of slavery" while in America (*CE* 17:230). But he confided to Bridge in March 1854 that he was "sick to death of the continual fuss, and tumult and excitement, and bad blood, which we keep up about political topics" (*CE* 17:188). "If compelled to choose, I go for the North," he wrote Bridge in 1857, but he acknowledged, "I have no kindred with nor leaning towards the Abolitionists" (*CE* 18:8). He was not alone in this feeling. Jared Sparks had written to Thomas Reade Rootes Cobb in Georgia much earlier, "Slavery in the abstract, I consider a great calamity and a reproach to free government, and one with which every true patriot should desire to see removed as soon as it can be done: but in the present state of things we have little to do with the question in the abstract. Slavery exists by the Constitution and the laws. . . . I hold it to be wrong, therefore, to interfere with these rights." Such opinions were often expressed. On August 4, 1835, the *Salem Gazette* came out against both slavery and abolitionism. In 1839, Leverett Saltonstall wrote his son, "I regret all anti-slavery excitement. I loathe and abhore slavery—but there are difficulties about it, which our zealous anti-slavery people dream not off [*sic*]." Many New Englanders who had those opinions in the 1820s, 1830s, and 1840s changed their minds later. But some did not. Lydia Maria Child, an ardent abolitionist, was a good friend of Marianne C. D. Silsbee, Jared Sparks's sister-in-law, but she was appalled in 1861 when she called on the Silsbees, and Nathaniel Silsbee Jr., a former mayor of Salem, "maintained that the slaves were much better off than the poor in Massachusetts, that the moral character of Southerners was much better than that of Northerners, that the South had been abominably abused by the North."[31] Examples could be multiplied of those who were to be called Copperheads and whose views were overcome by events.

In a matter of human reform by force, Hawthorne always felt that he would rather trust to God or Providence than to politicians. Sophia, much to the regret of her family, agreed. In 1863, she wistfully wrote General Ethan A. Hitchcock:

31. See Frederick Newberry, *Hawthorne's Divided Loyalties: England and America in His Works,* or M. Moore, "Hawthorne, Tories, and Oliver," 213–24; Herbert Baxter Adams, *The Life and Writings of Jared Sparks, Comprising Selections from His Journals and Correspondence,* 1:262–65; Saltonstall, *Papers, 1816–1845,* 2:152; Child, *Selected Letters,* 375.

> I was glad to find that you believe that GOD'S Law would without
> fail have removed slavery, without this dreadful convulsive action. It
> always seems to me that Man is very arrogant in taking such violent
> measures *to help GOD,* who needs no help. . . .
>
>   I find no one in Concord—or hardly in Boston to whom I can utter
> such sentiments without exciting fiery indignation—My sisters cannot
> hear me speak a word. . . . To my husband only I can speak. He is very
> all sided and can look serenely on opposing forces and do Justice to
> each.[32]

In his *Life of Franklin Pierce,* Hawthorne, in his loyalty to his friend,
articulated the same thought: "[Another view] . . . looks upon Slavery
as one of those evils, which Divine Providence does not leave to be
remedied by human contrivances, but which, in its own good time,
by some means impossible to be anticipated, but of the simplest and
easiest operation, when all its uses shall have been fulfilled, it causes
to vanish like a dream" (*CE* 23:352). Of course, slavery did not vanish
easily like a dream. Pierce became one of the most unpopular presidents
of this country, and Hawthorne's friendship with him became a liability
to the writer. It may not be too much to say that his loyalty to party also
figured in this view, and that he did not realize that many in his party
had already left this interpretation behind.

    Hawthorne was often criticized in Salem for not only his politics but
also his political friends. Dr. George B. Loring, for example, informed
Moncure Conway that "His daily official associates . . . were a group of
men, all of whom had remarkable characteristics, not of the best many
times, but original, strong, highly-flavored, defiant democrats." Conway
had called the Democratic party of Hawthorne's surveyor years a "party
of rowdies."[33] Even before that time Democrats were not seen in the best
light. When Collector George Bancroft spoke in Salem, he was chided
by the *Salem Gazette* (March 6, 1840) for repeating "profane ribaldry."
Abner Kneeland was another member of the party whose views were
despised by many. There were enough of such people around to shock
the sober Whigs of Salem.

    Hawthorne had both political friends and enemies in Salem. Frank B.
Sanborn, in commenting on the writer's political demise, later reported
that Sophia wrote him that "Mr. Upham . . . was not solely responsible.
A number of the leading men of Salem, for one reason or another,
disliked Hawthorne and joined in the intrigue."[34] Some of his allies were

---

    32. SPH to General Ethan Hitchcock, August 9, 1863, Nathaniel Hawthorne Collection
(#6249), Clifton Waller Barrett Library.
    33. Conway, *Life of Hawthorne,* 107.
    34. Frank B. Sanborn, *Hawthorne and His Friends: Reminiscence and Tribute,* 43.

Zachariah Burchmore Jr., William Baker Pike, and Benjamin F. Browne. I shall discuss each of these first, and then examine two enemies, Horace Lorenzo Conolly and Charles Wentworth Upham, who were at one point his friends.

ZACHARIAH BURCHMORE JR. (1809–1884)

Burchmore may well have been called a "defiant democrat." Grandson of a privateer in the Revolution and son of a Custom House inspector, he was a product of the Salem Custom House. When Hawthorne knew him, he was nominally the clerk, but in reality he was the chief officer. Almost of an age with Hawthorne, he was one of the most highly praised persons in the writer's "The Custom-House" as "the main-spring" that kept the custom house going and "the man of business" (*CE* 1:24). Though not named, Burchmore was described as giving a "new idea of talent," of being "prompt, acute, clear-minded; with an eye that saw through all the perplexities." He was, in short, "the ideal of his class" (*CE* 1:24). One wonders if Hawthorne spent so many words on Burchmore and none on Pike in the sketch because Burchmore was fired and Pike was not. Certainly the description contrasts strangely with Burchmore's later alcoholism and Hawthorne's description of him to Pike as a "poor, miserable, broken, drunken, disagreeable loafer, contemptible as an enemy, and only troublesome to his friends" (*CE* 16:690).

There were those who saw Burchmore as the evil genius of the Salem Democrats. On October 15, 1841, the *Salem Gazette* quoted a writer stating that he would "wait patiently in hopes in a few days to see one Burch-more than has grown from a Hickory stump, lopped off." It did not happen that year, but the Whigs were merely biding their time. Stephen Nissenbaum has characterized him as the real target of the Whig conspiracy that eventuated in Hawthorne's removal.[35] Burchmore wrote Hawthorne in 1849 that the "Whig party here have always charged me with doing every thing pertaining to party management" (*CE* 16:290). Hawthorne informed Fields in a letter on May 31, 1853, that "the Salem politicians are very watchful of my correspondence with this fellow [Burchmore]" (*CE* 16:689). Certainly the Custom House seemed to be the main interest of Burchmore's life. When he was no longer there, he gradually sank into alcoholism. One gets the impression that it was not so much the Democratic party as the Custom House around which his world revolved.

Yet it is difficult to see the reason for Hawthorne's somewhat extravagant praise and his long friendship with Burchmore. Edwin Haviland

35. Stephen Nissenbaum, "The Firing of Nathaniel Hawthorne," 74.

Miller believes that Hawthorne liked the rough set of men that Burch-more seemed to represent, that he liked to drink with them and to listen to their conversations, to "let his hair down," so to speak.[36] Did Hawthorne know Burchmore when he figured in the White trial? Whatever the attraction, Hawthorne retained his affection for Burchmore. When the latter could no longer hold down a job, Hawthorne asked Ticknor to pay Burchmore money but not to say anything that would let Sophia know what he was doing, since Sophia was not happy about Burchmore (*CE* 18:340).

WILLIAM BAKER PIKE (1811–1876)

The first mention of William B. Pike by Hawthorne was in his notebooks during their mutual Boston Custom House period. In February 1839, Hawthorne wrote at length of this fellow Salemite who had seen ghosts and who had been a carpenter (*CE* 8:189–92). Pike had also been the editor for six weeks in 1836 of the *Salem Advertiser,* a party organ for the Democrats. He was an assistant measurer at the Boston Custom House and a weigher and gauger at the Salem Custom House. He was not released from service there when Hawthorne was. Later he became collector from 1857 to 1861.[37] Thus, his party credentials were good, and he and Hawthorne had that in common.

What must have interested Hawthorne even more, however, was the spiritual dimension of the man. Pike was a seeker. He, indeed, had been a devout Methodist, even aspiring to be a minister of what was then a sect. When this hope was dashed by his failure to tell the Methodists that he had not been ordained, he left the Methodists and joined St. Peter's Episcopal Church. He and his sister Lucy Ann were communicants in December 1839 and were confirmed on June 28, 1840. This move coincided with the Boston Custom House experience. The Pikes left St. Peter's in 1845, and Pike became a Swedenborgian.[38] Pike was also interested in spiritualism and testified in favor of communication with the dead. Hawthorne was a skeptic, but he treated Pike's belief with respect. On July 24, 1851, he wrote Pike, "I should be very glad to believe that these rappers are, in any one instance, the spirits of the persons whom they profess themselves to be; but though I have talked with those who have had the freest communication, there has always been something that makes me doubt" (*CE* 16:466).

---

36. Miller, *Salem Is My Dwelling Place,* xv, 14, 88.
37. See the introduction to *CE* 15:64–66; "Portraits in the Essex Institute," 76–77; Little, "Salem Custom-House," 266.
38. G. Holden, "Hawthorne among Friends," 265; St. Peter's Church Records.

Julian Hawthorne maintained that Pike was a "man of remarkable depth of mind and tenderness of nature" and that he knew Hawthorne "more intimately than any other man." Rose Hawthorne Lathrop spoke of the "fragrance of his humility." She called him "one of the half-earthy intelligences which are capable of bloom, like a granite-strewn hill, revealing upon a closer glance unexpected imagination." The letter Pike wrote to Hawthorne about his reaction to *The Blithedale Romance* indicates clearly the side of Pike that appealed to Hawthorne. When he says that Hawthorne goes "down among the moody silences of the heart, and open[s] those depths whence come motives that give complexion to actions," he shows that he understands what Hawthorne is about.[39]

It was Pike who informed the Hawthornes of the death of Louisa, "at the request of the family," says Mellow. The Dikes asked him to go to them (*CE* 16:582). Sophia's description of the scene when Pike came from Salem and told the family the news is unforgettable. Hawthorne went to Salem, for the last time so far as we know, but he was too late for the funeral. Sophia was glad that he had not had to go through the ceremony "and to hear all the Calvinistic talk."[40]

It is regrettable that something happened to the memoirs Pike wrote toward the end of his life. He could have elucidated many mysteries about Hawthorne—especially the depth of Hawthorne's political leanings. After all, Hawthorne had written Pike on September 2, 1851, "I am getting damnably out of the beaten track, as regards politics; and I doubt whether I can claim fellowship with any party whatever" (*CE* 16:480). George H. Holden remarked that Pike's end was sad, that he was "abjectly poor" and blind, but that his mind was "unclouded," and his "soul kindly and serene."[41]

BENJAMIN FRANKLIN BROWNE (1793–1873)
Another of his Democratic friends was Benjamin F. Browne, who could not, I think, have been called a rowdy. Hawthorne must have known Browne by sight from the time he was a young boy, since Browne worked in an apothecary shop in the Union Building at the head of Essex and Union Streets. He began to know Browne well, however, after he in 1840 aspired to his position as Salem postmaster, a post that he did not get. Hawthorne offered to edit Browne's manuscript on his Dartmoor prison days and to try to get it published. As has

39. JH, *Hawthorne and Wife,* 1:443–44; RHL, *Memories,* 154.
40. Mellow, *Hawthorne in His Times,* 411–12.
41. G. Holden, "Hawthorne among Friends," 267.

been suggested, he probably had the ulterior motive of making some money on the manuscript and of helping himself politically, but he also thought that the manuscript had possibilities (*CE* 15:425).[42] The house on Chestnut Street in which the Hawthornes briefly lived belonged to Browne. That short stay resulted in the anecdote told by Robert S. Rantoul:

> [I]n 1865 I became Collector of the Port. . . . The delightful tale of his old neighbor and landlord, Dr. Benjamin Franklin Brown [*sic*], was not worn threadbare then. Hawthorne told Dr. Brown,—they were fellow Democrats and Hawthorne hired his near-by house of the Doctor, and fled to him by the back door, for refuge when cornered by an unwelcome caller—Hawthorne told Dr. Brown that of course he had the "Scarlet Letter" and would show it to him some day. Pressed repeatedly to make good, he finally said "Well Doctor, I did have it but one Sunday afternoon, when we were all away at meeting, the children got it and threw it in the fire."[43]

The Scarlet Letter, of course, was written in Mall Street, not in the Chestnut Street house, and the information about Hawthorne's going to meeting would have made Browne suspicious anyway, if he had taken it seriously. But the truth in the story, aside from revealing Hawthorne's sense of humor, was that Hawthorne probably did escape by the back door of the Chestnut Street house just as he did in Concord, and he would have gone to Browne's home after he and Dr. Browne became friends.

Browne was the product of many Salem families: not only the Brownes but also the Andrews, the Maules, the Higginsons, the Gerrishes, and many more. He was born on Winter Street in 1793, the son of Benjamin Browne and Elizabeth Andrew. In 1807 he entered the apothecary shop of E. S. Lang, where he served a five-year apprenticeship. When the War of 1812 made finding jobs very difficult, he became a surgeon's assistant on the privateer *Alfred*. In 1813 he served as a captain's clerk, purser, and sergeant of marines on the privateer *Frolic,*

---

42. Hawthorne wrote Pike (March 19, 1840) that he was returning Dr. Browne's manuscript. "It has afforded me much entertainment and instruction," he noted, "and I should suppose that the work might easily be made very acceptable to the public" (*CE* 15:425). Hawthorne had tried to interest Evert A. Duyckinck to no avail, so he finally edited it and had it published in the *United States Magazine and Democratic Review* in vols. 18 and 19. See *CE* 16:139, 153. Also see "Hawthorne's 'Privateer' Revealed at Last," 44–49.

43. Tolles with Tolles, *Architecture in Salem,* 196; R. S. Rantoul as quoted in Edward Waldo Emerson, *The Early Years of the Saturday Club, 1855–1870,* 209–10.

in which William Manning had one share. Unfortunately, this ship was captured, and Browne was held prisoner first at Barbados and then at Dartmoor Prison in England. Browne's own father had been a prisoner in England after serving in a privateer in the Revolutionary War. After the son's return to Salem, he went into business with William Stearns in an apothecary shop that sold everything from raisins to canary seed. That shop was opposite the house in which Hannah Crowninshield lived and in which Dr. William Bentley boarded. Browne was one of the first to get to Bentley when the clergyman collapsed and died. Browne's notebook sketch of Bentley ends the four-volume diary of the minister.[44]

In 1823 Browne opened his own shop. Soon active in Democratic circles, he was representative to the General Court in 1831; a state senator in 1843; replaced Caleb Foote, a Whig, as postmaster and served from 1845 until 1849, when he resigned the post, according to the *Salem Advertiser,* in a "satisfactory and highly credible manner."[45] As Hawthorne wrote George Hillard on June 18, 1849, "my present esteemed friend, Dr. Browne—contrary to what had been told me, was an excellent officer, and had the great bulk of the party with him" (*CE* 16:279). When Browne died in 1873, the *Salem Observer* said of him on November 29, "Even when Dr. Browne was active as a Democrat in this then Whig city, he always retained the respect and goodwill of all the people."

Browne was not only a Democrat and a druggist but also an antiquarian and a writer. When the *Essex Institute Historical Collections* began publication in 1859, Browne's articles were much in evidence. He annotated the books kept by the barbers Benjamin Blanchard and William Jelly, whose patrons would jot down items of historical interest. He also collected family histories. He copied church rolls, wrote poetry and his own reminiscences, and annotated those of others. Charles W. Upham in the introduction to his two-volume *Salem Witchcraft* cordially expressed his "acknowledgements to the Hon. Benjamin F. Browne of Salem, who retired from public life and the cares of business, is giving the leisure of his venerable years to the collection, preservation, and liberal contribution of an unequalled amount of knowledge respecting our local antiquities." Not long before Browne died his house burned, destroying a lifetime of notes. Fortunately, many of his facts had been

44. For the life of Browne, see the *DAB* or "The Memoir of Benjamin Franklin Browne," 81–89.
45. *Salem Advertiser,* January 31, 1849.

published.[46] He and Hawthorne may well have discussed Salem history and old Salem families; the latter could not have had a better contemporary source.

Benjamin F. Browne was also the first president of a fire club in Salem, as a member recalled:

> The druggist of antiquarian taste.
> Regular as a clock, but never in haste,
> As a Dartmoor Prisoner known in town,
> Was our first President—Doctor Browne.

To many in Salem of that time, then, it would have seemed unbelievable that in 1927 a contest had to be waged to discover who wrote the "Dartmoor Prisoner" after an unpublished segment was put back with the original work. It was first thought to be an unknown work by Hawthorne. But William Lyon Phelps and Irving Putnam discovered eventually that it was the work of Browne. That fact had been better known in Salem than many of the works of Hawthorne at the time. Nathaniel sent Browne copies of his books, but I do not think Browne's views of them are known. Such opinions on the early tales would be especially interesting, since Browne knew so many of the legends behind them.[47]

HORACE LORENZO CONOLLY (C. 1808–1894)

A friend and a later enemy of Hawthorne's was Horace Lorenzo Conolly, the adopted son of Susan Ingersoll. He was born in 1808 or 1809, but his parentage is not fully known, nor is the precise moment when he went to live with Susan. It must have been fairly early on, however, for she sent him to various Salem private schools: to the Quaker John Southwick, to James Gerrish from 1819 to 1823, and to Henry K. Oliver from 1823 until 1828.[48]

Susan Ingersoll evidently loved him "with almost fanatical devotion," as Caroline Emmerton claimed. She sent him to Yale from 1828 to 1831

---

46. These recollections were written in 1869. The first issues of the *EIHC* were replete with contributions of Browne; C. Upham, *Salem Witchcraft,* 1:xiii; "Memoir of Browne," 88.

47. Dennis, "Fire Clubs of Salem," 15, 17, 64; Benjamin F. Browne, *The Yarn of a Yankee Privateer;* "Hawthorne's 'Privateer' Revealed," 44–49; RHL to Rebecca Manning, December 8, 1925, Hawthorne-Manning Collection.

48. Conolly's obituary, *Salem Daily Gazette,* September 13, 1894. My sketch of Conolly is largely based upon this article. My thanks to Mark Nystedt, researcher in Salem, who sent me a copy of this obituary. Also see M. Hawthorne, "Hawthorne and Man of God," 262.

and then to Trinity College in Hartford from 1831 to 1832, after which he returned to Salem where he was confirmed in her church, St. Peter's, by Bishop Alexander Griswold on August 26, 1832. He studied theology with Griswold from 1832 to 1834. Possibly Hawthorne had seen or known him before he went to Yale, but the first knowledge we have of an acquaintance is from a recollection by Conolly of their meeting in New Haven in 1828 when Nathaniel was on a trip with his Uncle Samuel. Conolly's reminiscence was of a very different Hawthorne from the one we usually see: an irritable man who could hardly speak without some bit of profanity.[49] If this picture does not quite ring true, then we are entitled to some skepticism about Conolly's memories. Possibly they saw each other in New Haven in 1828, again when Samuel Manning and Nathaniel went that way in 1829, and then in 1832 when Conolly was in Salem.

From 1834 to 1838, Conolly was the rector of St. Matthew's Church in South Boston. It was probably during the latter part of this time that many whist games were played with the Duchess (Susan Ingersoll), the Chancellor (David Roberts), the Empress (Louisa), and the Emperor (Nathaniel). Conolly said they had a more intimate acquaintance in 1837. In May of 1839 Hawthorne wrote Longfellow that his friend Conolly was going south to establish "an Academy" (*CE* 15:310). He wrote Louis O'Sullivan that Conolly was going to Virginia and that he was "a man of talents and highly respectable attainments" (*CE* 15:313). In fact, Conolly did go south as far as Philadelphia and organized St. Mark's Church, where he was rector from 1839 to 1841, and to New Bedford to Grace Church in 1841. He must have become disenchanted with himself as a rector because he read the law in Philadelphia with John Devereaux and also in New Bedford. His obituary does not mention it, but perhaps he thought of studying law at Harvard in 1840; at least Hawthorne saw him in Boston with a Cambridge law student when he, Hawthorne, was in the Boston Custom House (*CE* 15:481). After Conolly returned to Salem, he read law with his friend, David Roberts, was admitted to the bar, and practiced law from 1846 to 1868. Thus, a daily acquaintance between Hawthorne and Conolly seems to have been possible only from 1837 to 1839, possibly a sporadic one in 1840, and then from 1846 to 1850, at which time Hawthorne left Salem. Already in 1840 Hawthorne had written Sophia Peabody that he was "sorely tried with Mr. Conolly" (*CE* 15:481). By 1842, Hawthorne queried his sister Louisa from Concord:

---

49. Caroline O. Emmerton, *The Chronicles of Three Old Houses,* 24; M. Hawthorne, "Hawthorne and Man of God," 207, 278.

"Do you ever see him? I don't think he deserves a letter; for he treated me very ill during my visit to Salem—not inviting me to come and see him, and being otherwise intolerably rude. He is a real blackguard" (*CE* 15:659).

Hawthorne often wrote in this vein to Louisa about Conolly, yet he had him come as a guest when Sophia was away in 1844; he was relieved, nevertheless, when Conolly left (*CE* 16:37, 39). When Hawthorne was sworn in as the surveyor at Salem, Conolly and Browne were cosigners of his oath of office (*CE* 16:154). By 1849, however, Conolly was a signer of the Whig petition to have him removed from office. Conolly reported that the break in their friendship originated in a dispute "over a dog," which sounds odd. The fact that Conolly as a converted Whig was opposed to him is clearly one reason for the break. They did reconcile, more or less, by September 1850, as Hawthorne remarked to Burchmore (*CE* 16:365).[50]

Hawthorne and Conolly stayed somewhat in touch. Conolly had given him the story that later became Longfellow's *Evangeline,* and he was aware of the reason for Hawthorne's calling his Salem book *The House of the Seven Gables*. He gave Hawthorne an Ingersoll heirloom when the writer was married. During his latter days he practiced as "a quack doctor," according to Caroline Emmerton. Conolly seems to have retained his friendship with David Roberts. In the latter's will he left some law books to Conolly, calling him "my friend of many years." After Susan Ingersoll died in 1858, leaving her home and wealth to Horace, he had his name legally changed to Ingersoll, he said by her wish. Since her will had been made in 1835 and was witnessed by David Roberts, one wonders if the will would have been the same, had she made it later. She did not, however, revoke it. Conolly proceeded to go through her considerable fortune, lost the house, and died in poverty in 1894. But when he did die, his long front-page obituary was headlined "Hawthorne's Companion."[51] One can almost see Hawthorne's sardonic grin.

CHARLES WENTWORTH UPHAM (1802–1876)
Another Salemite who helped eject Hawthorne from the Custom House and who was right at the top of his list of enemies was Charles Went-

50. The Conolly obituary quotes Conolly as saying, "My break with Hawthorne . . . came in 1847 and was caused by a row over a dog."

51. See G. Holden's report on an interview with EMH, August 30, 1882, Nathaniel Hawthorne Papers; Essex Probate Court, #51812, will of David Roberts, July 7, 1879; C. Emmerton, *Chronicles,* 25; Essex Probate Court, #43338, will of Susannah Ingersoll, November 25, 1835 (probated August 3, 1858); Essex Probate Court, #36031, petition to change name, Horace Conolly to Horace Ingersoll, October 6, 1858; Conolly's obituary notice.

worth Upham, initially a minister at Salem's First Church and then a politician, but always a writer. His story, however, is more complicated than that.

Upham was born in St. John, New Brunswick, on May 4, 1802, of Loyalist Joshua Upham and Mary Chandler Upham. Deprived of his father in 1808, the young lad worked first as an apothecary's clerk in St. John. He was then sent to Boston to work for a cousin, merchant Phineas Upham, who perceived that the boy was not interested in a merchant's life and sent him to learn Latin with Deacon Samuel Greele. Upham then was in the Harvard class of 1821 with Ralph Waldo Emerson. He taught school in the winter vacations to make expenses and then attended the Harvard Divinity School, from which he was graduated in 1824. His final oration had the provocative title, "The Necessary Ambiguity of Language."[52] He was soon called in November 1824 to be colleague pastor of Salem's First Church, where the Reverend John Prince was the senior minister, a post he advanced to after Prince's death in 1836 and kept until ill health forced him to resign in December 1844.

Very likely Hawthorne did not know him when he teased Mary Manning in November of 1824 (and before Upham had been ordained and installed) by saying that "Elizabeth says you are deeply in love with Mr. Upham. Is the passion reciprocal?" (*CE* 15:190). Hawthorne was home from college in March 1826 when Upham married Ann S. Holmes, the sister of Oliver Wendell Holmes. The minister began his writing career with a discourse on *Principles of Reformation* (1826) and *Letters on the Logos* (1828), both vigorous defenses of Unitarianism. In 1829 he wrote a life of Hugh Peters and gave a lecture on the "Leaders of New England" that dealt primarily with persons who had been connected with First Church, Salem.

Probably his study of the roles and records of this church led to his lifelong interest in events in Salem and in Essex County. His biographer for the Massachusetts Historical Society noted that "the place—then a town, now a city—may well be described as the center of his affections." In January 1831 he gave two lectures on "Salem Witchcraft," which were widely noticed and then printed (1835). This was, of course, at exactly the same time Hawthorne was delving into the historical records. In 1833 Upham held a protracted debate in the *Salem Gazette* with George B. Cheever on Unitarianism versus Orthodoxy. Hawthorne may not have been fascinated with the theological niceties, but Upham's opponent was his Bowdoin classmate, and Hawthorne visited him in jail frequently

52. For facts on Upham's life, see *DAB;* George E. Ellis, "Memoir of Charles Wentworth Upham," 182–221; "Remarks by Winthrop," 155; *Christian Disciple* 11 (1823): 314.

after he was convicted of libel. Upham, of course, was very interested in the fine points of doctrine. His brother-in-law, Oliver Wendell Holmes, wrote his sister from Paris in October 1834 about "the long talks over the fire and all the doctrines therein held" that he had had with Upham.[53]

It is not known precisely when Hawthorne and Upham became friends, if indeed they were ever more than acquaintances. They certainly knew each other in 1837/1838 when Hawthorne described a scene in David Roberts's office in which Judge Elisha Mack tried to persuade Upham to marry a man and the girl whom he had seduced and left with child, a ceremony Upham was not inclined to perform. "Upham," Hawthorne remarked, "seemed to be more hardened in the performance of his awful duty." The marriage did not take place, which Hawthorne regretted (*CE* 23:194–95). Upham had written *The Life of Sir Henry Vane* for the Library of American Biography, and in January 1838 Hawthorne had urged an autograph seeker to obtain Upham's signature: "No collection of American autographs can be considered complete, without a specimen from him" (*CE* 15:260).

Hawthorne also mentioned Upham in "Alice Doane's Appeal": "Recently, indeed, an historian has treated the subject in a manner that will keep his name alive, in the only desirable connection with the errors of our ancestry, by converting the hill of their disgrace into an honorable monument of his own antiquarian lore, and of that better wisdom, which draws the moral while it tells the tale" (*CE* 11:267). In this passage Hawthorne may indeed have been writing with irony, as Susan Schwartzlander says, especially if this part was added later.[54] Or if this sentence was there earlier, we may see the beginnings of a coolness between the two. In September 1838 when Jones Very was incarcerated in the McLean Asylum, Charles Upham was primarily responsible for Very's enforced stay in the asylum. This probably did not endear him to Hawthorne.

Upham resigned his position at First Church in December 1844 because of a persistent bronchial infection that barely enabled him to speak. He was guaranteed a year's salary, and sat in a pew in that church for the rest of his life. He visited New Brunswick again and also had dinner with Hawthorne and Emerson in Concord.[55] The former wrote his wife (December 6, 1844) that when Upham "returned from Concord,

53. Ellis, "Memoir of Upham," 194; Stewart, "Recollections of Hawthorne," 328; John T. Morse Jr., *Life and Letters of Oliver Wendell Holmes,* 1:145.

54. Susan Swartzlander, "Hawthorne's 'Alice Doane's Appeal,' " 127.

55. Ellis, "Memoir of Upham," 189, 199; [J. Stone], "Notes," 263.

he told the most pitiable stories about our poverty and misery, so as to almost make it appear that we were suffering for food" (*CE* 16:70).

Upham's treatment of Very and his gossip about the Hawthornes were cause enough for any unfavorable feeling that Hawthorne may have had about the minister. Elizabeth Peabody much later also declared that Hawthorne, upon mentioning his engagement to Sophia to Upham, was advised by the clergyman to keep his wife in subjection, and that this may have been a cause for a cooling friendship. That is possible, although Hawthorne seems not to have gone around mentioning that engagement to anybody, and Elizabeth had very strong feelings about Upham herself. She also said that "Upham appreciated and admired [Hawthorne], but may be supposed to have felt somewhat irked from the fact that although the Hawthorne family held a pew in his church, Nathl never went to hear him preach."[56]

During the year after Upham resigned his pastorship, he edited, in a very urbane manner, from March 1845 to March 1846, the Unitarian periodical, the *Christian Register.* He announced, in fact, upon assuming editorship on March 8, 1845, that "We shall endeavor as far as possible to avoid controversy." And he did, although controversies inevitably arose during the year. He turned to politics in 1848, and until 1860, when he retired from public office, he played a large part in Massachusetts affairs. He was head of the Whigs in Salem in 1849, was in the Massachusetts House of Representatives in 1849 and 1850, was a member of the U.S. Congress from 1853 to 1855, was president of the Massachusetts Senate from 1857 to 1858, and served in the state house again in 1859 to 1860. He was also mayor of Salem in 1852, reorganized the police department, and brought about the settling of a state normal school in the city, now Salem State College. He penned a biography of John C. Fremont in 1856 also. He spent the rest of his life writing such books as the two-volume *Salem Witchcraft* (1867) and volumes 2–4 of *The Life of Timothy Pickering* (1873). Volume one, based on an incomplete sketch by John Pickering, was written by another son, Octavius, who in 1867 asked Upham to complete the work. Upham also defended his position on Cotton Mather in several articles.[57]

All this upright behavior contrasts strangely with his actions in the removal of Hawthorne from the Custom House in 1849. He had told Hawthorne, in the presence of David Roberts, as Hawthorne wrote

56. G. Holden's interview with EPP, August 18, 1883, Nathaniel Hawthorne Papers.
57. *Christian Register,* March 8, 1845. He was editor until February 28, 1846; Octavius Pickering and Charles W. Upham, *The Life of Timothy Pickering,* 2:vi; *DAB.*

George S. Hillard on June 18, 1849, "that I need never fear removal under a Whig administration, inasmuch as my appointment had not displaced a Whig" (*CE* 16:280). And indeed it had not, since the writer replaced a Tyler Democrat. Nevertheless, Upham made every effort to evict Hawthorne, even to the extent of going to Washington twice, writing numbers of letters, and accusing Hawthorne of all sorts of malfeasance. Even if the political acts that occurred on Hawthorne's watch were true as charged, the "Memorial" Upham wrote was, as Nevins characterized it, "a curious medley" of bitter charges and sympathetic feeling. Either Hawthorne was "the abused instrument of others" or he was directly responsible for various kickbacks that occurred at that time. Many have gradually come to believe, as Nissenbaum concludes, that "Hawthorne was certainly not the practicing machine politician that the Salem Whigs made him out to be. But neither was he the political innocent pictured by his friends."[58]

Hawthorne wrote his intention to Horace Mann to do his "best to kill and scalp him [Upham] in the public prints" and to Longfellow that he would "select a victim, and let fall one little drop of venom on his heart" (*CE* 16:269–70, 293). Sophia described Upham to her mother in that fateful June: "He is, my husband says, the most satisfactory villain that ever was, for at every point he is consummate." Thomas Woodson believes he assuaged his rage by depicting Upham as a scoundrel in *The Scarlet Letter* as well as *The House of the Seven Gables*. Although Claudia Johnson considers the latter book "a legend of vengeance," she indicates that the vengeance may be against many of the patriarchs in Hawthorne's Salem: not only Upham, but his ancestor John Hathorne, his uncle Robert Manning, and "very likely" Justice Joseph Story, as Brook Thomas has also suggested.[59]

Although Hawthorne never acknowledged directly that he was satirizing Upham, most scholars believe that he was in part, if not in whole. But what has not been completely dealt with is the motivation for Upham to be so determined to remove Hawthorne from his post, nor has it been proved to my knowledge that Upham tried hard to find him another post, as Upham's friend, John Chapman, editor of the *Register,* maintained (*CE* 16:285). Upham's tone all through this episode seems unlike him. It is true that so long as Hawthorne stayed, the Whigs would not have complete control over one of the alleged perks of

58. Nissenbaum, "Firing of Hawthorne," 80.
59. RHL, *Memories,* 100; Woodson, "Hawthorne, Upham, and *The Scarlet Letter,"* 188–91; Claudia D. Johnson, "Unsettling Accounts in *The House of the Seven Gables,"* 84–85; Thomas, *Cross-Examinations,* 47.

their party's power in Washington. It was probably likewise true that Salemites resented all the outside interference in their own political affairs. Hawthorne had not then written his great works so that they may well have felt his literary pretensions were not important enough to keep him at his post. Upham may even have been somewhat jealous of all the literary talk since he too was an author with many works to his credit.

At the same time, Upham may well have resented remarks presumably made during the removal fracas. In September 1850 when Upham was running for political office, he could not obtain a majority in two tries and, therefore, did not succeed. As his friend, Nathaniel Silsbee Jr., said, "Upham had many warm friends but many determined enemies. A large portion of his own party voted for his opponent and others did not vote."[60] Whether that dislike had anything to do with his treatment of Hawthorne we do not know. In fact, it probably did not. But Hawthorne asked Zachariah Burchmore, "In the canvas against Upham did you remind the public of the fact of his refusing to read the Declaration of Independence one Fourth of July, some years ago, on the plea that he did not assent to its principles? Pike told it for a fact" (*CE* 16:366). Upham's father had been a Loyalist who had left the country at the beginning of the Revolution and had not come back. He was, in fact, an aide to Sir Guy Carleton for the remainder of the war and then became the judge of the highest court in New Brunswick. But as Upham says in volume two of his *Life of Pickering* in speaking of John Pickering, "his father and mine were class-mates and room-mates at college." And volume one includes a letter written by Joshua Upham to Timothy Pickering just after the war in which he says, "The public quarrel at an end, why should individuals continue the contest?"[61] Pickering evidently agreed, according to a chapter in volume 2, "Pickering and the Tories," in which Upham gives many details of Pickering's tolerance of those who took the opposite course from his during the war. Pickering did not approve of the confiscation of estates, nor of harsh treatment. Since Hawthorne's own feelings toward homegrown Tories seemed very similar, the only reason I can see for his suggestion to Burchmore was sheer political revenge. Upham may have realized that this charge had been made earlier and resented it.

On the other hand, Salemites could have resented Upham's repeated references to "our ancestors" who were so wrong during the witchcraft

60. "Autobiography of Nathaniel Silsbee Jr.," typescript, Silsbee Family Papers.
61. Pickering and Upham, *Timothy Pickering,* 2:vi, 111.

year. The Uphams did not come from Essex County; they had no known connection to the witchcraft accusations. Upham really did draw "the moral as it tells the tale," but the moral was pointed at Hawthorne's ancestors, not his own. Even though his treatment of John Hathorne was not nearly so trenchant in the earlier lectures as in his later book on the subject, the judge was singled out for cruelty to Elizabeth Carey. And even though Hawthorne said he would "take shame upon himself" for his ancestor's sin, he may have resented an outsider pointing the moral for the community.[62]

At any rate, each persona in this drama reacted with an excess of emotion that leads one to wonder if each was primarily a hypocrite. In Upham's "Memorial" there is a great deal of not very repressed rage. And in *The House of the Seven Gables* there is the same. Most of the characteristics of Judge Pyncheon were not true of Upham. He was not a judge, a horticulturalist, or mixed up with the White murder, but he did suffer from bronchitis, which could have led to the same clearing of the throat "rather habitual with him not altogether voluntary, yet indicative of nothing unless it were a slight bronchial complaint" (*CE* 2:124). And he did seem overinvolved in this case. Hawthorne, on the other hand, was not the figure of "corruption, iniquity, and fraud" portrayed in the "Memorial," but he was in charge of many of the underlings who were part of the Democratic machine, which worked for its own ends, and he did lend his name to the party in the newspapers and elsewhere. Perhaps he, too, was not so innocent as he professed to be, and yet, at the end, he may not have known "whereabouts his party was."

62. Charles W. Upham, *Lectures on Witchcraft, Comprising a History of the Delusion in Salem in 1692*, 75–76, and *Salem Witchcraft*, 1:15.

9

Salem Friendships

In the midst of cheerful society, I had often a feeling of loneliness. (*CE* 3:70)

DESPITE HIS reputation as a recluse, partially self-engendered, Nathaniel Hawthorne was not without friends, many of whom he kept all his life. There are great gaps in our consciousness of some of his Salem friends; about others there is information, but usually not from the writer himself. Knowledge of his boyhood friends is especially lacking. Yet there are hints here and there.

As was usually the case with large extended families, many of his companions were relatives. Manning Hawthorne asserted that Nathaniel had his youngest uncles, John and Samuel, to play with as well as his sisters. Another friend was John Stephen Dike, stepson of Aunt Priscilla. Hawthorne mentioned going to Nahant with John and his sister, Mary Dike, in the summer of 1818 (*CE* 15:107). Hawthorne was obviously fond of John; he shared with him all the gossip he knew of Salem after Dike moved to the West. Both boys had gone to Mr. Archer's school together, and Louisa heard them each "declaim" in the summer of 1820 (*CE* 15:125*n*).[1]

Nathaniel in the summer of 1819 was taken to visit some "country cousins," the Fosters in Danvers, and his Aunt Mary wrote her brother Robert that Nathaniel "went in the water with Benjamin." Later in his notebooks, he observed the spot where the Fosters lived, remembered damming up a brook with Benjamin, and chanced upon the gravestones

1. M. Hawthorne, "A Glimpse," 183; M. Hawthorne, "Hawthorne's Early Years," 4; Edward B. Hungerford, "Hawthorne Gossips about Salem," 445–69.

of the parents, but he forbore trying to see Benjamin. "I used to like him then," he noted plaintively (*CE* 8:276–77). Benjamin was two years older than Nathaniel and a second cousin on the Manning side. Another childhood playmate was Thorndike Deland (b. 1806), whose father was an auctioneer in Salem. Years later when Ralph Waldo Stoddard was collecting tributes to Hawthorne on the one hundredth anniversary of his birth, he heard on April 11, 1904, from novelist Ellen Douglas Deland, who reported, "My father, Thorndike DeLand, who was born in Salem in 1806, was a playmate of Hawthorne's and knew him well. They were near neighbors and close friends until my father went to boarding school at the age of thirteen. They met but once in after life as my father went to Philadelphia to live." Elizabeth, his sister, thought that Hawthorne was a normal boy in his teens, only retiring a bit from society after college. She wrote James T. Fields, "When he was a boy of fifteen he was not so very shy; he was too young to go into society, but he went to dancing school balls, for he was a good dancer, and he never avoided company, and talked as much as others of his age."[2]

Our concern is not with his companions in Maine, either in Raymond or at Bowdoin, although the latter produced several of his most cherished comrades. Fortunately we know a good deal about the Salem friends of his more mature years, but we must take some of the generalizations about them with caution. Especially is this true, I think, of the characterizations by Dr. George Bailey Loring, whose words to Moncure Conway have influenced many later writers. Loring did not move to Salem until 1851 and did not meet the Hawthornes until July 1852 when he paid them a visit in Concord (*CE* 16:676). He had married Mary Toppan Pickman, Sophia's cousin, and had reviewed *The Scarlet Letter* favorably for the *Massachusetts Quarterly Review;* hence, the Hawthornes were prepared to like him. Loring observed in 1890 to Moncure Conway, who was writing a biography of Hawthorne, "My first wife, a cousin of Mrs. Hawthorne, used often to urge Sophia to bring him to her house, but in vain. Salem was full of cultivated and brilliant people at that time, but Hawthorne could not be induced to visit them."

2. Mary Manning to Robert Manning, June 28 [1819], misdated 1818, Hawthorne-Manning Collection. Richard Manning Jr.'s sister, Elizabeth (b. 1734), had married Thomas Day of Ipswich; their daughter Anstiss (1767–1837) married Benjamin Foster (c. 1769–1844). Their son Benjamin (b. 1802) was Hawthorne's second cousin. See *Vital Records of Beverly*, 1:135; 2:120, 439, 440; Ellen Douglas Deland to Ralph Waldo Stoddard, April 11, 1904, in "Tributes from American Authors on the 100th Anniversary of His Birth," Nathaniel Hawthorne Collection (#6249), Clifton Waller Barrett Library; Stewart, "Recollections of Hawthorne," 325.

In 1888 Loring wrote a section on Salem's literature for the *History of Essex County, Massachusetts,* edited by Hamilton Hurd. He spent much more time in the Hawthorne portion on his love of solitude than on his writing. He did say, however, that "for his old official friends he had a tender affection; for the strong and practical young men with whom he set forth in life he had an abiding love and attachment; they satisfied the longings of one side at least of his existence." Loring warned those who accused Hawthorne of dissipation or vulgarity, however, that the accusations were not true.

When Loring first came to Salem, he was a Democrat. He tried hard to unseat Ephraim Miller as the collector of the port in 1853, tried to enlist Hawthorne's help, and probably thought that it was Hawthorne's influence with Pierce that enabled Miller to be collector, whereas Loring was appointed postmaster. He had also written Hawthorne that he would do nothing to get Burchmore a position (*CE* 16:629, 646, 687). Mary Toppan Pickman Loring died in December 1878. Joan Maloney details Loring's unethical treatment of Mary Pickman's money, showing a darker side to the man. Loring certainly seems to have influenced Conway, who in turn influenced others. That Loring's view of Hawthorne was so influential, despite the fact of very brief acquaintance, is puzzling.[3]

CALEB FOOTE (1803–1894)

One of the "strong and practical young men with whom he had set forth in life" may well have been Caleb Foote. Born of a family long settled in New England (his earliest known ancestor, Pasco Foote, came in 1636), Foote's grandfather, Caleb Foote, was a prizemaster on a privateer during the Revolution and a prisoner of war in Fortum Prison in England, an experience that left the family in poverty. His son, also named Caleb Foote (1778–1812), was a mariner who died at sea when the youngest Caleb was merely nine years old. That fact, in itself, could have been a strong bond between Foote and Hawthorne.

Foote, on the other hand, had a more difficult life than did Nathaniel. He was an only child and an orphan very early, since his mother also died prematurely. Caleb, with no huge family to fill in the empty spaces in his life, left school at the age of ten, and worked in an uncle's grocery store, then in Henry Whipple's and Samuel West's bookstores.

---

3. Conway, *Life of Hawthorne,* 116; *History of Essex County,* 1:144; Maloney, "George Bailey Loring: A Matter of Trust-s," 35–60. "Rose does not like Mr. Loring," reported EMH to Rebecca Manning, copy, November 22 [187?], Hawthorne-Manning Collection. Rose had lived with the Lorings in 1867. See Patricia Dunlavy Valenti, *To Myself a Stranger: A Biography of Rose Hawthorne Lathrop,* 37–38.

He learned arithmetic by making change in his uncle's store and gained a little Latin from an old grammar. Later he studied French and Spanish so that he could profit by the foreign newspapers that Salem sea captains brought him. He became an apprentice at the *Salem Gazette* office at the age of fourteen and remained with the paper seventy-one years. He was editor and proprietor, sometimes alone and sometimes sharing the responsibilities with other journalists. "It is difficult now," wrote Winslow Warren in 1893, "to realize the importance of the local editor of a prominent paper at that time in such a place as Salem, especially when, as in the case of Caleb Foote, he represented in a large degree the culture and social importance of the town."[4]

His activities were not, however, confined to his paper. He was admitted to the Essex Lodge of Freemasons on January 4, 1825, and was its master in 1830, 1831, and 1832. He lectured for the Salem Charitable Mechanic Association. He was one of the first directors of the Salem Lyceum, and was a member of the Massachusetts House of Representatives (1832–1833) and of the Governor's Council. In 1835 he married Mary Wilder White, daughter of Judge Daniel Appleton White. In fact, according to Sarah Freeman Clarke, it was at Judge White's that Elizabeth Peabody met Hawthorne, "which was the only house he visited and then only when the family was supposed to be alone."[5] Hawthorne had evidently witnessed or noticed the marriage of Caleb Foote and Mary White in October 1835, and had either observed or heard of the reactions of the new bride to a discussion of Halley's comet by Dr. John Brazer in North Church shortly thereafter (*CE* 23:139).

The Footes had six children, three of whom survived. Winslow Warren, who wrote a sketch of one of their children, describes the sort of parents they were: "Children's tales and histories were read together by the fireside, poetry was committed to memory and repeated, selections from religious books and the best of modern authors were studied and discussed." Their first child, Henry Wilder Foote (1838–1889) was the Unitarian minister of Boston's King's Chapel from 1861 to 1889. Their daughter, Mary Wilder White Foote Tileston (1843–1934), edited the letters of her parents and what was called "a widely loved anthology,"

4. Perley, *History of Salem,* 1:369; Henry W. Foote, "Caleb Foote," in *History of Essex County,* 1:247–48; Cantwell, *Nathaniel Hawthorne,* 130, 131; C. D. Phelps, "Printing, Publishing, and Bookselling," 275; Tapley, *Salem Imprints,* 93; Winslow Warren, "Memoir of Rev. Henry W. Foote," 238.

5. William Leavitt, "History of the Essex Lodge of Freemasons," 3:255, 4:257; C. Upham, "Francis Peabody," 49, 52, 53; H. W. Foote, "Caleb Foote," *History of Essex County,* 1:248; Norman Holmes Pearson, *Hawthorne's Two Engagements,* 2.

Daily Strength for Daily Needs, among other books. Arthur Foote, another son, was a well-known musician and composer who penned an autobiography that gives glimpses of Caleb Foote. "I look back," writes Arthur, "and realize how little I understood of my father's solitary life for almost forty years. . . . There was no eight-hour day for my father!"[6] Mrs. Foote's death in 1857 accounted in part for the solitary nature of Caleb Foote, but he also worked too assiduously to have much spare time.

That lack of time may in part explain what seems to have been a fairly meager friendship between Foote and Hawthorne. In 1873, James Upton, in explaining to his son that so few Salemites knew the writer before 1837, reported that he had asked Foote the day before "if *he* ever knew him or of him in the days of his obscurity. He said no; but he had printed quite a number of his anonymous productions which he could satisfactorily identify from internal evidence." It is strange that two boys of an age, both having lost mariner fathers early, both often watching all the preparations in the War of 1812, would not have met until 1837. There is a report that Hawthorne gave many of his stories to Foote's early partner, Ferdinand Andrews (which would have been from 1825 until April 1826), and then took them back and burned them since Andrews failed to publish them. Foote and Hawthorne could have met that way. In January 1835, Foote, in reviewing the *New-England Magazine,* remarked, "In the spirited sketch of 'The Gray Champion' we think we recognize the hand of one whose productions have occasionally adorned this *Gazette.*" When *Twice-Told Tales* was published, Foote affirmed in the *Salem Gazette* (March 17, 1837) that he knew who the author was: "Mr. Hawthorne is no man of straw, but a taxpayer in Salem, where he and his fathers before him, have lived these two hundred years supporting an honorable name." Foote published several of Hawthorne's early productions, two "Carrier's Addresses," and reprinted others.[7]

Caleb Foote was a Whig, and he edited what was then a Whig paper. From May 1841 to August 1844 he was postmaster of Salem, a position

6. W. Warren, "Memoir of H. W. Foote," 236, 238; Arthur Foote 2d, "Henry Wilder Foote, Hymnologist," 4; Arthur Foote, *Arthur Foote, 1853–1937: An Autobiography with Notes by Wilma Reid Cipolla,* 12, 27.

7. James Upton, "Hawthorne in the Salem Custom-House: An Unpublished Recollection," 114; G. Lathrop, *Study of Hawthorne,* 135. Ferdinand Andrews was partner from 1823 to 1825 with Caleb Cushing of the *SG* and partner with Foote in 1825 (Phelps, "Printing, Publishing, and Bookselling," 267); *SG,* January 9, 1835, August 26, 1825, November 2, November 12, November 23, December 7, and December 21, 1830, January 11, 1831, January 2, 1838, and January 1, 1839. It is possible that Andrews accepted the poem "The Ocean" (August 26, 1825) before Foote became a partner.

Hawthorne wanted. He was even at the Whig meeting on July 6, 1849, when Charles W. Upham read the "Memorial" to oust Hawthorne as surveyor; it was unanimously accepted. As Arlin Turner points out, Foote always went along with the party, both in 1849 and in reviewing Hawthorne's *Life of Pierce* in 1852.[8] Foote's political partisanship, however, seemed fairly moderate. His wife wrote a revealing letter to her sister-in-law on November 6, 1855:

> I never felt happy before in his position during an election, [she wrote]. It was what he could not help, but for years I have hated to have him forced along to endorse or work for the Whigs. This year he has really succeeded in maintaining an independent position. . . . This course is never a popular one, and people feel fully at liberty to call it cowardly, inconsistent, treacherous, and every way unsatisfactory. But, as he privately observed to me, "I have suited one person, and that has been one whom it has been hard to satisfy in many previous elections—*myself.*"[9]

Perhaps, then, Foote was always the sort of person with whom one could disagree without losing his friendship.

It is true, however, that Hawthorne's correspondence with Foote, so far as we know it, consisted of two letters from Hawthorne to Foote in the early 1840s (one asking advice about editing a newspaper with Longfellow, and the other requesting repayment of a loan); two others— one in 1846 about the birth of Julian and another in 1851 about the birth of Rose—were to Mary Foote, who had long been a friend of Sophia's (*CE* 15:489, 604; 16:175, 439). Not only is there not much recovered correspondence between the two men, but Hawthorne did not seem to send his books to Foote. Probably the publishers did. Members of Hawthorne's family and early biographers rarely mentioned the editor. George Lathrop gives a picture (which could have come from Foote himself) of Hawthorne in 1837 stopping by Foote's office "full of excitement" at his burgeoning social life.[10]

Hawthorne does not use such characters as newspaper editors often in his work. He stresses the importance of their work in "Old News,"

---

8. H. W. Foote, "Caleb Foote," *History of Essex County,* 1:247–48; Winfield S. Nevins, "Nathaniel Hawthorne's Removal from the Salem Custom House," 106; Turner, *Hawthorne,* 251.

9. Mary W. Tileston, *Caleb and Mary Wilder Foote: Reminiscences and Letters,* 222–23.

10. For some of Sophia's letters to Mary Foote, see RHL, *Memories,* 49, 50–57, 75–76, 82–83; Pearson, *Hawthorne's Two Engagements,* 2; Pearson, "Elizabeth Peabody on Hawthorne," 265; Tileston, *Caleb and Mary Foote,* 90–91; G. Lathrop, *Study of Hawthorne,* 169.

where he brilliantly reconstructs the Boston of the eighteenth century from the papers of the time. In "Old News," he remarks, "Happy are the editors of newspapers! Their productions excel all others in immediate popularity, and are certain to acquire another sort of value with the lapse of time. They scatter their leaves to the wind, as the sybil did, and posterity collects them, to be treasured up among the best materials of its wisdom. With hasty pens they write for immortality" (*CE* 11:132). He asserts that Holgrave was once a political editor of a newspaper, but then he alludes to many other occupations that Holgrave briefly held (*CE* 2:276). The very fact that he could always publish in the *Gazette* (even though he did not send original work after 1838, so far as we know) must have been helpful to Hawthorne.

Foote died in 1894 after a long life. His children appear in various encyclopedias or lists of famous persons, while he does not. Foote never received the sort of praise he merited. He appreciated the work of Hawthorne very early. For that, if nothing else, we should remember him.

DAVID ROBERTS (1804–1879)

Support for a friendship with another Salemite, however, is more directly available. Born the same year as Hawthorne, David Roberts was the son of Samuel Roberts (1768–1835) and Martha Stone Roberts (1772–1845) of Hamilton, Massachusetts. His father was a Mason and a charter member of the Salem Charitable Mechanic Association in 1817. David Roberts lived in the family home, 21 Winter Street, after his father died in 1835. He attended the Salem Latin Grammar School and Harvard, from which he was graduated in 1824. He read law for three years with Leverett Saltonstall in Salem and passed the Essex Bar in 1827.[11]

An active if somewhat unobtrusive citizen, he was a Freemason. The *Salem Gazette* on February 16, 1827, listed him as "Master of the Veil" (which may have amused Hawthorne). He was marshal of the Liberty Lodge in Beverly in 1828. During the "Morgan Excitement" of November 1831 he signed the petition defending Masonry. He was also among those who met in Topsfield to plan an Essex County Lyceum. He was a charter member of the Naumkeag Fire Club in July 1832 and later its president. At the Salem Lyceum in 1836/1837, he delivered a lecture on Benjamin Franklin. Hawthorne quite possibly heard the lecture or heard Roberts speak of it before he wrote his stories of Franklin in *True Stories* (*CE* 6:262–67, 268–74). Roberts also seems to have been fond

11. "Portraits in Essex Institute," 141–42; William D. Dennis, "The Salem Charitable Mechanics Association," 34; *Vital Records of Hamilton, Massachusetts to the End of the Year 1849,* 31.

of music. He signed a letter on behalf of the Musical Society of Salem, and he willed his Chickering piano to a niece at his death.[12]

Roberts was no Democrat, although many Hawthorne scholars have assumed he was. He was nominated on the National Republican ticket in May 1829 rather than on the Jackson ticket. He signed the Salem resolution opposing Jackson on March 21, 1834. He was listed as a Whig in November 1834. In May 1845, Hawthorne observed that "Conolly and Roberts have each an influence on different newspapers in Salem," and this usually referred to the political orientation of the papers (*CE* 16:96). Roberts was in the state legislature in 1833–1834. Charles P. Huntington, a fellow representative, noted in his diary that he "appears to be a pleasant fellow, with frightful whiskers and steel bow spectacles." In 1866 Roberts was mayor of Salem for a brief period but resigned because of a disagreement with the aldermen. Almost a decade earlier on February 14, 1857, he characterized his political stance in a letter to Hawthorne: "I assure you that my vote was most satisfactory to myself in the late election, as it was given from principle only. The Result delights me; but the scramble I loathe as you know & am now quiet as ever politically."[13]

We do not know when the friendship with Hawthorne began. Perhaps they became acquainted through the offices of Horace Conolly. Conolly and Roberts were always good friends. He was the "Chancellor" and Conolly the "Cardinal" in the little group that played cards with Susan Ingersoll and Nathaniel and Louisa Hawthorne (*CE* 15:62). Our concrete knowledge of the friendship starts in 1838 in allusions to Roberts in the notebooks and when Hawthorne, who had gone to North Adams, Massachusetts, with the firm resolve not to let anyone know of his location, wrote Roberts and asked him to tell him some Salem gossip (*CE* 23:193, 194; 15:274). The editors of the *Centenary Edition* believe this letter indicates that they had known each other since boyhood (*CE* 15:62).

Hawthorne went with Roberts in 1840 to Susan Ingersoll's and there discovered not only that the house had had seven gables but also

12. "Portraits in Essex Institute," 141–42; *SG,* January 4 and July 8, 1828, and March 21, 1834; Leavitt, "Freemasons," 3:88; Dennis, "Fire Clubs," 14, 16; Dennis, "Charitable Mechanics," 8; *Historical Sketch of Salem Lyceum,* 42; George M. Whipple, "A Sketch of the Musical Societies of Salem," 120; Essex Probate Court, #51812, will of David Roberts, July 7, 1879.

13. *SG,* May 15, 1829, and November 7, 1834. Stewart, Turner, and the editors of the *Centenary Edition* have all indicated that Roberts was a Democrat; Charles P. Huntington, "Diary and Letters of Charles P. Huntington," 258; David Roberts to NH, February 14, 1857, Hawthorne Family Papers, Bancroft Library. Roberts's comment apparently refers to the election of President Buchanan, a Democrat.

received from Ingersoll the suggestion for the general frame and title of *Grandfather's Chair*.[14] Roberts visited the Hawthornes in Concord in 1843; Sophia was not impressed. She wrote Louisa Hawthorne that he was an "intolerable heavy lump of stupidity and clownishness. . . . Nathaniel acknowledged he had no idea of him before" (*CE* 15:62). Louisa, who had spent much time playing whist with Roberts, may not have appreciated this opinion; one doubts that Hawthorne did. When the Hawthornes were hoping for the surveyorship in Salem, Roberts and Pike drew ground plots on Roberts's hearth of a possible spot on a hill for a house for them (*CE* 16:130).

We know little of the friendship when Hawthorne was "decapitated." What Roberts actually did to help, if anything, is unclear. His remark later that he loathed the "scramble" of politics and that he was now "quiet as ever politically" may be appropriate to remember. Louisa wrote Hawthorne in 1852 that David Roberts had mentioned all manner of possible appointments Hawthorne could have when Pierce was elected president, and she added: "I not by any means thinking office the most desired path to glory for you, very coolly told him I hoped you would have nothing to do with it. I believe he thought I was very ridiculous."[15]

Office did come Hawthorne's way. Appointed Consul at Liverpool, he wrote Roberts in 1855 asking him to get the facts on the ancestral Hathornes, and Roberts, who seemed by this time to be interested in genealogy too, researched the Salem Hathorne facts, some of them obtained from Ebe, and sent them. He remarked that "Wm. [Hathorne], Judge John, Capt. Daniel & others are characters & it is full of interest & novelty to me. I have copies of their Wills etc." In a following letter he acknowledged, "I have never thought of my ancestors till this past year."

Roberts showed his consideration of his friend in the same letter when he said:

> I should not be in a hurry to throw up your consulship at present. Be first sure to get yourself pecuniarily independent & then come home & "grow old quietly" if so disposed.
>
> But I give you one mark as from an old friend & that is—*Keep in the harness as long as possible*—if the pen wearies you—read if not for yourself at any rate for your children—mental culture is sometimes a riddle & one hardly knows when he is dropping seeds in the right place.
>
> I pray you let me hear often & give my love to your family; trusting

14. M. Hawthorne, "Hawthorne and Man of God," 269–82.
15. Turner, *Hawthorne,* 243.

that your children may yet still further adorn their father's name and race.[16]

Hawthorne sent a copy of each book to Roberts, who was himself something of a writer, having written an article on Matthew Cradock, first governor though nonresident of the Massachusetts Bay Colony, for the first volume of the *Historical Proceedings* (1848–1856), and another in 1860 for the *Collections* entitled "Paper on a Spared Record of the Salem Custom House." But most of all, he wrote *A Treatise on Admiralty and Prize* (1869), which sounds rather trifling until one holds its bulk of 709 pages in hand. He was also on the library committee of the Essex Institute from a very early date and was on the committee set up to study whether the chief business of the Essex Institute should be genealogy.[17]

After Hawthorne's return from England, he wrote Roberts on January 29, 1861, and asked him to visit Concord. "We have reached the age, now, when old friends ought to make the most of each other," he observed (*CE* 18:359). Roberts did visit for two days the next June. In September 1863 he was again asked to come. "Mrs Hawthorne wishes much to see you," Hawthorne affirmed (*CE* 18:601). Perhaps Sophia had changed her mind about this old friend.

When Roberts died in 1879, in his will written in 1877, he spoke of "the Harmony ever hitherto existing in the Family." He provided for his sisters and his nephews; he willed his "classical, philosophical & miscellaneous books" to the children of his sister Caroline. I do not agree with Hubert Hoeltje that Roberts was "a lonely man who had never apparently found his niche," but I do agree that there were "bonds of friendship with Hawthorne neither ever revealed."[18] It seems to me that we can surmise from the little we do know that this was a solid and supportive friendship, perhaps interrupted for a while by Sophia's dislike, but surely never ended.

DR. MALTHUS AUGUSTUS WARD (1794–1863)

Dr. Malthus Augustus Ward was another friend whom Hawthorne had apparently first met at Bowdoin, but who lived in Salem for a time, and

16. David Roberts to NH, September 17, 1856, Hawthorne Family Papers, Bancroft Library; Roberts to NH, February 14, 1857, Hawthorne Family Papers, Bancroft Library.

17. David Roberts, "Historic Discourse on the Life of Sir Matthew Cradock," 242–55; Roberts to NH, September 17, 1856, where he asks Hawthorne for any information he can find on Cradock in England; David Roberts, "Paper on a Spared Record of the Salem Custom House," 169–77; and David Roberts, *A Treatise on Admiralty and Prize . . .* ; *Proceedings,* Essex Institute, 2:82–91.

18. Essex Probate Court, #51812, Roberts will; Hoeltje, *Inward Sky,* 217.

then moved to Georgia. Nathaniel had written Louisa from Brunswick on May 4, 1823, "There is in the Medical Class a certain Dr. Ward of Salem, where he intends to settle after taking his degree of M.D. which will be given him this term. I shall give him a letter of introduction to you, when he returns to Salem, which he intends in about a fortnight. He is the best scholar among the Medicals, and I hope you will use your influence to get him into practice" (*CE* 15:177). In the Hargrett Rare Book Room and Manuscript Library at the University of Georgia, where some of Ward's notebooks are housed, on the back cover of an 1823 book is penciled, "Nathaniel Hathorne—Herbert Street."

Who was this certain Dr. Ward? His early life is not totally documented, but his biographers, William Barlow and David O. Powell, have unearthed enough shards to have suggested his interest to Hawthorne. The son of Joshua and Elizabeth Whitworth Ward, Malthus (originally spelled Maltis and thus a clue to pronunciation) was born in 1794 in Haverhill, New Hampshire, where his farmer father struggled to make a living for the family of five children. Ward somehow attended Haverhill Academy and Middlebury College in Vermont, according to his obituary in the Augusta, Georgia, *Southern Cultivator* in 1863. He certainly received a liberal education somewhere, as his notebooks attest with their numerous references to Shakespeare, Fielding, Aristotle, Euripides, and others.

Between 1812 and 1815, he served in the War of 1812, apprenticed himself for two years to Dr. Ezra Bartlett of Haverill, a son of a signer of the Declaration of Independence, and attended the new Medical Institution at Dartmouth College. Though he did not receive a degree there, he was a frontier physician in Pennsylvania and Indiana from 1815 to 1822. The *New-England Magazine* of September 1831 reported that "he has traversed the country from Kennebec to the Lakes—thence to Missouri and the Gulf of Mexico—crossed the Alleghenies at three distinct places, and resided six years westward of them."[19]

He attended the new Medical Institute of Maine at Bowdoin, and there he and Hawthorne were acquainted. His medical degree was awarded in September 1823, but, preceded by Hawthorne's letter, Ward went to Salem in May. His roots were in Salem; he was a descendant of Miles Ward and had innumerable kin among the Salemites. It soon

19. William Barlow and David O. Powell, "Malthus Augustus Whitworth Ward," in *Dictionary of Georgia Biography,* 2:1033–34; *New-England Magazine* 1 (1831): 274. This section on Ward was read before the Philological Society of the Carolinas at the University of North Carolina at Asheville, March 1995.

became clear that he was more interested in botany and horticulture than medicine, or perhaps he concluded the possibilities of a livelihood were greater in those fields. The *Observer* announced on May 31, 1823, that he proposed to give a course of Botanical Lectures. In the following October he discoursed on chemistry. Ward was also one of the founders of the Salem Lyceum and participated in its first year; in June 1830 he offered talks on botany and floriculture. A lecture on botany is copied into one of his notebooks. He wrote that "Botany appears to be peculiarly adapted to the study of ladies. . . . It is a science, too, within the range of female acquirement." He was also secretary of the Essex Lodge of Freemasons from 1828–1831 and was a trustee of the Salem Athenaeum in 1831. In addition, he practiced medicine and attended the sick at the almshouse. He was married in 1829 to Eliza Cheever of Salem. Altogether he was a very solid citizen.[20]

In 1825 he became superintendent of the East India Marine Society, later to become the Peabody Museum, which housed some very fine Polynesian and Asian marine artifacts brought by Salem mariners from around the world. A new building for the cabinet (as the display was called) had been built in 1824/1825. In February 1824 the superintendent of the museum was "authorized to purchase any article of curiosity for the use of this Society to render their Museum more complete." Ward was also chosen professor of botany and horticultural physiology for the Massachusetts Horticultural Society from 1829–1831, which he helped found. As he increasingly moved from the practice of medicine to horticulture, he came to know Robert Manning, who started his pomological garden in 1823, and was prominent in the Horticultural Society.[21]

In 1831 Ward was elected to be a professor of natural history at Franklin College (as the University of Georgia was then called) in Athens, Georgia, where he was to teach courses in botany, mineralogy, geology, and physiology. Before Ward left Salem for Athens, Hawthorne visited the East India Museum on March 22, 1832, with Samuel Dinsmore

20. George R. Curwen, "Materials for a Genealogy of the Ward Family and Notices of the Descendants of Miles Ward," 207–19. In his senior year Hawthorne himself took a medical course in anatomy and physiology. See Turner, *Hawthorne*, 39, and *General Catalogue of Bowdoin College and Medical School*, 56, 440; *Observer*, May 31, 1823, and October 18, 1823; C. Upham, "Francis Peabody," 52, 53, 55; *ER*, June 14 and 17, 1830; Dr. Malthus A. Ward Collection, Hargrett Rare Book Room and Manuscript Library; Leavitt, "Freemasons," 3:259; *SG*, January 4, 1828, and June 2, 1829.

21. Ernest D. Dodge, "Captain Collectors," 30; *History of the Massachusetts Horticultural Society, 1828–1878*, 48.

and Franklin Pierce from New Hampshire, in order to see their old college friend, whose 1831 museum catalogue listed nearly five thousand objects. Charles A. Goodspeed believes that this visit triggered Hawthorne's imagination and provided the idea for a collection of assorted objects that the writer later described in "A Virtuoso's Collection."[22]

In Georgia, Ward was not only to teach but also to have oversight over a botanical garden, established in 1833, that flourished greatly for a while. The garden eventually covered twenty-five acres with two thousand plants, and a lake, a waterfall, and a fountain. Ward was reported to have brought a cutting from the Cambridge Elm under which Washington had taken command of the Continental Army on July 3, 1775. The garden, meant for the practical study of botany as well as aesthetic experience, did well as long as Ward had supervision, but he and one other professor had to resign in 1842 because state appropriations were reduced. In 1846 he applied again for the post of professor of natural science, but one of his former students, John LeConte (later president twice of the University of California at Berkeley) was selected by one vote. The botanical garden was sold in 1856 for one thousand dollars, which was used to put a fence around the university. Despite his disappointment, Ward stayed on in Athens, practicing medicine and pursuing his horticultural interests, even after the Civil War began. He died there in 1863.[23]

To revisit the Salem (and probably only) phase of the friendship, Hawthorne had not only introduced (or reintroduced) Ward to Salem but also had put him in touch with his family. Ward's association with Robert Manning must have helped them both. In 1842, the year of Manning's death, James Camak, a member of the Board of Trust and first professor of mathematics at the University of Georgia, ordered innumerable plants and trees from Manning, whose name he had received from Ward, but Manning was probably too ill to comply, since he died that October.[24] Such friendship as there may have been between the older Ward and the younger Hawthorne probably would not have lasted after Ward left for Georgia.

22. *New-England Magazine,* 1:274; Charles E. Goodspeed, *Nathaniel Hawthorne and the Museum of the Salem East India Marine Society,* 7.

23. Barlow and Powell, "Ward," *Dictionary of Georgia Biography* 2:1033–35; Samuel Boykin, "Reminiscences of the Original Botanical Garden," 2:23–25; *Garden History of Georgia, 1733–1933,* 72. Also see E. Merton Coulter, *College Life in the Old South,* 66, and Coulter, "The Story of the Tree That Owned Itself," 237–39.

24. James Camak to Robert Manning, May 20, 1842, Hawthorne-Manning Collection.

Be that as it may, the connection with Ward may have been closer still. Frank Cousins and Phil M. Riley in their book, *The Colonial Architecture of Salem,* report:

> During Nathaniel Hawthorne's residence near by in the house at Numbers 10½ and 12 Herbert Street he was on very friendly terms with the family of a relative then occupying the Derby-Ward house, and frequently he ate and slept there in one of the spacious chambers reserved for him. In this room and in a little summer house among the lilacs and syringas, shaded by an old apple tree of the garden, he wrote some of his earliest stories.

The Derby-Ward House on the corner of Derby and Herbert Streets had been sold to the Wards by the Derbys after the Revolutionary War. Edward H. Garrett in *Romance and Reality of the Puritan Coast of the North Shore* (1902) has a drawing of that house, and comments on its surroundings: "the summer-house, where the romancer loved to sit, is tumbling to pieces, and the garden is forlorn in its neglect. All sorts of weeds grow rankly in its wastes, and a little thicket of crowding poplars nearly hides, with the gray silver of their leaves, the purple and white of the ancient lilacs and the weather-beaten grays of the lower story." Roderick C. Penfield calls the Miles Ward House "a favorite visiting place of Hawthorne's."[25]

These statements have long puzzled me. I knew the Ward family lived there, but the city directories were not published until 1837, after Ward had moved to Georgia. Who was the relative who lived there? In the tangled web of Salem genealogies, anything is possible. A Miles Ward (and there were lots of them) who died in 1792 had married as his second wife Hannah Derby Hathorne, the widow of Hawthorne's grandfather's brother. The Wards married Osgoods, Hodges, Briggses, Osbornes, and almost any other Salem family that could be mentioned. Malthus Ward's great-uncle may have been Ebenezer Ward, the father of the Wards listed in that first directory. Those listed for 19 Herbert Street were Chipman Ward, Mary Ann Ward, and Miles Ward.[26] What would be more likely than Malthus Ward moving in with cousins when he removed to Salem in 1823 until he married in 1829 or until he left for Georgia in 1832?

---

25. Frank Cousins and Phil M. Riley, *The Colonial Architecture of Salem,* 51; Tolles with Tolles, *Architecture in Salem,* 54; Edmund H. Garrett, *Romance and Reality of the Puritan Coast of the North Shore,* 118, 121; Roderick C. Penfield, "Pioneers of American Literature," in Cameron, *Hawthorne among His Contemporaries,* 408.

26. Curwen, "Genealogy of the Ward Family," 208; *Salem Directory and City Register,* 1837.

If this be the case, it changes the picture of Nathaniel holed up in his top-floor room, isolated from the world. It would mean that he had written some of those early stories in the midst of flowers and sunshine! And its influence may be seen in the description of the Pyncheon garden in *The House of the Seven Gables* in which the summer house is called "this green play-place of flickering light" or the garden is "this one green nook, in the dusty town" (*CE* 2:145, 148). Furthermore, James Duncan Phillips, without mentioning Hawthorne, describes the Derby house as "the lovely old gray unpainted house then in the midst of a tangled garden, shaded by a magnificent elm tree," which we all know was a tree that graced a house that had seven gables.[27]

JONES VERY (1813–1889)

Jones Very too might be called a friend of Hawthorne's—for a limited time and with restrictions. He was the son of Captain Jones Very and Lydia Very, one of those women who made the idea of women in Salem a complex one. She was fiercely passionate and independent, an atheist until her son considered that God spoke through himself. There are those who feel, with good reason, that her qualities contributed significantly to the person whom Very was briefly to become in the late 1830s. He was described in Charles Archer's notebooks in clippings from the *Salem Evening News* (May 31, 1922) as "a very tall man quite plain, with a long, long face and hollow cheeks, beardless but for a small turf of down on the sides, his countenance inclined to be somewhat melancholy. . . . He looked as though he had just stepped out of an old family portrait." Very's story has been well told by Helen R. Deese and Edwin Gittleman. As Very moved from student days at West School, Isaac Hacker's school, through two voyages with his mariner father, to becoming an assistant to Henry Kemble Oliver in another Salem school, he was more and more interested in Transcendentalism and in a belief that one must sacrifice his own will to God and let God speak through him. His Harvard days, both as an undergraduate and as a student in the Divinity School and a tutor in Greek to undergraduates, confirmed and escalated his struggle. He began preaching more and more to his students. He also lectured (speaking as one having authority) some of the stalwarts on the Divinity School faculty, such as Henry Ware Jr. Very at this time was completely convinced of his mission. His immediate reward was to be asked to leave Harvard. He then attempted the same conversations in Salem, especially with his own minister, John Brazer

27. James Duncan Phillips, "Salem in the Nineties," 302.

of North Church. Lucius Bolles of the Baptist Church "put him bodily out of the house," and agreed with Charles W. Upham of First Church that Very was dangerously insane, so he was sent to McLean Asylum in Charlestown, Massachusetts, for a month.[28]

He was a poet of remarkable potency during his time of empowerment by the Holy Spirit. He then spent an aftertime of writing poetry and gentle preaching in a voice no one could hear. His crucial period lasted from December 23, 1837, until sometime in 1840—also a very important time for Nathaniel Hawthorne—and it was during this interval that they became friends. Elizabeth Palmer Peabody was, as usual, the intermediator. She had gone to hear one of Very's lectures at the Lyceum, offered her hand, which he grasped "like a drowning man," and invited him to come to the Charter Street home. Soon Hawthorne and Very met there to everyone's best recollection. Sarah Freeman Clarke remembered seeing Hawthorne and Very, "both new treasures of Elizabeth's," possibly in January 1838. The Peabody sisters and the two men attended Miss Susan Burley's club on Saturday nights. When Very was forced to leave Harvard, he visited each of these people in September 1838 to offer them his gifts of baptism as the embodiment of Christ. He also revisited them after his return from the asylum. Miss Burley and the Frederick Howes were discomforted by him. Elizabeth Peabody was a concerned listener and helper. Sophia was the most receptive to his message except when he told everyone his sin and pointed hers out as "the love of imagination," which, if she would give up, she would no longer feel pain.[29]

Very also delivered his message to Hawthorne from 1838 to sometime in 1840. Elizabeth Palmer Peabody described to Emerson one of his visits:

> Hawthorne received [his message] in the loveliest manner—with the same abandonment with which it was given—for he has that confidence in truth—which delivers him from all mean fears—& it was curious to see the respect of Very for *him*—and the reverence with which he treated his genius. . . . He says Very was always vain in his eyes—though it was always an innocent vanity—arising greatly from want of sense of the ludicrous & sanctified by his real piety & goodness.[30]

Mary Peabody wrote Sophia on January 5, 1839, that Hawthorne has concluded that Very "wants a brother and is trying to convert him

28. Gittleman, *Jones Very,* 157, 190; *The Complete Poems,* ed. Deese; Helen R. Deese, "The Peabody Family and the Jones Very 'Insanity': Two Letters of Mary Peabody," 218.
29. Gittleman, *Jones Very,* 188–89, 219, 223; EPP, *Letters,* 220.
30. EPP, *Letters,* 221.

and goes there very often. What shall I do? says he" (*CE* 15:482). In July of 1840 when Hawthorne was in Boston, he wrote Sophia, "Night before last came Mr. Jones Very; and thou knowest that he is somewhat unconscionable as to the length of his calls" (*CE* 15:481).

Hawthorne referred to Very in two of his works. In "A Virtuoso's Collection," which appeared in the *Boston Miscellany* in 1842, he spoke of "Jones Very,—a poet whose voice is scarcely heard among us by reason of its depth" (*CE* 10:491). In "The Hall of Fantasy," which appeared in Lowell's *Pioneer* in 1843, in a part later cut, he described "Jones Very [who] stood alone, within a circle which no other of mortal race could enter, nor himself escape from" (*CE* 10:638). After Nathaniel met Very, he told Elizabeth Peabody that Very "more than realised the conception of entire subjectiveness he had tried to describe in the preacher of 'The Story Teller.'" As Michael Colacurcio has pointed out, Very is also likely to have been in Hawthorne's mind when he wrote "Egotism: or the Bosom Serpent."[31] When Very went around pointing to each person's sin, it must have been very like the hissing of the snake in Roderick Elliston's breast (*CE* 10:275–77).

From our very lack of knowledge about the relationship between these two writers, we can see something of Hawthorne's manner of friendship. He was kind to Very and believed him totally sincere; he refused to ridicule him, though he was cognizant of Very's own lack of a sense of humor. It seems to me that this relationship, brief though it seems to have been, shows us that quality of loyalty which Edwin Haviland Miller has pointed out. Furthermore, the friendship may have lasted longer. Helen Deese remarks that, according to one source, Very in 1849 "along with Thomas Treadwell Stone and Nathaniel and Sophia Hawthorne helped arrange a series of conversations for Alcott in Salem," although she does say that her assumption "is that they were not really close after Very's 'ecstatic' period subsided."[32] Nevertheless, the coldness that is so often ascribed to Hawthorne does not seem evident here.

ELEANOR BARSTOW CONDIT (1822–1886)
Hawthorne always seemed to have a special affinity with children. He not only wrote books for them but also described the activities of his own children with unusually pleased interest. Mrs. Ora Gannett Sedgwick later recorded some of her experiences at Brook Farm. The

31. EPP, *Letters,* 408; Colacurcio, *Province of Piety,* 507, 516.
32. Miller, *Salem Is My Dwelling Place,* 88; *The Complete Poems,* ed. Deese, xxviii. My thanks to Helen Deese for her letter, February 6, 1995.

writer of a newspaper clipping at the Peabody Essex Museum is grateful for her giving

> us such charming pictures of Hawthorne, walking along the brook, it may be, with his hands clasped behind his back, closely followed by a delighted group of children, who seemed to stoop at intervals, and, then, faces all smiles, pick up something and go on after their leader. On being closely watched, it was found that Hawthorne dropped an occasional penny, without apparently looking back or paying the slightest attention to the children, much to the latter's edification and profit.

Another glimpse of the Salem writer with children comes from Edward Waldo Emerson, son of the man who felt he could not achieve friendship with Hawthorne. The younger Emerson observed, "His smile when we suddenly came upon him was delightful; for children were not to him little half-molded and untamed lumps of creation, but rather estrays from Paradise bringing some of its airs with them, important in saving the human man from corruption."[33]

Hawthorne's friends were not all male, by any means. One friend was a little female cousin. Horatio Bridge wrote Hawthorne, after reading "Little Annie's Ramble," on March 19, 1837, "It must be that you had some particular child in your mind's eye, and perhaps did actually take the walk?" And that was probably true. Eleanor Barstow was Hawthorne's cousin; they seemed to have a special bond between them. According to James T. Fields, Eleanor remembered "before Hawthorne had printed any of his stories, she used to sit on his knee and lean her head on his shoulder, while by the hour he would fascinate her with delightful legends, much more wonderful and beautiful than any she has ever read since in printed books." Elizabeth Hawthorne also commented on the Hawthorne-Barstow friendship, and Randall Stewart has recorded her reminiscences: "Elinor [*sic*] . . . was a very affectionate child. She was almost the only person out of his immediate family who knew my brother; and I believe people liked to tease her about him—to say something to his disadvantage, in order to see her kindle into wrath in his defense. She told me about it the last time I saw her. She said that she was a perfect little tempest." Eleanor does seem to have been a "perfect little tempest." Annie Barstow, Eleanor's sister, explained to her friend, Mary Silsbee Sparks, when there was a proposed visit to Cambridge including Eleanor, that "Mother has some fears of trusting

---

33. "A Girl of Sixteen at Brook Farm," undated newspaper clipping in the Nathaniel Hawthorne Papers; E. W. Emerson, *Early Years of Saturday Club,* 212.

Ellen on so hazardous an expedition. She is so wild and thoughtless that she don't know what you and Mr. Sparks may think of her—but Ellen makes great promises of sobriety of demeanour & seems so anxious to avail herself of your kindness that I think it will terminate in your supporting her good company for a week."[34]

When a bit younger, this is the little Annie with whom Hawthorne rambled. Of course, no character is the exact copy of someone the writer has known in life, nor is the first-person narrator always Hawthorne himself. Every writer transforms his characters from people that he may know to an amalgamation of those known and those imagined. Yet in this case, Eleanor Barstow thought she was Annie; as did Elizabeth Hawthorne; as did almost everyone in Salem. She was about three or four years old when Hawthorne returned from college. It is difficult to tell exact age because the Barstows seemed to have had their children baptized in batches. Elizabeth Lathrop Chandler thought the earliest possible date for the writing of "Little Annie's Ramble" was September 1825 and the latest date was June 1834. Hawthorne says that the little girl was five years old and would commence reading the *Juvenile Rambler* soon, a periodical that first appeared in 1826 (*CE* 9:124).[35]

Little Annie was even then "longing after the mystery of the great world," and was the "giddy child" who loved "the silks of sunny hue, that glow within the darkened premises of the spruce dry-goods men" (*CE* 9:121, 123). She is also the "Ellen" who brought an "exquisite crimson rose" to Sophia Peabody with such evident delight in her gift. It has been said that Hawthorne did not like her later, that he thought her unnatural, or so Sophia informed Elizabeth Peabody probably in the summer of 1838 and continued, "he expressed a sense of her brilliant powers, her wit and acuteness, and then said he thought 'women were always jealous of such a kind of remarkability' (that was his word) 'in their own sex' and endeavored to deprecate it."[36] He seems to be explaining, however, women's dislike of her, not his own.

Eleanor went to St. Augustine with her father and mother in 1852, where Dr. Barstow died. Perhaps it was in Florida that she met Caleb Harrison Condit of a wealthy and influential New Jersey family and

34. JH, *Hawthorne and Wife,* 1:151; R. S. Rantoul, "Opening Remarks," 6. Rantoul identified Eleanor Condit as Annie, as did Elizabeth Hawthorne in Stewart, "Recollections of Hawthorne," 329–30; Fields, *Yesterdays with Authors,* 47; Annie Barstow to Mary Silsbee Sparks, February 19 [184?], Richards and Ashburner Papers, Mss. 20368, f. 153.

35. Elizabeth Lathrop Chandler, "A Study of Sources of the Tales and Romances Written by Nathaniel Hawthorne before 1853," 57.

36. RHL, *Memories,* 9; JH, *Hawthorne and Wife,* 1:193.

married him as his second wife. She then went to live in Newark, New Jersey, where her children were born. At some point her husband was confined to a mental hospital, and she seems either to have lived with her mother or in Europe. In 1869 she published her book, pseudonymously, *Philip English's Two Cups, "1692,"* and others later.[37]

She kept up her friendship with Elizabeth Hawthorne and visited her cousin often at Montserrat. Eleanor asked Elizabeth once if she thought Sophia appreciated Nathaniel. "I told her that she believed herself worthy of him; at which Eleanor was indignant," wrote Elizabeth.[38] Eleanor Barstow Condit was clearly still on Hawthorne's side, although the friendship with Hawthorne seemed to be restricted to Eleanor's childhood.

SUSAN INGERSOLL (C. 1785–1858)

Susannah Ingersoll, another female friend, is fairly well known in Hawthorne scholarship. She was baptized Susannah after her mother, but, as she acknowledged in her will, she was commonly called Susan. She was the surviving child of Captain Samuel Ingersoll (1744–1804) and Susannah Hathorne (1749–1811) who lived in the old Turner house, popularly thought of as a model of the house with seven gables. Her grandmother, Susannah Touzel Hathorne, lived until 1802 in the old English house, the home of Philip English, who had been accused, along with his wife, of witchcraft. William Bentley was interested in the old lady and the stories she had to tell of the Englishes and the Touzels, of the founding of St. Peter's Church, and in the books, papers, silver, and crystal she owned. When her daughter Mrs. Ingersoll died, the minister believed he had to rescue Susan from the avarice of her cousins, the family of Colonel John Hathorne (1749–1834). Bentley wrote in his diary, "This morning I was with her only daughter who has been beset by the Col's family with the ferocity of tigers. They insisted upon entrance into the house and apartments. The daughter had swooned upon the death of her mother and was very low. I took such charge as she desired me for which I expect their vengeance." Bentley felt he had to hide Susan's money and the keys to the house from "the hungry expectants."[39] Thereafter, Susan lived alone except for a housekeeper and the young man named Horace Conolly of unknown antecedents.

37. Gideon Barstow to Anne Ashburner, March 8, 1852, Richards and Ashburner Papers, Mss. 20368, f. 188; Annie Ashburner to Mary Silsbee Sparks, January 13 [1857] and October 15 [1858?], Richards and Ashburner Papers, Mss. 20368, ff. 204, 221; M. B., *Philip English's Two Cups, "1692."*

38. EMH to Robert Manning, March 6 [no year], copy, Hawthorne-Manning Collection.

39. Essex Probate Court, #43338, will of Susannah Ingersoll (written November 25, 1835; probated August 3, 1858); Perley, *History of Salem,* 1:132; Lillian Drake Avery,

In her youth Ingersoll was celebrated for her "beauty and accomplishments." According to Caroline Emmerton, Susan was "a tall, stately young woman, fond of society, so it is said, until an unfortunate love affair with a naval officer, who sailed away, turned her into a recluse and more or less of a man hater." Perhaps there was a naval officer, but even more likely there was a courtship for a time by Dr. Seth Bass (1780–1867), later librarian at the Boston Athenaeum. In March 1817, Benjamin H. Hathorne wrote his sister Elizabeth Ranney that "once in about six months we accidentally see Susan Ingersoll & we hear of her being visited yet by Doctor Bass but we do not know whether they will make a match of it or not." George H. Holden reported that Elizabeth Hawthorne said in 1882 that "the doctor who was engaged to Miss Ingersoll was married (Miss [Ann] Savage thinks)" and then, by itself, the word "Bass." Bass was superintendent of the East India Marine Society until he was succeeded by Malthus Ward in 1825. He had studied medicine at Dartmouth in 1815, married Ann Lovett Harmon at Beverly in 1826, and was librarian at the Boston Athenaeum from 1825 to 1846.[40]

Whether Susan or Dr. Bass broke off this affair, surely something happened to make her a recluse. Emmerton noted that "Miss Ingersoll was a recluse with something in her past which made her shrink from any form of publicity." Eleanor Putnam later described Susan and her house: "In the days of my childhood its mistress was a lonely woman, about whom hung the mystery of one whose solitude is peopled by the weird visions that opium brings. We regarded her with something of awe, and I have wondered, in later days, what strange and eldrich beings walked with her about those shadowy rooms, or flitted noiselessly up and down the fine old staircase." The former curator of the house, David Goss, proposes that those "eldrich beings" were runaway slaves. A secret staircase, discovered later, contained an ancient book of prayers and hymns with the inscription "Cuffy—his book." Goss says that Caroline Emmerton, who was told of this find by the new owner, believed that slaves were hidden there from about 1830 to about 1860. Were this true, slaves were there all during the times Hawthorne was visiting the Duchess, as he called her. Emmerton also says that she saw in an old letter an allusion to the secret staircase that Hawthorne used

A Genealogy of the Ingersoll Family in America, 1629–1925, 45; WB, *Diary,* 2:385, 446–47; 4:71–72, 73.

40. C. Emmerton, *Chronicles,* 23; Benjamin H. Hathorne to Elizabeth Ranney, March 1817, copy, English/Touzel/Hathorne Papers; George Holden's interview with Ann Savage, August 18, 1888, Nathaniel Hawthorne Papers; Nathaniel Ingersoll Bowditch, "Death and Funeral of Doctor Spurzheim," 79; *SG,* March 11, 1825.

in "the first draft of *The House of the Seven Gables* or outline of his romance, but on showing it to Miss Ingersoll encountered her strong objection to anything which should arouse the interest of the curious in her house."[41] This could support Goss's view, but it would also indicate that Hawthorne had written the first draft or outline even earlier than has been thought. It could also mean that Ingersoll just did not like curious strangers.

Hawthorne may have known Susan Ingersoll since his childhood in the vague way that children know their older relatives, but his formal introduction to her occurred later, according to an unsigned, undated letter at the Peabody Essex Museum in which "Miss Savage" acknowledged that Hawthorne had "expressed a wish to become acquainted with Miss Ingersoll," and, on inquiring, announced that Ingersoll "desired him to take tea with her" and to bring his sisters. Francis H. Lee also commented on this meeting in his diary on January 6, 1878, recollecting that he had called on Miss Savage, who reported that "Mr. H's first visit to Susie Ingersoll was made with her and her sister, she introducing him. It was when he was a young man, and lived down town. He escorted them home, stopping as it was quite cold, for them to rest at his house. He went in and sat in the dark, telling them stories and expressing his fondness for chattering in the dark." Further evidence of this meeting comes from George Holden's interview with Ann Savage. She said that on that visit "the Dutchess [*sic*] . . . had much to say about the Hawthornes as a striking race, as peculiar as the Jews & remarkably handsome."[42]

In *Hawthorne's Country* (1910), Helen Clarke quotes an octogenarian in Salem who remembered Hawthorne, Conolly, and the others "having a jolly, not to say convivial time" in the kitchen of the Turner house, that "punch or some other not entirely innocuous beverage played a

41. C. Emmerton, *Chronicles,* 39, 28; Eleanor Putnam [Harriet Leonora Vose Bates], *Old Salem,* 79; Howard Parnell, "Secret Staircase Indicates Seven Gables Railway Stop," 4.

42. [Ann Savage] to NH [n.d.], Hawthorne-Manning Collection. This visit must have been before 1828 or after 1832, the time when Hawthorne lived in North Salem. His name is spelled with a "w", which indicates it was after his college years; Francis H. Lee, "Forty Years Ago in Salem," 102; George Holden's interview with Ann Savage, August 18, 1888, Nathaniel Hawthorne Papers. JH inaccurately recorded this passage as the "Hawthornes were to other people what Jews are to Christians, says Miss Ingersoll or somebody who knew them." Norman Holmes Pearson added dryly: "Precisely what Susan Ingersoll, or 'somebody' meant is not clear." It is not clear because that is not what Ingersoll said. See Norman Holmes Pearson's article, "Hawthorne and the Mannings," 171.

not unimportant part."[43] Thus, the use of either opium or alcohol was rumored about Susan Ingersoll's gatherings. Neither one would seem to be conducive to the efficient running of an underground railway stop. The fact that Horace Conolly did not know about the secret staircase, as Caroline Emmerton thought, appears to undermine that supposition. It is possible that Hawthorne would not know of such activities, but not probable for Conolly who lived there. However, since Conolly did not have a reputation for strict veracity, he may have only said he did not know.

The house in which Susan Ingersoll lived was a prototype for the seven-gabled house in Hawthorne's novel, according to Horace Conolly. Susan Ingersoll had mentioned that the Turner house had once had seven gables. "The expression was new and struck me very forcibly," said Hawthorne, "I think I shall make something of it." The Duchess led him to the attic and explained where the last two gables, now missing, had been. She also urged him to write something, and when he said he had nothing to write about, she pointed to an old Puritan chair and suggested that he deal with that. From that one visit, if Conolly is right, Hawthorne received ideas for *The House of the Seven Gables* and for *Grandfather's Chair*. Conolly confirmed the story with David Roberts and mistakenly added that the novel was written at odd times while Hawthorne lived in Mall Street. Actually (unless Emmerton's story that he showed the first draft to Ingersoll is true), it was drafted in Lenox after he had finished *The Scarlet Letter*, although many of its ideas had been in his mind for a long time.[44]

During his stay in Salem between 1825 and 1839, Hawthorne and his sister Louisa often went to the Ingersoll house to play cards with Horace Conolly and David Roberts and Susan Ingersoll. Eleanor Putnam describes going to the house herself as a child; she felt that the house was beautiful but not an easy place for a child. She describes a cupboard full of sparkling cut glass, "an array of frail and icy splendor." Bentley had mentioned this same crystal at great grandmother Susannah Touzel Hathorne's house.[45] Hawthorne in his notebooks remarks on "[an] ancient wineglass . . . long-stalked, with a small, cup-like bowl, round which is wreathed a branch of grape-vine, with a rich cluster of grapes, and leaves spread out" (*CE* 8:181). This glass stayed long in Hawthorne's memory. In the manuscript "Septimius Felton"

43. Helen A. Clarke, *Hawthorne's Country,* 64, 151.
44. Streeter, "Historic Streets," 210–12.
45. Putnam, *Old Salem,* 79–80; WB, *Diary,* 1:147.

he speaks of "a most pure kind of glass, with a long stalk, within which was a curious elaboration of fancy work, wreathed and twisted" (*CE* 13:186).

Susan Ingersoll probably inspired various fictional characters. Gilbert L. Streeter observed that she was said to be Alice Pyncheon in *The House of the Seven Gables.* "If ever there was a lady born, and set apart from the world's vulgar mass by a certain gentle and cold stateliness, it was this very Alice Pyncheon," he affirmed. She was very likely to have inspired the picture of Ursula Hillsworth in Eleanor Barstow Condit's *Philip English's Two Cups, "1692,"* who was "nearer kin to the English's than any one in town." Edward Wagenknecht suggests that Hepzibah Pyncheon may owe some part of her character to Susan.[46]

After Hawthorne left Salem, he does not to my knowledge mention Miss Ingersoll except once when he wrote to Horace Conolly, and once after her death in *The American Claimant Manuscripts* (*CE* 16:346; 12:220). He did not seem to send her books. When he worked at the Custom House, he was very close to her home, but we have no record that he went to see her in his last years in Salem. Hawthorne was in England when Susan Ingersoll died.

SUSAN BURLEY (1791–1850)

Miss Susannah Burley was the black-haired, high-minded lady with luminous eyes who appears fleetingly in the letters of and scholarship about the Peabody sisters—Elizabeth, Mary, and Sophia—Jones Very, Mary and Caleb Foote, and, above all, Nathaniel Hawthorne. She seems to have been the centripetal force, drawing various Salemites toward her literary salons or "Hurley-Burleys" to converse with like-minded souls on Saturday evenings. She was what would now be called an "enabler," but we know more about those drawn to her than we know about her. Who was she and how did she get into such a position?

What we have known is that her sister, Elizabeth Burley, married Frederick Howes, an influential lawyer in Salem; that she was wealthy; that she financed the thrice-told edition of Hawthorne's "The Gentle Boy," which has illustrations by Sophia Peabody; that she arranged for Hawthorne to have a guest ticket at the Boston Athenaeum in 1846; and that she was an ever-present help in times of trouble, save perhaps to Jones Very. The most helpful sources of knowledge have been Edwin

46. Streeter, "Historic Streets," 208; M. B., *Philip English's Two Cups, "1692."* Ursula was, according to the narrator, "hardly a relative, although we might have claimed cousinship" (28); Edward Wagenknecht, *Nathaniel Hawthorne: The Man, His Tales and Romances,* 100.

Gittleman, a Jones Very scholar, and two Salem writers of reminiscences, Marianne Cabot Devereaux Silsbee and Caroline Howard King.[47] Burley's name is sprinkled through Hawthorne biographies without much elucidation. Some more scholarly excavation of facts may help, but it still does not fully illuminate this rather remarkable lady.

Susannah Burley was born the third child of William and Susannah Farley Burley in Boston on September 2, 1791. Her mother was the daughter of General Michael Farley, a delegate to the Provincial Congress from Ipswich. Her grandfather, Andrew Burley, was a graduate of Harvard in 1742. Susan Burley's father was a fascinating man. He was active in the Revolution, "enlisting as a soldier and while a lieutenant . . . was taken prisoner near White Plains, New York, remaining in captivity a year and nine months." After the war he set himself up as a banker and broker in Boston, and amassed a fortune. According to a handwritten obituary notice in the Beverly Historical Society, he retired to Beverly, "where his time has been alternately devoted to the cultivation of his farm and the moral qualities of the heart." During his Beverly years he established one of the first cotton factories in the country, but he had to abandon it with the decline of a waterfall. He bought Browne Hall, once resplendent on Browne Hill, built by Loyalist William Browne, who had had to move the home downhill when it was rendered unsafe by an earthquake. Browne had to flee to London with the advent of the Revolution. The house, purchased by William Burley, was removed in three parts to Danvers. Hawthorne had roamed the hill as a child and had heard stories of the house before it became triplets. In 1860 when his cousin, Richard Manning, asked for a sketch from Hawthorne to be published for some worthy cause, the writer obliged with the true sketch "Browne's Folly" (*CE* 23:399–402).[48]

An insight into another aspect of William Burley is offered by "Oliver Oldschool"—not Joseph Dennie, but probably Nathan Sargent (1794–1875)—who wrote a series of articles that the *Salem Gazette* copied from

47. Some of the best accounts of Susan Burley are found in Gittleman, *Jones Very,* 156–57; King, *When I Lived in Salem,* 166–68; M. C. D. Silsbee, *A Half-Century,* 97. This part on Burley was presented at the South Atlantic Modern Language Association in Baltimore in November 1994.

48. *A Report of . . . Boston Births from A.D. 1700 to A.D. 1800,* 339, 336; Charles Burleigh, *The Genealogy of the Burley or Burleigh Family of America,* 33, 17; *Vital Records of Beverly,* 1:59; 2:49, 30; Felt, *History of Ipswich, Essex, and Hamilton,* 154, 183; "William Burley legacy," June 28, 1823, a copy by Frederick Howes in the Beverly Historical Society. There is also a handwritten obituary of William Burley. Also see Edwin M. Stone, *History of Beverly,* 4; Robert S. Rantoul, "The First Cotton Mill in America," 1–43; Ezra D. Hines, "Browne Hill," 201–38.

the *New York Gazette* on July 18, 1837, in which the author reported that, as a lad, he was present at the Salem jail when

> Mr. Burley came in to enquire into the circumstances under which one of his unfortunate townsmen had been confined. The keeper informed him that he was incarcerated by an importunate and unrelenting creditor and that his case was one of peculiar hardship and distress. As soon as the circumstances were made known, the prison doors were unlocked and the captive set free, with a purse of relief for his family. Nor did Mr. Burley stop here. "What other suffering debtors have you on your list," said he to his friend the keeper. The list was shown him, when he not only visited them but paid their debts, and liberated them all.

William Bentley, on the other hand, thought that Burley (which he spelled Burleigh) was a singular and rather strange person. Possibly that was due to Burley's seeming preference for conservative theology. Bentley described him as "the speculator of lower Beverly" and a "vulgar man" in 1794, which was Bentley's way of identifying those not leaning toward his own liberal religious predilections. In 1796 he called him a "curious man." In 1802 Bentley noted in his diary that Burley had given one thousand of the six thousand dollars spent on the new meetinghouse in Beverly, and by August 26, 1819, Bentley allowed himself to be socially entertained by Burley.[49]

One of the charities for which Burley was most noted was his provision in his will for the poor children in Beverly and Ipswich. He left one hundred dollars per year for ten years (which was a large sum in those days) to each town "to be applied for the instruction of poor children in reading and the principles of the Christian religion." Burley died on December 22, 1822.[50] Beverly stretched the sum for the whole ten years, whereas Ipswich applied the whole amount at once. Susan Burley was left comparatively wealthy by her father, as was her sister, Elizabeth, and her surviving half brother, Edward Burley, who later gave the first bequest to the Beverly Library and bequeathed his home, the old Cabot house, to be used as the Beverly Historical Society. Susan went to Salem to live with the Howes shortly after the legal work had been completed on her father's will. An understanding of Susan Burley rests on some knowledge of her father.[51]

It is quite clear that her father valued education, but where Susan received her instruction is not known. It was probably at the school set

49. WB, *Diary*, 2:346, 203; 4:159, 608.
50. Felt, *History of Ipswich, Essex, and Hamilton*, 89–91.
51. William Burley Papers.

up for both sexes in Beverly shortly after the Revolution. This school was a "small, plain building, heated by a large open fireplace." About forty students attended, paying "tuition of four dollars per quarter." A class in Latin and Greek was offered. "None of the teachers, all college graduates, received over five hundred dollars salary." Among the teachers was William Prescott, the father of the famous historian.[52]

Living with this father (her mother had died when she was two years old) indelibly stamped Susan Burley. She was not only well educated but also believed in lifelong learning. She was a mentor to the Peabody sisters and Jones Very, and she knew German as well as she knew English. Burley, with her "shining black hair" and "brilliant eyes," made free translations of the Grimms's fairy tales for Caroline King and her friends. Marianne Silsbee called her "a highly educated woman" who valued both "acquisition of varied knowledge" and "bestowing it with the devotion of a loving heart" on those around her.[53]

Before 1837 Susan Burley and the Howes lived on Chestnut Street in Salem, but moved to Federal Street in that year, and that is where the "Hurley-Burleys" were held. These occasions were always attributed to Susan Burley, although the residence belonged to the Howes. In November 1837 Hawthorne made his first visit to Charter Street and there met the Peabodys; the next day Elizabeth procured an invitation for him to dinner at the Howes'. Thereafter Hawthorne and one or several of the Peabody sisters went to the weekly meetings, and Burley's opinions were often quoted. Sophia told her sister Elizabeth in an undated letter that Hawthorne had said that now he "could not do" without going to Miss Burley's. She also reported a good-bye call on Burley by Hawthorne just before his trip to North Adams in 1838.[54] Hawthorne wrote Sophia from Boston in August 1840 that in Salem he had gone to the Hurley-Burley, and "considering that it was the first time I had been there without thee. . . . I enjoyed it very well." He also reported that Burley wanted him to write an address of some kind for the Bunker Hill Fair (*CE* 15:486, 487).

The Peabody sisters had known Susan Burley a long time, since child-hood, James R. Mellow says. In December 1836 when Elizabeth Peabody was back in Salem, she wrote Elizabeth Bliss of the mental stagnation of the place, but she clearly found an intellectual companion in Burley.[55]

---

52. *History of Essex County,* 1:739.
53. King, *When I Lived in Salem,* 166–68; M. C. D. Silsbee, *A Half-Century,* 97.
54. EPP, *Letters,* 207, 210–11, 216, 220; Gittleman, *Jones Very,* 56–57.
55. Mellow, *Hawthorne in His Times,* 116; EPP, *Letters,* 190.

The other Peabody girls were also encouraged by her: Sophia in her love for art and Greek sculpture, by borrowing drawings and engravings; Mary Peabody probably in her general high-mindedness.

Another attendant at the Hurley-Burleys was Jones Very. He tried to convert Burley. She thought he was "not capable of complete *views all round subjects.*" She said he talked violently at her house, "tells them they are wicked—and truth itself is a poison to them & says to them . . . there has been no good man since the apostles until himself." Elizabeth Peabody reported all these modest pronouncements to Emerson, and added that Very did not frighten Burley, but that "his conversation torments her & affects her dreams at night." Being a mentor to Very clearly had its price.[56]

Other participants in the Burley evenings were Mary Wilder and Caleb Foote, both of whom were extremely interested in books and in the ideas of Unitarianism. All the group, save for Hawthorne, were members of the Unitarian North Church and were distinctly responsive to Transcendentalism.[57]

Burley was also good with children. In Salem she had had what Marianne Silsbee called "working parties" to which young people went with their mothers and listened to the conversations. Sophia wrote Louisa that she had taken Una to see Susan to give her a copy of *Mosses from an Old Manse.* "Miss Burley played with her, rolling cushions across the floor and peeping at her in a facetious manner" (*CE* 16:172).[58]

In 1840 Susan Burley moved to Boston. On November 27, 1840, Hawthorne apprised Sophia that he had met Frederick Howes, who had asked him to come to the conversations that night, "although he seemed to think that Miss Burley will be in Boston." Hawthorne also wondered if Burley might go with them to Brook Farm (*CE* 15:505). She did not, but perhaps there was some hint of Burley in the description of the stateliness and dark-haired beauty of Zenobia in *The Blithedale Romance.* Mary Wilder Foote wrote her sister Eliza A. Dwight on December 20, 1840, that "Miss Burley's removal [to Boston] is an unmingled source of regret and truly the dearth of all intellectual stimulous in our society is appalling."[59]

In Boston Burley continued to be in their thoughts. Hawthorne saw her on the street, April 4, 1841, and declared to Sophia that "her face

56. EPP, *Letters,* 220; Gittleman, *Jones Very,* 266.
57. Tileston, *Caleb and Mary Foote,* 170.
58. M. C. D. Silsbee, *A Half-Century,* 97.
59. Tileston, *Caleb and Mary Foote,* 155, 156, 170.

seemed actually to beam and radiate with kindness and goodness" and that he thought she looked "really beautiful" (*CE* 15:524). By 1842 Burley had attended Margaret Fuller's Conversations. In November Fuller exclaimed to Elizabeth Hoar that "Miss S. Burley has joined the class and hers is a presence so positive as to be of great value to me." Emerson noted in the *Memoirs* of Margaret Fuller Ossoli that "the late Miss Susan Burley had many points of attraction for her, not only in her elegant studies, but also in the deep interest which that lady took in securing the highest culture for women. She was very well read, and avoiding abstractions, knew how to help herself with examples and facts." Even after she left Salem, she returned and in 1848 "instituted" the Salem Book Club, in which twenty women participated.[60]

Susan Burley was also a lady with good common sense. When Hawthorne seemed in imminent danger of permanently losing his position at the Salem Custom House, Burley was very concerned. Mrs. Peabody described her solicitude to Sophia. She was "very desirous that your husband should come out with the whole truth, at all risks and notwithstanding all delicacies," to do it soon, or "Mr. Upham might get possessed of political power which he had no moral right to have." She also thought that since Hawthorne had denied the first charges "which were of things morally innocent, this acquiescence under more grave charges might seem, to people at a distance, to imply confession."[61]

Unfortunately, Susan Burley died the next June. In a letter to her sister Eliza Dwight, Mary Foote declared despondently, "It seemed so sad and so sudden. She lived in the contemplation of the highest objects and she lived for duty exclusively." To S. C. Higginson, Mary Foote wrote, "she was one of the most remarkable beings I have ever known."[62] One can only ponder the encouragement and hope she gave to Hawthorne. She never thought he was idle; she thought his writings wove "a golden web"; and she lived just long enough to read, one supposes, *The Scarlet Letter.*

Hawthorne depicted his "ideal of a friend" in a letter to Sophia in February 1856, as one who would stir him "to any depth below my surface" (*CE* 17:438). Measured by Hawthorne's ideal of a friend, perhaps

60. Margaret Fuller, *The Letters of Margaret Fuller,* 3:101, 103; *Memoirs of Margaret Fuller Ossoli,* ed. Ralph W. Emerson and James F. Clarke, 1:320; Cynthia B. Wiggin, "History of the Salem Book Club," 137, mentions that books were given by Caroline King and Mrs. Joseph S. Cabot (a niece of Susan Burley), but the author does not mention Burley herself. King, *When I Lived in Salem,* however, does (168).

61. EPP, *Letters,* 224; JH, *Hawthorne and Wife,* 1:338–39.

62. Tileston, *Caleb and Mary Foote,* 155, 156, 170.

no one could stand up, but in his real Salem world, he did have those who fit lesser requirements. Nevertheless, these friends of Hawthorne's reveal some of his own qualities. His work appealed to Caleb Foote, and he, I think, did too. Certainly some sort of relationship persisted. His friendship with Susan Ingersoll may possibly have foundered on the rocks of Conolly's uneven affections; if she doted on her protégé as much as was reported, it would have been difficult to maintain the relationship. But for a time at least, Hawthorne had a friend who gave him ideas and contributed to his feeling for the past. The friendship with Malthus Ward probably did not survive Ward's removal to Georgia, but there are only suggestions of anything more than mere acquaintance. The relationship with Jones Very burned briefly and seemingly was extinguished, but perhaps not. Eleanor Condit was always his loyal friend. So were David Roberts and Susan Burley, and he continued loyal to them. They were a varied lot with different appeals. Taken with his political friends, they reveal Hawthorne's capacity to appreciate diversity. They also illustrate the variety of people that Salem and the North Shore produced. Even though Hawthorne could feel lonely in a crowd, he had friends in that crowd.

10

The Place of Women
ALL ABOUT EVE

And the Lord God said, It is not good that the man should be alone; I will make an help meet for him. (Genesis 2:18)

THE PLACE that woman should occupy has long intrigued human beings. Many Christians of Hawthorne's time believed that her sphere had been settled when God took Eve from Adam's rib as a helpmeet for him. Unfortunately for men's peace of mind, this patriarchal point of view continued to be debated. For both men and women, the lines kept fluctuating. Just as the whole question seemed settled, new questions would arise, sometimes with greater urgency. Was Eve's role always to be a helpmeet, or, alternatively, a snare and tempter? How much of the tree of knowledge should she be allowed?

The early nineteenth century was a time of increasing demand for education and more opportunities for women. Every newspaper or magazine that Hawthorne may have read would have touched on the topic, not always with approval. A writer in the *Boston Recorder* (April 17, 1819) stated that for woman "the proper end of acquiring knowledge is not to enable her to shine but to do good." In February 1828 the *New England Galaxy* took advantage of its editor's temporary absence to print a long article entitled "Blue Stockings," for which Joseph Tinker Buckingham, the editor, later apologized. The piece in question said that the "province" of women was "to superintend the affairs of the household," to dispense charity, and to educate their children. Women should be educated not to write "books and pamphlets to enlighten the age, but . . . [to] be enabled to do a more important duty," to "succeed well in works on education, and juvenile tales . . . [and] in their peculiar task of instructing the young." "They have adequate means and powers," the writer concludes, for this "immense field for their labors."[1]

This author may well have had in mind, among others, Sarah Savage of Salem, a writer as well as a teacher, who published at least twelve books, anonymously, which were very popular just at this time. These works, many of them for children, urged submission to duty and to God. But she also depicted women who educated themselves far beyond the usual practice of that age, although always in order to do good. It is conceivable that she wrote an editorial in a short-lived Salem newspaper, the *Ladies' Miscellany* (1830), under the name of Evelina, asking

> If female minds are inferior to those of the other sex, is it not because
> their mental faculties have never been called into action? Whilst the
> numerous colleges and public schools furnish every means of facili-
> tating the acquisition of knowledge by the one sex, how seldom have
> institutions been found devoted exclusively to the other; and females
> have been taught from infancy to distrust their own abilities; who then
> can wonder that so few females have yet appeared to advantage in the
> literary world?

Evelina continues her remarks by expressing gratitude that many "noble minds" were now willing "to promote the cultivation of female talent, and thereby raise woman to that elevated sphere which was assigned her by her Creator." These at least were probably the sentiments of Savage. Her first cousin was James Savage (1794–1871), a graduate of Harvard in 1803, president of the Massachusetts Historical Society and founder of the Boston Athenaeum. Had her education been the equal of his and the opportunities as ample, she must have sometimes thought that her sphere of doing good would have been so much wider.[2]

The question of women also involved not only their right to education but also their ability to write poems, novels, or treatises. Many scholars have of late concentrated on the role Hawthorne assigned to women, especially women writers. From his early piece on "Mrs. Hutchinson" to

---

1. S., "Female Education," *Boston Recorder,* April 17, 1819. Six years later in "On Female Education" *(Port Folio,* 20:413–15) Constantia remarked that even if women "should enjoy the rare distinction" of writing, they did not have to leave home to do it; Right [pseudonym], "Blue Stockings," *New England Galaxy,* February 8 and 22, 1828. An answer to "Blue Stockings," perhaps, appeared in a favorable review of *Hope Leslie* in the *North American Review,* n.s. 26:403–20.

2. M. Moore, "Sarah Savage," 240–59; Evelina [pseudonym], "For the Miscellany," 2:29. For James Savage, see Park, "The Savage Family," 323, or *DAB.*

his remarks about "scribbling women," Hawthorne has been castigated (*CE* 23:66–67; 17:304). Critics may and do differ on this question. Jane Tompkins in *Sensational Designs* (1985) argues that Hawthorne was deemed more worthy as a writer than Susan Warner because he was male and had "old boy" connections. He made the canon, and she did not. Louise DeSalvo in her feminist reading in *Nathaniel Hawthorne* (1987) deplores Hawthorne's ancestors, who "epitomize everything that feminist historians have identified as the characteristics of patriarchy," and believes that Hawthorne "aligns himself with his own ancestors." But James D. Wallace maintains that Hawthorne's opinion of "women writers was more complicated than any account of that opinion has recognized."[3]

Surely Hawthorne's opinion not only of women writers but also of women in general springs, in part at least, from his formative Salem years. From his birth until he went to college, he lived in a world largely peopled by women. In the section of Salem in which he lived there were many households run by women, either because their husbands were away at sea (sometimes for years at a time), or they had died in its service. In a limited sense, this was a matriarchal world. That is not to say, however, that women were dominant in Salem. Men still controlled the property and most of the decisions. But in a seaport, from which so many men were away so much of the time, women often were in de facto positions of control of the household.

In addition, women were not always confined to washtub or kitchen. Even a cursory glance at the pages of the *Salem Gazette* from 1808 to 1821 reveals women managing shops, tailoring, teaching school, operating boardinghouses, painting profiles, writing books, and leading benevolent societies. Women from poorer families were going into domestic service. Girls were also being recruited to work at the cotton factory in nearby Danvers. As early as 1814, Sarah Savage published a book entitled *The Factory Girl.* She also produced another on advice to female domestics. Many women held powers of attorney for their absent husbands (Margaret Heussler Felt for one), and paid all the bills when due. As Ann Douglas illustrates in *The Feminization of American Culture,* it was the women who first joined churches and did most of the church work, although they had to follow males out of the building after service and held no positions of authority. Furthermore, some women shared the lives of their husbands, as Harriet Martineau pointed out after

3. Tompkins, *Sensational Designs,* 3–39; Louise A. DeSalvo, *Nathaniel Hawthorne,* 4, 7; James D. Wallace, "Hawthorne and the Scribbling Women Reconsidered," 203.

visiting America in 1839; some sailed with their husbands, "trafficking around the world."[4]

But of all this, the lad Hawthorne was probably not aware. His experiences with his own family and his first teacher, Elizabeth Carlton, may have led him to believe that most women were private and submissive. For instance, when Priscilla Manning and Betsey Hawthorne wanted to go to Maine during the War of 1812, they meekly obeyed their brother Robert when he vetoed the idea. Other experiences in Salem tended to be the same. Hawthorne's earliest teacher may have been a woman, but all the others were male, as were his classmates. The same was true of his college days. It was only later, perhaps, in Salem that he began to see women in all their variety. He had a growing knowledge of some of his cousins: Ann Savage and her sisters, the Barstows, the Forresters, the Archers, Susan Burley, and Susan Ingersoll. He occasionally met young women on the various summer journeys he undertook. Some of the friendships he suggested may have been fueled by his imagination. Elizabeth said that he "had *fancies* like this whenever he went from home." His notebooks do show his awareness of females in all his travels. Randall Stewart has recorded a rumored engagement with an Eliza Gibbs of Edgartown. Hawthorne certainly was aware of a "Susan" who appears in "The Village Uncle." Elizabeth Hawthorne reported that "Susan's sister lived at John Forrester's, and so the affair became known. He never would tell us her name." He called her "a mermaid" and brought home a pink sugar heart to remember her by, but appetite overcame memory and he ate it.[5] Susan was certainly lovingly portrayed in "The Village Uncle": "You seemed a daughter of the viewless wind, a creature of the ocean foam and the crimson light, whose merry life was spent in dancing on the crests of the billows, that threw up their spray to support your footsteps" (*CE* 9:312).

Another eye-opening experience was his reading in the early history. For the most part, if we take the early records seriously, it was women who were among the primary dissenters, who demonstrated minds of their own. He would not have to have known all his familial connections to have recognized the importance of Hannah Phelps in the

4. [Sarah Savage], *The Factory Girl* and *Advice to a Young Woman at Service, in a Letter from a Friend;* Ann Douglas, *The Feminization of American Culture,* 159–62; Harriet Martineau, *Society in America,* 2:67.

5. Priscilla Manning to Robert Manning, August 29, 1814, Hawthorne-Manning Collection; JH, *Hawthorne and Wife,* 1:128; Maurice Bassan, "Julian Hawthorne Edits Aunt Ebe," 274–78; Randall Stewart, *Nathaniel Hawthorne: A Biography,* 43–44; [EMH], "The Susan Affair: An Unpublished Manuscript," 12; Turner, *Hawthorne,* 94.

story of the Quakers. The preponderance of women named as witches was evident.[6]

When he began to write stories about those early times in Salem, his tales often featured women. Dorothy Pearson in "The Gentle Boy" was an example of the warm, nurturing woman, whereas Catharine the Quaker was the sterile woman of monomaniacal ideas (*CE* 9:75, 104). Pride was the primary feature of Lady Eleanore in "Lady Eleanore's Mantle" (*CE* 9:276). Perhaps Hawthorne had heard the story that Dr. Bentley learned from Susan Ingersoll's mother, that Eleanor Storer came to America to marry her lover. There was a mix-up and she married Hollingworth instead. But, says Bentley, "She preserved her ideas of importance, as she never went abroad in the evening, unless with a servant before, & another behind her."[7] Perseverance characterized Esther in "Old Esther Dudley" (*CE* 9:294). Witches such as Martha Carrier entered his pages with gleams of "unquenchable pride" in "Main Street," or old crones such as Tabitha Porter in "Peter Goldthwaite's Treasure" (*CE* 11:75; 9:386–87).

Nathaniel Hawthorne's mixed statements on women reflect, I believe, his awareness of their infinite variety. His later famous remark about the "damned mob of scribbling women" must be balanced by his knowledge that the women had accomplished what earlier writers had talked about. There was a "mob" of such women, and they were "scribbling" (*CE* 17:304). But Hawthorne's depictions of women are more complex than this statement suggests. Sometimes they are portrayed as simple as Miriam in "The Canterbury Pilgrims" who has the "feelings of a nun," or as bitter as the victim of "estranged affection" in the wife of the unprosperous yeoman in that tale (*CE* 11:123, 130). They can be proclaimed as "sinless" as Alice in "Alice Doane's Appeal" or with ambiguous claims to the name of Faith in "Young Goodman Brown" (*CE* 11:227). Women may be saluted as "a stirring sisterhood" as are "our great-grandmothers in 'The Old French War,'" or as "innocent as naked Eve" as was Susan in "The Village Uncle" (*CE* 11:149; 9:316). In other words, these women were of all sorts and varieties, given the times in which they lived and the prevailing modes of expression.

Actual recollections by Salem women of Hawthorne's time are often nostalgic memories in which all the women are beautiful and all the children are above average. Two of the best such recollections are

6. See Carol F. Karlsen, *The Devil in the Shape of a Woman,* for a discussion of the role of women in the witchcraft story.

7. WB, *Diary,* 2:82.

those of Marianne Silsbee and Caroline King. Silsbee remarked that in Salem "to be handsome was almost a birthright," and King was greatly disturbed by Elizabeth Barstow Stoddard's mockery in *The Morgesons* of the Salem custom of wearing "splendid camel's hair shawls over calico dresses." Collections of letters, such as those of Leverett Saltonstall and his family, make plain some of the women of Hawthorne's day. Saltonstall's mother-in-law, Elizabeth Sanders, for example, wrote voluminously about the plight of the Indian, practiced good health habits long before many people knew they were good, and encouraged her family to speak up on all occasions. The reminiscences gathered by Francis H. Lee in the 1880s parade before our eyes the women of an earlier time as beautiful and effective. Private diaries and letters may sometimes show that this was surface stuff, that some women were miserable and—perish the thought—even ugly. Harriet Martineau wrote that for American women "indulgence was given . . . as a substitute for justice."[8] The prevailing view of women in Salem accorded with the predominant opinion of the country, but no alert citizen could have avoided knowledge of the discussion of "the woman question." Most Salemites—indeed most Americans probably—would have agreed with what Hawthorne had said in his essay on Ann Hutchinson, that there were "strong division lines of Nature" (*CE* 23:66). Woman had a place, and she should stay in it.

Hawthorne's experiences with women in his own adult life in Salem indicate what the town had to offer. In the late 1830s he emerged from his so-called seclusion, during which he interacted primarily with the women in his family. In his notebooks [perhaps 1837?] he recorded enigmatically that "[t]hose who are very difficult in choosing wives seem as they would take none of Nature's ready-made articles, but want a woman manufactured purposely to their order" (*CE* 23:154). Surely he was thinking about himself.

The role of women became personal for Hawthorne in the years 1837 and 1838. The publication of *Twice-Told Tales* led to his acquaintance with the Peabody sisters, especially Elizabeth, who was determined to know the author of the tales. From then on she promoted him in every possible way: she wrote reviews of his books; she helped to arrange his political appointment as weigher and gauger at the Boston Custom House; she published his histories for children that make up *True Stories (Grandfather's Chair, Famous Old People, Liberty Tree, and*

8. M. C. D. Silsbee, *A Half-Century,* 101; King, *When I Lived in Salem,* 21; Saltonstall, *Papers, 1816–1845;* E. E. Sanders, *Conversations;* Francis Henry Lee Papers; Martineau, *Society in America,* 2:226.

Biographical Stories, 1840–1842); and she printed "Main Street" in her one issue of *Aesthetic Papers* (1849).[9] But, perhaps, more important than any of these, she opened up for him a social world in Salem. The Peabody daughters (Elizabeth, Mary, and Sophia) were an education in themselves. If Nathaniel harbored thoughts of sweet, retiring womanhood, Elizabeth Peabody would have soon changed his mind. It was through the Peabodys that he began to know Susan Burley, an emancipated, intelligent woman who was still intensely feminine. He also met or continued to know Mary Wilder White, daughter of Judge Daniel Appleton White and wife of Caleb Foote. They were all intelligent readers, abreast of the latest currents of thought, and in touch with most of the intelligentsia of Massachusetts.

In the years 1837 to 1838 two women in particular captured his attention: Mary Crowninshield Silsbee and Sophia Amelia Peabody. There are those who would add Elizabeth Peabody to the list. Years later Caroline H. Dall said that Nathaniel and Elizabeth had been engaged, and that Nathaniel was always "in terror" that Sophia would find out. George W. Curtis had also heard the rumor and asked Hawthorne's cousin, Robert Manning, if it were true. Hawthorne wrote Catharine C. Ainsworth on April 12, 1838, according to Arlin Turner, that there was a rumor in Salem that he was engaged to two ladies there, and Turner believed they were Mary Silsbee and Elizabeth Peabody. The mystification lingered. On April 25, 1842, Benjamin Merrill wrote to Leverett Saltonstall, "I heard a rumor that N. Hawthorne and Miss E.P. Peabody or some of the sisters are betrothed—so the world may be blessed with transcendental literary productions—hope they will preserve their Copy-Right."[10]

The rumor aside, the facts were surely otherwise. Elizabeth may have had some such fantasy, but it is hard to fathom such a possibility. She was certainly a vital part of the events, and Hawthorne was probably pleased with the attention she provided. But it was Mary Silsbee and Sophia Peabody who were very much in the writer's thoughts in these years. Nathaniel met Sophia Peabody for the first time on November 11, 1837. There are various conjectures about his first meeting with Mary Silsbee. The year 1838 was the crucial one for both relationships.

Mary Crowninshield Silsbee (1809–1887) was the product of established Salem families. She was born on Daniels Street in eastern Salem, "in the oldest house in Salem," to Nathaniel Silsbee, a former sea captain,

9. EPP, *Letters,* 199*n,* 213, 217–18; Mellow, *Hawthorne in His Times,* 175, 285.
10. Norman Holmes Pearson, "Hawthorne's Duel," 238; George W. Curtis to Richard Manning, November 29, 1880, Hawthorne-Manning Collection; Turner, *Hawthorne,* 95; Saltonstall, *Papers, 1816–1845,* 4:84.

merchant, and United States Senator. The family built in 1818/1819 a much admired mansion on Washington Square. According to Jonathan Porter Felt, Silsbee (1773–1850) was "one of the earliest East India captains, and a member of the East India Marine Society, and afterwards a successful merchant trader to the East Indies." When Silsbee went to Washington in 1817, the capitol was in ruins from the War of 1812. He was in the House of Representatives (1817–1821) and later in the Senate (1826–1835). He was highly thought of by Leverett Saltonstall. Caroline Howard King described him as having a "dignified presence, silvery hair, and a very, very long nose."[11] Her mother was Mary Crowninshield, daughter of George Crowninshield and Mary Derby, a union that combined two of the most important merchant families of Salem. She was an aunt of the two Crowninshield boys involved in the White murder, but also the sister of the powerful Crowninshield men. The Silsbees and the Crowninshields were members of the Unitarian East Church.

Mary, along with her brother, Nathaniel Jr., went to a private school in the Franklin Building (where the Hawthorne Inn is now) to a John Clark. She went later to the well-known girls' school taught by Thomas Cole on Marlboro Street near the Tabernacle Church. She often accompanied her parents to Washington when Congress was in session. Hence, her education was not confined to Salem. Her father retired in 1835, and her mother died soon after.[12]

Nathaniel Hawthorne and Mary Silsbee may well have known of each other since childhood, since they lived in the same area of town and Nathaniel's father had sailed for Captain Silsbee. By 1837/1838, however, Hawthorne was smitten with Mary for a while and then disillusioned. According to Elizabeth Peabody who relayed the story much later to Julian Hawthorne, Mary used her wiles on Nathaniel to the point that he was ready to fight a duel with John Louis O'Sullivan, editor of the *United States Magazine and Democratic Review,* over something O'Sullivan supposedly had done to her. In addition, Elizabeth felt that this action encouraged Hawthorne's friend, Jonathan Cilley, to engage in his own fatal duel.[13] Hawthorne and O'Sullivan did not fight, largely

11. WB, *Diary,* 2:79; Whitney, "Crowninshields," 15; James A. Emmerton, "Henry Silsbee and Some of His Descendants," 286, 296; Tolles with Tolles, *Architecture in Salem,* 29–30; J. P. Felt in *Life of Manasseh Cutler,* 2:364*n;* "Autobiography of Nathaniel Silsbee, Jr.," typescript, Silsbee Family Papers; *History of Essex County,* 2:248 a, b; King, *When I Lived in Salem,* 51.

12. Crowninshield Family Papers; WB, *Diary,* 4:617; list of Cole's scholars, Scrapbook, 3:202, Francis Henry Lee Papers.

13. Pearson, "Hawthorne's Duel," 232. Cilley's death occurred on February 24, 1838.

because Hawthorne's gauntlet was a letter, and O'Sullivan explained the situation to his satisfaction.

It is not known exactly how Mary and Nathaniel began their more intimate friendship. Perhaps as Edwin Miller has suggested, she sought out Hawthorne after *Twice-Told Tales* was published in March 1837, or they may have been properly introduced by O'Sullivan, as Arlin Turner asserts. James R. Mellow believes that they may have met earlier in 1837 and that Mary was the object of Bridge's matrimonial inquiries in 1837. Whether Hawthorne "crushed" Mary after he discovered her duplicity or not, she married Jared Sparks as his second wife on May 21, 1839, and went to Cambridge to live. Sparks alluded to his engagement in a letter on November 19, 1838. The historian had been warned by his friend, Ann Storrow, about Mary Silsbee earlier in 1830 when he courted the Salem belle in Washington. Storrow had written Sparks, "But her thirst for display and admiration is so utterly insatiable that it leads her I verily believe to sacrifice for the sake of it much that is lovely and beautiful in a woman's character—properties which you, my susceptible friend, love and admire as much as anybody when you have clear possession of your faculties."[14]

Sparks was not at that time the only susceptible man in Washington. In April 1831 Anne E. Saltonstall wrote her sister, "We are all just going up to Mary Silsbee's where I fear we may interrupt a tête à tête. Mr. Buchanan is devotion itself. I never witnessed anything like it." There are several other references to the future president and his attendance on Mary Silsbee. In addition, by February 8, 1839, Leverett Saltonstall informed his daughter, Anne, that a friend [Daniel Jennifer] was thoroughly acquainted with Mary—"and with all her peculiarities."[15]

Edwin Haviland Miller, having read Silsbee's book of poetry, "[p]rinted not published," finds a melancholy, sensitive strain in the "Star of Salem" and believes that she was maligned by Julian, who followed Elizabeth Peabody's account with its undertones of "suppressed rage." Certainly the picture given by Julian is devastating. She was, according to Julian and Elizabeth Peabody, a liar, a manipulator of men with her "Armida-like" wiles. It is very clear that there was something of the sorceress Armida about her. She was able to charm Hawthorne into the very uncharacteristic gesture of challenging O'Sullivan to a duel. The

14. Miller, *Salem Is My Dwelling Place*, 145; Turner, *Hawthorne*, 96; Mellow, *Hawthorne in His Times*, 103–4. For Bridge's inquiries, see JH, *Hawthorne and Wife*, 1:158, 161, 162, 164; Adams, *Life and Writings of Sparks*, 2:541–42; Ann Gillam Storrow, "Letters of Ann Gillam Storrow to Jared Sparks," 201–31.

15. Saltonstall, *Papers, 1816–1845*, 2:13–14, 195.

aftermath left him depressed. He observed to Mrs. Lydia T. Fessenden on April 22, 1838, "It has been a winter of much anxiety and of very little pleasure or profit" (*CE* 15:269). The death of Cilley on February 24, 1838, in addition to his feeling of betrayal by Mary, was hard to bear. Elizabeth Peabody wrote Elizabeth Hawthorne about Hawthorne's "unequal spirits last spring" when she began to suspect that "M.C.S. was coquetting."[16]

On May 1, Sophia apprised her sister Elizabeth about a visit she and Mary had made to the home of Mary Silsbee to see a picture:

> We were put into the drawing room before Miss Mary appeared, [were] received very simply and pleasantly, and I was very agreeably impressed with her. But the picture—I should call it a huntsman, and not a bandit. It was sometime before I saw it—except the resemblance to Miss Silsbee which is at first very striking. But then I did so wish to be alone with it, as soon as I began to comprehend and kindle. I wanted to put Miss Mary out of the window. . . . I tried to keep silent and abstracted before the delicate nobleness of the form and the countenance of the huntsman. . . . What very much impressed me was the motion in his hushed attitude—the head almost imperceptibly bent on one side to listen. So full of life and grace and energy!

It seems very clear that Sophia saw in the tilted head and the countenance of the huntsman the portrait of Hawthorne with Mary Silsbee, and it made her furious.[17]

After O'Sullivan had disabused Nathaniel of his faith in Mary Silsbee, Hawthorne, according to Elizabeth Peabody, went to see Mary and "crushed her." On May 31, 1838, Nathaniel Silsbee took his two daughters on a long trip to the Midwest. When they returned in August, Mary was ill. Hawthorne himself had left Salem on July 23 and did not return until September 21, saying to Sophia that he wanted no one to know where he was, including his own mother. He spent that time in western Massachusetts and filled his notebooks with descriptions of new people and scenes. His only surviving letter of this period is to David Roberts in July (*CE* 15:274). In fact, all the players had left the scene. Sophia was not present to greet Hawthorne on his return. She had gone to Marblehead to visit the home of Samuel Hooper in the latter part of September (*CE* 15:297).[18]

16. Miller, *Salem Is My Dwelling Place*, 148, 147; JH, *Hawthorne and Wife*, 168–69; EPP to EMH, as cited by Mellow, *Hawthorne in His Times*, 120.

17. SPH to EPP, May 1, 1838, Berg Collection.

18. JH, *Hawthorne and Wife*, 1:173, 192; Mellow, *Hawthorne in His Times*, 119; SPH to EPP, September 21 and 25, 1838, Berg Collection.

Leaving town was not the end of Hawthorne's seeing Mary and perhaps not the end of his infatuation. Elizabeth Peabody wrote [October 19, 1838] to Elizabeth Hawthorne, "In my hurry last evening I forgot to say that M. Silsbee is downstairs—I asked the Dr. if she was ready to see company—& the Dr. said she hardly feels like it I guess but nevertheless I [EPP] guess your brother would not be refused if he were to send in his name—and very like it would be a pleasure that would help on her recovery." Bruce A. Ronda thinks that the *she* who was ready to see company was most likely Sophia Peabody, but it seems more likely to me that she was Mary Silsbee.[19] In November of that momentous year of 1838, Hawthorne wrote O'Sullivan that he had seen "our fair friend." He felt manipulated by her, but now he recognized it for what it was. Even though she had expressed a "desire and a determination to break off all intercourse," and even though she had invited him to come to see her, she nevertheless managed to make him feel the villain. "All the glory was on her side," he ruefully observed, and "no small glory it is, to have made a wronged man feel like an offender—and that, too, without permitting any direct allusion to the matter in dispute" (*CE* 15:278).

He left that interview feeling that "there was no real sympathy between us" and that it was his "duty to stop here, and to make her aware that I have no further aims." He goes on to say that she probably acted honorably toward him and that her remark about a "secret spring" concerned something about herself, not her father's disapproval (*CE* 15:278–79). Elizabeth Peabody thought the "secret spring" was his ability to make three thousand dollars a year, a salary unlikely for Hawthorne.[20] It is interesting to note, however, that in that same letter to O'Sullivan, Hawthorne urges, "do not you be one whit the less zealous to get me the Post-Office; for the salary may purchase other comforts as well as matrimonial ones" (*CE* 15:279).

The affair seemed to be over. Hawthorne wrote Longfellow on January 12, 1839, that he had seen Mr. Sparks at Miss Silsbee's "some time since" (*CE* 15:288). Having taken the job of weigher and gauger in Boston, he informed O'Sullivan on May 19, 1839, that he was returning a letter of O'Sullivan's to Mary Silsbee, and that she had burned all of his correspondence. He continued:

> [N]ow certainly the last knot of our entanglement is loosed. She is to
> be married, I believe, this week—an event which, I am almost sorry to

19. EPP, *Letters,* 214*n*5.
20. Norman Holmes Pearson, "A 'Good Thing' for Hawthorne," 304; Miller, *Salem Is My Dwelling Place,* 152.

think, will cause a throb in neither of our bosoms. My visits to Salem
have been so short and hurried, that I have found no time to call on
her these three months; but I understand that I am still in good odor
with her. As for me, I have neither resentment nor regrets, liking nor
dislike—having fallen in love with someone else. (*CE* 15:312)

Another source of knowledge of Silsbee is through the Barstows,
Hawthorne's cousins. Annie Meade Barstow (1820–1895) was one of
Silsbee's good friends, although she was eleven years younger. There
are extant in the National Library of Scotland at least thirty-seven letters
that Annie wrote to Mary beginning on April 23 [1839] in the month
before Silsbee and Sparks were married. It is clear from these letters
that Mary and Annie knew each other well and had known each other
for a long time. Until Annie married Samuel Ashburner in 1845, she
retailed Salem news.

Annie did not mention the Hawthornes to Mary nor, one would
speculate, did Mary. After 1845 Annie lived in Hartford, Connecticut,
with her railroading husband and then in Jamaica Plain, Massachusetts.
The friendship flourished, but then Mary's "peculiarities" must have
irritated Annie. In July, perhaps in 1866, Annie wrote her daughter, Nan,
of a journey to Cambridge with her husband:

> as we passed Mrs. Sparks house, we were called after and your father
> was brought face to face with Mrs. Sparks. She wished to ask some
> RRd [railroad] questions as she and the girls and Willie are going on a
> journey. When I went with the information to her the next day she told
> me she was going to Niagara and asked me to go with her. I should
> like to see Niagara again exceedingly but I should not enjoy it so much
> in her society. When I went to see Mrs. Sparks the second time I took
> Wat [Walter Ashburner, her son] with me and we were to go to "Harbers
> Quare" and then make the call but he would not budge an inch down
> Quincy Street and when I said "Why not see Mrs. Sparks, Walter?" he
> looked most solemnly and replied "becod I do not like the family." I
> could not move him & I feared if I did take him he might take some
> uncomplimentary notice of Mrs. S.[21]

It is not clear what Mary Sparks's "peculiarities" were exactly; it is only
evident that various people noticed them.

Annie Barstow Ashburner moved to England in the 1870s and lived
there for the rest of her life. Her sister-in-law, Grace Ashburner, notified

---

21. Annie Barstow Ashburner to her daughter Anne Ashburner, July [1866?], Richards
and Ashburner Papers, Mss. 20364, ff. 54, 56. Walter Ashburner became a professor
of jurisprudence at Oxford; Mary Sparks's children were Florence, William Eliot, and
Elizabeth.

her from Cambridge about the condition of Mary Sparks, and Annie replied on March 18 [1884?]:

> your letter of March 3d arrived with its information about Mrs. Sparks. I am very much grieved to hear it, but not wholly unprepared as when I saw her two summers since she spoke at times in a confused way & her letters have been difficult to understand—tho she has not corresponded as she used to do. . . . She has always showed to me great kindness from very early days and her great intelligence & love of reading, fun, & experience of the world has made M[ary] in serious conversation a most agreeable companion who knew all my family—all the Salem circle—and we could talked [*sic*] over past events in the old time to which I was a most interested listener. . . . it is sad to see such mental decay coming upon one whose gifts have been so much above the ordinary.[22]

If this letter did emanate from the year 1884 (and there the National Library of Scotland has placed it), that would explain Mary Sparks's lack of response to Julian's and Elizabeth Peabody's allegations that she never denied their story about her relationship with Hawthorne and O'Sullivan. She may have been too confused by that time, and her children may not have wanted to spotlight that confusion by answering the charges.

But it was not only Annie's husband and her child Walter who did not want to see Mrs. Sparks. Alice James, sister of Henry and William, wrote Anne Ashburner, Annie Barstow Ashburner's daughter, on November 2, 1873:

> I don't think I told you of our going down to breakfast one day at St. John & finding Mrs. Sparks and family arrived. We became intimate for the first time with the former & our vague plan of departure for the next day became in the course of a few hours fixed as fate. Was there ever such a horror? Her children are marvels of patience and virtue I think & as for the noble Pickering what can we do to testify to his courage. The only possible explanation must be that he is in love with Lizzie as few men are with women . . . But don't let's say another word about her, she seems to me to be an unholy object.

Alice James retained that opinion of Mary Sparks and expressed it vigorously. "Did you ever know such a creature," she asked Anne Ashburner in 1874.[23] Mary Silsbee Sparks was obviously one of the most

22. Annie Barstow Ashburner to Grace Ashburner, April 25, 1874, Richards and Ashburner Papers, Mss. 20369, ff. 69–70.
23. [Alice James], *The Death and Letters of Alice James,* ed. Ruth Yeazell, 59. The "noble Pickering" was Ed C. Pickering, who married Elizabeth W. Sparks in 1876.

interesting women from Salem that Hawthorne knew, but it is clear that opinions differed about her.

This, of course, is also true of Sophia Amelia Peabody (1809–1871), at least among Hawthorne scholars. She was the third daughter of Nathaniel and Elizabeth Palmer Peabody, who had met while teaching school in Andover and had married in 1802. Their daughter, Elizabeth Palmer, was born in Billerica, Massachusetts, in 1804. In 1806 they moved to Cambridgeport so that Mr. Peabody, who had graduated from Dartmouth in 1800, could hear medical lectures at nearby Harvard. Their next child, Mary Tyler, was born there. When they moved to Salem in 1808, Dr. Peabody practiced medicine and dentistry while Mrs. Peabody taught school.[24]

Sophia was born on Summer Street in 1809. In 1810 the Peabodys lived in the Union Building at the corner of Union and Essex Streets, the long brick edifice still there. The Union Street Corporation, with Benjamin Pickman as president, was built in 1808, and so was very new. In addition to space for several businesses, there were four dwellings in the block building. The Peabodys were in one of these. It was at that point that Elizabeth remembered seeing the little boy with "clustering locks" playing in the Manning and Hathorne yards. That was also the time when Mrs. Peabody taught little Elizabeth Hawthorne. But for the most part the Peabodys lived before 1820 in the side of the house at the corner of Essex and Cambridge owned by Miss Susy Hathorne, a daughter of William Hathorne, brother to Daniel, Nathaniel's grandfather.[25]

Mrs. Peabody was a granddaughter of General Joseph Palmer of Revolutionary fame, and she seems always to have felt superior to her husband because of that. It is true that her income from teaching school was usually needed, but the Peabodys were not alone in that predicament. A well-educated woman, she found time to write and to teach her own six surviving children as well as many others. In fact, she advertised in the *Salem Gazette* (January 16, 1818) that she could board as many as thirty students in addition to her own family of eight in her

---

Alice expressed her opinion of Mary Sparks in letters to Anne Richards, Annie Barstow Ashburner's daughter. The letters are in the Richards and Ashburner Papers, Mss. 20367, ff. 41, 44, 45, 50, 62, 74.

24. Edwin P. Hoyt, *The Peabody Influence: How a Great New England Family Helped to Build America,* 170–90; Selim Peabody, *The Peabody (Paybody, Pabody, Pabodie) Genealogy,* 85; EPP, *Letters,* 9–10, 49; Louise Hall Tharp, *The Peabody Sisters of Salem,* 17–18.

25. A. Archer, "Essex Street in 1820"; *SG,* February 7, 1890, March 2, 1813, and January 23, 1818; EPP, *Letters,* 451.

half of the double house. She wrote two books during her teaching days.[26] She was very close to her daughters especially, and she kept Sophia protected when perhaps her youngest daughter did not need such oversight.

Dr. Peabody seems to have been dominated by his wife. She once characterized her husband to Sophia: "I doubt not your father's motives, but I know he has no knowledge of human nature."[27] Hawthorne's opinion of him, according to Sophia, was entirely different. She wrote Elizabeth after their father's death:

> Mr. Hawthorne thinks father a very rare person & valued him more sincerely than any body else ever did. His sincerity, his childlike guilelessness, his good sense & rectitude—his singleness & unaffected piety—all & each of his qualities made him interesting & never tedious to my husband. I really do not believe anyone else ever listened to his stories & his conversation with love & interest excepting him. (*CE* 17:302*n*)

For a while Dr. Peabody continued to practice some medicine. He was, in fact, one of the physicians who tried to cure Nathaniel Hawthorne's lameness (*CE* 15:106). Then he turned more and more to the practice of dentistry in Salem. He advertised "Teeth Brushes" for sale, and he announced in the *Gazette* (July 26, 1808) that "teeth can be filled, cleaned and ingrafted in a neat manner." He published in 1824 *The Art of Preserving Teeth*. He was also secretary of the Medical Society in 1817. In that year and the next he was on the Salem School Committee, a task not unrelated to that of the instruction of his children in Latin. In 1834 he was a manager of the Lyceum. After the family moved to the Charter Street home bordering on the Charter Street Burying Ground in 1835, he took as dental partner a Dr. Joseph E. Fiske, who later mesmerized Sophia in an effort to cure her of her headaches. The Peabodys moved to Lancaster in 1820, then to Boston, but back to Salem in 1828. Had they stayed put, Dr. Peabody might have enjoyed his share of civic honors. It could not have helped his feelings of adequacy to meet often a kinsman, Joseph Peabody, one of the wealthiest merchants in Salem.[28]

The Peabodys were members by 1816 of North Church under Dr. Thomas Barnard. When Dr. Barnard obtained "the obliteration of the Trinity from the confession of the church under his care," Dr. William

26. [EPP Sr.], *Sabbath Lessons, or an Abstract of Sacred History* and *Holiness: or the Legend of St. George, a Tale from Spenser's Fairie Queen by a Mother*.

27. JH, *Hawthorne and Wife*, 1:70.

28. Miller, *Salem Is My Dwelling Place*, 125; Russell Leigh Jackson, "Physicians of Essex County," 184; *SG*, August 26 and April 25, 1817, March 13, 1810, and March 13, 1818; Tharp, *Peabody Sisters of Salem*, 24, 43, 102.

Bentley recorded in his diary, "Col. Butman told me that Dr. Peabody, half Physician and Schoolmaster & perhaps half of something else, had told him as a member of the society the change would be unpleasing etc."[29] If so, Dr. Peabody was overruled. His wife was adamantly liberal in her opinions. Elizabeth Peabody reported:

> The religious controversies that ended in changing all the old Puritan churches of Boston and Salem from Calvinism to Liberal and Unitarian Christianity, denying the total depravity of man and the vicarious atonement of Jesus and affirming his unfallen humanity,—were raging in my early childhood and divided all families. Some of our relatives became Calvinists; our own family, and especially our mother, who was very devout, remained Liberal.[30]

Dr. Peabody seems to have gone along with his strong-willed wife in this as in many other things. Perhaps it is no wonder that the family seemed to divide: Mrs. Peabody with three strong daughters, Elizabeth, Mary, and Sophia; and Dr. Peabody with three sons who either were fairly ineffectual or who died early: Nathaniel (1811–1881), George (1813–1839), and Wellington (1816–1838). Another daughter, Catherine, lived only a few weeks in 1819. James Upton in 1873 remembered Dr. Peabody "as an old & rather crusty man who first, to my knowledge, made a speciality of teeth doctoring & put out a shingle as 'dentist.' "[31]

Their youngest daughter, Sophia Amelia, was five years younger than Elizabeth. When she was teething, she was given medicine that was said to have afflicted her with headaches for much of her life. Taylor Stoehr remarks that Dr. Peabody later regretted the "allopathic doses of paregoric" that she had been given. It is difficult to tell her actual infirmity from her mother's smothering protection. Some of her pain was certainly real, but she did seem to improve when she was away from her mother and sometimes from her sisters. When her brother George was ill, her sister Mary wrote Elizabeth, "We do not tell all our fears to Sophia, whom we wish to keep cheerfully employed as long as we can."[32] Treated like a child, she often retreated from the world.

When the Peabodys moved to Boston in the 1820s, Sophia began to write. She composed a continuation of Coleridge's "Christabel," and she took drawing lessons from Francis Graeter, who taught art in Elizabeth's school in Boston, and from the landscape artist Thomas Doughty (1793–1856) and portrait painter Chester Harding (1792–1866). She was also

29. *First Centenary of North Church,* 212; *SG,* July 4, 1814; WB, *Diary,* 4:342.
30. Pearson, "E. Peabody on Hawthorne," 270.
31. J. Upton, "Hawthorne in Salem Custom House," 114.
32. Stoehr, *Hawthorne's Mad Scientists,* 108; RHL, *Memories,* 8.

favorably noticed by the painter Washington Alston (1779–1856). Since she and her family assumed she would never marry because of her invalidism, she worked hard at her painting. Patricia Valenti considers her not only as "one of the earliest female painters in America" but also as an artist of considerable talent. She worked at her art with so much intensity that she became quite ill.[33]

Mrs. Richard Cleveland of Lancaster was responsible for seeing that Sophia had a recuperative stay in Cuba from 1833 to 1835, while sister Mary tutored the children of a Cuban planter. Sophia bloomed in that atmosphere, went horseback riding, and kept on with her painting, at which she was becoming proficient. Sophia also wrote letters that, bound together as a journal, were read later by Hawthorne and others. He thought the letters ought to be published. In Cuba Sophia also captivated James Burroughs, an agent for sugar planters and an older man. Rumors about him reached Salem, and Sophia began to have headaches again.[34]

Sophia learned French under Salem teacher Peter Louvrier (1778–1846), and she also knew Italian, Greek, Hebrew, and Latin. She was quite an accomplished invalid. She wrote letters at times in the language of the Peabodys, a speech that Rebecca B. Manning later characterized as one that "needed to be translated to be intelligible to common people."[35]

Hawthorne finally met Sophia through the persistence of her sister Elizabeth on November 11, 1837, the year when his anonymity lifted with the publication of *Twice-Told Tales*. He was shy, but he was also thirty-three years old and ready to venture forth from his "owl's nest." The Peabody sisters and Hawthorne began going to Susan Burley's "Hurley-Burleys" on Saturday evenings. Sophia drew illustrations of Ilbrahim in Hawthorne's "The Gentle Boy," which he liked and, with Susan Burley's financial aid, published in a separate edition dedicated to her. She in turn dedicated the last portion of her "Cuba Journal" to him. Sophia with her wide gray eyes and light brown ringlets was more and more the object of Hawthorne's affection.

What we know about that first year comes primarily from the two participants, and one must allow for the romantic aura that surrounds

33. Patricia Dunlavy Valenti, "Sophia Peabody Hawthorne's Continuation to 'Christabel,'" 14–16; Valenti, "Sophia Peabody Hawthorne: A Study of Artistic Influence," 1–21.
34. Tharp, *Peabody Sisters of Salem*, 71, 85, 82, 104; Pearson, "E. Peabody on Hawthorne," 271; Gaeddert, *A New England Love Story*, 60–65.
35. Rebecca B. Manning, "Some Facts," Nathaniel Hawthorne Papers. Also see Gollin and Idol, *Prophetic Pictures*.

their love. Some say they were engaged by the time he went to Boston to work in the Custom House in January 1839. On January 5, 1839, Mary Peabody wrote Sophia what Arlin Turner calls "a cryptic letter." Mary Foote, it seems, had been asked "what she thought of the *report*—and whether she thought it ever *would be true.*" Mary Foote had said she was "possessed with another idea," with which Mary Peabody agreed. Turner believes they both thought that Sophia, not Elizabeth, would in time be engaged to Nathaniel.[36] He had been seeing Sophia all through 1838, when her health permitted, but events certainly speeded up when Mary Silsbee was out of the way.

It had been agreed between Nathaniel and Sophia that she must be able physically to marry. Her crippling headaches would make it impossible otherwise. Taylor Stoehr believes that Dr. Joseph Fiske (1811–1882) treated Sophia almost daily with mesmerism until 1840 when the Peabodys moved again to Boston. There Sophia found Cornelia Park, an old friend, who also practiced mesmerism.[37] When she mentioned this to Hawthorne (she had kept her treatment by Dr. Fiske from him), Hawthorne replied with horror:

> I am unwilling that a power should be exercised on thee, of which we know neither the origin nor consequence, and the phenomena of which seem rather calculated to bewilder us, than to teach us any truths about the present or the future state of being. . . .
> [T]hou wilt know that the view which I take of this matter is caused by no want of faith in mysteries, but from a deep reverence of the soul. . . . (*CE* 15:588–89)

Hawthorne finally acquiesced to some treatments to relieve her headaches, but he wrote on June 30, 1842, "My feeling on this point is so strong, that it would be wronging us both to conceal it from thee" (*CE* 15:634).

This is not to say that their love was one of unequal partners. Their three-year engagement, his love letters (he later burned hers), his attempts to find remunerative employment with which he could support a wife: all testify to a solid and genuine love. They also testify to a man and a woman who were ready for love and marriage. Leland Person writes that "Sophia not only complemented his character, but enabled him to become a new self in relation to her."[38] She, like Elizabeth Barrett, got up from her invalid's bed, and Nathaniel grew to know what sort of employment he was unsuited for. The Custom House and then Brook

36. Turner, *Hawthorne,* 115, 116.
37. Stoehr, *Hawthorne's Mad Scientists,* 41.
38. Leland S. Person Jr., "Hawthorne's Love Letters: Writing and Relationships," 213.

Farm turned out not to be the best. They were married on July 9, 1842, with the prospects only of his writer's wages and a possible recovery of the funds he had sunk in Brook Farm.

So much has been written about Sophia and their marriage that I shall not attempt to repeat what is generally known. Hawthorne scholars tend to divide on their like and dislike of Sophia (and of late on their opinion of Hawthorne too). These views are usually clearly evident in their books. Her bubbling naïveté, her adoration of her husband, her protection of her own children are either seen as hindrances to his career or as absolute guarantees of it. Some of those then living who did not like her would probably not have liked any wife Nathaniel had chosen. Chief among these was his sister Elizabeth. It would be hard to imagine any two women less alike. Difficult, individualistic Elizabeth, who adamantly went her own way and spoke her own mind, would have been hard put to it to like a woman she saw as selfish, clinging, and a facilitator of all the worst elements in her brother. "Sophia," she wrote later, "is the only human being whom I really dislike." The ethereal quality of Sophia's talk was bound to irritate Ebe. She remarked sarcastically that Julian "has enough of the Peabody element in him to make all his talents available." She thought Sophia kept all her children in dependence on her, that she had in effect shortened her husband's life by dragging him around Rome, that she was never satisfied in any place for long.[39] On the other hand, Sophia was not very fond of Elizabeth either, and she could be just as strong-minded as Elizabeth, but in a more subtle way. Her views of religion, of homeopathic medicine, of the education of children, and of the immense significance of art all influenced Nathaniel in greater or lesser degrees.

There were many who thought the marriage of Sophia and Nathaniel was the best thing that could happen to them. This was certainly Julian's view, and not many sons would write a biography of a well-known writer by giving his wife equal billing. Julian said that "Sophia Peabody was Hawthorne's true guardian and re-creating angel." Margaret Fuller wrote Sophia, "if ever I saw a man who combined delicate tenderness to understand the heart of a woman, with quiet depth and manliness enough to satisfy her, it is Mr. Hawthorne."[40]

Mary White Foote was also pleased with their match. In January 1838, as has been said, she had intimated her wish to see the two united at a time others thought Elizabeth might be the chosen one.

39. EMH to Rebecca Manning, August 7 [1879?], May 8 [1872?]; EMH to cousin, March 6 [1870?], copies, Hawthorne-Manning Collection.

40. JH, *Hawthorne and Wife,* 1:196; Fuller, *Letters,* 3:66.

Various scholars have advanced different views of the marriage. T. Walter Herbert does not think it endured as a happy marriage. Joyce W. Warren, however, supports Hawthorne's conviction that Sophia was an independent being, significant in her own right, and that their marriage was good. Richard Brodhead observes that Hawthorne "was in fact the most perfectly domestic of all American writers, the one most devoted to the family as the scene of fulfilling relation."[41]

It is in the context of Salem, however, that my interest lies. In what way were Mary Silsbee and Sophia Peabody products of Hawthorne's Salem world, and in what way, if any, was his choice dictated by that world? Both young women were Salemites in the sense that they were born there and lived a good part of their lives there. Yet each was in some ways different from it. Mary Silsbee had spent some of her youth in Washington, D.C., where she knew many famous and widely traveled people. Sophia's life had alternated between Salem, Lancaster, and Boston, with three years in Cuba thrown in. So neither was a typical Salemite, in the sense that their boundaries were limited to Salem. From the little we know, each wanted more from life than a typical Salem wife would expect. Mary may have wanted wealth (if the report about the three-thousand-dollar requirement is true), but she seems also to have wanted excitement, fame, position. She achieved some of that as the wife of the president of Harvard who was a famous historian to boot. In an obituary of her father in the *Salem Register,* the writer noted, "his eldest daughter graces and adorns the classic shades of Harvard in presiding over the elegant hospitalities of President Sparks's mansion."[42]

Sophia, once she decided that she could marry after all, seemed to want a life of intellect in which stimulating artistic people were available, but perhaps most of all she wanted a husband whom she could adore and whom other people admired. This is not to say that she had no personal goals. She was probably often frustrated in her desire to paint original work, not do copying, and she may well have wanted to write, as she finally did after her husband's death when she edited his notebooks. She was not the first, nor indeed the last, woman to chafe at times at the restrictions that come with motherhood. She could not always go on trips with him, but in Rome she seemed to be setting the pace.

41. Herbert, *Dearest Beloved,* 210, 270–71; Joyce W. Warren, *The American Narcissus: Individualism and Women in Nineteenth-Century Fiction,* 200, 202; Richard H. Brodhead, *The School of Hawthorne,* 48.
42. *Salem Register* (formerly *ER*), obituary notice in the Silsbee Family Papers.

There was, of course, no such thing as a typical woman at that time any more than there is today. Many Salem women grew up, married sea captains or merchants, had many children, managed affairs when husbands were absent, and quite often died young. Margaret Heussler Felt was at least partly typical. She was born in Newburyport, but came at an early age to Salem. Her mother died when she was quite young, and her father, a landscape gardener for Elias Haskett Derby, married again. Margaret married the son of a sea captain who became a sea captain himself. Jonathan Porter Felt was gone for much of their early married life, sailing around the world while she had children and tended those who early left the world. She managed business affairs in his absence, assumed responsibility for his family as well as her own, attended church faithfully, and acceded to his various but failed schemes to make money in gold mining and silkworm manufacture in the commonwealth of Virginia. She read newspapers avidly, but I know of only one novel that she read: Catharine Sedgwick's *The Linwoods*. She often spoke her mind on topics political or social, but she seemed content with her lot; she felt that this was the way life should be. We could find many women in the Salem of that time who were like her.[43]

But other kinds of women were there also. Mary Silsbee seems less typical of the Salem woman than does Sophia. She fails to fit into the Adam and Eve story as Sophia does. That metaphor was used over and over by Nathaniel to illustrate his perception of their love. He perhaps came to see Silsbee as belonging in "that Eden of poisonous flowers" with Rappaccini's daughter, but she was never Eve (*CE* 10:115). She belonged in the elite group of fairly wealthy families that ruled Salem then, but she did not, to my knowledge, reflect the intellectual currents permeating Salem in the 1840s. Sophia did. She inclined to the Transcendentalist point of view (at least before her marriage), to the interest in mesmerism, homeopathy, and to the ideas and educational theories of German and French origin. These opinions were also held, to a greater or lesser degree, by her sisters, Susan Burley, Mary Foote, and other liberal ladies of the town. Sophia never was a woman's rights advocate, however; she was feminine, but not feminist.

The role of women was often bound up in the idea of woman as writer. Was it wrong for her to shine in just that way? Salem had a fair number of women writers in the early nineteenth century, but they often hid their accomplishments under pseudonyms or published

---

43. The facts about Margaret Heussler Felt may be found in my unpublished manuscript, "Talking on Paper: The Letters of Margaret Heussler Felt, 1811–1861."

anonymously. There is not much difference between the sexes, however, in the practice in this regard. Sarah Savage was not identified until the end of her writing career in 1835. Elizabeth Sanders (1762–1851) wrote on Indian topics and Shakespeare without identifying herself. Mary Louise Horton (1805–1831) published much poetry in the *Register* under the pseudonyms of M.L.H. or M.Louisa or H.L.M., causing some people to think that Louisa Hawthorne was versifying. The elder Elizabeth Palmer Peabody wrote anonymously or with a pseudonym. As the century wore on, women as well as men used their own names. Maria Cummins (1827–1866) of Salem and Dorchester; Lydia Louisa Ann Very, sister of Jones Very; and Hannah G. Creamer claimed their writings. But Caroline R. Derby, who wrote of the Salem witch trials, used the pseudonym "D. R. Castleton." Despite these women writers (and there were a great many more outside of Salem), Hawthorne did express some uneasiness about the breed. It seems to me that James Wallace is right when he comments, "For Hawthorne's anxiety about women as writers has something to do with his own intense privacy."[44] What Hawthorne objected to was the lack of decorum in yielding so much of the personal. And with this Sophia agreed. She wrote James T. Fields in November 1859, when he asked her to submit her own writings to the *Atlantic:* "You forget that Mr. Hawthorne is the Belleslettres portion of my being and besides that I have a repugnance to female authoresses in general" (*CE* 18:202). But once that portion of her being was gone, she did write, as much to glorify him or to pay the bills as to shine for herself.

Hawthorne was certainly aware of and sympathetic to the restrictions on women. Of Hilda in *The Marble Faun,* he remarks, "whenever we admit woman to a wider scope of pursuits and professions, we must also remove the shackles of our present conventional rules, which would then become an insufferable restraint on either maid or wife" (*CE* 4:55). He admires Hester in *The Scarlet Letter,* who despite her sin grows from that experience into helping others. He depicts the women "wounded, wasted, wronged, misplaced, or erring" who "with the dreary burden of a heart unyielded, became unvalued and unsought' and came to Hester's cottage, "demanding why they were so wretched, and what the

---

44. For one example of the confusion caused by Horton's pen names see F. Clark, "Unexplored Areas of Hawthorne Bibliography," 49. Many more female writers could probably be found then in Salem, since so many wrote anonymously. For some description of writers in Salem, see among others, John Wright Buckham, "Literary Salem"; Loring, "Literature," in *The History of Essex County;* Sidney Perley, *The Poets of Essex County, Massachusetts;* Joseph B. Saunders, *A Short Study of Three Centuries of Salem, 1626–1926,* chapter six; Wallace, "Hawthorne and the 'Scribbling Women,' " 210.

remedy!" (*CE* 1:263). Zenobia, in talking about Priscilla in *The Blithedale Romance,* exclaims to Coverdale, "Did you ever see a happy woman in your life? How can she be happy, after discovering that fate has assigned her but one single event, which she must contrive to make the substance of her whole life? A man has his choice of innumerable events" (*CE* 3:60).

In addition to the undervalued woman, Hawthorne sympathizes that so much work around the house is laid on her. Sybil in "Septimius Felton" wonders why "woman gets so large a share of human misery laid on her weak shoulders." Kezia longs for the other world where there "won't be all house-work, and keeping decent and doing like other people" (*CE* 13:171, 123). Yet when Septimius Felton finally translates part of the old manuscript with its rules for living, one reads, "On the whole, shun woman, for she is apt to be a disturbing influence" (*CE* 13:105).

Disturbing or not, one would not expect a writer of more than common talent and sensitivity to pick an ordinary kind of wife, or for such a woman to pick him. It sometimes surprises me that he chose Sophia; she seems so unlike him in so many ways. She was so unerringly optimistic, so confident of the goodness of people that it must have grated on him at times. But then he was the one who saw (in his imagination anyway) "the power of blackness" in persons and situations. They complemented each other; she had a Greek mind perhaps, whereas his was Hebrew. Yet had he chosen another, his married life and hence his writing life would have been unrecognizably different. "Thou wast the only possible one," wrote Nathaniel to Sophia, and with that we must be content (*CE* 15:565).

From the early time when Hawthorne pondered the life of Ann Hutchinson, he was clear about one thing. He did not really mind women writing or professing anything, so long as they retained some femininity and privacy in the process. He did not want them to display their "naked minds" to the world, but to retain some aura of mystery. He would have agreed with Hugh Peters, who said to Ann Hutchinson, "You have stept out of your place, you have rather bine a Husband than a wife, and a preacher than a Hearer, and a magistrate than a subject."[45] Sophia had found her place with Hawthorne and seemed to rejoice in it, as much as he did. She was her own person, but she was also part of him, a helpmeet. For the Hawthornes, the role of this woman was clear.

45. Battis, *Saints and Sectaries,* 44.

Postscript

WILLIAM DEAN Howells, in recalling his first visit to New England, remarked that "we are always finding new Hawthornes." There could be no more appropriate characterization of Hawthorne scholarship. It is almost as if we see in this complex man what we are prepared to see, as though we are trying to mold this unmalleable writer into our own ideology. And, indeed, if we change our minds, we can find enough substance to prove the opposite. Howells goes on to say, "but the illusion soon wears away, and then we perceive that they were not Hawthornes at all; that he had some peculiar difference from them, which, by-and-by, we shall no doubt consent must be his difference from all men evermore."[1]

The doubleness of Hawthorne's meanings has struck many readers. In the 1860s, a writer in the *North British Review* noticed that "he seems endowed with a sort of intellectual polarity." A critic in the *London Review* observed in 1868 that "Hawthorne, without the smallest design to unsettle anything, doubted, and knew he doubted; saw two sides to everything, and knew that he presented them to his readers." In his own time, when Samuel G. Goodrich was pondering publication of Hawthorne's short tales, he showed them to John Pickering, then president of the American Stationers Company. Pickering discerned "a kind of double vision, a sort of second sight, which revealed, beyond the outward forms of life and being, a sort of spirit world." More recently, Malcolm Cowley has noticed that "everywhere in his characters

1. Howells, *Literary Friends and Acquaintance,* 52.

one finds a sort of doubleness." Charles Swann mentions Hawthorne's "predilection . . . for alternative explanations," and George Dekker has remarked that "we do well to remember that readers who try to fix an unwavering 'position' for Hawthorne by the customary nineteenth-century political landmarks do so at their peril."[2]

Hawthorne himself not only recognized this doubleness, but celebrated it. In *Our Old Home,* he declared, "It is only one-eyed people who love to advise, or have any spontaneous promptitude of action. When a man opens both his eyes, he generally sees about as many reasons for acting in any one way as in any other, and quite as many for acting in neither" (*CE* 5:30). Hawthorne did not like reformers for that very reason. They saw one side only in whatever cause they had taken up. Hollingsworth in *The Blithedale Romance* was only one example. The writer saw two sides to the Revolutionary War and was also aware that there was another side to the Civil War. He realized that many

> warm-hearted, sympathetic, and impulsive persons have joined the rebels, not from any real zeal for the cause, but because, between two conflicting loyalties, they chose that which necessarily lay nearest the heart. . . . If a man loves his own State, therefore, and is content to be ruined with her, let us shoot him, if we can, but allow him an honorable burial in the soil he fights for.

Characteristically, however, he ironically states in a note that his tone is "reprehensible, and its tendency impolitic in the present state of our national difficulties" (*CE* 23:416, 417).

Such views led many in Hawthorne's time and later to think him odd, but it should be remembered, especially today, that Salem itself was not without its peculiarities. I hope I have shown that Salem was never monolithic in its views, and such divisiveness often manifests itself in various eccentricities. Hawthorne himself indirectly commented on these in *The House of the Seven Gables.* The narrator, for example, describes "a town noted for its frugal, discreet, well-ordered, and home-loving inhabitants, as well as for the somewhat confined scope of its sympathies; but in which, be it said, there are odder individuals and, now and then, stranger occurrences, than one meets with almost anywhere else" (*CE* 2:21–22).

---

2. *Littell's Living Age* 99 (1868) reprinted an article from the *North British Review,* which can be found in Cameron, *Hawthorne among His Contemporaries,* 118; "Hawthorne," *London Review* (1868) in Cameron, *Hawthorne among His Contemporaries,* 119; S. G. Goodrich, *Recollections of a Lifetime,* 2:271; Malcolm Cowley, "Hawthorne in the Looking Glass," 551; Swann, *Nathaniel Hawthorne,* 30; Dekker, *American Historical Romance,* 130.

Others noted these characteristics too. In a letter to Annie Barstow Ashburner, written probably in the 1880s, Francis H. Lee acknowledged, "We are all odd here in Salem. Think of the Stones and Mr. Foote and John P. Andrews and the Nichols and Gov. Andrews and a host of others." George P. Lathrop and Rose Hawthorne Lathrop apparently shared that sentiment. George Lathrop remarked that Salem was "fecund of eccentricities," and Rose Lathrop recollected a conversation she had with Oliver Wendell Holmes in which she suggested, "The people are rich in extraordinary oddities. At every turn a stranger is astonished by some intense characteristic. One feels strongly its different atmosphere."[3]

It is in the context of this town that we should see Hawthorne. From his roots in Salem he drew many of his characteristics. It must be remembered that the Hathorne family—all the way back to that first bearded ancestor—had some eccentricities and "a twist aside" as had Holgrave (*CE* 2:218). One purpose of *Seven Gables* is to trace the way traits are passed down from one generation to another. The early Hathornes were known for their stubborn adherence to their beliefs. Nathaniel could be mule-headed as well. Reading Sophia's attempts to make him go to various affairs of Mrs. Anna Maria Heywood of Norris Green in Liverpool clearly indicates this. "He does not choose to do as the Romans do while in Rome," she wrote her father in exasperation in 1853 (*CE* 17:176). Hawthorne recognized this quality in himself. In refusing to accept an invitation to Crewe Hall, he wrote Richard Monckton Milnes that he was an "absurdly shy sort of person" who had "missed a vast deal of enjoyment, in the course of my life, by an inveterate habit (or more than habit for I believe it was born with me) of keeping out of people's way" (*CE* 17:272).

But it is not only through his heredity that we begin to understand Hawthorne but also through the Salem context of his own day. His family, his friends, his teachers all affected him in some way. The very consciousness of the past, which is and was so evident in Salem, helped shape him. He simply cannot be divorced entirely from that context, and the more we know about it, the more we may know about him. He should not be judged merely by present-day standards either. Take the matter of privacy, for example. The reticent Hawthorne would be unable to believe the absolute abandonment by the current generation of strictures on disclosure. Reluctance to expose "the naked mind" was not then unusual, but rather expected. Early nineteenth-century

3. Francis H. Lee to Annie Barstow Ashburner, copy, n.d., Francis Henry Lee Papers; G. P. Lathrop, *Study of Hawthorne,* 38; RHL, *Memories of Hawthorne,* 459.

manners, as well as formalities, were different. Teachers were called "Master." A recent scholar has said that the fact that Betsey Hawthorne was addressed as "Madame" by her family was "not quite a taunt," but the words, "Sir" and "Madame" were used, according to John Pickering, "in some parts of New England for Father and Mother."[4] The Felt family of Salem used these as expressions of respect throughout Hawthorne's lifetime. Words change and customs change, of course, but we must be aware as much as possible of what was contemporary practice in Hawthorne's own day.

That is not to say that Hawthorne can be completely revealed through knowledge of his ancestors or his town. They touched him, but they did not confine him. If there is one clue to Hawthorne, I think it is his insistence on the sanctity of the human heart and its mystery. He was forever trying to burrow "into the depths of our common nature," but his conclusions were tentative (*CE* 11:4). That is the reason he spoke more in the subjunctive mood rather than in the indicative, I believe. Howells speaks of Hawthorne's "impalpability." "[I]f he was not there to your touch, it was no fault of his; it was because your touch was dull, and wanted the use of contact with such natures. The hand passes through the veridical phantom without a sense of its presence, but the phantom is none the less veridical for all that."[5] Hawthorne remains elusive. With all our separate Hawthornes, the real one keeps slipping away. But the real one lived in a time and place that contribute significantly to our understanding of the man and his work.

4. Herbert, *Dearest Beloved,* 65; J. Pickering, *Vocabulary,* 172.
5. Howells, *Literary Friends and Acquaintance,* 53.

Selected Bibliography

This bibliography is selective; not all sources are shown, due to space limitations. Others not listed but used specifically for this work may be found in the notes.

MANUSCRIPT COLLECTIONS
Henry W. and Albert A. Berg Collection, New York Public Library, New York, Astor, Lenox, and Tilden Foundation.
Burley Papers, Beverly Historical Society, Beverly, Massachusetts.
Felt-White Collection, the Charles White Family of Virginia, a private collection.
Hargrett Rare Book and Manuscript Collection, The Ilah Dunlap Little Library, University of Georgia, Athens, Georgia.
Manning Hawthorne Papers, Bowdoin Library, Hawthorne-Longfellow Library, Brunswick, Maine.
Nathaniel Hawthorne Collection (#6249), Clifton Waller Barrett Library, Special Collections Department, University of Virginia Library, Charlottesville, Virginia.
Hawthorne Family Papers, The Bancroft Library, University of California, Berkeley, California.
James Duncan Phillips Library, Peabody Essex Museum, Salem, Massachusetts. I used the following collections:
Benjamin Frederick Browne Papers
Crowninshield Family Papers
Perley Derby Papers
Andrew Dunlap Papers
East Church Records

English/Touzel/Hathorne Papers
Felt Family Collection
Jonathan Porter Felt Papers
First Church of Salem Records
First Baptist Church Records
Forrester Family Papers
Hawthorne-Manning Collection
Nathaniel Hawthorne Collection
Francis Henry Lee Papers
St. Peter's Church Records
Salem and Boston Stage Company Records
Silsbee Family Papers
Tabernacle Church of Salem Records
Richards and Ashburner Papers, National Library of Scotland, Edinburgh,
     Scotland.

BOOKS AND PAMPHLETS

Adams, Herbert Baxter. *The Life and Writings of Jared Sparks, Compris-
     ing Selections from His Journals and Correspondence.* 2 vols. 1893.
     Reprint, Freeport, New York: Books for Libraries Press, 1970.
Allen, Thomas J. *The Accomplice: The Truth of Vigilanti Salem: Haw-
     thorne, Melville, Robert Rantoul, Jr., and the Captain White Murder
     Case.* Salem: Common School Press, 1865.
*Articles and Covenant of the Tabernacle Church in Salem Adopted May
     8, 1786.* Boston: Perkins and Marvin, 1833.
Avery, Lillian Drake. *A Genealogy of the Ingersoll Family in America,
     1629–1925.* New York: Grafton Press, 1926.
B., M. [Eleanor Barstow Condit]. *Philip English's Two Cups, "1692."* New
     York: Anson D. F. Randolph and Company, 1869.
Bacon, Edwin M. *Literary Pilgrimages in New England.* New York: Silver,
     Burdette and Company, 1902.
Banks, Charles Edward. *The Planters of the Commonwealth: The Study
     of the Emigrants and Emigration in Colonial Times: To Which Are
     Added Lists.* Baltimore: Genealogical Publishing, 1967.
Battis, Emery John. *Saints and Sectaries: Anne Hutchinson and the
     Antinomian Controversy in the Massachusetts Bay Colony.* Chapel
     Hill: University of North Carolina Press, 1962.
Belknap, Henry W. *Trades and Tradesmen of Essex County, Massachu-
     setts.* Salem: Essex Institute, 1929.
Benson, Allan L. *Daniel Webster.* New York: Cosmopolitan Book Cor-
     poration, 1929.

Bentley, William. *The Diary of William Bentley, D.D.* 4 vols. 1905–1914. Reprint, Gloucester, Mass.: Peter Smith, 1962.

Biographical Dictionary of the American Congress, 1774–1971. Washington, D.C.: Government Printing Office, 1971.

Bishop, George. *New England Judged by the Spirit of the Lord.* 1661. Reprint, London: T. Sowle, 1703.

Bodge, George Madison. *Soldiers in King Philip's War.* 3d ed. 1906. Reprint, Baltimore: Genealogical Publishing, 1967.

Bowden, James. *The History of the Society of Friends in America.* 1850. Reprint, New York: Arno Press, 1972.

Boyer, Paul S., and Stephen Nissenbaum. *Salem Possessed: The Social Origins of Witchcraft.* Cambridge: Harvard University Press, 1974.

[Bridge, Horatio]. *Journal of an African Cruiser, by an Officer of the United States Navy. . . .* Ed. Nathaniel Hawthorne. New York: Wiley and Putnam, 1845.

Bridge, Horatio. *Personal Recollections of Nathaniel Hawthorne.* 1893. Reprint, New York: Haskell House, 1968.

Brodhead, Richard H. *The School of Hawthorne.* New York: Oxford University Press, 1986.

Browne, Benjamin F. *The Yarn of a Yankee Privateer.* Ed. Nathaniel Hawthorne. Introduction by Clifford Smythe. New York: Funk and Wagnalls, 1926.

Burleigh, Charles. *The Genealogy of the Burley or Burleigh Family of America.* Portland, Maine: B. Thurston and Company, 1880.

Cahill, Robert Ellis. *New England's Cruel and Unusual Punishments.* Salem: Old Saltbox, 1994.

Cameron, Kenneth Walter. *Hawthorne among His Contemporaries: A Harvest of Estimates, Insights, and Anecdotes from the Victorian Literary World and an Index.* Hartford: Transcendental Books [c. 1968].

Cantwell, Robert. *Nathaniel Hawthorne: The American Years.* New York: Rinehart, 1948.

Caruthers, J. Wade. *Octavius Brooks Frothingham, Gentle Radical.* Tuscaloosa: University of Alabama Press, 1977.

Catalogue of the Books Belonging to the Salem Athenaeum. Salem: Warwick Palfrey, Jr., 1826.

[Child, Lydia Maria]. *Hobomok and Other Writings on Indians.* Ed. Carolyn L. Karcher. American Women Writers Series. New Brunswick: Rutgers University Press, 1986.

———. *Lydia Maria Child: Selected Letters, 1817–1880.* Ed. Milton

Meltzer and Patricia G. Holland. Amherst: University of Massachusetts Press, 1982.

Choate, Rufus. *A Discourse Delivered before the Faculty, Students, and Alumni of Dartmouth College on the Day Preceding Commencement, July 27, 1853, Commemorative of Daniel Webster.* Boston: James Munroe, 1853.

Chu, Jonathan M. *Neighbors, Friends, or Madmen: The Puritan Adjustment to Quakerism in Seventeenth-Century Massachusetts Bay.* Westport, Conn.: Greenwood Press, 1985.

Clarke, Helen A. *Hawthorne's Country.* New York: Baker and Taylor, 1910.

[Clayton, W. Woodford]. *History of Cumberland County, Maine.* Philadelphia: Everts and Peck, 1880.

Colacurcio, Michael J. *The Province of Piety: Moral History in Hawthorne's Early Tales.* Cambridge: Harvard University Press, 1984.

Conway, Moncure D. *Life of Nathaniel Hawthorne.* London: Walter Scott [1880].

Cooke, George Alexander. *Cooke's Topographical Library of Great Britain: Berkshire.* London: Sherwood, Gilbert and Piper [n.d.].

Cooke, George Willis. *Unitarianism in America: A History of Its Origin and Development.* 1902. Reprint, New York: AMS Press, 1971.

Coulter, E. Merton. *College Life in the Old South.* 1928. Reprint, Athens: University of Georgia Press, 1951.

Cousins, Frank and Phil M. Riley. *The Colonial Architecture of Salem.* Boston: Little, Brown, 1919.

Cressy, David. *Coming Over: Migration and Communication between England and New England in the Seventeenth Century.* Cambridge, England: Cambridge University Press, 1987.

Crews, Frederick C. *The Sins of the Fathers: Hawthorne's Psychological Themes.* 1966. Reprint, Berkeley: University of California Press, 1989.

[Crowninshield, Clara]. *The Diary of Clara Crowninshield: A European Tour with Longfellow, 1835–1836.* Ed. Andrew Hilen. Seattle: University of Washington Press, 1956.

Currier, John J. *History of Newburyport, Mass. 1764–1905.* 2 vols. 1906–1909. Reprint, Somersworth: New Hampshire Publishing, 1977–1978.

Curtis, George Ticknor. *Life of Daniel Webster.* 2 vols. New York: D. Appleton, 1870.

Darling, Arthur B. *Political Changes in Massachusetts 1824–1848: A*

Study of Liberal Movements in Politics. Cos Cob, Conn.: John E. Edwards, 1968.

D'Arusmont, Frances Wright. *Biography, Notes, and Political Letters.* Dundee: J. Myles, 1844.

————. *Views of Society and Manners in America.* 2d ed. New York: E. Bliss and E. White, 1821.

Dekker, George. *The American Historical Romance.* New York: Cambridge University Press, 1987.

Deland, Thorndike. *Auction Catalogue.* Salem: John D. Cushing, 1824.

Derby, John Barton. *Political Reminiscences Including a Sketch of the Origin and History of the 'Statesman Party' of Boston.* Boston: Homer and Palm, 1835.

DeSalvo, Louise A. *Nathaniel Hawthorne.* Brighton, Sussex: The Harvester Press, 1987.

Donnan, Elizabeth. *Documents Illustrative of the History of the Slave Trade to America,* 4 vols. Vol. 3: *New England and the Middle Colonies.* Washington, D.C.: Carnegie Institute of Washington, 1932.

Donohue, Agnes McNeill. *Hawthorne: Calvin's Ironic Stepchild.* Kent, Ohio: Kent State University Press, 1985.

Douglas, Ann. *The Feminization of American Culture.* New York: Alfred A. Knopf, 1977.

Dubois, William Edward Burghardt. *The Suppression of the African Slave-Trade to the United States of America, 1638–1870.* 1898. Reprint, New York: Russell and Russell, 1965.

Dunne, Michael. *Hawthorne's Narrative Strategies.* Jackson: University Press of Mississippi, 1995.

Duyckinck, Evert A., and George L. Duyckinck. *Cyclopedia of American Literature.* 2 vols. New York: Charles Scribner, 1856.

Eliot, John. *A Biographical Dictionary Containing a Brief Account of the First Settlers and Other Eminent Characters.* Salem: Cushing and Appleton, 1809.

Emerson, Edward Waldo. *The Early Years of the Saturday Club, 1855–1870.* Boston: Houghton, Mifflin, 1918.

Emmerton, Caroline O. *The Chronicles of Three Old Houses.* Boston: Thomas Todd, 1935.

Endicott, Charles M. *Account of Leslie's Retreat at the North Bridge on Sunday, Feb'y 26, 1775.* Salem: William Ives and George W. Pease, 1856.

Erikson, Kai Theodore. *Wayward Puritans: A Study in the Sociology of Deviance.* New York: Wiley [1966].

Erlich, Gloria. *Family Themes and Hawthorne's Fiction: The Tenacious Web*. New Brunswick: Rutgers University Press, 1984.

Faces of a Family. Comp. Andrew Oliver. Portland, Maine: The Anthoeson Press, 1960.

Fairbanks, Henry G. *The Lasting Loneliness of Nathaniel Hawthorne: A Study of the Sources of Alienation in Modern Man*. Albany, N.Y.: Magi Books, 1965.

Felt, Joseph Barlow. *Annals of Salem from Its First Settlement*. Salem: W. and S. B. Ives, 1827. 2d ed. 2 vols., 1845, 1849.

——. *History of Ipswich, Essex, and Hamilton*. Cambridge, Mass.: Charles Folsom, 1834.

Fick, Leonard J. *The Light Beyond: A Study of Hawthorne's Theology*. 1955. Reprint, Folcroft, Pa.: Folcroft Press, 1969.

Fields, James T. *Yesterdays with Authors*. 1871. Reprint, Boston: Houghton, Mifflin, 1891.

The First Centenary of the North Church and Society in Salem, Massachusetts. Salem: Printed for the Society, 1873.

Fischer, David Hackett. *Albion's Seed: Four British Folkways in America*, Vol. 1 of *America: A Cultural History*. New York: Oxford University Press, 1989.

Foote, Arthur. *Arthur Foote, 1853–1937: An Autobiography with Notes by Wilma Reid Cipolla*. New York: DaCapo Press, 1979.

Fuess, Claude Moore. *Daniel Webster*. 2 vols. Boston: Little, Brown, 1930.

Fuller, Margaret. *The Letters of Margaret Fuller*. Ed. Robert N. Hudspeth. 5 vols. Ithaca: Cornell University Press, 1983–1988.

Gaeddert, Lou Ann. *A New England Love Story: Nathaniel Hawthorne and Sophia Peabody*. New York: Dial Press, 1980.

Gale, Robert L. *A Nathaniel Hawthorne Encyclopedia*. New York: Greenwood Press, 1991.

Garden History of Georgia, 1733–1933. Comp. Lorraine M. Cooney. Atlanta: Peachtree Garden Club, 1933.

Garland, Joseph E. *Boston's North Shore*. Boston: Little, Brown, 1978.

Garrett, Edmund H. *Romance and Reality of the Puritan Coast of the North Shore*. Boston: Little, Brown, 1902.

A General Catalogue of Bowdoin College and Medical School of Maine: A Biographical Record of Alumni and Officers, 1794–1950. Brunswick, Maine: Anthoeson Press, 1950.

Gildrie, Richard P. *Salem, Massachusetts, 1626–1683: A Covenant Community*. Charlottesville: University Press of Virginia, 1975.

Gittleman, Edwin. *Jones Very: The Effective Years, 1833–1840*. New York: Columbia University Press, 1967.

Gollin, Rita K. *Portraits of Nathaniel Hawthorne: An Iconography*. DeKalb: Northern Illinois University Press, 1983.

Gollin, Rita K., and John L. Idol Jr. with assistance from Sterling K. Eisiminger. *Prophetic Pictures: Nathaniel Hawthorne's Knowledge and Uses of the Visual Arts*. New York: Greenwood Press, 1991.

Goodrich, Samuel G. *Recollections of a Lifetime or Men and Things I Have Seen*. 2 vols. New York: Miller, Orton and Company, 1857.

Goodspeed, Charles E. *Nathaniel Hawthorne and the Museum of the Salem East India Marine Society*. Salem: Peabody Museum, 1946.

Grimké, Charlotte Forten. *The Journals of Charlotte Forten Grimké*. Ed. Brenda Stevenson. New York: Oxford University Press, 1988.

Hammatt, Abraham. *The Hammatt Papers: Early Inhabitants of Ipswich, Massachusetts 1633–1700*. 1854. Reprint, Baltimore: Genealogical Publishing, 1980.

Hanson, Chadwick. *Witchcraft at Salem*. New York: George Braziller, 1969.

Hawthorne, Julian. *Hawthorne and His Circle*. New York: Harper and Brothers, 1903.

———. *Nathaniel Hawthorne and His Wife*. 2 vols. Boston: Houghton, Mifflin, 1884.

———. *The Memoirs of Julian Hawthorne*. Ed. Edith Garrigues Hawthorne. New York: Macmillan, 1938.

Hawthorne, Nathaniel. *The Centenary Edition of Nathaniel Hawthorne*. Ed. William Charvat et al. 23 vols. Columbus: Ohio State University Press, 1962–1997.

———. *Main Street with an Introduction by Julian Hawthorne*. Canton, Pa.: Kirkgate Press, 1901.

———. *Our Old Home and English Note-Books*. 2 vols. Boston: Houghton, Mifflin, 1892.

Herbert, T. Walter. *Dearest Beloved: The Hawthornes and the Making of the Middle-Class Family*. Berkeley: University of California Press, 1993.

Heyrman, Christine. *Commerce and Culture: The Maritime Communities of Colonial Massachusetts, 1690–1750*. New York: W. W. Norton, 1984.

Higginson, Thomas Wentworth. *Old Cambridge*. New York: Macmillan, 1900.

Historical Sketch of the Salem Lyceum with a List of Officers and Lecturers since its Formation in 1830 and an Extract from the Address by General Henry K. Oliver. Salem: *Salem Gazette,* 1879.

History of Essex County, Massachusetts. Ed. D. Hamilton Hurd. 2 vols. Philadelphia: Lewis, 1888.

History of the Massachusetts Horticultural Society, 1828–1878. Ed. Robert Manning. Boston: The Society, 1880.

Hoeltje, Hubert H. *Inward Sky: The Mind and Heart of Nathaniel Hawthorne.* Durham: Duke University Press, 1962.

Holmes, Frank R. *Directory of the Ancestral Heads of New England Families, 1620–1700.* Baltimore: Genealogical Publishing, 1964.

Howe, Mark Anthony DeWolfe. *Memories of a Hostess: A Chronicle of Eminent Friendships Drawn Chiefly from the Diaries of Mrs. James T. Fields.* Boston: Atlantic Monthly Press, [1922].

Howells, William Dean. *Literary Friends and Acquaintance: A Personal Retrospect of American Authorship.* Ed. David F. Hiatt and Edwin H. Cady. Bloomington: Indiana University Press, 1968.

Hoyt, Edwin P. *The Peabody Influence: How a Great New England Family Helped to Build America.* New York: Dodd, Mead, 1968.

Hutchinson, Thomas. *The History of the Colony and Province of Massachusetts Bay.* Ed. Lawrence Shaw Mayo. 3 vols. Vol. 1, 1765. Reprint, Cambridge: Harvard University Press, 1936.

[James, Alice]. *The Death and Letters of Alice James.* Ed. Ruth Bernard Yeazell. Berkeley: University of California Press, 1981.

James, Henry. *Hawthorne.* 1879. Reprint, Ithaca: Cornell University Press, 1956.

Karlsen, Carol F. *The Devil in the Shape of a Woman.* New York: Vintage Books, 1989.

Kenny, Herbert A. *Cape Ann: Cape America.* Philadelphia: J. B. Lippincott, 1971.

King, Caroline Howard. *When I Lived in Salem, 1822–1866.* Brattleboro, Vt.: Stephen Daye Press, 1937.

Lang, Amy Schraeger. *Prophetic Woman: Anne Hutchinson and the Problem of Dissent in the Literature of New England.* Berkeley: University of California Press, 1987.

Lathrop, George Parsons. *A Study of Hawthorne.* Boston: James R. Osgood and Company, 1876.

Lathrop, Rose Hawthorne. *Memories of Hawthorne.* Boston: Houghton, Mifflin, 1897.

Lewis, Alonzo, and James R. Newhall. *The History of Lynn, Including Nahant.* 2d ed. Boston: Samuel N. Dickinson, 1844.

Loggins, Vernon. *The Hawthornes: The Story of Seven Generations of an American Family.* New York: Columbia University Press, 1951.

Longfellow, Henry Wadsworth. *The Letters of Henry Wadsworth Longfellow.* Ed. Andrew Hilen. 6 vols. Cambridge: Belknap Press, 1966–1982.

Lord, Priscilla Sawyer, and Virginia Clegg Gamage. *Marblehead: The Spirit of '76 Lives Here.* Updated ed. Radnor, Pa.: Chilton Book Company, 1972.

Lyttle, David. *Studies in Religion in Early American Literature: Edwards, Poe, Channing, Emerson, Some Minor Transcendentalists, Hawthorne and Thoreau.* Lanham, Md.: University Press of America, 1983.

McLoughlin, William Gerald. *The Cherokees and Christianity, 1794–1870.* Ed. Walter H. Conser Jr. Athens: University of Georgia Press, 1994.

McMillen, Persis W. *Currents of Malice: Mary Town Esty and Her Family in Salem Witchcraft.* Portsmouth, N.H.: Peter E. Randall, 1990.

Mais, Stuart Petre Brodie. *Glorious Devon.* London: Great Western Railway, 1928.

Manning, William H. *The Genealogical and Biographical History of the Manning Families of New England and Descendants.* Salem: Salem Press, 1902.

Mansfield, Howard. *In the Memory House.* Golden, Colo.: Fulcrum, 1993.

Martin, Edward Sandford. *The Life of Joseph Hodges Choate as Gathered Chiefly from His Letters.* 2 vols. New York: Charles Scribner's Sons, 1927.

Martineau, Harriet. *Society in America.* 2d ed. 2 vols. New York: Saunders and Otley, 1837.

Matthiessen, Francis Otto. *American Renaissance: Art and Expression in the Age of Emerson and Whitman.* New York: Oxford University Press, 1941.

Mellow, James R. *Nathaniel Hawthorne in His Times.* Boston: Houghton, Mifflin, 1980.

Memoirs of Margaret Fuller Ossoli. Ed. Ralph W. Emerson and James F. Clarke. 2 vols. Boston: Phillips, Sampson and Company, 1852.

Miller, Edwin Haviland. *Salem Is My Dwelling Place.* Iowa City: University of Iowa Press, 1991.

Miller, Perry. *Roger Williams: His Contribution to the American Tradition.* Indianapolis: Bobbs-Merrill, 1953.

Moore, George H. *Notes on the History of Slavery in Massachusetts.* New York: D. Appleton and Company, 1866.

Morris, John E. *The Felt Genealogy: A Record of the Descendants of George Felt of Casco Bay.* Hartford, Conn.: Case, Lockwood and Brainard, 1893.

Morse, John T., Jr. *Life and Letters of Oliver Wendell Holmes.* 2 vols. Boston: Houghton, Mifflin, 1896.

Nagel, Paul C. *The Adams Women: Abigail and Louisa Adams.* New York: Oxford University Press, 1987.

Newberry, Frederick. *Hawthorne's Divided Loyalties: England and America in His Works.* Rutherford, N.J.: Fairleigh Dickinson University Press, 1987.

Newhall, James Robinson. *The Essex Memorial for 1836: Embracing a Register of the County.* Salem: Henry Whipple, 1836.

Normand, Jean. *Nathaniel Hawthorne: An Approach to an Analysis of Artistic Creation.* Cleveland: The Press of Case Western Reserve University, 1970.

Norton, Mary Beth. *The British-Americans: The Loyalist Exiles in England, 1774–1789.* Boston: Little, Brown, 1972.

Nylander, Jane C. *Our Own Snug Fireside: Images of the New England Home, 1760–1860.* New York: Alfred A. Knopf, 1993.

Oliver, Benjamin Lynde, Jr. *Hints for an Essay on the Pursuit of Happiness (Designed for Common Use).* Cambridge, Mass.: Hilliard and Metcalf, 1818.

———. *The Rights of an American Citizen with a Commentary on State Rights.* . . . Boston: Marsh, Capen and Lyon, 1832.

Osgood, Charles S., and Henry M. Batchelder. *Historical Sketch of Salem, 1626–1879.* Salem: Essex Institute, 1879.

Paige, Lucius R. *History of Cambridge, Massachusetts, 1630–1877.* Boston: H.O. Houghton, 1877.

Paine, Ralph D. *The Ships and Sailors of Old Salem.* New York: Outing, 1909.

[Peabody, Elizabeth Palmer, Sr.]. *Holiness: or the Legend of St. George, a Tale from Spenser's Fairie Queen by a Mother.* Boston: E. R. Broaders, 1836.

———. *Sabbath Lessons, or an Abstract of Sacred History.* Salem: Cushing, 1810.

Peabody, Elizabeth Palmer. *Letters of Elizabeth Palmer Peabody: American Renaissance Woman.* Ed. Bruce A. Ronda. Middletown, Conn.: Wesleyan University Press, 1984.

Peabody, Selim Hobart. *The Peabody (Paybody, Pabody, Pabodie) Genealogy.* Ed. Charles H. Pope. Boston: Charles H. Pope, 1909.

Pearson, Norman Holmes. *Hawthorne's Two Engagements*. Northampton: Smith College, 1963.

Perley, Sidney. *The Poets of Essex County, Massachusetts*. Salem: Sidney Perley, 1889.

———. *A History of Salem, Massachusetts*. 3 vols. Salem: Sidney Perley, 1924–1928.

Pfister, Joel. *The Production of Personal Life: Class, Gender, and the Psychological in Hawthorne's Fiction*. Stanford: Stanford University Press, 1992.

Phelps, Oliver Seymour, and Andrew T. Servin. *The Phelps Family of America*. 2 vols. Pittsfield, Mass.: Eagle, 1899.

Phillips, James Duncan. *Salem and the Indies*. Boston: Houghton, Mifflin, 1947.

———. *Salem in the Eighteenth Century*. Boston: Houghton, Mifflin, 1937.

———. *Salem in the Seventeenth Century*. Boston: Houghton, Mifflin, 1933.

Pickering, John. *A Vocabulary; or Collection of Words and Phrases Which Have Been Supposed to be Peculiar to the United States of America*. 1816. Reprint, New York: Burt Franklin, 1974.

Pickering, Octavius, and Charles W. Upham. *The Life of Timothy Pickering*. 4 vols. Boston: Little, Brown, 1867–1873.

Ponder, Melinda M. *Hawthorne's Early Narrative Art*. Studies in American Literature, no. 9. Lewiston, N.Y.: Edwin Mellen Press, 1990.

Pope-Hennessy, James. *Sins of the Fathers*. New York: Alfred A. Knopf, 1968.

Pope, Charles Henry. *Pioneers of Massachusetts*. Facsimile reprint, Bowie, Md.: Heritage Books, 1991.

The Probate Records of Essex County, Massachusetts. 3 vols. Salem: Essex Institute, 1920.

Putnam, Eleanor [Harriet Leonora Vose Bates]. *Old Salem*. Ed. Arlo Bates. Boston: Houghton, Mifflin, 1899.

Pynchon, William. *The Diary of William Pynchon*. Ed. Edward Oliver Fitch. 1890. Reprint, New York: AMS, 1971.

Quinquennial Catalogue of the Officers and Graduates of Harvard University, 1636–1905. Cambridge: Harvard University Press, 1905.

Records and Files of the Quarterly Courts of Essex County, Massachusetts. Ed. George Francis Dow. 8 vols. Salem: Essex Institute, 1911. Vol. 9, Ed. Mary G. Thrasher. Salem: Essex Institute, 1975.

Records of the Court of Assistants of the Colony of Massachusetts Bay,

1630–1692. 3 vols. 1901–1928. Reprint, Boston: County of Suffolk, 1984.

The Records of the First Church in Salem, Massachusetts, 1629–1736. Ed. Richard D. Pierce. Salem: Essex Institute, 1974.

A Report of the Record Commissioners of the City of Boston Containing Boston Births from A.D. 1700 to A.D. 1800. Boston: Rockwell Churchill, 1894.

Reynolds, David S. *Beneath the American Renaissance: The Subversive Imagination in the Age of Emerson and Melville.* New York: Alfred A. Knopf, 1988.

Ridlon, Gideon Tibbetts. *Saco Valley Settlements and Families.* 1895. Reprint, Rutland, Vt.: Charles E. Tuttle, 1969.

Roberts, David. *A Treatise on Admiralty and Prize Together with Some Suggestions for the Guide and Government of the United States Naval Commanders in Maritime Wars.* New York: Hurd and Houghton, 1869.

Robotti, Frances Dianne. *Chronicles of Old Salem: A History in Miniature.* New York: Bonanza Books, 1948.

Rosa, Alfred. *Salem, Transcendentalism, and Hawthorne.* Rutherford, N.J.: Fairleigh Dickinson University Press, 1980.

Rosenthal, Bernard. *Salem Story: Reading the Witch Trials of 1692.* Cambridge Studies in American Literature and Culture. Cambridge, England: Cambridge University Press, 1993.

Rust, Albert D. *Record of the Rust Family.* Waco, Tex.: privately printed, 1891.

The Salem Directory and City Register. Salem: Henry Whipple, 1837, 1842, 1846.

Salem Witchcraft Papers: Verbatim Transcripts of the Legal Documents of the Salem Witchcraft Outbreak of 1692. Ed. Paul S. Boyer and Stephen Nissenbaum. 3 vols. New York: Da Capo Press, 1977.

Saltonstall, Leverett. *The Papers of Leverett Saltonstall, 1816–1845.* Ed. Robert E. Moody. 5 vols. Boston: Massachusetts Historical Society, 1978–1992.

The Saltonstall Papers, 1607–1815. Ed. Robert E. Moody. 2 vols. Boston: Massachusetts Historical Society, 1974.

Sanborn, Frank B. *Hawthorne and His Friends: Reminiscence and Tribute.* Cedar Rapids, Iowa: Torch Press, 1908.

Sanders, Elizabeth Elkins. *Conversations, Principally on the Aborigines of North America.* Salem: W. and S. B. Ives, 1828.

Saunders, Joseph B. *A Short Study of Three Centuries of Salem, 1626–1926.* Salem: Deschamps Brothers, 1926.

[Savage, Sarah]. *Advice to a Young Woman at Service, in a Letter from a Friend,* by the author of "James Talbot," "The Factory Girl," etc. Boston: Printed for the Publishing Fund by John R. Russell, 1823.

[————]. *The Badge: A Moral Tale for Children.* By the author of "The Factory Girl," "James Talbot," etc. Boston: T. G. Wells, 1824.

[————]. *Blind Miriam, Restored to Sight.* Salem: Register Office, 1833.

[————]. *The Factory Girl,* by a Lady. Boston: Munroe, Francis, and Parker, 1814.

[————]. *Filial Affection: or, The Clergyman's Granddaughter. A Moral Tale.* Boston: Cummings and Hilliard, 1820.

[————]. *Life of Philip the Indian Chief.* By the Author of "The Factory Girl," "The Badge," and "Two Birth Days" etc. Salem: Whipple and Lawrence, 1827.

[————]. *Trial and Self Discipline.* No. 1 in *Scenes and Characters Illustrating Christian Truth.* By the author of "James Talbot," "The Factory Girl," etc. Boston and Cambridge: James Munroe and Company, 1835.

Seaburg, Carl, and Stanley Paterson. *Merchant Prince of Boston: Colonel Thomas Handasyd Perkins, 1764–1854.* Cambridge: Harvard University Press, 1971.

Sewel, William. *The History of the Rise, Increase, and Progress of the Christian People Called Quakers.* 2 vols. 1774. Reprint, Philadelphia: Friends' Book Store, 1856.

Shipton, Clifford K. *New England Life in the Eighteenth Century: Representative Biographies from Sibley's Harvard Graduates.* Cambridge: Harvard University Press, 1963.

Silsbee, Marianne C. D. *A Half-Century in Salem.* Boston: Houghton, Mifflin, 1887.

Sprague, William Buell. *Annals of the American Pulpit.* 9 vols. New York: Robert Carter and Brothers, 1857–1869.

Stearns, Frank Preston. *The Life and Genius of Nathaniel Hawthorne.* Philadelphia: J. B. Lippincott, 1906.

Stewart, Randall. *Nathaniel Hawthorne: A Biography.* New Haven: Yale University Press, 1948.

Stoddard, Elizabeth Barstow. *The Morgesons and Other Writings, Published and Unpublished.* Ed. Lawrence Buell and Sandra A. Zagarell. Philadelphia: University of Pennsylvania Press, 1984.

Stoddard, Richard Henry. *Recollections, Personal and Literary.* 1903. Reprint, New York: AMS Press, 1971.

Stoehr, Taylor. *Hawthorne's Mad Scientists: Pseudoscience and Social*

Science in Nineteenth-Century Life and Letters. Hamden, Conn.: Shoe String Press, 1978.

Stone, Edwin M. *History of Beverly.* Boston: James Munroe, 1843.

The Story of Essex County. Ed. Claude M. Fuess. 4 vols. New York: American Historical Society, 1935.

Swann, Charles. *Nathaniel Hawthorne: Tradition and Revolution.* Cambridge, England: Cambridge University Press, 1991.

Tapley, Harriet S. *Salem Imprints, 1768–1825: A History of the First Fifty Years of Printing in Salem, Massachusetts.* Salem: Essex Institute, 1927.

Tharp, Louise Hall. *The Peabody Sisters of Salem.* Boston: Little, Brown, 1950.

Thomas, Brook. *Cross-Examinations of Law and Literature: Cooper, Hawthorne, Stowe, and Melville.* New York: Cambridge University Press, 1987.

Thompson, Gary Richard. *The Art of Authorial Presence: Hawthorne's Provincial Tales.* Durham: Duke University Press, 1993.

Thompson, Roger. *Mobility and Migration: East Anglian Founders of New England, 1629–1640.* Amherst: University of Massachusetts Press, 1994.

Tileston, Mary W. *Caleb and Mary Wilder Foote: Reminiscences and Letters.* Boston: Houghton, Mifflin, 1918.

Tolles, Bryant F., Jr., with Carolyn K. Tolles. *Architecture in Salem: An Illustrated Guide.* Salem: Essex Institute, 1983.

Tompkins, Jane. *Sensational Designs: The Cultural Work of American Fiction, 1790–1860.* New York: Oxford University Press, 1985.

Travels in the Old South: A Bibliography. Ed. Thomas D. Clark. 3 vols. Norman: University of Oklahoma Press, 1956–1959.

Trollope, Frances. *Domestic Manners of the Americans.* 2 vols. 1832. Reprint, ed. Donald Smalley. New York: Alfred A. Knopf, 1949.

Trow, Charles Edward. *The Old Shipmasters of Salem.* New York: G. P. Putnam's Sons, 1905.

Turner, Arlin. *Nathaniel Hawthorne: A Biography.* New York: Oxford University Press, 1980.

Upham, Charles W. *Lectures on Witchcraft, Comprising a History of the Delusion in Salem in 1692.* Boston: Hendee and Babcock, 1831.

———. *Salem Witchcraft. With an Account of Salem Village and a History of Opinions on Witchcraft and Kindred Subjects.* 2 vols. 1867. Reprint, New York: Frederick Ungar, [1959].

Upham, William P. *Town Records of Salem, 1634–1659.* 3 vols. Salem: Essex Institute, 1868.

Valenti, Patricia Dunlavy. *To Myself a Stranger: A Biography of Rose Hawthorne Lathrop*. Baton Rouge: Louisiana State University Press, 1991.

Very, Jones. *The Complete Poems*. Ed. Helen R. Deese. Athens: University of Georgia Press, 1993.

Vital Records of Andover, Massachusetts, to the End of the Year 1849. 2 vols. Topsfield: Topsfield Historical Society, 1912.

Vital Records of Beverly, Massachusetts to the End of the Year 1849. 2 vols. Topsfield: Topsfield Historical Society, 1906–1907.

Vital Records of Hamilton, Massachusetts to the End of the Year 1849. Salem: Essex Institute, 1908.

Vital Records of Ipswich, Massachusetts to the End of the Year 1849. 3 vols. Salem: Essex Institute, 1910, 1919.

Vital Records of Lynn, Massachusetts to the End of the Year 1849. 2 vols. Salem: Essex Institute, 1905–1906.

Vital Records of Reading, Massachusetts to the Year 1850. Boston: Wright and Potter, 1912.

Vital Records of Salem to the End of the Year 1849. 6 vols. Salem: Essex Institute, 1916–1925.

Wagenknecht, Edward. *Nathaniel Hawthorne: The Man, His Tales and Romances*. New York: Continuum, 1989.

Waggoner, Hyatt Howe. *The Presence of Hawthorne*. Baton Rouge: Louisiana State University Press, 1979.

Ward, George Atkinson. *Journal and Letters of the Late Samuel Curwen, Judge of Admiralty, etc., an American Refugee from 1775*. New York: C. S. Francis, 1842.

Warren, Austin. *New England Saints*. Ann Arbor: University of Michigan Press, 1956.

Warren, Henry P. et al. *The History of Waterford, Oxford County, Maine, Comprising Historical Address by Henry P. Warren, Record of Families by Rev. William Warren, and Centennial Proceedings by Samuel Warren*. Portland, Maine: Hoyt, Fogg, and Donham, 1879.

Warren, Joyce W. *The American Narcissus: Individualism and Women in Nineteenth-Century Fiction*. New Brunswick, N.J.: Rutgers University Press, 1984.

Webster, Daniel. *The Papers of Daniel Webster*. Vol. 3. *Correspondence, 1830–1834*. Ed. Charles M. Wiltse and David G. Allen. Hanover, N.H.: University Press of New England, 1977.

Wells, John A. *The Peabody Story*. Salem: Essex Institute, 1973.

Wells, Ronald A. *Dictionaries and the Authoritarian Tradition*. The Hague: Mouton, 1973.

Whitmore, William Henry. *A Brief Genealogy of Descendants of William Hutchinson and Thomas Oliver.* Boston: S. G. Drake, 1865.

Willard, Joseph A. *Half a Century with Judges and Lawyers.* Boston: Houghton, Mifflin, 1895.

Wilson, Fred A. *Some Annals of Nahant, Massachusetts.* Boston: Old Corner Book Store, 1928.

Worrall, Arthur J. *Quakers in the Colonial Northeast.* Hanover, N.H.: University Press of New England, 1980.

Wyman, Thomas Bellows. *The Genealogies and Estates of Charlestown, Massachusetts, 1629–1818.* 1879. Reprint, Somersworth: New England History Press, 1982.

Young, Christine Alice. *From "Good Order" to Glorious Revolution, Salem, Massachusetts, 1628–1689.* Ann Arbor: UMI Research Press, 1980.

Young, Philip. *Hawthorne's Secret: An Untold Tale.* Boston: David R. Godine, 1984.

ARTICLES

Almy, James F. "A History of Methodism in Salem." *EIHC* 24 (1887): 275–301.

Amory, Thomas C., Jr., "Reminiscences." *NEHGR* 18 (1864): 228–30.

Annable, Irving Kinsman. "Historical Notes of the Crombie Street Congregational Church, Salem, Massachusetts." *EIHC* 77 (1941): 203–17.

Barlow, William, and David O. Powell. "Malthus Augustus Whitworth Ward." *Dictionary of Georgia Biography.* 2 vols. Ed. Kenneth Coleman and Charles Stephen Gurr. 2:1033–34.

Bassan, Maurice. "Julian Hawthorne Edits Aunt Ebe." *EIHC* 100 (1964): 274–78.

Baughman, Ernest W. "Excommunications and Banishments from the First Church in Salem and the Town of Salem, 1629–1680." *EIHC* 113 (1977): 89–104.

Baym, Nina. "Nathaniel Hawthorne and His Mother: A Biographical Speculation." *AL* 54 (1982): 1–27.

Beaman, Charles Cotesworth. "The Branch or Howard Street Church." *EIHC* 3 (1861): 272–83.

Belknap, Henry W. "Check List of Salem Privateers in the War of 1812." *EIHC* 78 (1942): 247–48 to 80 (1944): 158–76.

———. "Philip English, Commerce Builder." *American Antiquarian Society Proceedings* n.s. 41 (1931): 17–24.

———. "Simon Forrester and His Descendants." *EIHC* 71 (1935): 17–64.

"Bent of the Mind." (From *Curiosities of Literature.*) *AMUEK* 2 (1836): 294.

Bentley, William. "Description and History of Salem." *Massachusetts Historical Society Collections* 6 (1800): 212–88.

[————]. "Parish List of Deaths Begun 1785." *EIHC* 14 (1877): 129–48 to 18 (1881): 206–23.

Bjorkman, Gwen Boyer. "Hannah (Baskel) Phelps Phelps Hill: A Quaker Woman and Her Offspring." *National Genealogical Society Quarterly* 75 (1987): 289–302.

Bogin, Ruth. "Sarah Parker Remond: Black Abolitionist from Salem." *EIHC* 110 (1974): 120–50.

Bolton, Theodore. "New England Portrait Painters in Miniature: A Checklist." *Old-Time New England* 12 (1922): 131–34.

Bowditch, Nathaniel Ingersoll. "Death and Funeral of Doctor Spurzheim." *Colonial Society of Massachusetts Publications* 10 (1904): 77–81.

————. "The Witchcraft Papers." *MHSP* 5 (1860–1862): 31–37.

Boykin, Samuel. "Reminiscences of the Original Botanical Garden." *Newsletter,* Friends of the Botanical Garden, University of Georgia 2 (1982): 15–29.

Brancaccio, Patrick. "The Black Man's Paradise: Hawthorne's Editing of the 'Journal of an African Cruiser.'" *NEQ* 53 (1980): 23–41.

Breslaw, Elaine G. "The Salem Witch from Barbados: In Search of Tituba's Roots." *EIHC* 128 (1992): 217–38.

Brodhead, Richard. "Veiled Ladies: Toward a History of Ante-bellum Entertainment." *American Literary History* 1 (1989): 273–94.

Brooks, Charles Timothy. "Poem" in "An Account of the Commemoration, by the Essex Institute, of the Fifth Half-Century of the Landing of John Endicott in Salem, Massachusetts." *EIHC* 15 (1878): 195–215.

Brooks, Henry M. "Some Localities about Salem." *EIHC* 31 (1894): 103–26.

Browne, Benjamin F. "Youthful Recollections of Salem." *EIHC* 49 (1913): 193–209 to 51 (1915): 297–305.

Buckham, John Wright. "Literary Salem." *EIHC* 43 (1907): 193–98.

Burkholder, Robert E. "Emerson, Kneeland, and the Divinity School Address." *AL* 58 (1986): 1–14.

Burstyn, Harold D. "Salem Philosophical Library: Its History and Importance for American Science." *EIHC* 96 (1960): 169–206.

"Catalogue of Portraits in the Essex Museum, Salem, Massachusetts." *EIHC* 70 (1934): 169–84 to 73 (1937): 60–88.

Chandler, Elizabeth Lathrop. "A Study of Sources of the Tales and Romances Written by Nathaniel Hawthorne before 1853." *Smith College Studies in Modern Languages* 7, no. 4 (1926): 1–64.

Chapple, William Dismore. "Salem and the War of 1812." *EIHC* 59 (1923): 289–304; 60 (1924): 49–74.

Chever, George Francis. "Some Remarks on the Commerce of Salem from 1626 to 1740—with a sketch of Philip English—a Merchant in Salem from About 1670 to About 1733–4." *EIHC* 1 (1859): 67–76 to 3 (1861): 111–20.

Chipley, Louise. "The Financial Anxieties of New England's Congregational Clergy during the Early National Era: The Case of William Bentley, 1783–1819." *EIHC* 127 (1991): 277–96.

Choate, Joseph H. "Nathaniel Hawthorne: A Letter on the Centennial of His Birth at Salem, July 4, 1904." In Cameron, *Hawthorne among His Contemporaries,* 472–75.

Clark, C. E. Frazer, Jr. "Unexplored Areas of Hawthorne Bibliography." *NHJ 1972,* 47–51.

———. "New Light on the Editing of the 1842 Edition of *Twice-Told Tales:* Discovery of a Family Copy of the 1833 *Token* Annotated by Hawthorne." *NHJ 1972,* 91–103.

Commager, Henry Steele. "The Blasphemy of Abner Kneeland." *NEQ* 8 (1935): 29–41.

Constantia [pseudonym]. "On Female Education." *Portfolio* 20 (1825): 413–18.

Cowley, Malcolm. "Hawthorne in the Looking Glass." *Sewanee Review* 56 (1948): 545–63.

Coulter, E. Merton. "The Story of the Tree That Owned Itself." *Georgia Historical Quarterly* 46 (1962): 237–49.

Cox, James M. "Reflections on Hawthorne's Nature." In *American Letters and the Historical Consciousness: Essays in Honor of Lewis Simpson,* ed. J. Gerald Kennedy and Daniel Mark Fogel. Baton Rouge: Louisiana State University Press, 1987, 137–57.

Crothers, Samuel M. "Address." *EIHC* 41 (1905): 9–20.

Crowninshield, B. B. "An Account of the Private Armed Ship 'America' of Salem." *EIHC* 37 (1901): 1–76.

Cummings, Abbott Lowell. "The House and Its People." *EIHC* 97 (1961): 82–97.

Curwen, George R. "Materials for a Genealogy of the Ward Family and Notices of the Descendants of Miles Ward." *EIHC* 5 (1863): 207–19.

Davis, Sarah I. "The Bank and the Old Pyncheon Family." *Studies in the Novel* 16, no. 2 (1984): 150–65.

Deese, Helen R. "The Peabody Family and the Jones Very 'Insanity': Two Letters of Mary Peabody." *Harvard Library Bulletin,* 35 (1987): 218–29.

Dennis, William D. "The Fire Clubs of Salem." *EIHC* 39 (1903): 1–28.

———. "The Salem Charitable Mechanics Association." *EIHC* 42 (1906): 1–35.

Derby, Perley. "Inscriptions from Charter Street Burial Ground, Salem, Massachusetts." *EIHC* 13 (1875): 67–80, 107–14.

Dodge, Ernest D. "Captain Collectors." *EIHC* 81 (1945): 27–34.

Donnan, Elizabeth. "The New England Slave Trade after the Revolution." *NEQ* 3 (1930): 251–78.

Downing, Lucy. "Letters of Lucy Downing [1626–1674]." In *The Winthrop Papers,* III. *MHSC* 1, 5th ser. (1871): 3–63.

Drake, Samuel G. "Early Settlers of Essex and Old Norfolk." *NEHGR* 6 (1852): 205–8 to 7 (1853): 357–60.

Edwards, Mrs. Henry. "Lady Deborah Moody." *EIHC* 31 (1894): 96–102.

Ellis, George E. "Memoir of Charles Wentworth Upham." *MHSP* 15 (1876): 182–220.

Emmerton, James A. "Henry Silsbee and Some of His Descendants." *EIHC* 17 (1880): 257–311.

Evelina [pseudonym]. "For the Miscellany." *Ladies' Miscellany* 2 (1830): 29.

Farmer, John. "Memoirs of Graduates of Harvard College." *NEHGR* 1 (1847): 34–39.

Flibbert, Joseph. "Hawthorne, Salem, and the Sea." *Sextant: The Journal of Salem State College* 5 (1994): 2–9.

Foote, Arthur, 2d. "Henry Wilder Foote, Hymnologist." *Papers of the Hymn Society* 26 (1968): 3–24.

[Foote, Caleb]. Review of "Main-Street." *SG,* May 18, 1849.

[———]. Review of *Trial and Self-Discipline. SG,* March 31, 1835.

Foote, Henry W. "Caleb Foote" in *History of Essex County,* vol. 1, 247–48.

French, Elizabeth. "Genealogical Research in England." *NEHGR* 63 (1909): 356–63 to 71 (1917): 227–57.

French, Roderick S. "Liberation from Man and God in Boston: Abner Kneeland's Free-Thought Campaign, 1830–1839." *American Quarterly* 32 (1980): 202–21.

Gardner, Frank A. "Thomas Gardner, Planter, and Some of His Descendants." *EIHC* 37 (1901): 81–104 to 40 (1904): 353–74.

Gildrie, Richard. "Visions of Evil: Popular Culture, Puritanism, and the Massachusetts Witchcraft Crisis of 1692." *Journal of American Culture* 8 (1985): 17–33.

Goodell, Abner Cheney. "A Biographical Notice of the Officers of Probate for Essex County, from the Commencement of the Colony to the Present Time." *EIHC* 2 (1860): 156–66; 4 (1862): 97–111.

―――. "A Biographical Sketch of Thomas Maule of Salem Together with a Review of the Early Antinomians of New England." *EIHC* 3 (1861): 238–42, 243–53.

―――. "Essex County Court Records." *EIHC* 7 (1865): 17–19 to 8 (1866): 63–64.

Goodrich, Merton Taylor. "The Children of Eleanor Trusler." *American Genealogist* 10 (1932): 15–16.

Greene, David L. "The English Origin of George Giddings of Ipswich, Massachusetts." *NEHGR* 135 (1981): 274–86.

―――. "The Third Wife of the Rev. George Burroughs." *American Genealogist* 56 (1980): 43–45.

Harrington, Arthur H. "Hathorne Hill in Danvers with Some Account of Major William Hathorne." *EIHC* 48 (1912): 97–112.

[Hawthorne, Elizabeth M.] "The Susan Affair: An Unpublished Manuscript." Ed. C. E. Frazer Clark Jr. *NHJ 1971,* 12–17.

Hawthorne, Julian. "Nathaniel Hawthorne's Blue Cloak, a Son's Reminiscences." *The Bookman* 75 (1932): 501–6.

―――. "The Salem of Hawthorne." *The Century Magazine* 28 (1884): 3–17.

Hawthorne, Manning. "Aunt Ebe—Some Letters of Elizabeth M. Hawthorne." *NEQ* 20 (1947): 209–31.

―――. "A Glimpse of Hawthorne's Boyhood." *EIHC* 83 (1947): 178–84.

―――. "Hawthorne and the Man of God." *The Colophon* n.s. 11 (1937): 262–82.

―――. "Hawthorne's Early Years." *EIHC* 74 (1938): 1–21.

―――. "Maria Louisa Hawthorne." *EIHC* 75 (1939): 103–34.

―――. "Nathaniel Hawthorne Prepares for College." *NEQ* 11 (1938): 66–88.

―――. "Parental and Family Influences on Hawthorne." *EIHC* 76 (1940): 1–13.

[Hawthorne, Nathaniel]. "April Fools." *AMUEK* 2 (1836): 339–40.

―――. "Churches and Cathedrals." *AMUEK* 2 (1836): 497–98.

―――. "The Duston Family." *AMUEK* 2 (1836): 395–97.

―――. "John C. Calhoun." *AMUEK* 2 (1836): 359–60.

―――. "Revolutionary Sentiments." *AMUEK* 2 (1836): 496.

―――. "Sketch of the Fur Trade." *AMUEK* 2 (1836): 509–10.

"Hawthorne's 'Privateer' Revealed at Last." *Literary Digest* 93 (1927): 44–49.

Heyrman, Christine. "Specters of Subversion, Societies of Friends: Dissent and the Devil in Provincial Essex County, Massachusetts." In *Saints and Revolutionaries: Essays on Early American History,* ed. David D. Hall et al. New York: W. W. Norton, 1984, 38–74.

Hill, Mrs. Georgie A. "Passenger Arrivals at Salem and Beverly, Massachusetts, 1798–1800." *NEHGR* 106 (1952): 203–9.

Hines, Ezra D. "Browne Hill (Formerly Called Long Hill and Leach's Hill) and Some History Connected with It." *EIHC* 32 (1896): 201–38.

Hitchings, A. Frank. "Ship Registers of the District of Salem and Beverly, 1789–1900." *EIHC* 39 (1903): 185–208 to 42 (1906): 89–112.

Hoeltje, Hubert J. "Captain Nathaniel Hathorne." *EIHC* 89 (1953): 329–56.

Holden, George H. "Hawthorne among His Friends." *Harper's New Monthly Magazine* 63 (1881): 260–67.

Holden, Robert J. "General James Miller: Collector of the Port of Salem, Massachusetts, 1825–1849." *EIHC* 104 (1968): 283–302.

Hope Leslie (Review). *North American Review.* n.s. 26 (1828): 403–20.

Howe, Samuel Gridley. "Atheism in New England." *New England Magazine* 7 (1834): 500–509; 8 (1835): 53–62.

Howells, William Dean. "The Personality of Hawthorne." *North American Review* 177 (1903): 872–82.

Hungerford, Edward B. "Hawthorne Gossips about Salem." *NEQ* 6 (1933): 445–69.

Huntington, Charles P. "Diary and Letters of Charles P. Huntington." *MHSP* 57 (1924): 244–77.

"Ipswich Court Records and Files." *EA* 10 (1906): 37.

Jackson, Russell Leigh. "Additions to the Catalogue of Portraits in the Essex Institute." *EIHC* 85 (1949): 311–34; 86 (1950): 155–84.

———. "Physicians of Essex County." *EIHC* 83 (1947): 162–77 to 84 (1948): 331–48.

James, Henry. "A Letter From Henry James." *EIHC* 41 (1905): 55–62.

Johnson, Claudia D. "Unsettling Accounts in *The House of the Seven Gables.*" *ATQ* n.s. 5:2 (1991): 83–94.

Johnson, Edward. "Wonder-Working Providence of Sion's Saviour." *MHSC* 2d ser. 2 (1814): 51–95 to 8 (1826): 1–39.

Kesselring, Marion L. "Hawthorne's Reading, 1828–1850: A Transcription and Identification of Titles Recorded in the Charge-Books of the Salem Athenaeum." *New York Public Library Bulletin* 53 (1949): 55–71, 121–38, 173–94.

Lanikainen, Dean T. "New Insights into the Early History of the 1804

Gardner-Pingree House in Salem, Massachusetts." *EIHC* 116 (1980): 223–47.

Leavitt, William. "History of the Essex Lodge of Freemasons." *EIHC* 3 (1861): 37–47 to 4 (1862): 255–63.

———. "Notice of the Southward Family in Salem." *EIHC* 14 (1877): 77–88.

Lee, Francis H. "Forty Years Ago in Salem." *EIHC* 59 (1923): 102–4 to 61 (1925): 396–400.

[———]. "Notes on Old Times in Salem." *EIHC* 74 (1938): 365–72.

Lee, Thomas Amory. "The Lee Family of Marblehead." *EIHC* 52 (1916): 33–36 to 53 (1917): 281–85.

Little, David Mason. "Documentary History of the Salem Custom-House." *EIHC* 67 (1931): 1–26, 145–60, 265–80.

Loring, George Bailey. "Literature" in *History of Essex County,* vol. 1, 135–54.

———. "Nathaniel Hawthorne." In Cameron, *Hawthorne among His Contemporaries,* 213–18.

McCracken, George E. "The Salem Gardners: Comments and Clues." *American Genealogist* 30 (1954): 155–68.

Maloney, Joan M. "George Bailey Loring: A Matter of Trust-s." *EIHC* 122 (1986): 35–60.

Manning, Elizabeth. "The Boyhood of Hawthorne." In Cameron, *Hawthorne among His Contemporaries,* 354–70.

Marks, Alfred H. "Hawthorne, G. B. Cheever and Salem's Pump." *EIHC* 123 (1987): 260–77.

"Members of the Essex Bar." *EIHC* 23 (1886): 31–35.

"The Memoir of Benjamin Frederick Browne." *EIHC* 13 (1875): 81–89.

Moore, Margaret B. "Elizabeth Manning Hawthorne: Nathaniel's Enigmatic Sister." *NHR* 20 (1994): 1–9.

———. "Gold-Gathering Expedition[s]: Three Possible Sources for 'Peter Goldthwaite's Treasure.'" *Hawthorne Society Newsletter* 11 (1985): 13–16.

———. "Hawthorne and the Five-Dollar School." *Postscript* 6 (1989): 1–9.

———. "Hawthorne and the Lord's Anointed." In *SAR 1988,* 27–36.

———. "Hawthorne, the Tories, and Benjamin Lynde Oliver, Jr." In *SAR 1991,* 213–24.

———. "Hawthorne's Uncle John Dike." In *SAR 1984,* 325–30.

———. "Salem Sea Captains and Carolina Gold." *EIHC* 122 (1986): 69–89.

————. "Sarah Savage of Salem: A Forgotten Writer." *EIHC* 127 (1991): 240–59.

Moriarty, G. Andrews, Jr. "The Kitchen Family of Salem." *EIHC* 51 (1915): 126–30.

Moriarty, G. Andrews. "The Carleton Family of Salem." *EIHC* 86 (1950): 146–47.

————. "The Wife of George Gardner of Salem." *EIHC* 90 (1954): 105–6.

"Nathaniel Hawthorne." *Littell's Living Age,* from the *North British Review.* In Cameron, *Hawthorne among His Contemporaries,* 108–18.

Neal, David Augustus. "Salem Men in the Early Nineteenth Century." *EIHC* 75 (1939): 1–14.

Nevins, Winfield S. "Nathaniel Hawthorne's Removal from the Salem Custom House." *EIHC* 53 (1917): 97–132.

Newell, William. "Memoir of Joseph E. Worcester, LL.D." *MHSP* 18 (1880): 169–73.

Nissenbaum, Stephen. "The Firing of Nathaniel Hawthorne." *EIHC* 114 (1978): 57–86.

Northend, Mary H. "Historic Salem." *New England Magazine* 31 (1904): 507–23.

"Obituary" [of Adams Bailey]. *NEHGR* 13 (1859): 85.

"Obituary" [of Caleb Bradley]. *NEHGR* 15 (1861): 358.

Park, Lawrence. "Old Boston Families, No. 3: The Savage Family." *NEHGR* 67 (1913): 198–215 to 68 (1914): 119–26.

Parnell, Howard. "Secret Staircase Indicates Seven Gables Railway Stop." *North Shore Magazine,* November 15, 1990.

Pearson, Norman Holmes. "Elizabeth Peabody on Hawthorne." *EIHC* 94 (1958): 256–76.

————. "A 'Good Thing' for Hawthorne." *EIHC* 100 (1964): 300–305.

————. "Hawthorne and the Mannings." *EIHC* 94 (1958): 170–93.

————. "Hawthorne's Duel." *EIHC* 94 (1958): 229–42.

Penfield, Roderick C. "Pioneers of American Literature." In Cameron, *Hawthorne among His Contemporaries,* 400–409.

Perley, Sidney. "Part of Salem in 1700. No. 5." *EA* 4 (1900): 161–70.

————. "Salem in 1700, No. 14." *EA* 8 (1904): 20–37, 152–64.

————. "Salem in 1700. No. 21." *EA* 9 (1905): 162–71.

————. "Salem in 1700. No. 25." *EA* 10 (1906): 152–66.

————. "The Woods, Salem in 1700." *EIHC* 51 (1915): 177–96.

Person, Leland S., Jr. "Hawthorne's Love Letters: Writing and Relationships." *AL* 59 (1987): 211–27.

Phelps, C. Deidre. "Printing, Publishing, and Bookselling in Salem, Massachusetts, 1825–1900." *EIHC* 124 (1988): 265–95.

Phillips, James Duncan. "Political Fights and Local Squabbles in Salem 1800–1806." *EIHC* 82 (1946): 1–11.

———. "Salem in the Nineties." *EIHC* 89 (1953): 295–328; 90 (1954): 17–57.

Porter, Dorothy Burnett. "The Remonds of Salem, Massachusetts: A Nineteenth-Century Family Revisited." *American Antiquarian Society Proceedings* 95 (1985): 259–95.

Rantoul, Robert, Sr. "Negro Slavery in Massachusetts." *EIHC* 24 (1887): 81–108.

———. "Mr. Rantoul's Youth and Apprenticeship." *EIHC* 5 (1863): 193–96.

Rantoul, Robert S. "Opening Remarks." *EIHC* 41 (1905): 3–6.

———. "The First Cotton Mill in America." *EIHC* 33 (1897): 1–43.

———. "Some Notes on Old Modes of Travel." *EIHC* 11 (1871): 19–73.

———. "William Phineas Upham: A Memoir." *EIHC* 56 (1920): 161–76.

"Remarks by the Honorable Robert C. Winthrop." *MHSP* 14 (1875): 153–56.

Right [pseudonym]. "Blue Stockings." *New England Galaxy,* February 8 and 22, 1818.

Roberts, David. "Historic Discourse on the Life of Sir Matthew Cradock." *EIHP* 1 (1848–56): 242–55.

———. "Paper on a Spared Record of the Salem Custom House." *EIHC* 2 (1860): 169–77.

Roberts, Gary Boyd. "Additions, Corrections, and Further Documentation for Previous Columns." *NEXUS* 8 (1991): 67.

S [pseudonym]. "Female Education." *Boston Recorder,* April 17, 1819.

"Salem Social Life in the Early Nineteenth Century." *EIHC* 36 (1900): 105–27, 233–44.

Saltonstall, Leverett [Jr.]. "Leverett Saltonstall's Reminiscences of Salem Written in 1885." *EIHC* 81 (1945): 55–65.

"The Sea Serpent." *AMUEK* 2 (1835): 122–23.

Sharf, Frederick Alan. "Charles Osgood: The Life and Times of a Salem Portrait Painter." *EIHC* 102 (1966): 204–12.

Shuffelton, Frank. "Nathaniel Hawthorne and the Revival Movement." *ATQ* 44 (1979): 311–23.

Solomon, Barbara M. "The Growth of the Population in Essex County, 1850–1860." *EIHC* 95 (1959): 82–103.

Stewart, Randall. "Recollections of Hawthorne by His Sister Elizabeth." *AL* 16 (1945): 316–31.

Stoddard, Richard Henry. "Nathaniel Hawthorne." *Harper's New Monthly Magazine* 45 (1872): 683–97.

[Stone, John]. "Notes from the Memorandum Book of John Stone, Deacon, First Church, Salem." *EIHC* 61 (1925): 97–112.

Storrow, Ann Gillam. "Letters of Ann Gillam Storrow to Jared Sparks." Ed. Frances Bradshaw Blanshard. *Smith College Studies in History* 6 (1921): 185–252.

Streeter, Gilbert L. "Some Historic Streets and Colonial Houses of Salem." *EIHC* 36 (1900): 185–213.

Swartzlander, Susan. " 'Amid Sunshine and Shadow': Charles Wentworth Upham and Nathaniel Hawthorne." *Studies in American Fiction* 15 (1987): 227–33.

————. "Hawthorne's 'Alice Doane's Appeal.' " *Studies in Short Fiction* 25 (1988): 121–28.

Thayer, Oliver. "Early Recollections of the Upper Portion of Essex Street." *EIHC* 21 (1884): 211–24.

Thompson, James W. "Tribute to the Memory of Rev. Henry Colman." *Monthly Religious Magazine,* quoted in the *Christian Register,* November 17, 1849.

Upham, Charles W. "Memoir of Francis Peabody." *EIHC* 9, part 2 (1869): 3–80.

————. "Memorial for John Prince." *MHSC* 3d ser. 5 (1836): 271–81.

Upham, William P. "Beverly First Church Records." *EIHC* 35 (1899): 177–211 to 41 (1905): 193–226.

Upton, James. "Hawthorne in the Salem Custom-House: An Unpublished Recollection." Ed. Matthew J. Bruccoli. In *NHJ 1971,* 113–15.

Upton, William B. "List of Deaths Recorded by the Rev. John Prince LL.D." *EIHC* 9, part 2 (1869): 91–111.

Usrey, Miriam L. "Charles Lenox Remond: Garrison's Ebony Echo World Anti-Slavery Convention, 1840." *EIHC* 106 (1970): 112–25.

Valenti, Patricia Dunlavy. "Sophia Peabody Hawthorne: A Study of Artistic Influence." In *SAR 1990,* 1–21.

————. "Sophia Peabody Hawthorne's Continuation to 'Christabel.' " *NHR* 13 (1987): 14–16.

Wallace, James D. "Hawthorne and the Scribbling Women Reconsidered." *AL* 62 (1990): 201–22.

Ward, Gerald W. R. "The Andrew-Safford House." *EIHC* 112 (1976): 59–88.

Warren, Winslow. "Memoir of Rev. Henry W. Foote." *MHSP* 2d ser. 8 (1893): 236–51.

Waters, Edward Stanley. "Genealogical Notes of the Webb Family." *EIHC* 16 (1879): 213–34.

Waters, Henry F. "Genealogical Gleanings in England." *NEHGR* 38 (1884): 60–74, 193–208, 301–25.

———. "More Passengers to New-England, 1679." *NEHGR* 28 (1874): 375–78.

Waters, Joseph E. "A Biographical Sketch of Rev. William Bentley." *EIHC* 41 (1905): 237–50.

Watkins, Lura Woodside. "Water Mills of Middleton." *EIHC* 99 (1963): 311–43.

Whipple, George M. "History of the Salem Light Infantry." *EIHC* 26 (1889): 161–242.

———. "A Sketch of the Musical Societies of Salem." *EIHC* 23 (1885): 72–80, 113–33.

White, Arthur O. "Salem's Antebellum Black Community: Seedbed of the School Integration Movement." *EIHC* 108 (1972): 99–118.

Whitney, William T., Jr. "The Crowninshields of Salem, 1800–1808." *EIHC* 94 (1958): 1–36, 79–118.

Wiggin, Cynthia B. "History of the Salem Book Club." *EIHC* 105 (1969): 137–41.

Willson, E. B. "Ecclesiastical History." In *History of Essex County,* vol. 1, 17–63.

———. "Memorial of Charles T. Brooks: Birth and Beyond." *EIHC* 21 (1884): 1–12.

Woodson, Thomas. "Hawthorne, Upham, and *The Scarlet Letter.*" In *Critical Essays on Hawthorne's The Scarlet Letter,* ed. David B. Kesterson. Boston: G. K. Hall, 1988, 183–93.

Wright, Conrad Edick. "Institutional Reconstruction in the Unitarian Controversy." In *American Unitarianism, 1805–1865,* ed. Conrad E. Wright. Boston: Massachusetts Historical Society and Northeastern University Press, 1989, 3–29.

Index